MEN OF STEEL

MEN OF STEEL

**The Story
of the
Family that
Built the
World Trade
Center**

KARL KOCH III
with RICHARD FIRSTMAN

 Crown Publishers • New York

Grateful acknowledgment is made to Pantheon Books, a division of Random House, Inc., for permission to reprint an excerpt from "The Mohawks in High Steel" from *Up in the Old Hotel* by Joseph Mitchell. Copyright © 1992 by Joseph Mitchell. Reprinted by permission of Pantheon Books, a division of Random House, Inc.

Illustrations in chapters 14 and 18 were originally published in *The World Trade Center: A Building Project Like No Other*, published by The Port of New York Authority. Illustrations by George V. Kelvin

Endpaper illustrations are courtesy of Richard Welling and the drawings were donated to the New-York Historical Society.

Published by Crown Publishers, New York, New York.
Member of the Crown Publishing Group, a division of Random House, Inc.
New York, Toronto, London, Sydney, Auckland
www.randomhouse.com

CROWN is a trademark and the Crown colophon is a registered trademark of Random House, Inc.

Printed in the United States of America

Design by Lauren Dong

Library of Congress Cataloging-in-Publication Data is available upon request

ISBN 1-4000-4601-7

10 9 8 7 6 5 6 4 3 2 1

First Edition

CONTENTS

This book is dedicated to my beautiful wife,
Vivian, who was with me every step of the way;
and to the memory of my father, Karl Koch, Jr.,
who was truly a man of steel.

Brick and stone and steel that gird our structures,
All must crumble, in their time be shattered.
Naught remains of all our pride and vaunting
Save our blessed deeds that are eternal.
When the memories of our dear departed
Spur us on to nobler aspiration
In our hearts they live enshrined forever,
Though removed from earthly habitation.

When hypocrisy and hate we banish,
When our efforts loose the bonds of evil,
When we strive for peace, for righteousness and justice—
Yea, 'tis then that we become immortal,
Deathless, timeless, living on in others.

—FROM THE JEWISH PRAYER FOR THE DEAD

PROLOGUE

September 2001

I WANT TO GO—it's where I should be. So why am I not there?

It is five days in: Sunday, September 16, 2001. My partner Andy Zosuls calls to say he's been asked to come into the city and work on the recovery. Francis Lee, whose construction company we've both been working for as consultants, has been hired to repair the Verizon building, one of the structures ringing the World Trade Center still standing, but with holes gashed into its side from hurled pieces of the fallen towers. Francis has called in his whole team, Andy says—engineers, project managers, ironworkers. Are you going in? he asks. We can drive in together.

Francis hasn't called me, I tell him.

"I didn't think you could manage walking the site," Francis is saying a minute later when I call him on his cell phone. He's talking about my legs, of course. But he could just as easily be talking about my head. Going down there isn't easy for anybody, but Francis knows it might be that much harder for me. It's true that I've been in an emotional fog for much of the past five days. But I know where I have to be. I've always resisted using my legs as an excuse, even now, thirty-seven years after the accident, months away from my seventieth birthday. And I'm sure as hell not staying away because I don't have the stomach for it.

Don't worry about me, I tell Francis. I'll be all right. I call Andy back and we arrange to meet the next morning at five-thirty at the Oyster Bay train station and drive in together.

Monday morning at 6:45, Andy and I are downtown, talking our way past the police line at Canal and Varick and then heading for a building Verizon is using as a temporary command post. We have our photos taken and get passes to hang around our necks. We continue south on foot—the entire downtown area seems like one of those horrible fighting zones we're used to seeing on TV from the Middle East. A National Guardsman stops us at the next block and tells us we need another pass, a red one being issued by the city. "That's the issuing point over there," he says, pointing toward a line of people. We get our red tags. "Mayor's Office of Emergency Management," it reads. "World Trade Center Emergency." Now we're walking toward what they've started calling Ground Zero. Someone hands each of us a box containing a gas mask.

It's becoming almost a cliché: *It's much worse when you see it with your own eyes.* The mayor said it first, and then the politicians from Washington—the president said it while looking down from a helicopter—and then the ballplayers paying visits to the weary rescue workers. They all say the same thing. *It's surreal. Like a movie.* And it's true. Television flattens everything anyway, makes it seem artificial. Isolated and condensed in that little box, this just looks like a crazy mess. But when you're here and you see it and smell it and feel it—when you look down and your shoes are covered with pasty dust—the magnitude of the destruction seems *beyond* reality. Beyond *possibility.* The grand orderliness of the financial district, rock solid as the country itself, has given way to chaos and obliteration. The crushed buildings are piled up in small mountains fifty feet high. Even the buildings that are only injured are a shock to see: Thousands of windows shattered, chunks missing, exteriors ripped off. You can see their bones, the steel. And then I gaze beyond the Trade Center, all the way across West Street. My God, I think—you shouldn't be able to see the Winter Garden from here. It's behind the towers. But the towers are . . . *gone.*

The scene is the same for everyone: a nightmarish tableau of twisted steel and pulverized, smoldering wreckage. But not everyone sees the same thing. For me, the emotional force of what's happened sends me back to another time. My mind reverts more than thirty years, to the last time there were no towers, only cranes and ironworkers. The World Trade Center was then a work in progress, a steel skeleton rising up methodically, floor-by-floor, from the mammoth foundation dug seventy feet into the earth at the southern tip of Manhattan.

The images, the time, will forever be frozen in my memory. It's 1968 and I'm in my mid-30s. I have long sideburns and four little kids and another under construction. I have spent most of the past four years literally trying to get back on my feet after an accident that almost killed me. Two tons of steel came tumbling down onto my legs when I came to deliver the payroll to a jobsite and saw something that didn't look right. So now I'm helping supervise the construction of the World Trade Center from an office across the street, on the sixth floor of a building on Liberty Street. I'm not quite mobile yet, so binoculars have become primary equipment—to the dismay of our men up above, ironworkers who don't like the feeling of being watched. I put the glasses down and gaze up at the evolving steel arrangement with pride and awe. I'm not yet aware that these great structures, these towers that will stand closer to the heavens than any other building on earth, will mark both the pinnacle of accomplishment for the construction company that bears my grandfather's name—and my father's and mine—and the beginning of its demise as a proud family enterprise.

Now, on this grim day thirty-three years later, all of that is just a backdrop to the panorama of annihilation in front of me. I am wearing my red construction helmet with KOCH branded across the side—the very helmet I wore during the construction of the Twin Towers. I look at the spot where they stood only five days earlier and for three decades before and wonder where the hell they went. The mound of rubble seems way too small for all that came down. I'm told most of it is now below ground level—the pounded and incinerated contents of a thousand offices, and, horribly, the corpses of so many of the people who worked in those offices, who fell with the floors we put up.

A jumble of emotions ricochets in my head. There are familiar things everywhere, or versions of them. I see some exterior wall panels still standing, leaning at crazy angles, like ghosts. *We put those up.* I see a firefighter hosing down another pile of panels that are crushed and smoldering. We brought them in, and all the others, from Pacific Car & Foundry. They weighed twenty-two tons apiece, and every one had a square hole cut into it so the men could stick their hands through and bolt the beam onto the previous section. I can see the square cut-out on this piece of beam. And I can see the number stamped onto it, showing exactly where the beam was supposed to go according to the construction drawings. I see the rolled steel, the heavy weldments, all twisted and bent and torn. Some look like they just came from the fabricator. They're still smoking hot. I don't know what possesses me—it's like putting your head in the lion's mouth—but I feel myself being pulled to the base of a pile. I want to touch the steel. And then I hear a National Guardsman's voice behind me. "One more step and you'll be leaving here in handcuffs."

✖   ✖

FIVE DAYS EARLIER, I had been home in Mattituck, Long Island, eighty miles east of Ground Zero. My daughter, Jill, had called from her apartment in Midtown Manhattan, screaming that a plane had just hit the Trade Center. Jill lives on the thirty-sixth floor of a building on East Thirty-ninth Street, a clear shot downtown. She didn't need the TV to tell her what was going on. A little while later, she called back, crying, saying that the south tower had collapsed. I was sure she was wrong. I was sure the people on TV were wrong. It's just the angle and all the smoke, I assured her. It *had* to be the angle. The south tower *had* to be hiding behind its twin.

Later that morning, an hour after I knew that the south tower wasn't hiding, that it was gone and so was the north one, I found myself looking out my window at Long Island Sound, trying to fathom what forces could possibly have pushed those buildings to the earth with such speed and ferocity. They weren't beautiful structures in everyone's eyes, but they had come to represent something great in a great city. And they were strong. Or so we thought. Now thousands of people had died absolutely horrendous deaths on live television. And my first thought was: I killed them.

Of course it was an irrational thought. I didn't hijack any airplane. I didn't design the buildings. But it was my family that built the structures that now lay in ruin, entombing thousands of poor workaday souls in the churned rubble of their own offices and cubicles. It was the 200,000 tons of structural steel and six million square feet of floor that we brought across from New Jersey and hoisted up with enormous cranes we imported from Australia that fell to earth and took the lives of all those rescuers. It was my family's company, started by my grandfather and father in 1922, that found itself forty-five years later with the job of the century and a workforce of six hundred. It was our men, hundreds of them, who, day after day for three years, hoisted and bolted the girders and beams and joists that now lay twisted and crushed and melted on the ground. If we hadn't built it, someone else would have. But we did. It was we who, on a blustery December day in 1970, reached the summit of the first tower and ceremoniously raised an American flag, a venerated tradition among American ironworkers when a new building is topped out. A picture was snapped—I'm on the left, holding up a corner of the flag—freezing the moment. But now when I look at that picture, the symbolism is unbearable.

For our closely held family company, a diminutive outfit by the standards that might be expected of the World Trade Center, erecting these towers was a feat of technology and finance, and, ultimately, of sheer will. But it was also, always, something much less triumphant. The World Trade Center provided the foundation for a fatal betrayal of family trust that would be the defining saga of my life. For years, the loss of the family business I cherished, a company I expected to inherit and one day pass down to my own sons, was a pain so acute that for a long time I could not look at the skyline of Lower Manhattan. I literally averted my eyes. To me, the World Trade Center was both the best thing and the worst thing that ever happened to the Koch Family.

And now it was gone. How did it happen? How could the buildings collapse like that, both of them in seconds? Looking out over Long Island Sound, I closed my eyes and pictured the floor plan: The details, the numbers, flooded my brain. The building was 200 feet square; each floor had some 32,000 square feet of floor space. There was a center core made of structural steel. From the ninth floor the perimeter was made up of bearing-wall panels that were ten feet wide and thirty-six feet high. The panels were composed of three columns, each fourteen inches square tied together with fifty-four-inch spandrels. There were 5,828 of these shop-assembled panels, and each weighed up to 22 tons. These numbers were imprinted on my brain. Quick math: More than 100,000 tons of steel were holding up each of the towers. But it wasn't how much those vital supports weighed, but where they were—and where they weren't.

I knew almost immediately why the towers collapsed the way they did. And I sat there and cried. I wept for the thousands who had to have died. I wept because we built the damn things.

High Steel

Building skyscrapers is the nearest peacetime equivalent of war . . . and these men are the soldiers of a great creative effort.

—COL. WILLIAM A. STARRETT,
one of the builders of the Empire State Building, in
his 1928 book *Skyscrapers and the Men Who Build Them*

1

RIVETS
AND
RIVERS

In the winter of 1908, my grandfather fell off the Manhattan Bridge.

He had come to New York just a few months before, from western Pennsylvania by way of Buffalo. In those days, a man of his trade went where the work was, and in the first decade of the last century, that meant going to New York City. Grandpa was twenty-six at the time, married with a two-year-old son and a three-month-old daughter. The baby was named Gladys. The toddler was Karl Koch II. He was my father.

Grandpa was an ironworker, a bridgeman. He was the man wielding the sledgehammer on the rivet gang, each of his blows pushing New York City and America just a tiny bit further into the new century. When I was young, I would run across old-timers who told me my grandfather's strength was legendary. It was said that there was not a union ironworker in New York who could put a beater to a rivet like my grandpa.

On this particular day in the winter of 1908, he was banging rivets on the Manhattan Bridge, the third and last of the great suspension bridges built around that time to link Manhattan and Brooklyn, which had been separate cities until a decade before. This span would connect Canal Street on one side and Flatbush Avenue on the other, and after seven years of construction, the bridge was almost finished. It was about eleven o'clock in the morning when Grandpa lost his footing, or his balance, or his grip, while working on one of the bridge towers. This detail escaped my grandmother's reporting when she wrote about the mishap in the seventy-chapter (a page or two per chapter) personal history she typed up in 1964, when she was eighty, and left behind for posterity.

According to Grandma, the East River was nearly frozen that day, and when Grandpa slipped off the bridge he went right through the ice. Fortunately for him (and for the eight more children he was to father), he was close enough to shore that his brother ironworkers were able to fish him from the river and drag him to the Manhattan side. Unconscious, he was rushed to the nearest hospital, which happened to be a private one not meant for a lowly ironworker, even a hypothermic one. Turned away, the ambulance driver tried the next-nearest hospital. Another private hospital, another refusal. Taking no more chances, he took Grandpa to the oldest public hospital in America, Bellevue, which hadn't turned anyone away since it opened in 1736.

Grandma didn't hear about any of this until six hours after Grandpa hit the water, when two policemen came to their apartment in the Bronx. Grandma grabbed her neighbor, Mrs. Kopsky, and they hired a taxicab—something an ironworker's wife would do only in an emergency—and headed downtown to Bellevue, where they found Grandpa, still wearing his wet clothes. "Get me outta here," he said when he saw Grandma. He explained that when he got to the hospital, a nurse told him to undress. "I told her, 'If I was able to undress, I wouldn't be here.' " The nurse told him she couldn't handle a big man like him and that he would have to wait for the orderly, who was out for dinner. Grandma, Mrs. Kopsky, and the orderly eventually managed to get Grandpa into a wheelchair, onto the elevator, and into the taxi, which took him home to the Bronx. Grandma kept him covered in hot water bottles for two days, and by the end of the week, he was back banging rivets on the Manhattan Bridge.

KARL WILLIAM KOCH was born in Williamsport, Pennsylvania, in the late spring of 1882—"Class of eighty-two," he liked to say—three years after his parents emigrated from Baden-Württemberg, Germany. His father and my great grandfather, Charles Koch, settled the family in a burgeoning community of German immigrants who might have been reminded of their homeland when they looked out at the mountains beyond the Susquehanna River. Charles was one of fifteen or so Koches who had come to Williamsport from Germany since the beginning of the century. The trailblazer was August Koch, a successful builder who arrived in 1807 and later became one of Williamsport's most prominent citizens. He was one of the few successful men in the booming city who didn't make his fortune in the lumber industry. He and his brother operated a brewery. There was a lot of drinking to good times in Williamsport, which produced more lumber—350 million board feet a day at its peak—than any place in the world. Millionaires were coming out of the woodwork.

Charles Koch arrived with little but his willingness to reinvent himself in a land full of promise. He started as a laborer in a sawmill. He ended there, too. At half-past eleven on the morning of May 2, 1884, a fire broke out at Valentine Luppert's Saw Mill, next to the Luppert & Kline furniture factory on the south side of town. "The fire started in some wood rubbish between the mill and the river," reported the evening edition of the *Sun-Gazette*. "How the fire got there is a mystery to some; to others it is not, as it is quite probable that a spark from one of the smoke stacks or a locomotive lodged there and was fanned into a flame by the high wind prevailing. In a few minutes the fire had rushed up to the mill—there being so much inflammable material for it to work upon—and soon that structure was one sheet of flame from front to rear, its destruction being complete. At this writing, it may be said that the rolling mill and furniture factory are not out of danger, as a very large lot of lumber between the saw mill and furniture factory is on fire, and the wind furious." There were two casualties so far, the newspaper said. One employee was burned on his hands and face. The other got his belt caught while he was trying to flee and was cut badly by a flying piece of shattered blade. He was Charles Koch. His youngest child, Karl, was two years old when he died.

When he was a teenager, Grandpa hopped a freighter and got off just outside Pittsburgh, where there was a living wage to be found in ironwork, which had become the modern means of erecting buildings and bridges. It was suitable work for Grandpa, who had a strong pair of hands, an old-world work ethic, and a sense of adventure and fearlessness that were among the job requirements in a trade which often forced men to go both farther and higher than they had ever been.

In the winter of 1903, Grandpa and a cousin of his traveled three hundred miles by train to Rochester, New York, to see Buffalo Bill Cody appear at the Pan American Ball. One night during their visit, they went to a masquerade ball. Grandpa declined to wear a costume but his cousin went as Martha Washington. Grandpa, who was twenty-one, was smitten by the First Prize winner, a girl of nineteen dressed as an Indian princess. Her name was Julia Charitus Weigand—everyone called her Cora—and it turned out that she had noticed him as well. In fact she had asked the hostess, Ella Curtis, who the stranger was and whether they could be introduced. But Ella told her to forget it. "He's engaged to Martha Washington," she told Cora, who did forget about it. She was a pretty girl not wanting for suitors and danced the night away with anyone who asked. But as the evening was winding down, Grandpa decided to introduce himself and ask for a dance.

"I wanted to come over all evening but I didn't have the nerve," he confessed as they were dancing. "I was afraid I was going to get a Virginia Throwdown."

"Or maybe your fiancée Martha wouldn't let you."

"You have it all wrong," Grandpa said. "Martha, as you call her, is my cousin."

"So what's a Virginia Throwdown?" Grandma asked.

"In the play at the Star Theater, a fellow asks a girl to dance and when she refuses, he goes out and shoots himself. They call it a Virginia Throwdown. Could I take you to see it?"

"You already saw the show," Cora said coolly. "Why should you see it again? Besides, for a quarter I can go with the girls on Saturday afternoon and sit in the top balcony and shoot beans at the villain."

Grandpa decided to extend his visit to Rochester. He showed up at Cora's door nearly every night with candy or flowers. She enjoyed the attention, though it wasn't entirely unfamiliar to her. "Most single men I met in those days acted a little silly," she wrote, "as did some married ones." One night she took Grandpa to the dance hall where she taught two nights a week with a partner, a big, blonde Irishman named Eddie, who considered her his girl. "As soon as we entered the hall and I saw Eddie, I knew I had made a mistake," she recalled. "In those days, there was at least one fight at every dance. I persuaded Eddie to let us alone and told him my friendship with Karl wasn't serious."

She meant it. Cora had it in her mind that she shouldn't get married until she was at least twenty-five. But Grandpa was neither a patient man nor a passive one. He told her he had no interest in waiting six years and was going straight to her father to state his intentions. Cora tried to stop him, to no avail. She hid behind the drapes and heard her father tell him: "You don't want her. One fellow came with a gun in order to shoot them both, and I had to talk him out of it. Another was going to end it all and I talked him out of it." Cora stuffed the drapes in her mouth to keep from bursting out in laughter at her father's ridiculous tales. He tried another tack: "You're German. Germans usually want to be the boss. Cora has bossed us ever since she was three. She won't take much from you." To which Grandpa responded: "I'm not afraid of her. We're going to be married."

And they were, on July 2, 1904, though barely. When the minister got to the part about taking this man till death do you part, Cora panicked and bolted. Karl chased her outside and coaxed her back to the altar, an ironic beginning since it was Grandma whose powers of persuasion we would all get to know.

Grandma—"Mrs. K," as Grandpa took to calling her—arranged for them to spend their honeymoon at her Aunt Kate's lakefront house near Rochester. They had a room downstairs, and Grandma recalled that Grandpa, ever the alert one, crawled under the bed and dislodged a bell that had been wired to the spring. I'm not sure who the warning system was meant to catch, or how Grandpa knew to look for it. All I know is that their first child was born the following year. Grandma described him as "a handsome, intelligent-looking child weighing twelve pounds." He was Karl W. Koch II, my father. No sooner was he born than he caused his very first family fight: a battle royale over what religion he would be raised in. Grandpa was Lutheran. Grandma was Catholic—devoutly so. After arguing about it for days, Grandpa knew Grandma wouldn't budge and threw in the towel.

He didn't go much for religion or spirituality, anyway; he had much more earthbound concerns. Like supporting his new family. Though living in his mother-in-law's house in Rochester, he got a job at a construction site seventy-five miles away, in Buffalo, where his uncle George was the superintendent. It meant living on the road during the week, but Grandpa didn't think twice about it. He was an extremely industrious worker, a working man to the core. He was no less demanding of the people he worked with. As a supervisor, he was, in the opinion of his wife, "more or less a slave driver." He allowed workers a lunch break only begrudgingly. His advice: "Eat a big breakfast."

Grandpa was riveting one day when he told a man to go back to the anchorage and bring him back a keg of bolts. The man couldn't believe Grandpa wanted him to carry an entire keg of bolts. "Throw it on your shoulder and bring it out to the heater," Grandpa told him. The man said, "I'm gonna bust the keg open and bring you out a bucketful." Grandpa told him to get the keg. The man told Grandpa to go to hell. Grandpa began taking his coat off to fight him when Uncle George came along and asked, "Karl, vas ees dees?"

"He told me to go to hell," Grandpa said.

"Vell, put your coat back on," replied Uncle George. "You don't have to go, do you?"

One bitter cold day in Buffalo, Grandpa told two men to climb a high pole outside the plant and repair some broken wires. The men wore fur-lined caps and heavy gloves, but still couldn't handle the cold and came down without finishing. Grandpa, fuming, climbed the pole and finished the job himself—but not before one of his ears became so frozen that he was left nearly deaf in that ear for the rest of his life.

That winter, 1907, my grandparents went to visit a friend of Grandpa's who was sick. They didn't know until they got there that the man had typhoid fever. The air in the room had a stench, and Grandma made a quick exit and waited outside. But Grandpa stayed about an hour. Two weeks later he had typhoid himself, such a severe case that he had to go to the hospital, where he was put in a straitjacket and placed in a tub filled with ice cubes to try to reduce the fever. A doctor told Grandma that his chances weren't good, and at one point she was called and told to hurry to the hospital. The only transportation available was the trolley, which ran hours apart. Grandma waited two hours in the December cold, wondering if Grandpa would die before she could get there. When she finally made it to the hospital, Grandpa was barely hanging on. He was gaunt, his face drawn. He had dark, sunken gray eyes and a thick growth of red beard. He later said he had hallucinated that he was being flattened by a steamroller. Somehow, Grandpa fought his way back and eventually was deemed well enough to let some other poor soul have his bed. He had lost eighty pounds, which put him very close to dipping below a hundred.

By the time Grandpa recuperated, the money was all but gone and work was scarce. He found some new work out of town with his uncle George, rebuilding Dole's Slaughter House in Buffalo. He hated the job, hated the smell and being around cattle being slaughtered. Uncle George knew Grandpa was only doing it because he was penniless, and got some kind of pleasure tormenting Grandma about it. "Never mind," she told him, "we will be hiring *you* some day."

Grandpa tried to ease their struggles with fanciful dreams. He would read the society pages of the New York papers and tell Grandma where all the Morgans, Astors, and Vanderbilts were staying and what they were doing. He promised her that someday they would live in a brownstone house just like the Vanderbilts, with servants to open the doors for her and a chauffeur to drive her anywhere she wanted to go, in a carriage drawn by high-stepping horses. Grandma allowed herself a moment's fantasy, but then it was back to reality. When the work at the slaughterhouse ended, Grandpa had to borrow a quarter from Grandma's sister Belle for carfare to get to another job prospect. After he left, Belle berated Grandma for having married a man who put her through such financial stress. Belle was still lecturing when in walked Grandpa with a fifteen-cent bag of chocolate drops. Grandma was furious. "What's *wrong* with you, Karl?" she bellowed. "Spending our last pennies on candy!" Grandpa smiled and said, "It's to celebrate. I got the job." But it was just more temporary work on the road, and the pressures grew when Grandma had a second child, a girl she and Grandpa named Gladys—after Gladys Vanderbilt.

Grandma's answer to everything was prayer, so she prayed that Grandpa would get a steady job in one city and in exchange promised God she would go to church more regularly. Evidently the deal had a quick turnaround, because within the week Grandpa got a letter from his brother Jack in New York telling him about a good job working on the Manhattan Bridge. Grandpa made his way down to the city, figuring it was just another out-of-town job for an itinerant ironworker, and that it would eventually end and he'd be back. Grandma, though, had faith that there would be unlimited work in New York and started to pack as soon as Grandpa left, not bothering to tell him.

The Manhattan Bridge was a two-level suspension bridge anchored by a pair of steel towers. Flanked by the Brooklyn and Williamsburg bridges, its upper level was designed for cars and pedestrians while the lower level would carry subway cars between the two boroughs. The entrance on Canal Street had a majestic steel arch, and the two towers—made of fifty-two-ton pieces of steel that had been carried 300 feet into the air by massive guy derricks—framed the span in crisscrossed girders. They were topped by four ornamental steel turrets.

Grandpa became a member of Ironworkers Local 35, which was based in Brooklyn, and joined a rivet gang. A gang was composed of four men: the heater, the catcher, the bucker-up, and the star of the operation, the riveter, otherwise known as the gunman. That was Grandpa. The heater would stand by his forge, a four-legged, round trough filled with coal with a hand-operated bellows mounted on the side. You could always recognize a heater in a gang of ironworkers because he would have folded newspapers in his back pocket, always ready to start his fire. His was a special art. Not only did he have to heat the rivets—and not overheat them—to get them to the precise temperature and size required, but he had to pluck each one with a pair of long tongs and swing it underhand, releasing it at just the right moment so that it flew through the air to be snared in a cone-shaped metal can by the catcher. The rivet-catching can was a major innovation. Not only did it make riveting infinitely easier and the gang more productive, but it gave people on the ground something to look at. Crowds would gather, gazing up at the "cannon ball catchers."

After the hot rivet landed in his can, the catcher—who was also known as the "sticker-in"—would extract it with his short tongs and insert it in the hole. The third member of the gang, the bucker-up, was a catcher of another sort. He had a tool called a dolly bar that matched the mushroom-cap-shaped head of the rivet, and after the catcher inserted the rivet in the hole, the bucker-up would stand on the other side of the steel, holding his weight against it with the dolly bar. Now the riveter raised his sledgehammer—called the beater—and pounded the rivet with all his force. Being a riveter on a gang required exceptional strength and endurance and was by far the toughest job on the bridge. Years later the job got a lot easier when the pneumatic rivet gun replaced the beater.

All the jobs on the rivet gang were interchangeable and paid the same 52.5 cents an hour (in 1908). But as a matter of honor the riveter rarely asked to be relieved, lest his fellow workers think he was tiring, or worse—that he was becoming "sissified." The other member of the gang who generally - didn't change positions was the heater. He was most often a man who was crippled from an accident on a previous job, and this was the one job in ironwork that didn't require much mobility of the legs. At the beginning of the shift, he would find a safe spot, away from other activity, and stay there. This meant that his tosses might have to be forty feet or more. The whole operation—the whole gang—depended on his technique. Rivet men were hired and fired as a gang. They learned from each other and grew with each other. The best ones became a real unit, coordinated and smoothly efficient, capable of driving twice as many rivets in a day than a less experienced or skillful gang. If one member didn't show up for work, the entire gang was replaced. The highest compliment one rivet man could pay another was, "You can be on my gang anytime." All this for a job that promised no advancement, or even regular employment, and whose only guarantee was that a certain number of men who did the work would die in the process.

I've often envisioned Grandpa up there on the Manhattan Bridge, pounding rivets in those steel towers after the catcher took them from his can and put them in the hole as the bucker-up prepared for the impact. One day many years ago when I was just starting out in the business, an old man stopped me as I walked by on my way to lunch. He asked if it was true that I was a Koch, as someone had told him. I told him I was the third Karl W.

Koch. "I used to work in a gang with your grandpappy," he said. He grabbed my forearm and told me, "Hell, he could drive a rivet with one blow." I asked what that meant. "Goddammit," he said, "it means he could drive a rivet with one blow."

He grabbed my arm again and nodded toward the building we were putting up. It was a high-rise apartment building in midtown Manhattan, and all over the site were ironworkers in red hardhats with KOCH emblazoned across the front. A crane had the family name in large block letters. "He learned a lot climbing back and forth over that barbed wire fence to have put an outfit like this together," the old man said. I asked what *that* meant. "Goddammit," he said, "it means he's learned a lot."

Walking away, I thought about what the old-timer had told me. Sure, Grandpa was a big man, and he did have terrific strength. He was an ironworker from a young age and a hard worker. But driving a rivet with just one bang? I had knocked rivets out with an eight-pound beater, but that wasn't the same thing. A rivet with one blow? Amazing. I told Grandpa what the old man had said about his riveting abilities. Could you really drive a rivet with a single blow? I asked. "That's what they say," he said, as he cut a rubber air hose into sections. I looked at his hands. They were big, but soft and clean as a surgeon's. He always wore deerskin gloves at work.

"But is it true?" I pressed.

"Get some more line off the truck," he said.

I was happy to believe my "grandpappy" could have done it and carried this assumption proudly with me for forty years, until someone informed me that while Grandpa was one hell of an ironworker, even he could not have driven a rivet with just one blow. But I still wonder.

WHILE GRANDPA WAS driving rivets with one or more blows, back in Rochester Grandma was busy getting ready to move. She sold most of the furniture to four German workmen, who paid her in cash and soup. A neighbor, Mr. Clifford, helped pack her things in crates. Grateful, Grandma gave Mr. Clifford her new stove.

She could have used it on the trip. With her two-year-old and infant, she took an unheated night train in February with no berths. She put Karl and Gladys together on one seat and covered them first with paper and then swaddled them in her coat. The conductor insisted she wear his coat, boots, and hat, without which Grandma swore she would have arrived at Grand

Central Station frozen. Arriving in the city, she headed downtown. Grandpa had arranged for the family to board with a woman whose husband, an iron-worker, had recently been killed on the Manhattan Bridge.

The furniture arrived a few weeks later, and they found an apartment in the Bronx. The family was barely settled when Grandpa fell off the bridge, almost making Grandma a widow herself. And then another crisis: Grandma learned she was pregnant again, very distressing news that she kept from Grandpa. Her first thought was that she couldn't have this baby. The woman they had boarded with told her she could help and handed her a piece of paper with the name and address of a doctor who would "take care of it." But Grandma felt terrible about what she was contemplating. She concluded that if she went through with an abortion, God would punish her by taking her husband, which of course was a real possibility on a daily basis, even if she was not thinking of doing something that might offend God. "I sat down and thought that if I do this thing, the place next to me in bed would soon be empty," she wrote. In January 1909, Madeline was born. Fifteen months later, the baby contracted spinal meningitis and died.

"YOUNG KARL WAS a scrapper and could lick any boy he met, even ones a head taller," Grandma wrote of my father. "His head was so hard that his father called it solid ivory. When he was little, he used to bang it on the side-walk when he was mad."

Grandpa's mother, Mary, was living with them at the time. She was a sweet, even-tempered woman whose life had been filled with tragedy. After her husband's death in the fire at the sawmill, she had married again, but the man lived only two more years himself. Meanwhile, between her two hus-bands, she had given birth to fifteen children, but ten of them died of a vari-ety of illnesses that killed children routinely in those days. Mary loved her grandson and always called him "Mein Karl." (When she began talking, his baby sister Gladys assumed this was his name and called him "Mein Karl" too.) My father played drums with the kettles in the kitchen, and his grand-mother couldn't stand the racket so she hid them. He got even by nailing her shoes to the floor. "Mein Karl is smart," his grandmother remarked, more amused than annoyed.

Sometimes, my father's famous mischievousness wasn't so harmless. One day, a policeman came to the apartment and told my grandmother not to strike any matches. There seemed to be a gas leak somewhere in the neighborhood. Grandma looked out and saw a policeman on each corner keeping people from smoking. A terrible thought crossed her mind. She had heard banging in the cellar every day that week. She had gone down to investigate and found Karl innocently hammering on a board. Now she went down again, and found that he had been standing on a box with a baseball bat and had worked a wooden gas plug loose. "Nothing was sacred to him," Grandma said.

By now she had come to expect calamities and catastrophes and bizarre events. Coming home after a trip to Pennsylvania, she and my grandfather were met by the woman they had hired to stay with the children. She gave them the horrible news that the police had been there and had taken young Karl to the morgue. Grandma, frantic and weeping, went to the neighbors to see what they knew. A dozen different stories were going around. Grandpa was calling the police when in walked Karl. By now Grandma was used to bizarre things happening and then finding out what the story was. This was the best one yet. Karl had played hooky and was hitching a ride on the back of a truck. He had gotten knocked off the truck and landed in the street, unconscious—and was hit by a passing hearse. The hearse driver brought him to the funeral parlor. The undertaker was calling for an ambulance when Karl came to and sneaked out and made his way home. By now, Grandma, who tended to ascribe other-worldly qualities to every noteworthy event, was beginning to suspect that the family was under some kind of wicked spell. "I believe that some houses have an aura of disaster about them," she recalled, "and this was one."

The house was getting more crowded. In 1913, three years after Madeline died, Cornelia was born. And a year later, Delores. Then Patricia, Robert, Jerome, Julia, and Daniel—seven babies in eleven years for a grand total of ten. (There were eighteen years between the oldest and youngest children, and thirteen between the first boy, Karl Junior, and the second, Robert.) But by Grandma's account, it was a long time before she lost her youthful appeal. One day she went to a beauty parlor and a man claiming to be a movie producer told her that her hair was "perfect for the part, and also your figure." He wanted her to come to California. In those early days of silent movies, people really did get discovered this way.

"Don't be silly," Grandma said. "I'm married with children. My husband is an ironworker."

"That's all right. He can come too. There's plenty to do there."

Grandma knew that Grandpa would damn well have no part of it. Years later, she confessed that sometimes when things were tough she would won-der if she had given up a career as a famous movie star, or even an obscure one. But life as an ironworker's wife turned out to be pretty good, especially once her firstborn child, the boy with the ivory head and the inclination for mischief, grew up.

2

TAKING
OFF

Skinny Crocker and Toots Garrity. Jimmy the Bear Baird and Jerry the Deacon Feltham. Pop Miles, Rubberlegs Martinsen, and Hole in the Head Himpler—I can only guess how he got *his* nickname. They are some of the legendary names from the early days of the culture of ironworkers in New York City, men my grandfather worked with after he arrived from upstate. In those days, only a decade removed from the founding of the first Ironworkers local by a group of German immigrants, there were no limits to the risks these men took just to make a living. Death and injury were so commonplace that the ironworkers had a motto: "We don't die. We are killed." Years later, during the Depression, work was so coveted that each day groups of ironworkers would gather outside job sites, waiting for someone to get hurt or fall off so they could go in and apply for his job.

Ironworkers didn't work with iron, really. They erected structural steel, which is made from iron. But it wasn't wise to call them steelworkers, because a steelworker was some guy in Pennsylvania or West Virginia making steel in a mill. Nothing wrong with that, but a steel mill was down on terra firma, a much safer place to put in nine hours than the workplace in the air that was the province of what were sometimes called high-steel workers. Somehow, the term "high steel worker" never caught on. So Skinny and Rubberlegs and Hole in the Head were ironworkers, as are the 130,000 members of today's International Association of Bridge, Structural, Ornamental and Reinforcing Iron Workers.

It was an industry born in the 1880s, when, almost overnight, steel replaced wood and stone as the principal material used for bearing loads in bridges and large buildings. "Bridge carpenters" became "bridgemen" and "blacksmiths" became "architectural ironworkers" or "house smiths." Structural steel allowed everything to get bigger and taller, but it also meant that a whole new culture of workers had to be created. Men not only with skills but guts—daredevil workers with more courage and endurance than any blue-collar workers before them. Fearlessness of heights and impeccable balance were job requirements one and two in an occupation whose mortality rates were higher than in any other trade. Carrying planks and tools as they ambled along four-inch-wide beams at stunning heights and in all kinds of weather, the early ironworkers became known as "cowboys of the skies." Down below, pedestrians stopped and watched them, peering up as if Barnum & Bailey had just rolled into town.

From down there, it was hard to appreciate how precarious a workplace it was. The men worked on loose planks thrown across beams yet to be fastened tight. They were dependent on the skill of the derrick operator, who couldn't even see what he was doing because he was feeding these enormous and unwieldy beams to men a floor above him. The boom, meanwhile, was driven by an engine operated by a man more than a dozen stories down who decided what moves to make on the basis of bells that he had better hear clearly through the clatter of pounding rivets and the ambient growl of heavy construction.

These men knew what they were getting into, and did their work with a certain amount of bravado and pride. A lot of them carried flasks of whiskey in their back pockets. Drinking on the job would not seem to be the smartest thing to do when the job is to walk on steel beams a couple of hundred feet in the air. But these weren't reckless belts they were taking. For many of the men, a carefully calibrated nip would steady their nerves and actually make them more agile. Years later, photographers Margaret Bourke-White and Lewis W. Hine showed courage of their own in going up and photographing the construction of the Empire State and Chrysler buildings, giving us images such as the famous one showing a dozen ironworkers eating their lunches on a beam a thousand feet in the air, feet dangling and nothing but death beneath them, leaning over and joking around as casually as if they were munching their sandwiches on a bench in Bryant Park. I remember once reading a quote from an early ironworker who remarked that, given the choice, he'd rather work up high than down below. At the bottom, you could get hit with something dropped from above. Up there, at least nothing could fall on you.

Not that there was a whole lot of attention paid to safety. The ironworkers of my grandfather's generation wore beat-up felt fedoras. The first local ironworkers organizations—they weren't called unions yet—were formed around the country not to fight for better wages or even better working conditions, but to ensure decent burials for fallen workers and to help them when they were merely injured. In 1902, for a nine-hour day that paid $3.50, New York City ironworkers had the privilege of working in a trade in which 12 percent of them were killed. One of those was a man who fell a hundred-fifty feet during the construction of the Williamsburg Bridge by the Pennsylvania Steel Company. When his body wasn't recovered, his brother ironworkers—who didn't let much keep them from showing up for work and earning their thirty-nine cents an hour—took an unprecedented action. Normally after a fatal accident, the men would knock off for the day and spend the rest of their shift in the nearest gin mill trying to wash away the image of the poor bastard dropping to his demise. But this time they refused to go back to work in protest. All they wanted was for the company to put boats under the span to recover bodies.

FROM THE EARLIEST part of the twentieth century, the ironworkers on any building or bridge construction were a melting pot. There were groups of Germans, Scandinavians, Irish, Newfoundlanders, and Americans from the South, each with a nickname. The men from Newfoundland were "fish," "herring chokers," or "goofy-noofies." The Swedes and Norwegians were "square heads." Southerners were "tar heels" or "deacons." Though ironworkers came to see themselves as a brotherhood, and the nicknames were affectionate, ethnic pride wasn't lost. There were some squabbles up there over which of them was the better ironworker, which gave rise to the tradition of segregating rivet gangs. It seemed that more work got done when rivet gangs were made up of men from the same ethnic group.

The North American and European ironworkers had their quirks, but by far the most distinctive ethnic group among the old ironworkers were the Indians—the men from the Caughnawaga band of Mohawks who started streaming down from Quebec in 1907. As the story has been told on countless job sites and barstools—and which I remember hearing when I was a kid—the Caughnawagas got into high-steel work by a kind of divine happenstance. Their reservation was on the south shore of the St. Lawrence River just north of Montreal, and they had a succession of trades through the centuries—fishing and farming and hunting—before most became canoe men at the beginning of the eighteenth century, carrying goods from Montreal to ports upriver, returning with canoes laden with furs. This was the Caughnawaga way of life for 150 years, until the fur trade waned and the men started disbursing to other lines of work. According to a 1949 essay on the Caughnawagas by the renowned *New Yorker* writer Joseph Mitchell, some joined the timber-rafting industry on the St. Lawrence, becoming famous for running huge sections of oak and pine over the rapids at the French-Canadian village of Lachine. Others performed old Mohawk dances in circuses that traveled the United States or went around New England on horse-drawn buggies selling homemade tonics the women made on the reservation. And more than a few stopped working, got depressed, and hung out in Montreal and drank.

In the spring of 1886, the Dominion Bridge Company, Canada's biggest steel erector, their version of Bethlehem Steel, began building a rail bridge across the Lachine rapids, connecting the village with a point at the south end of the Caughnawaga reservation. The plans called for the bridge abutment to be on reservation land, which meant Dominion and the rail company, Canadian Pacific, had to make friends with the Caughnawagas. The Indians didn't ask much. In exchange for letting the companies use their land, all they wanted was a promise to employ Caughnawaga men on the job. That was an easy deal for Dominion Bridge to make. They would need laborers to unload materials anyway. But the Caughnawagas had more than that in mind.

As a company official explained to Mitchell sixty years later: "They were dissatisfied with this arrangement and would come out on the bridge itself every chance they got. It was quite impossible to keep them off. As the work progressed, it became apparent to all concerned that these Indians were very odd in that they did not have any fear of heights. If not watched, they would climb up the spans and walk around up there as cool and collected as the toughest of our riveters, most of whom at that period were old sailing-ship men especially picked for their experience in working aloft. These Indians were as agile as goats. They would walk a narrow beam high up in the air with nothing below them but the river, which is rough there and ugly to look down on, and it wouldn't mean any more to them than walking on the solid ground.

"They seemed immune to the noise of the riveting, which goes right through you and is often enough in itself to make you feel sick and dizzy. They were inquisitive about the riveting and were continually bothering our foremen by requesting that they be allowed to take a crack at it. This happens to be the most dangerous work in all construction, and the highest paid. Men who want to do it are rare and men who can do it are even rarer, and in good construction years there are sometimes not enough of them to go around. We decided it would be mutually advantageous to see what these Indians could do, so we picked out some and gave them a little training, and it turned out that putting riveting tools in their hands was like putting ham with eggs. They were natural-born bridgemen."

This was no surprise to the Caughnawagas. *They* knew they weren't afraid of heights. After the Canadian Pacific Bridge was finished, Dominion began work on the Soo Bridge, which connected two cities with the same name, Sault Sainte Marie, one in Ontario and the other in Michigan. The first Caughnawaga riveting gangs moved onto the new bridge and very cleverly recruited apprentices from the reservation to come with them. As soon as the apprentice was trained, they'd send for another one. When four new men were trained, a new rivet gang was born. But instead of putting the new men together, they would shuffle themselves, so that two new men would always be paired with two of the more experienced ones. Over the next twenty years, the ranks of Caughnawaga bridgemen grew to more than seventy. But then came what is commonly referred to among the Caughnawagas as "the disaster."

On August 29, 1907, a span of the Quebec Bridge collapsed during construction, the result of inept design work by unqualified engineers that sent 20,000 tons of steel and ninety men crashing three hundred feet into the St. Lawrence. Thirty-six Caughnawagas—half the band's force of ironworkers— were killed. The accident left twenty-five widows and dozens of fatherless children, and began a tradition that survives to this day: The bodies of Caughnawaga ironworkers who perished on the job were sent back to the reservation for burial, not beneath standard tombstones but under huge crosses made from steel I-beams.

The Quebec Bridge disaster had a strange effect on the Caughnawagas: It made ironwork *more* alluring. "People thought the disaster would scare the Indians away from high steel for good," the patriarch of the Caughnawagas in the 1940s, an eighty-year-old one-time riveter named Old Mr. Jacobs, told Joseph Mitchell. "Instead of which, the general effect it had, it made high steel much more interesting to them. It made them take pride in themselves that they could do such dangerous work. Up to then, the majority of them, they didn't consider it any more dangerous than timber-rafting. Also, it made them the most looked-up-to men on the reservation. The little boys in Caughnawaga used to look up to the men that went out with circuses in the summer and danced and war-whooped all over the States and came back to the reservation in the winter and holed up and sat by the stove and drank whiskey and bragged. That's what they wanted to do. Either that, or work on the timber rafts. After the disaster, they changed their minds—they all wanted to go into high steel."

Caughnawaga women weren't nearly so appreciative of how "interesting" the Quebec Bridge disaster made high-steel work. They insisted that the men who continued no longer work all together on one bridge. Some gangs would go to one job, some to another. That way, if there were another disaster, the reservation wouldn't be quite so devastated as it was after Quebec City. Ironically, this was what led the Caughnawagas to work even higher in the sky. Because there weren't enough bridge jobs, they went to work on all kinds of steel structures: office buildings, hospitals, hotels, distilleries, grain elevators. "Anything and everything," Old Mr. Jacobs said. "In a few years, every steel structure of any size that went up in Canada, there were Indians on it. Then Canada got too small and they began crossing the border. They began going down to Buffalo and Cleveland and Detroit."

New York's first Caughnawaga bridgeman arrived in 1915. John Diabo got hired as the bucker-up on an Irish rivet gang working on the Hell Gate Bridge up the East River. The Irishmen called him Indian Joe. A few months after he arrived, three other Caughnawagas came down and they formed the city's first Indian rivet gang. But one day John took a wrong step on a scaffold, fell into the river, and drowned. The others took him home to be buried on the reservation and never came back. That was the last New York saw of a Caughnawaga working on high steel until a decade later.

THE EARLY-CENTURY BUILDING boom in New York saw the construction of one East River bridge after another and a series of skyscrapers proclaimed "tallest building in the world," culminating with the 56-story Woolworth Building. This "cathedral of commerce," as it was envisioned by five-and-dime magnate Frank W. Woolworth, opened in 1913 on Park Place at Barclay Street, two blocks from where two successors to the crown, cathedrals of commerce in their own right, would be erected sixty years later.

The boom times for structural steel erectors and the rest of the construction industry came to a crashing end in every major city when World War I began and thousands of ironworkers were shipped off to fight in Europe or were put to work by the government in shipyards. There was so little going on that the ironworker union locals all but disbanded.

Grandpa, thirty-two and the father of five when the war broke out in 1914, scrambled to earn a living. He teamed up with a friend of his, an Irish ironworker named Larabee. They bought a pickup truck and spent the war years going around the Bronx doing little steel jobs, putting up storefronts and small buildings. By necessity Grandpa had to master more of the process of steel erecting than riveting. He became a rigger, learning the ins and outs of using lines, chains, steel cable and blocks and tackle to hoist steel with derricks and cranes.

My father was fascinated by his father's work. Ever since Dad was a little kid, Grandpa would take him to jobs he was working on and describe everything that was going on, how each of these men had a specific job to do at a specific point in the sequence of events, and how somehow it all came together in the end. Grandpa would explain that ironworkers were divided into three groups: the raising gangs, the fitting-up gangs, and the riveting gangs. He showed Dad the big sections of steel piled high, and explained that they came from the fabricator, already cut and built into columns, beams, and girders according to the engineering plans. He would point to the numbers painted onto each piece. "That's so the men will know where it goes."

Dad watched the raising gang use the derrick to hoist the pieces of steel up and set them, putting temporary bolts through pre-drilled holes to hold them in place. Then he saw the men in the fitting-up gang take over, as Grandpa explained how they were making sure the pieces were plumb before tightening them with guy wires and turnbuckles. And how they spread plank at every floor so that if a man slipped, he couldn't fall more than twenty feet. Finally the four-man riveting gang comes in to finish the process. The heater with his forge set up shop on a plank he laid across a pair of beams. The other men used ropes to hang a plank on either side of the spot they were working on, then climbed down with their tools. Dad would be entranced as the rivet gang performed its relay of high steel: the heater plucking the hot rivet from the forge, tossing it thirty or forty feet in the air; the sticker-in catching the rivet in his cone-shaped can, picking it out with his tongs, pushing it through the hole, stem end first; the bucker-up bracing the sizzling rivet with his dolly bar; the riveter smashing the stem end with his beater until it matched the button head on the other side.

As much as Dad loved watching the ironworkers, being around them and helping out by carrying tools and loading trucks, he never wanted to be one of them, not really. His real interest was in the blueprints Grandpa began to bring home when he went out on his own with Larabee. Dad was a math whiz; he once went on a radio show and, computing numbers in his head, won a calculation competition against a Chinese man who used an abacus.

So he was a natural at estimating steel jobs. Grandpa would spread a set of plans across the kitchen table, and Dad would pore over it, counting. He would count the beams and the rivets and calculate how much steel the job required. This was—still is—called taking off. The contractor takes off, or records, all the members of steel in the job, counting them and noting their nomenclature and length and weight, all the key information he needs to estimate the cost of the job. A typical takeoff item looks like this: 10-36WF230 x 30'6"=7015 lbs. This reads ten pieces of thirty-six-inch-wide flange beam with a weight of two hundred-thirty pounds per foot, each piece thirty feet, six inches long. The total weight of these pieces is 7,015 pounds—30.5 feet times 230 pounds. After he finishes the takeoff, he knows how many pieces must be erected, what the heaviest piece weighs, what the total tonnage of the job is—information that he needs to price out the job.

After Dad did the takeoff, Grandpa would describe the labor: how many beams could be unloaded and set in a day, how many rivets could be driven in a day, how many men he would need and what they would be paid, what equipment would have to be rented. From all this Dad would calculate the total cost of labor, materials, and equipment, then add a reasonable profit. And that would be Grandpa's bid. And often as not, he won the bid. Dad was only a teenager, but Grandpa was only doing small jobs. Even as they got bigger, he came to depend on his son, not only for his precise calculations—which was just basic math, after all—but for his uncanny instinct for how long the different facets of the job would take. Since a steel erector's bid was all about labor, his calculations had to be all about time.

Dad was not unaware of Grandpa's growing dependence on him. "Grandpa was a great rigger," my father used to tell me, "but he was no businessman." Larabee was no better. Dad was still in high school when he started thinking that he would make a better partner for his father. I have no trouble envisioning him as a ballsy teenager with big plans.

One day when he was seventeen, Dad came to Grandpa with a proposition. "You know rigging and I know how to bid a job," he said. "Come on, Dad, let's form a company." Though it was usually a father in business asking his son to join him rather than the other way around, I don't imagine my grandparents were surprised by Dad's brashness. They both knew he was already more sophisticated than his country-born father. He had proven himself to be a fast study, and amazed both his parents with his ability to make elaborate calculations in his head. But what made him more than a whiz-kid bean counter was that he already seemed to have a grasp of the business as a whole, along with the personality to deal with people on both ends—contractors and builders and union business agents and ironworkers. Not only that, he had saved up $1,200, an incredible sum, from caddying at golf courses. They could use that, along with some money Grandma had gotten from her mother, to get their business off the ground. Grandma especially thought this was a fine idea. Grandpa dumped Larabee, and he and Dad looked for a place to use as an office. The cheapest one they could find was at a goat yard in the Bronx. And so with goats bleating in the background, the Karl Koch Erecting Company was born.

While working their first small jobs, Dad enrolled in night school, studying engineering at Brooklyn Polytechnical College. After his last class of the night, instead of going home he'd park his car in front of the job site to cut down on his travel time. He'd fall asleep in the car, and the beat cops looked out for him through the night. The foreman would wake him up each morning at seven, and he'd be the first one on the job. But eventually it was too exhausting and he quit school to devote all his energies to the fledgling family business. He didn't really want to be an engineer, anyway. Nor did he want to be up there erecting steel like his father. He wanted to be down on the ground, making the deals and organizing the work.

In the early days of their business, Grandpa and Dad went on the road, bidding on jobs. Dad would do the estimating and presenting—and even though he wasn't yet out of his teens, Dad was very presentable. He was tall, handsome, and articulate. He exuded self-assurance, and he could talk numbers with men of any age. And Grandpa had more than enough experience as an ironworker, foreman, and rigger. If they got the job Dad would handle the contracts and then drop in at the ironworkers' union hall and meet with the local's business agent. We're coming into town, he'd say, and we need some good men. We'll pay good money. After the deals were made, Grandpa went out and built the job, doing the steelwork at first with locals and later with a corps of loyal ironworkers, including some from the second wave of Caughnawaga from Canada who began traveling with them.

BUSINESS WAS GOING well enough for Grandma and Grandpa to move the family from the Bronx to a house in Jamaica, Queens. But apparently they brought the "aura of disaster" with them. On her eighth birthday, my aunt Delores was hit by a car on her way home from church. She couldn't walk for three months, never mind using the shiny new skates she had gotten for her birthday. A few months later, Grandma gave birth to the last of her ten children, Daniel. When he was two months old, she had what she later called a nervous breakdown—probably what's now called postpartum depression—and had to be taken to the hospital. It was summer, and with Grandpa and my father at work during the day, seventeen-year-old Gladys was left in charge of seven kids.

One day, Grandpa and Dad were coming home from work in Grandpa's Buick when something didn't look right as they got close to the house. Usually they could see their roof from around the corner. When they pulled onto their street, they saw that not only was the roof missing but so was most of the second floor. Three-year-old Jerome had set fire to a mattress in the attic and then hid under a bed. Miraculously he and everyone else escaped, but Grandpa had to figure out what to do with a houseful of kids and a wife in a psychiatric hospital. He and the children stayed with friends for a few weeks, and then he rented a summer house in Island Park, on the South Shore of Long Island, until the house in Jamaica was rebuilt. Grandma eventually came home, fully recovered from whatever had taken hold of her, and she and Grandpa wound up building their own house in Island Park, where the family spent its summers for years. Except for Julia contracting polio when she was eight, the skies over the Koch family seemed to brighten.

In 1924, Dad had the idea that it was time to go for something big. He heard about a job going out for bid that Grandpa would have had every right to consider out of their league. It was the new Biltmore Hotel in Coral Gables, Florida. The area around Miami was booming, and the Biltmore, a few miles south of the city, would be a landmark for its time and place. The building was designed by two of the most eminent hotel architects of the era, the team of Leonard Schultze and S. Fullerton Weaver, who conceived it in what they called the Mediterranean Revival style, which was to become a South Florida trademark. With its centerpiece, inspired by the Giralda tower of the Cathedral of Seville in Spain, the Biltmore would have the feel of an old-world European luxury hotel.

Bidding on the Biltmore was a nervy move for two guys—a rigger and his twenty-year-old son—who were not experienced contractors. But Dad couldn't see why the Biltmore people wouldn't look at this as an advantage. An experienced contractor, he reasoned, wouldn't be as hands-on as he and Grandpa would be. And they could submit a much leaner bid, because the bigger contractors could be relied upon to pad theirs with contingency costs and overhead. And indeed, the Biltmore people found themselves sitting at a table with these two ambitious and sincere erectors who were offering to build their hotel for a low, low price. After Dad presented their number, the hotel men asked them to step outside so they could talk among themselves.

Leaving the room, Dad, nervous, lit a cigarette. "You don't have to smoke, I never did," Grandpa told him, and Dad snuffed his cigarette.

Inside, the Biltmore guys calculated their risk. All the engineering work was done, and they were buying the steel from the fabricator themselves. So really all these Koches have to do is erect it. The father has a lot of experience and the kid seems to know his stuff. If they do what they're saying, we'll beat our budget.

They gave them a shot, and more than seventy-five years later the Biltmore in Coral Gables remains regal, the jewel of a four-star golf resort. Of course, when my grandfather and father were finished with their part of the work, the hotel was only as regal as a skeleton of structural steel could be. But they contributed something beyond workmanship. They and their corps of traveling ironworkers finished the steelwork so quickly that the hotel had its grand opening in January 1926—just ten months after ground was broken. People came to see this mad pace as a symbol of the go-go real estate and building fervor that swept South Florida in the Twenties. The Biltmore established the bona fides of the Karl Koch Erecting Company and led to a lot of work in and around Miami, including Burdines department store and the McFadden Urban Hotel, owned by Bernard McFadden, the century's first health and fitness guru, who sponsored a "World's Most Perfectly Developed Man" contest at the original Madison Square Garden. My father and grandfather had parlayed their own audacity and the hotel company's gamble into the big break they needed.

To Grandma, who well remembered the bitter cold and the struggle for work in upstate New York, following the work to Florida was like going to paradise. She considered the Biltmore a godsend. "From then on," she recalled, "I spent the winters in the sunny south, mostly in Miami, as my men were busy building bridges and buildings in booming Florida." She brought the younger children with her, while the older ones stayed north, except during school vacations. They often drove, though Grandma preferred to book passage on a Clyde-Mallory ocean liner, which sailed regularly between New York and Miami.

One year when school was about to start up, Grandma put Patty, Bob, and Jerome on a ship for New York. She wasn't ready to go home and thought the children were old enough—Patty was thirteen, her brothers twelve and ten—to travel on their own, under the strict supervision of the ship's stewards, of course. Their big brother Karl, who was at home with the younger children, would meet them when the boat docked. The three made it home, but when Grandma boarded the same boat a few weeks later, she heard that they'd had maybe a little too much fun. Apparently the stewards had kept an eye on the kids when they could have used two. Patty had been in charge on the high seas, and she was anything but timid. One at a time, each of the boys had walked on the ship's rail, with Patty holding his hand. She played shuffleboard and pool for money, winning seventy dollars, sharing her fortune with all hands. Any of the stewards who did anything for the kids got five-dollar tips. Fearing her brother Karl's reaction if she had any money left when he met them in New York, she gave away the rest.

For my grandfather and father, the success of the Biltmore in Coral Gables meant something more than escaping the New York winters. Dad knew that breaking their backs on such a high-profile job—and impressing the likes of Leonard Schultze and Fullerton Weaver—would pay off. And it did. Three years later, another Schultze and Weaver hotel came up, this one in their own backyard. It was the Hotel Pierre, one of the city's first skyscraper hotels.

The builder was the George A. Fuller Company, the company whose founder is credited with coming up with the modern contractor system. In 1902, Fuller built its own headquarters, which became one of New York's most eccentric and beloved buildings and is now, at twenty-two stories and one hundred years, the oldest remaining skyscraper in the city. Originally called the Fuller Building, it has long been known as the Flatiron Building. When the Fuller company was hired to build the Pierre, Dad and Grandpa decided to bid on the steel erection. Dad worked the numbers for weeks, and came up with a lean bid. After all the bids were considered, the Fuller people told him that while they would love to give him the job, he wasn't the low bidder, a not-uncommon lie. "Give us a cut," the Fuller man said. And Dad did. "That's not enough," he was told. But he knew the man was bluffing and told him he and his father were sticking with their number. "Well, that's too bad," the man said. "We would have liked to see you get the job."

Dad left the office, and a week later the man called. "Come on back," he said. "You've got the job." On the way to the Flatiron Building to accept the job, Dad started second-guessing himself. He knew the general contractor had tried to peddle his last number to other, more experienced erectors and couldn't find any to even match it, let alone beat it. Was the bid too low? Could they really bring the job in for that? What the hell, he thought, finally, we can do it. He sealed the deal with a handshake. That, and some letters back and forth, were what constituted a contract in those days.

Grandpa and Dad bought their first derrick and rented a two-drum clyde hoist and a whole series of guys and turnbuckles for plumbing up the building and holding it rigid while the rivets were being driven. What they didn't have was money to meet the payroll for the three dozen or so men they would be hiring. So their deal with the Fuller people was that they would be paid weekly. In effect, Dad and Grandpa were like construction managers—hiring the men, acquiring the equipment, and running the erection—but using the financial wherewithal of the builder to raise themselves up into the big leagues.

The Pierre was a more difficult project than the Biltmore. The 42-story central tower rose from an exceptionally large and complex base to take advantage of the hotel's location in a residential neighborhood, which meant there would be no stores on the ground floor. And with 714 good-sized rooms, this hotel was no ten-month job.

In those days, it started with beer cans. The steel base plates that would anchor all the steel columns of the project were secured with bolts that were placed inside beer cans with the top and bottom lids removed. That's how they contained the wet concrete that was poured in as a derrick lifted the base plate and placed it over the anchor bolts. The first truckload of steel was for the columns. A man called a hooker-on (another self-descriptive job title) put a cable called a choker around the beam and put the eye of the choker on the lifting hook of the derrick. Another man tied a half-inch line onto the beam, and the signal man called to the hoist operator to take 'er away. If they were low enough for the operator to see, the signal man would use hand gestures. If they were higher up, he used bells. Then the piece was raised and swung to its setting location, where successive gangs of men connected, bolted, and riveted the piece.

Each time the men erected two floors of steel, they would spread plank over the higher floor so that the derricks could jump to their new location. My father once told me that if an ironworker gave a foreman like Jack Finnel or Steve Burkhardt a lot of lip, he was likely to find himself assigned to the lowly plank gang. One foreman liked to taunt any man who was a special pain in the ass with the threat that he was getting only a half-day's pay because every time he put a piece of plank down he came back with his hands empty. If an ironworker wasn't producing enough, or was a risk to himself or other men, or if he simply rubbed him the wrong way, the foreman would tell him, "Go downstairs and say good-bye to the timekeeper." When that happened, there was a line of men outside the job waiting to take his place. It was foremen like Jack and Steve—each the sort of man one magazine writer at the time compared to "a profane orchestra conductor, directing the derrick, yelling at the bull-stick man who turns the boom, signaling with his arms and his hands to the man who yanks the engineer's bells, jerking his head at the tag line pair whose line guides the dangling column"—who allowed the Koch company to bring in its first big New York job without going under.

After its completion in 1930, the Pierre, which was named for its manager Charles Pierre, became known as the most lavish of the hotels in the area of the city known as the Plaza District. It was famous for opulent entertainment and as a tony address for temporary residents, even though it opened only a few months after the crash that started the Depression. The Pierre, on Fifth Avenue at Sixty-first Street, and another Schultze-Weaver hotel, the Sherry-Netherland two blocks down Fifth, formed a famous duo, posing together grandly in many photographs, including some by the legendary Alfred Stieglitz. Taking pictures from his apartment and gallery windows, Stieglitz turned images of the city's architecture into art. A famous one was shot from his seventeenth-floor gallery, An American Place, on Madison Avenue and showed the two hotels in romantic silhouette against the sky. Together the two hotels raised the prestige of the neighborhood and were largely responsible for the area eventually becoming New York's third skyline district, after Times Square and Lower Manhattan.

As soon as they were done with the Pierre, Grandpa and Dad moved a few blocks down to Fifty-seventh Street, erecting the steel for the Fuller Company's new headquarters. And then came their biggest project of these years: the Hotel New Yorker, on Eighth Avenue at Thirty-fourth Street, adjacent to Pennsylvania Station. With 2,503 guest rooms and a structure of massive, stepped sections and dramatic lighting at night, it made the Pierre look practically like a country inn. The New Yorker was built and operated on such a grand scale that when it opened in 1930 it became the largest hotel in the city. It had five restaurants staffed by thirty-five master chefs and a barber shop with forty-two chairs and twenty manicurists. There were ninety-two telephone operators and a laundry staff of 150 that washed more than 300,000 pieces a day. The nation's largest private power plant ran the whole operation from the sub-basement. In its heyday, through the Thirties and Forties, the New Yorker was what would now be called a happening place. All the big bands played the ballroom and guests came from the highest ranks of New York society. Joe DiMaggio lived there. (The hotel started declining in the Fifties, and closed down in 1972. It was renovated and reopened on a much more modest scale twenty years later. Today it's a Ramada franchise.)

I grew up knowing that Grandpa and Dad had built the Pierre and the New Yorker, and every time I walked by and gazed up at them, I imagined them up there. While Grandpa and the foremen ran the ironworkers, Dad handled the administrative duties. He was a timekeeper, a paymaster, a project engineer. He monitored the flow of steel and made sure all the planks and bolts and tools were on hand. He kept track of everything with endless, perfunctory notes to himself scribbled on yellow pads. On Fridays he would go to the bank and then back to the job to hand out envelopes stuffed with cash. On the Pierre, he also helped plumb the job, keeping the building level as it climbed skyward. For the rest of his life this provided him with one of his favorite self-deprecating jokes. "I got another call from the concierge at the Pierre today," he loved to say. "The guests are complaining that the water won't run out of the bathtubs."

He could joke about it because he more than compensated for his modest ability and lesser interest in manual work with the kind of business acumen that made it possible for his father, a journeyman ironworker, to become the proprietor of a major construction company. I've always been amazed by how young Dad was, still in his teens when he started negotiating contracts and only in his mid-twenties when he helped oversee the construction of these mammoth buildings. After putting up the Biltmore, the Pierre, and the New Yorker, the family was actually wealthy enough to stay in these famous hotels. They were pivotal projects in my father's career, and were always his favorites.

With the money flowing, my father used company money to buy his parents a fifteen-room Tudor mansion in the wealthy suburb of Scarsdale, north of the city in Westchester County. It was 1931, an odd time to be doing well, not to mention buying a house that looked like a medieval European cathedral. The house, in fact, was designed by a prominent architect who had intended to live there until he lost his fortune in the stock market crash and committed suicide. Grandma was always the first to spot omens, wary in particular of houses that might have auras of disaster. Apparently, though, she had no such qualms about the Scarsdale manse.

3

THE
ORANGE BLOSSOM
EXPRESS

As AMBITIOUS AND industrious as my father was, he was also something of a man about town. Especially after the money started rolling in. He was a hard drinker, drove a two-seat Packard, and was a regular at the Cotton Club, even if he was just a kid from Queens. One night in 1929, he was at a club in Hollis, Queens, which had a bar on the ground floor and a dance hall upstairs. There was a teenager playing the piano, really pounding the keys, and a girl leaning against the piano, tapping her foot. She noticed my father sitting in a chair, watching her. "He was very dignified, very quiet," my mother recalls. "He was just watching, so I went over and said hi and asked if he would like to dance." The one thing Dad was never good at and never liked to do was dance. He politely declined, but kept on watching her when she returned to the piano. She had an hibiscus flower behind her ear.

Marie Palffy was only seventeen at the time, but already working as a chorus line dancer. She was the younger of two daughters of Hungarian immigrants. Family lore has it that her father, Eugene Palffy, was a count born into an aristocratic family whose origins dated to the twelfth century. But as the younger son in a culture of primogeniture, he stood to inherit nothing and worked as a wine merchant. He and my grandmother had been married in the Old Country and sailed across the Atlantic to New York in late August of 1912, only months after the *Titanic* sank in the same waters. My grandmother was well into her eighth month of pregnancy, and it was anyone's guess which would arrive first—the ship or the baby. Mom was considerate enough to wait until two weeks after her mother waddled through Ellis Island and got settled on the Lower East Side of Manhattan. She gave real meaning to the term "first-generation American," though her first words were Hungarian, and she grew up bilingual.

Despite his noble lineage and respectable occupation in Hungary, my mother's father was just another of the millions of European immigrants early in the century. "He was a nobody," my mother told me one day in the kitchen of her apartment in Florida. "He worked in a furniture warehouse." (But he was more than that. In the 1980s, I met an old Hungarian gentleman who told me that Eugene Palffy was illustrious among the immigrants in the Little Hungary section of New York for having helped many of them get settled.)

My mother's parents separated when she was three. Mom's sister Christine, eleven years her senior, was probably the biggest influence on her. By sixteen, Christine was already in show business, dancing in nightclubs. "I was about five when my sister taught me her dance," Mom said. "The song was 'I'll Be Down to Get You in a Taxi, Honey.' The dance was the shimmy, where you shake your shoulders. They called it jazz dance or a 'specialty dance.' We went to some kind of nightclub where my sister was performing. It wasn't a really nice one—they didn't even serve dinner. I got up and did my dance." Recalling this moment some eighty-five years later, Mom got up from the table in her kitchen and broke into a demonstration of the shimmy, accompanying herself with a chorus of "I'll Be Down to Get You in a Taxi, Honey." "Everybody was bringing money to the table. My mother stopped them. But she let me keep what was there, I think it was like five or ten dollars, and with that she bought me white and blue silk gloves and a pair of black patent leather shoes with a strap."

My mother's family moved out of the city, as Manhattan was called, to Jamaica, in Queens. When she was fourteen her sister paid for her to have ballet lessons in Manhattan, but during the first lesson the teacher, an older man, made an inappropriate advance. "That creep," she said. "He was about seventy, he was very gray with a wrinkled, skinny face. So that was the end of my ballet lessons." Instead, Christine taught her how to be a showgirl, showing her the routines until she thought she was good enough to join her on the Loew's circuit. Christine was by now a solo performer and married to a bandleader named Irving Aaronson, whom she had met while they were both performing on the circuit. Irving's band, the Commanders, included the young Gene Krupa and Artie Shaw. They were in Cole Porter's Broadway show *Paris* and recorded four songs with Bing Crosby, including a number one hit, "Love in Bloom."

At sixteen my mother quit high school when Irving and Christine arranged for her to start dancing for Loew's, which had opened enormous theaters—movie palaces that also had live shows—in all the boroughs and in New Jersey. "My sister said, 'I have a job for you,' " Mom said. "They made me a showgirl, not a big showgirl, just decorating the scenery." She would make thirty dollars a week and live in rented rooms "on the road," which meant the Bronx or Brooklyn. "I didn't want to leave school, and later on I resented it," Mom said. "She was my big sister, so I thought I had to do it. My mother didn't say anything. I sent her fifteen or twenty dollars every week."

The night my father was watching her in the upstairs club in Jamaica, she was hanging around with her friend Harry, the piano player, before going to work. She was dancing that night at the newest Loew's, the Valencia on Jamaica Avenue, a 3,500-seat palace that had opened just months before and was to go on to become a landmark. When she came out the stage door after the show, my father was waiting for her. And a few feet away was Harry, who walked her home. Dad tried this two or three times, but Harry was always there.

Some months later, Mom was on the road, dancing at the Paramount Theater in Washington, D.C. After the show she emerged from the stage door, and there he was. "I just happened to be in town," he said. The next time he was home, he drove over to her house and took her for a ride in the Packard. He had taken her out only a dozen times when they were sitting in the driveway in Island Park. Dad shut the ignition and said, "I have a little ring here. Would you wear it?" Mom, oblivious to the implication, said, "All right."

"He takes out this ring and it's like a two-and-half-carat diamond," my mother recalled. "He gave it to me and put it on my finger, and then we left to take me home. After I got home it dawned on me what just happened. I didn't know. He didn't say anything. He was never very talkative. He was very smart but he never explained anything. So it didn't dawn on me until I got home and I told my mother, 'I think I'm engaged.' "

They were married the following summer, at City Hall in Manhattan. After the ceremony, my father took his bride on a romantic honeymoon: to Jersey City for a meeting with the business agent for the ironworkers local and some New Jersey politicians. He introduced her, then got down to business over drinks. He had a contract to negotiate for a section of the Pulaski Skyway, an intricate span that would link Newark with Jersey City and Hoboken and be one of the first freeway-bridge structures in the country. My mother was so annoyed when Dad took her to a rundown hotel after the meeting, and then promptly fell asleep, that she packed her things and got on a train for Queens. As far as she was concerned, the marriage was over.

When Dad woke up in the morning, he was frantic. He thought someone might have kidnapped her. Jersey City was a tough town. Then he realized she had probably gone home and so drove to Queens to apologize. She came downstairs only reluctantly, and then only after he promised to be an attentive husband and never treat her as he had on their wedding night. It was an unpromising beginning to their marriage, even though the Pulaski Skyway was later named "Most Beautiful Steel Structure" by the American Institute of Steel Construction. (It was also immortalized as an escape route in Orson Welles' *War of the Worlds* radio broadcast in 1939.)

So there was no annulment, and almost immediately my parents began filling their little second-story apartment in Jamaica with the next generation of Koches. My sister Marie was born first, in 1931, and I followed her by a year, becoming the third Karl William Koch. There would be four more girls and two more boys for a total of eight—a mighty burden for my poor mother, who after all had not really thought through my father's marriage proposal and now found his promise of attentiveness wanting. Their marriage was constantly interrupted by Dad's long absences demanded by his business.

ANY NOTION THAT the Depression didn't apply to the Koch family was quickly vanquished. There was little work and a lot of competition, so Grandpa and Dad found themselves bidding jobs at a loss, and even then not always getting the contract. My father told me he always carried Mom's engagement ring with him in those days in case he couldn't make payroll. He once managed to stay afloat on a job—and escape what might have turned into a mob of unhappy ironworkers—by drawing a miraculous hand at the card table. At one point Grandpa heard there was work in Georgia. Grandma stood on the porch, watching him drive off. Then she fell onto the porch swing and cried. Grandpa came back from Georgia a few weeks later, tired and discouraged. And then along came a beautiful thing called the New Deal.

It's hard to consider the Depression a boom time, but that's what it became for builders who got in on the wealth of government contracts to construct buildings for all the government agencies created and expanded under President Franklin D. Roosevelt. For an up-and-coming steel erector like the Koch company, it was crucial to cultivate good relationships with the biggest general contractors and steel fabricators because they held the keys to the kingdom. When the government, or a private company for that matter, announced a project and invited bids from the major general contractors, the G.C.'s would then break up the job into all the trades, from plumbing to roofing. Structural steel was a major and pivotal piece, of course. In some cases the steel subcontract would be divided further into two sub-subgroups—one contract for furnishing and fabricating the steel and another for erecting it. In other cases, the general contractor sought bids from a steel fabricator who submitted a price that covered everything—buying the steel from the mill, fabricating it to specification, shipping to the job site, and erecting it—up to and including pounding the last rivet into place.

On those jobs, Dad and Grandpa had to partner up with a fabricator and try to work out a combined number low enough to beat the bids of other fabricator-erector teams. Dad's most frequent partner was Bristol Steel, a company from the Virginia-Tennessee border run by the Tilley Brothers, Jim and Bill, who became his good friends. He would go down to their office or to a hotel and the three of them would spread the blueprints across a big table, with a bottle of whiskey in the middle. Then they'd spend hours poring over the plans and pouring drinks, talking about how much steel they would need, what kind of delivery and erecting schedule they'd need to keep to, and finally how much they wanted out of it. For Dad and Grandpa, it was all about labor, and the numbers always flowed from the question of how many derricks would be needed. For each one, they needed six men on the raising gang, an operating engineer to run the hoist, and several four-man riveting gangs (the number depended on the size of the job and on whether they were using heavy structural steel that required more rivets). They needed one apprentice—they called them punks in those days—and they needed a foreman for the raising gang and another for the riveting gang.

By the end of the day, Dad and the Tilley brothers would have one price, to furnish and erect the steel, to submit to the general contractor. Then they had to hope, first, that theirs was the lowest bid among those submitted by all the teams of fabricators and erectors, and then, that the general contractor they were submitting their figure to had the lowest complete bid to get the job over other contractors. "If we get the job, you get the job," were the words Dad heard over and over.

Dad and Grandpa were little guys, scrappy underdogs to the heavy-weights of the industry, American Bridge—the steel-erecting division of United States Steel—and Bethlehem Steel. American Bridge was especially hard to beat because they were owned by the largest steel mill in the United

States. They poured and rolled their own steel. They had their own fabricating shops. It was common knowledge—and infuriating to my father—that American Bridge was essentially a sales arm of U.S. Steel. All they and Bethlehem really wanted to do was sell their steel, so they offered a single "furnish and erect" price that was barely more than the price of the steel itself. The erection price was essentially a loss leader. Once he realized this, Dad began pressing builders and procurement officers on government jobs to require steel contractors to break out their prices, one for the steel, one to put it up. He knew that if the giants were forced to submit a separate bid for erection, he could beat their price. And in the rare instances where the general contractors did break down the bids that way, Dad easily underbid the men of Big Steel. Among other projects, this was what happened with the Hotel New Yorker and the Department of Commerce building in Washington. In those cases, the steel our men raised, set, and riveted came from the mills and fabricating shops of my father's archrival, American Bridge.

By the early Thirties, Dad and Grandpa's company had established a reputation for bringing projects in. "Gentlemen," wrote general contractor Algernon Blair of Montgomery, Alabama, in April of 1933, "I have had real pleasure in observing the efficiency of your organization which resulted in the extraordinary achievement at Jacksonville in the erection of 2,600 tons of structural steel required in connection with my contract for construction of US Courthouse and Post Office buildings there. The service you rendered was perfect, and the time within which you erected this work was less than I believed practicable. I want you to know that I shall seek an opportunity for having other work with you." In those days, you could take a letter like that to the bank. Literally.

The really big contracting companies of the time—Fuller, Kelly, McCloskey, and McShain, who is considered the man who built modern Washington—were also giving work to the company. I'm sure it was their low bids and quality work that kept them busy, but somewhere in there was my father's deft social touch. He was well aware of the value of being an insider. Jack Kelly was Grace Kelly's father, and years later when she made the headlines, Dad would tell me, "I used to play cards with her old man." He played cards and drank with anyone in business who was willing. It didn't get him any jobs, but it sure didn't cost him any. My father's whole life was centered around the family and business, which were one and the same. He didn't have a single friend who wasn't somehow involved in the business. "Karl," he once told me, "in life your best friends are your banker and your lawyer."

His lawyer, who incorporated the company in 1931, was Grant Horner, who ran a one-man show on Forty-second Street. Mr. Horner's office was packed to the gills with papers and files. He had one little light and no secretary. "He's the smartest lawyer in the country," Dad said. Years later when I was starting out, I remember Horner, by then the very picture of the old, white-haired legal scholar, leaning close to me and saying, "Karl, I'm very fond of your father. We've been close a very long time. I want to give you a piece of advice that I hope you will remember all your life." Yes, Mr. Horner? "Don't put pepper on your food." He meant it—that's how serious a lawyer he was. The other lawyers my father considered his best friends were the Weiss brothers, Joe and Walter. "They used to call Dad a *Yiddisher cup*, which means 'Jewish head,' " my sister Marie recalled. "They could not believe that with his head he wasn't Jewish. He was too smart to be a *goyisher cup*." Dad reveled in the affection of his Jewish friends. When he took me to lunch as a boy it was usually to a kosher deli, where he would utter a few words in Yiddish to get his order.

THE DAY THAT bids were to be submitted and opened publicly was a big event for the general contractors, and for all the subcontractors and sub-subcontractors waiting to hear if they had made good choices in who to work with and how much to bid. After spending months collecting and calculating their numbers from the different trades, the general contractors convened at a government office and presented the procurement officer with their envelopes, nodding brusque acknowledgments to their competitors before sitting down in wooden chairs, pads and pencils resting on their laps. One by one, the officer unsealed each bid and read it aloud. If there were other requirements for the submission—say, a certified check for 10 percent of the bid amount to serve as a bond, or an acknowledgment that the bidder had received all of the addenda to the proposal—the officer would say whether the bidder had complied with them. If everything was not in order, he would fold the bid, return it to its envelope, and say, "Bid not acceptable." The sloppy contractor would slink out of the room.

After all the bids were read and the winner declared, the losers stood and start filing out of the room, offering grudging congratulations to the low man as they passed his chair. "Looks like you got a job," one might say. If the bid was *very* low, far beneath the next-lowest bid, he would say with a smirk, "You left a lot of money on the table." That meant that the winning bidder was seemingly so anxious to get the job that he had bid much lower than he had to. The money between his bid and the next-lowest was money he could have had if he'd submitted a sharper number.

The news of the winning bid on a major project triggered dozens of phone calls up and down the line. Sometimes contractors like Koch didn't know where they stood even when a general contractor to which they'd submitted a bid came up the winner, because the contractor didn't always tell them whether he had used *their* bid in *his* bid. The words they wanted to hear were: "I used your number. You've got a job." But it was common for the announcement to spark all kinds of jockeying. "You're not low bidder," the general contractor might say to any number of erectors and fabricators, "but you're in there." It was a ploy. The contractor was in the driver's seat and could give the vying steel subcontractors the opportunity to help him increase his profit. He would invite them in to go over their prices and schedules, trying to lower the number he'd used in his winning bid. The eventual winner could turn out to be a loser, if he lowered his number so much that, having gotten the job, he had to knock himself out just to break even.

Dad quickly picked up on the game, and before long let it be known that he wasn't playing. "I'm giving you my best price," he would say before the general contractor submitted his complete bid to the government. "If you use it, I expect you to give me the job." Eventually, he didn't have to say it. Everyone knew it. He would not negotiate after the fact.

On private jobs, the bids were considered in secret by the owners, who were of course not obliged to award the job to the lowest bidder. It was their building, their money, and their right to play favorites—though this was rarely based on anything but merit. It was not unusual for a contractor to reject a low bidder because of his performance on previous jobs. A low bid was all-but-irrelevant if the erector (or any subcontractor) failed to keep his schedules, if he overcharged for extra work, or his field-management team was impossible to control and refused to take direction.

It wasn't unusual for losing bidders to think a job was fixed. Sometimes they were right and sometimes they were just mad. When bids were put out for the Empire State Building in 1930, Dad and Grandpa were invited to bid on it by the general contractor, Starrett Brothers & Eken. Dad brought the company's bid to the Starrett office on the designated day, while my mother waited for him in an outer office. When he came out a while later, he went straight to the bathroom and threw up. "Let's get out of here," he told Mom when he emerged. "They gave it to American Bridge. We were third. It was rigged."

My father prided himself in his skill as an estimator, his ability to calcu-late the perfect bid, high enough to make money but low enough to win. He didn't suffer losing easily, and getting screwed even less. Sometimes he made no distinction between the two, especially if American Bridge or Bethlehem Steel was involved. Years later, when I asked my father if he'd ever wanted to build the Empire State Building, he told me, "No, we were too small." It was his way of both acknowledging and avoiding a subject that was still painful for him. The Koch company *was* seen as too small and unseasoned to trust with a building of the magnitude of the Empire State. But he never stopped believing that they could have done it every bit as well as American Bridge.

Instead, Dad looked to Washington for sustenance. His first winning bid on a government building was a project that you could say also got our fam-ily started. It was the Department of Commerce building, the project that brought Dad to Washington while my mother was dancing there. Commerce was a huge building. Its facade on Fifteenth Street was a thou-sand feet long, and when it opened in 1932 its one million square feet of space would make it the largest office building in the country. It was a mon-strous job for the Koch company, and it opened the door to three other major projects: the U.S. Supreme Court, the Federal Reserve Bank, and the Department of the Interior buildings. The company also built additions to two nineteenth-century buildings. One was the Adams Building, a free-standing annex to the Library of Congress built in 1936, and the other was an extension to the Civil War–era Government Printing Office, in 1939.

When you look at these buildings, steel isn't the first thing that comes to mind, especially in the case of the Supreme Court building. Designed by the architect Cass Gilbert (who also designed the Woolworth Building in New York) the Supreme Court was all neoclassical pillars and Vermont marble. But years later my father took my sisters Marie and Roberta on a business trip to Washington and went to the Supreme Court building. The marshal knew Dad, and told the girls, "I want to show you something your father did." He took them to a circular stair behind the justices's chambers, which allowed them private access to the courtroom below. The stairway was made of marble and had no visible support. "Your dad built this," he said. "It wasn't in the original building plans. Your father created it."

Even as they were putting up the buildings in Washington, Dad could often be found in their office back in New York doing takeoffs for government jobs around the country. There were post offices and courthouses and bridges in major cities from Philadelphia to Chattanooga. He loved building post offices and other buildings in which heavy equipment would be housed because they required stronger steel. Stronger steel meant heavier steel, and they were paid by the pound. "The derrick doesn't know how much the steel weighs," he told me once. If they got the contract, Dad would go out on the road to make arrangements with the union local, and again months later to see how things were going. He would drive to the nearby cities but ride the trains to those more distant—or occasionally fly when the job was really far, like Sacramento or Detroit, in planes that had canvas sides and wooden frames.

If flying took guts, riding trains took stamina. Dad would sit in coach and stay up all night. Arriving at his destination in the morning, he'd go directly to the union hall and meet with the business agent and usually go out to a restaurant or a bar. Dad would tell the agent about the job, its size, the start date, the anticipated completion date, the number of men that he would need, the name of the foreman he was bringing into town, and assure the agent that they wanted the best of relations possible with the union. He would recite all the jobs that the company had built with union labor and how he respected and admired the hardworking and dedicated ironworkers. This was music to the ears of the business agent. The years after the end of World War I were hard ones for the Ironworkers International. Trying to break the union (whose demands had advanced from boats in the water for fishing out bodies to better pay, shorter hours, and more safety) many contractors refused to negotiate or hire union labor. So most of the jobs at that time were non-union, especially in New York—most notably the Empire State Building. The union tried to discourage members from working on non-union job sites, but it was a lost cause. Men needed to work. Finally, on May Day 1924 the International called a strike against the Iron League and the National Erectors Association. It was to last fourteen years.

With Grandpa running one job, Dad took care to cultivate a cadre of dependable foremen to send out from New York to run the others. There was Jack Finnel, who chomped on a cigar and talked out of the side of his mouth, brusque and hard-nosed, completely sure of himself. Steve Burkhardt was snarling, loud, cussing, but ultimately fair. And there was the best of them all, Charlie Ruddy, a slightly built man with a quiet voice whose style was to observe silently and be aware of everything going on, always ready to fix a problem as soon as it happened, if not stepping in to avoid it altogether. My father truly loved these men. He once told me you could put any one of them on a job and never have to go back.

To my father, a foreman had several functions, and one of them was to be a babysitter, or in some cases a referee. "Every week I would give the foreman a bag full of money over his pay, and I'd tell him: 'Keep the Indians away from the Irishmen,' " my father told me. There were always arguments between members of the different ethnic groups about who was the better man, and the fact that pint bottles of whiskey were nearly as commonplace on the job as rivet beaters didn't help keep the peace. The union didn't like Dad's policy of paying off the foremen to keep its men in line—the whole idea of the union was to treat everyone equally, nobody getting paid more or less than the negotiated rate—and one man accused him of being a crook. "Yes, I pay them off," Dad replied. "To keep the Irish and the Indians sober till five o'clock."

It was in 1930 that the company first went into the kind of work that had first brought Grandpa to New York and which was to become a mainstay for the Koch Company: building bridges. The first project was a section of the Pulaski Skyway in New Jersey—the job that preempted my parents' wedding night. Originally called the Diagonal Highway, the Pulaski was New Jersey's answer to the Golden Gate Bridge, which was conceived and built at the same time. It was a 1.3-mile series of spans that crossed the Hackensack River, the Passaic River, and the town of Kearney, at a height of 135 feet above high tide to meet government requirements that American warships be able to pass under it. It was an extraordinary engineering and construction project for its time, and a treacherous one for the ironworkers who built it. Sixteen men died during its construction, including one who was murdered in a labor dispute.

Grandpa remembered one of these accidents. A group of ironworkers rigged a system so they could make quick exits at quitting time or lunchtime. They put a line through a pulley and tied one end to the deck they were working on. The other end went down to a bucket full of rivets. Rather than wait in line to climb down a ladder a hundred feet when the whistle sounded, the ironworkers would grab the line and step off the bridge. The bucket would rise and the ironworker would descend. But one day, someone apparently needed an empty bucket. Clueless, he spotted this particular bucket, untied it, dumped out the rivets, and took it away. A while later he returned the bucket, retied it to the line, but neglected to put the rivets back in. At the end of the day a couple of the men raced for the line. The winner grabbed the line, stepped off the bridge, and fell fifty feet to his death. Needless to say, this was decades before OSHA, before every job employed a man whose sole job was to go around looking for safety infractions.

✖ ✖

BY 1935, DAD had been working with his father for ten years. But while it was his business savvy that had been largely responsible for building the company into a highly regarded steel erector, he technically was nothing more than his father's employee. Grandpa owned the company and paid my father a salary. Dad, now thirty and with a growing family of his own, decided to do something about this equity imbalance. He went to his father and demanded to be made an equal partner. "I'm getting the jobs, I'm negotiating them, we're making money on them," he said, "and then you're taking the money and just giving me a paycheck." Left unsaid was that it was Dad who had convinced Grandpa to go into business in the first place. Also obvious was that while my father, being a good son, had taken money out of the company to buy his parents a beautiful home in a wealthy town, he and my mother and we kids were still living in the same rented second-story apartment in a three-family house in Jamaica. Though he had driven a high-powered Packard when he was single, Dad now drove a Pontiac. As busy as he and Grandpa were in the Thirties, it was mostly because they worked cheap. My father preferred low bids built on slight profits to bigger numbers that would likely land in a pile with all the other losing bids. Indications were that Dad was spending what he was earning. As he said, "We're all eating."

Grandpa—an obstinate German, let's face it—didn't see the need to make his son his partner. In his view, it was *his* name on the company—the irony was lost on him—and in the relationship between father and son there could be no equal footing, even now. There could be only one boss. Dad said he would quit if he wasn't made an equal partner. Grandpa held fast. My mother, knowing that the company's success was owed more to Dad's smarts than to his father's rigging skill, was not happy. "Your grandfather was the boss," she tells me. "But he knew nothing. The old guy was an ironworker. Catch a hot rivet in the thing, that's all he knew. But he was the big boss." Grandma basically agreed. "You can't run this business without Karl," she told Grandpa. "You're not a businessman. You're an ironworker."

But Grandpa wouldn't budge. "Your grandfather was steady, dependable, thoughtful, kind—and stubborn as a mule," my grandmother once told me. But Dad could be just as willful. So he quit. He decided to do something completely different. In Florida years earlier he had met a man named Earl Collins, whose father was a judge. Collins, his brother Lorene, and Dad started a movie promotion company. In those days, before multiplexes, movie distributors hired promoters to travel the country and try to get individual theater owners to show their movies. "Dad and Earl Collins went into business together, and they would hire trucks or cars with signs on them, and someone would drive through the towns to advertise the movie," my mother said. "They were paid according to the cash receipts." Dad and Collins promoted movies such as *Strike Me Pink,* a 1936 Samuel Goldwyn musical comedy starring Eddie Cantor and Ethel Merman, about a guy who runs an amusement park in trouble with racketeers.

Dad was just breaking into Hollywood when the pressure was mounting for him to come home. This new business put him even farther from the family than when he was working with Grandpa. At one point he came home with a large prancing Doberman pinscher, gleefully announcing that it was a pet for my mother, protection for her and the children while he was out of town. My mother was unenthusiastic, to say the least. "I have three little kids," she said. "How am I going to find time to feed the dog and take him for walks? Anyway, he's too big. He's frightening."

"Oh, no, no, he's very friendly," Dad said. "See?" He let go of the leash, and the dog leaped toward my terrified mother. His front paws landed on her shoulders and pushed her over backward. "He loves you!" Dad said, helping her up. "Get that dog out of here!" she screamed, and chased both man and beast from the house. "I need *you* here, not a dog," she yelled after him. My father was crushed. He had really gotten the dog for me, hoping my mother would go along with it if she thought it was for protection.

As unimpressed as she was with the Doberman, Mom had an even worse feeling about Earl Collins. "I think he's cheating you," she told Dad. "I don't trust him." She convinced him to go to California and check, "and sure enough," Mom said, "the guy was screwing him."

In his heart, Dad wanted to go back to the steel business. He loved it, it was what he knew best, and doing other work made him feel uncomfortable. But he was not about to come crawling back to Grandpa, hat in hand.

Grandma stepped in on her oldest child's behalf. "She said, 'You make him a partner,' " my mother told me. "And she was tough. She had black, black hair and these black eyes, like an Indian. They thought she was an Indian when she was young. Cora got to the old guy. She pretty much ordered Pop to make Karl an equal partner." Grandpa knew she was right. He couldn't continue the business without Dad. He sorely missed both his vast contacts in the industry and his estimating and bidding abilities, which were like magic. Building plans were bound in immense books that had to be wheeled around on a dolly. Each one was the size of a small area rug, an inch and a half thick, and weighing in at fifty pounds. Dad was so nimble with numbers that he could just look at the plans and come up with a bid, doing all the calculations without benefit of pencil and paper, as if he were a human calculator.

Now the negotiating power was completely tipped. Dad not only wanted to have an equal stake in the company. More than that, he wanted control. He'd already been in control of the money as the company's treasurer since its inception. Now he also wanted the power. He wanted to be the president of the company. He suggested Grandpa be "Chairman of the Board," though it seemed that the board consisted of the two of them and Grandma. But if Grandpa wanted Dad back, he would have to take him on his terms, especially since Grandma was now squarely on Dad's side. What man can fight both his wife and son and win? There wasn't much to discuss. Dad was back in the steel business.

Picking up where they left off, they erected post offices, federal buildings, and courthouses all over the country. They built Charity Hospital in New Orleans and the Philadelphia Savings Bank headquarters. They built bridges. Dad by now was well known to ironworkers everywhere. Coming home, he would tell me how, when he arrived in the city where they were starting up a job, he would get off the train and see ironworkers crawling out from underneath, dusting themselves off. They would gather behind him in pairs or threesomes, harking, "Where's the job, Chief? We're ready to go." Dozens of men would follow him to Florida in the winter, riding the rails, hiding in boxcars, hitchhiking, and, in some cases, hopping aboard Dad's Pontiac and speeding off to Florida, nonstop to Miami. Years later when I started traveling with my father during summers and school vacations, I met a few of those ironworkers. "Ever drive to Florida with your daddy?" one of them once asked, grinning and slapping my back. His buddy said, "I did it once and never again. We outran the cops in four states."

While my mother never came on the road with Dad, Grandma was used to it. She spent a lot of time in hotels, or even in rented apartments in Florida. Late in 1939, the family was in Atlanta, where they were putting up a new main post office. Grandma looked out her hotel window and saw a huge crowd lining the street, cheering as Clark Gable and Vivien Leigh passed in an old-fashioned carriage drawn by two elaborately decorated horses. It was the world premiere of *Gone With the Wind*, a huge event that had drawn all the stars, thousands of fans, and governors from five states. Seeing the glamorous actors in their carriage reminded Grandma of when she and Grandpa were nearly penniless in Buffalo, and he promised that one day she would have servants to drive her in a carriage drawn by high-stepping horses. She didn't live in quite that much opulence, but thirty years later her life was a lot more splendid than she could have imagined when she and my father and Aunt Gladys almost froze to death on the train to New York in 1908. "I turned away from the hotel window with a heavy heart," Grandma wrote. She was as homesick as Scarlett O'Hara. She couldn't wait to get home to the mansion in Scarsdale, her Tara.

THE ORANGE BLOSSOM EXPRESS pulls into Union Station in Washington, D.C., and thirty-three-year-old Karl W. Koch II gets off. He's coming in from Florida, trying to land a new job. He's gone two nights without sleep after passing on an opportunity to build a hotel in Miami. The owners had offered him the job if he would accept a percentage of ownership in the hotel as payment. Exhausted after chasing the job for three weeks and then negotiating all night, he finally got up from the table and said, "Gentlemen, I'm in the steel business. I'm not in the hotel business."

Now on this morning in late January of 1938, he has a date at the Washington Statler to meet Jim Smith from Fort Pitt Iron Works. The Pennsylvania fabricator has invited him to join its bid to build an annex to the Government Printing Office. It's a last-minute thing, and Dad is coming in cold. He had expected to be working on the hotel, which would have been Karl Koch Erecting's first major job since Karl Koch II became president and 50 percent stockholder. But when it fell through he called Smith and asked if he could still put in a bid on the Printing Office. Smith said sure, but that he'd better catch the next train to Washington. We're putting our bid in to McCloskey on Tuesday, he said, and unless you come in lower and do it in twenty-four hours, our erector is American Bridge. This is on Sunday night. Dad hasn't even seen the plans. But the mere mention of the words "American Bridge" is enough to send him scurrying for the Miami train station.

He arrives in Washington Monday night, checks in at the Statler, goes to his room, drops his suitcase by the door, and throws his coat over the nearest chair. He sits on the bed next to the phone and sails his fedora toward the mirror. It lands squarely on top of the bureau. He picks up the phone and asks for Mr. Smith as he yanks off his tie and shirt.

"Hi, Karl, when'd you get in?"

"Just walked in the door. Are you guys ready?"

"Yeah, we're in room six-twenty-three. Where are you?"

"Nine-fifty-nine. I'll be right down."

Dad goes into the bathroom, splashes water under his armpits and across his chest and on the back of his neck, blotting his body with a towel before the water can run down toward his pants. Back in the room, he unfastens the straps of his leather suitcase and flips the snap locks open. He's traveled thousands of miles with this leather beauty, but it still has its shape and the letters KWK are intact, still standing out from the softened patina. He takes out a freshly laundered white shirt and stands in front of the mirror buttoning it and then ties his tie with a simple once-over knot, which he prefers to the more complicated Windsor.

It's the heart of winter, but Jim Smith answers the door in shirt sleeves, his tie loosened. "Come on in, Karl," he says. "Good to see you." The room has twin beds and a round table by the window, where two other men are sitting. "That's Warren and over here is Russell," Smith says, and they all shake hands. "You've got all the brains of Fort Pitt's estimating department right here in this room, and the only thing we need now is you so we can button up this bid."

Dad has worked with Fort Pitt before, and the men trust him. They're bidding to the McCloskey Company of Philadelphia, whose founder, Matthew McCloskey, started out as a seven-dollar-a-week apprentice and built one of the nation's largest construction and development firms. Their buildings are all over Washington and Philadelphia, everything from the Rayburn and Senate office buildings to the U.S. Mint and, decades later, Veteran's Stadium. There's a bottle of whiskey and a bucket of ice on the bureau. The other men's glasses are already half empty. "Karl, grab a scotch and a chair and come on over here and tell us how you're gonna do this job. We need to know when you'll start, when you'll finish, and most of all how you're gonna give us a price that'll knock the hat off American Bridge's number."

"We can make this a very short evening, fellas," Dad says, pouring himself a drink. "Just tell me what American Bridge's number is."

"Now, Karl, you know we can't do that," Smith says. "And, besides, there are too many contingencies. It wouldn't be fair to just throw you a number."

Dad steps over to the table but doesn't sit down. The huge drawings are spread out in front of him, and he leans over them, planting his hands on the edges, and quickly looks at the dimensions of the building. It's about seven hundred feet long and three hundred feet wide. Seven stories high. "How's it going up?" he asks. "All at once or are you building it in stages?"

"It's in stages," Jim says, turning toward Warren. "Isn't it?"

"Yes, sir," replies Warren. "It's in two stages. The first stage runs to about here."

About three-hundred-fifty feet of the building, Dad figures. About half the job. That makes it easy. "Four derricks for each section," Dad mutters, mostly to himself. "Four hoists." He turns to Smith. "Piece of cake. We'll go up two floors a week."

"I know you've got the equipment," Smith says. "I saw it all down the street when you were doing the Interior Building for Fuller."

Dad flips through the enormous pages, figuring out how many crews, how many men, how many derricks he'll need for the first section, and then the second. He has a running tally of how many man-days he'll need to do the job. Then he turns to the section of the drawings that shows the tie-in of the annex to the existing building at all seven levels. He counts a hundred and eighty-two connections to existing columns in the old building. They're built-up members, which means knocking out rivets to prepare the connection. He estimates the number of holes that have to be drilled to connect the new steel, taking into account how many of the existing holes can be re-used. Figure ninety or so man-days for that. So far he's got 4,554 man-days. He always adds a hundred man-days and rounds up to the nearest hundred in a job this size, which brings him to 4,700, to which he now adds thirty man-days for weather and other contingencies, to bring it up to a nice, round 5,000 man-days. He multiplies that by the thirty dollars that each man-day costs him, adds the cost of equipment, and then the "add-on." This means the profit, but it's never called that. It's considered presumptuous in this industry to assume that any job will yield a profit. As a matter of fact, it's almost impossible to find a contractor who will admit he made a profit on any job.

"Boys," Dad says finally, "I can do it for $220,000. I can start when you're ready, and I'll finish in two-and-a-quarter months. Now remember, you've got to add on to that number Russell's six weeks."

Jim grabs the whiskey bottle and throws a splash in everyone's glass.

"Karl," he says, "son of a bitch if you don't have the right price. Is a handshake good enough for you?"

"Jim, you know my word is my bond. You run a good shop, and your steel fits better than most any we've ever used."

"Let's drink on it," says Jim, sealing the partnership. The next day, Smith submits the bid to McCloskey and they both win the job. By late spring, the steel for the new annex to the Government Printing Office will be up.

4

HELLION

I was six years old when Dad was finally able to move us out of our little apartment in Jamaica. He had told his boyhood friend, Joe Sherry, that he was looking for a house, and Mr. Sherry, who worked in the city tax assessor's office, directed him to the one right across the street from his. It was a big house on the corner of Thornhill and Redfield streets in Douglaston, which in 1938 constituted suburbia. It was still within the city limits, but barely. Douglaston occupied the last acre of Queens before Gatsby country, the Gold Coast of Long Island's North Shore.

The house on Thornhill was stucco and brick, with a Spanish-tile slate roof. There were so many large rooms—one of them was mine—that to my young eyes it seemed we must have suddenly become rich. Watching the movers bringing in Oriental rugs, Havilland china, and great pieces of art deco satin wood furniture—much of which my father acquired at auctions in the Bronx—some of our new neighbors might have thought we were already rich. One of them remarked, "Oooh, look at what they're bringing in. They've got to be millionaires."

Joe Sherry's son, Joe Junior, and I became boyhood buddies, just as our fathers had. We and most of the kids in the neighborhood went to St. Anastasia School, walking the mile and a half to school, walking home for lunch, and then back to school, then home again. I had a series of lethal nuns who noticed very quickly that I was the first one to sit down during spelling bees and the last one to turn in a good homework assignment. I was no more a mother's dream than a teacher's. I was a little too independent, and with the man of the house on the road so much, a kid found it easy to get away with a lot if he wanted to, and I wanted to.

The same year we moved to Douglaston, my parents bought a little summer bungalow in Long Beach, one oceanfront community over from my grandparents' house in Island Park. In Long Beach the streets with the big houses were named for the presidents. The other streets, the ones with the little bungalows, were named for the states. We lived on Vermont Avenue. Our bungalow had two bedrooms, and all the kids were stuffed into one of them. Years later, when I was driving my youngest daughter around on a leisurely Sunday in the middle of winter, I pulled in front of the bungalow on Vermont Avenue and told her that this was where my family spent the summers when I was very young. Jill looked out the window at the tiny bungalow, so close to the one next to it that there was hardly room to walk between them. "Oh, Daddy, you were so poor," Jill said.

It was in Long Beach, when I was just seven, that I developed a taste for freedom and adventure. I would get up, get myself some breakfast, and be out of the house by seven. I would go around stealing milk bottles for the nickel deposit. That would be my cash for the day. I'd go to the boardwalk and watch all the acts and see the shows and sit in on the auctions. I would go down to the bicycle store and wish I could steal enough milk bottles to buy a bike. I went to the Bohack grocery store and bought a box of animal crackers, and that would be lunch. I'd go down to the water and eat. One day I was standing on a dock watching some teenagers jumping into the water and swimming around. One of them asked, "Hey, kid, can you swim?" I said no. "Well, come on over here and we'll teach you." I went to the edge and someone pushed me in, a good ten-foot drop to the water. I came up, desperately dogpaddling to the ladder. And that's how I learned to swim. Around five in the afternoon, I'd start getting hungry and head back to our bungalow.

As the oldest boy in a house with a father who traveled too much, I was dutiful about the chores, but not an easy son to govern. If my father was in town, Mom beseeched him to take me off her hands. On Saturdays he would take me to the office in the Bronx and send me out to the shop, where the yard men would give me work to do. I'd sit on a pile of bolts three feet high winding the nuts down, separating the good from the bad, hour after hour. I'd go up to the backyard and watch the operation of the yard derrick. I would sit next to Louie as he worked the levers, moving the boom up and down, watching the drums picking and lowering the loads. The yard men would send truckloads of material and equipment out to the jobs and unload the trucks that were returning. They stacked the Douglas fir planks high into the air, putting spaces every few layers to allow the air to circulate so the planks wouldn't rot. The men showed me the tools of the trade and the various parts of the derrick. They delighted in telling me the peculiar names used to identify them: the spider, the bull wheel, the horse's cock. I would relate all my newfound knowledge to my father when we drove home, and he would laugh. He would constantly remind me to be careful, but he was happy that I apparently found the steel business as interesting as he did. Some days he would ask me to come back and hang around with him in the office, but I found it boring and escaped to the yard as quickly as possible.

My friend Joe Sherry caddied at the Douglaston North Hills Golf Club and encouraged me to join him. I went down and talked to the caddy master, Mike Ryan. He asked if I had any experience, and I assured him I had plenty, though all I really knew about the job was that the tips were good. With impeccable timing, I picked up a golf bag backwards and the clubs clattered to the ground.

One fall day, word spread that Babe Ruth, a retired legend by now, was at the club. He was reclining in a chaise longue facing the eighteenth green, bundled up in his camel-hair overcoat, with an afghan tucked around his legs. We caddies stared at him from our pen, taking turns scooting out for autographs when Ryan wasn't looking. I didn't get a chance the first time the Babe came to the club, but every day I caddied after that I made sure to bring a scorecard. One Sunday he was there and I dared to take my turn. I scampered over to the Babe, thrusting the scorecard toward his hands, which were resting on his chest with his fingers interlaced.

"Would you sign this for me, Mr. Ruth?" I asked.

"Got a pencil?" replied the Babe.

I held out my pencil. He scrawled his name across the folded card. "Thanks!" I cried, and ran back to the pen.

Later, I showed the autograph to my dad. He studied the signature and smiled. "When we worked on Yankee Stadium, I used to sit in the grandstand and watch the Babe at batting practice," he said. "One after the other, he hit the ball over the fence."

"Did you build Yankee Stadium, Dad?" I asked, so stunned by the possibility—the first I'd ever heard of it—that I forgot about the Babe for a moment.

"No," Dad said, chuckling. "Just some extensions."

"Oh," I said, but decided that "some extensions" meant that Dad had at least had a hand in building the house that Ruth built.

✖   ✖

I WAS PLAYING December stickball in the street outside our house one day when my mother called me inside and sat me down in front of the radio. "Listen to this," she said. "President Roosevelt is declaring war." I couldn't wait until he was finished so I could go back outside and play. My father was on the road, on a job that in retrospect seems eerily ironic. He and my grandparents were in St. Simon's Island, on the Georgia seacoast. The company was building a hangar for the military when Pearl Harbor was bombed half a world away.

A few months later, our school had a scrap-metal drive for the war effort. My father sent Pete, our yard foreman, over to the school in one of the company's pickup trucks. Pete pulled up, and unloaded a huge pile of metal in front of the school. Everyone came out to see it, and the impressive delivery—by a truck with *my name* on the door—earned me celebrity among my schoolmates and, for once, the good graces of the nuns. Something like that has a way of burnishing a son's wonderment about his father's place in the world, and brightening his reflected glory just a notch. With war rationing you were lucky to get a can of Crisco, but Dad seemed to have a direct pipeline into the black market. He had a bunch of kids to feed and a wife at home who didn't drive. Somehow he would get cases of food and bring them home. He had ration stamps on the window of his Pontiac that allowed him to buy as much gas as he needed, and sometimes on school vacations or weekends he would take me with him on business trips.

My father had been too young for the first World War and was now too old for the second, but his three younger brothers all joined the service. Bob, the oldest of the three, enlisted in the Navy. Jerome joined the Army, and Daniel, only seventeen when war was declared but anxious to fly combat missions, was a cadet in the Army Air Corps. Like tens of thousands of mothers, Grandma fretted at the prospect of three of her sons going off to war, maybe never to return. She worried most about Daniel, her baby, the only one among them who was gung ho for combat. But one night when he was almost through with his training, he was leaning on a Ping-Pong table and fell, cutting his hand on a Coke bottle so severely that he washed out of flight school. To his great disappointment and Grandma's relief, he never saw action. "Most of the boys in that division never came back," Grandma recalled. "I saw it as an act of God."

Grandma's credo was that everything good was from God and everything bad was from the Devil. During the war, every time we visited Scarsdale, she would without notice command everyone to get on their knees. "Let's pray for the boys," she would say, and we did.

Grandma's most often-recited prayer was that Grandpa would convert to Catholicism. Grandpa's favorite was that Grandma would leave him alone about it. He would turn off his hearing aid when the conversation became unbearable. I remember a time in Scarsdale when Grandma was looking for Grandpa, shouting for him all over the house and employing several of the kids in finding him. I decided to look in the garage to see if he was whittling a stick out there. I found him sitting in the car, the garage door closed, reading the Sunday newspaper. I ran back in shouting, "He's in the garage, he's in the garage." Grandpa came back in the house sheepishly, but not before whispering to me, "Karlie, we men have to have our secrets."

Though Dad missed the draft for both World Wars, he served in other ways. Within hours of the attack on Pearl Harbor, he and Grandpa got what must have been one of the first wartime military construction contracts. They were hired by the government to build a huge supply depot for the quartermaster general of the Army in Virginia. The company erected 9,400 tons of steel in only seventy-five days by building the equivalent of a 122-by-180-foot building every day. On one especially productive day, the men responded to Dad's challenge by erecting three times that much. By now the company was known in the industry for the pace of its work—"Organized for Speed" was the slogan Dad came up with, and never was speed more in demand than in the early months of the war.

He and Grandpa let it be known that they would take any contract that furthered the war effort. They put up a large airplane factory in Kentucky and hangers at naval air bases in Florida and Georgia. One night my father told me the company was under consideration for an exciting job in Panama. He showed me where it was on the map and said the job was to build two dirigible hangars to house "blimps" that would patrol the seas, looking for submarines that were sinking oil tankers arriving from South America. Each hanger would be an enormous open-air arch held up by fifty-one trusses. It looked like what the opening to the Queens-Midtown Tunnel might look like if it were designed for cars the size of the *Queen Elizabeth*. But besides looking unlike anything Dad and Grandpa had ever built, the hangars were to be made of material that was foreign to them: wood. Without any experience, they would have to learn and then teach their crews to handle timber.

Dad really wanted this job, but had to convince a somewhat skeptical procurement officer. He took the man out to dinner at his favorite restaurant, Snorers Steak House in the Bronx, where the first thing you felt when you came through the door was the sawdust underfoot and the first thing you saw were the huge slabs of beef hanging by the hook before being butchered. Dad and the government man drank mugs of beer until the white-aproned waiter delivered oversized pewter plates that barely held their steaks. Leaving the restaurant, Dad suggested they go up to the yard and he would show him the company's equipment. They drove up to the Bronx and Dad walked the officer up to the chain-link fence and rattled the gate. It was late at night and the place was locked up. Dad jingled the gate and apologized for not having the key with him. But he peered in and started pointing things out. "There's our plank over there. There's the derricks, Number Two and Number Three Terrys. The hoisting engines are over there in the shed."

With all the right equipment and a low bid, Dad won the job and went on to build the hangars in four months, which thrilled the general contractor, Carroll Griffin. "The excellent time record made on these two hangers is entirely due to your fine organization, suitable equipment, and the personal supervision of Mssrs. Koch, senior and junior," he wrote after the job was done. "You are especially to be commended for your versatility in handling this piece of construction, which was novel in its design and entirely foreign to your usual practice of erection." What Griffin didn't know was that Dad had done something else novel to help get the job. Back on that night when he wined and dined the government procurement officer in Manhattan, he had called the office in the Bronx and told Pete, the yard foreman, to take a drive down the street after dark—to American Bridge's yard. Take their sign off the fence, he told Pete, and wire a Koch sign to the fence in its place. When Dad took the man from the government to the yard after dinner, those derricks and hoisting engines he proudly pointed out were actually the property of his nemesis.

DAD WAS AWAY a lot in the winter of 1943. This wasn't unusual, of course. What *was* unusual was how secretive he seemed to be about what he was doing and where. "I've got a job in the South," was about all he said. The job lasted until the end of the year, and then he resumed telling us about the jobs he was bidding and working on.

Two years later, on August 7, 1945, Dad was sitting on the porch swing when Mom called all of us over. We had already heard that our country had dropped an atomic bomb on the Japanese city of Hiroshima, wiping it off the map. "Daddy has something to tell us," Mom said. When my brothers and sisters and I gathered around, we saw that there was a telegram resting on his lap. "This letter just arrived," he said, picking up the telegram. "It's from Henry L. Stimson. He is the secretary of war." He began reading to us:

> Today the whole world knows the secret which you have helped us keep for many months. I am pleased to be able to add that the warlords of Japan now know its effects better even than we ourselves. The atomic bomb which you have helped to develop with high devotion to patriotic duty is the most devastating military weapon that any country has ever been able to turn against its enemy. No one has worked on the entire project or known the whole story. Each has done his own job and kept his own secret, and so today I speak for a grateful nation when I say congratulations and thank you. I hope you will continue to keep the secrets you have kept so well.

As Dad read the letter, Mom's eyes glistened. Now she understood his long, mysterious absences. He had been building the plant in which the government had developed the atomic bomb that had just been dropped over Hiroshima.

"I always wondered what those seven-foot concrete walls were for," Dad said. When I pressed him for details, he said he'd had to sign a security agreement under the Espionage Act that prevented him from disclosing any information. Then he laughed and said, "I don't think there's any big secrets about setting steel." The secret, of course, was what was underneath the steel.

In 1939, Germany had discovered uranium fission, and when the United States entered the war, there was serious fear among American scientists that the breakthrough would allow the Nazis to develop a bomb capable of unimaginable destruction. There was no choice but to beat them to it. President Roosevelt appointed Leslie Groves, a brigadier general who was the deputy chief of the Army Corps of Engineers, to be director of what came to be called the Manhattan Project.

One of the first things Groves did (aside from appointing Robert J. Oppenheimer to be director of the Los Alamos National Laboratory) was to order the takeover of 59,000 remote acres in Tennessee, a broad swath between Black Oak Ridge and the Clinch River, for plants and labs that would secretly develop nuclear reactors. Groves arranged for the region to be designated as a federal reserve and gave it the code name Kingston Demolition Range, after the nearest town to the south. The Army opened a real estate office near the site and began condemnation proceedings, employing a good ol' boy from Kentucky to soothe the thousand or so families who would have to leave homes that in many cases they had occupied for generations.

The families were paid for their land and were immediately replaced by the first of thousands of construction workers, scientists, and engineers. Inside the walls of what would eventually be three facilities, they would conduct secret, scientific work of unprecedented sophistication and urgency, research that would change the world forever. A city of workers grew on the northern edge of the reserve, and it was named Oak Ridge.

On February 1, 1943, laborers began clearing land near the reserve's southwest corner for the construction of a building called X-10. This would be the site for the Graphite Reactor, whose job it would be to produce a self-sustaining chain reaction that would demonstrate that plutonium could be extracted from irradiated uranium. "The reason Leslie Groves wanted it so far out of the way was the possibility of a catastrophe," my father explained a few years later, when he was a little more forthcoming. "If it blew up, it could wipe out everything and put radioactive material into the atmosphere."

The entire Oak Ridge construction was run by EI du Pont de Nemours & Company, which Groves had pressed into service in spite of the protestations of the company's president, W.S. Carpenter, that du Pont was a chemical company with virtually no experience with nuclear physics. Groves, as well as Secretary of War Stimson and President Roosevelt himself, felt du Pont was the one company with the wherewithal to orchestrate what would be one of the largest and fastest constructions in history, and appealed to the company's patriotic impulses. Du Pont finally accepted, and refused to earn any profit or to take any patents that came out of the work.

X-10 was really a complex of buildings. Besides the main plant for the graphite reactor, there were separate structures for chemistry, physics, and health physics labs; machine and instrument shops; warehouses and administration buildings. And with construction also starting on other plants and smaller buildings elsewhere on the reserve, there was a mad scramble for labor. Du Pont sent out an army of recruiters and signed up three thousand workers, who began streaming in from many states. They built some 150 structures that summer of 1943. There was a makeshift cafeteria for workers in a striped circus tent. An old schoolhouse was converted into offices and a dormitory. The New Bethel Baptist Church was used for meetings and storage, and the occasional lab experiment. The facilities were racially segregated. The men typically worked seventy-hour weeks, and the people in charge did what they could to keep them happy. In the main cafeteria for black workers, which served men from different regions of the South, there were two lines, one with food that was more heavily spiced than the other.

Oak Ridge was like a national barn-raising. Six thousand trailers were brought in from all over the East and placed around central bathhouses. There were also prefabricated military barracks, and ninety-eight dormitories. Drugstores and barbershops were constructed, along with schools and churches, though many people attended services in the makeshift theaters that were also built, or in school gyms. A water distribution system and sewer and power lines were installed, and road-grading went on round-the-clock.

While I was researching Oak Ridge, Amy Rothrock, the Freedom of Information Act officer at what is now called Oak Ridge National Laboratories, told me that the barracks that housed many of the men who worked on the reserve were still there. "That's probably where your father stayed," she said, and offered to show it to me. I could only smile. Army barracks weren't my father's style. He stayed in the Andrew Johnson Hotel in Knoxville, and sometimes in the guest house in Oak Ridge that was General Groves' quarters when he was in Tennessee. "When the general came into town, I got the hell out," he once told me. Dad didn't care much for Groves. The general had been in charge of the Pentagon construction before the war—another job Dad had lost to American Bridge.

It was through his contacts in Washington that Dad, along with the Tilley Brothers at Bristol Steel, had been invited to bid on the Oak Ridge project. They weren't told anything about its purpose, of course, but saw that the plans for the main building called for individual rooms, or cells, with concrete walls seven feet thick, with removable slab tops to allow equipment to be brought in and taken out. The job called for the slabs to be supported by steel. Dad got the job, got his top-secret clearance and security badge (which remains a family treasure), signed his secrecy agreement, and headed for Tennessee for this mysterious job "in the South."

He and Grandpa supervised construction of a number of structures, but their key job came in September, after the reactor's thick concrete shield was in place and crews stacked seventy-three layers of graphite blocks inside to form a twenty-four-foot cube. At that point they erected the steel trusses to support the concrete lid that—unbeknownst to them—would cap the graphite reactor. The first uranium was loaded into the reactor on the afternoon of November 3, 1943, and just before dawn the following morning Enrico Fermi was summoned from the guest house in Oak Ridge. The reactor reached critical mass at five that morning, and less than two months later it was producing nearly seven hundred pounds of irradiated uranium a day. And two months after that, Oak Ridge chemists produced the world's first few grams of plutonium. But Dad and Grandpa didn't know about any of this until the day, nearly two years later, when the bomb was dropped on Hiroshima.

In his role as the director of the Manhattan Project, Groves had not only overseen all the research and development of the bomb, but also chaired the committee that recommended Hiroshima and Nagasaki as targets. Groves, in fact, personally wrote the order for the Air Force to "deliver its first special bomb as soon as weather will permit visual bombing after about 3 April 1945."

After his work in Oak Ridge was done, my father was offered a commission as a lieutenant colonel in the Army Corps of Engineers. He turned it down. "Can you imagine me taking orders from a colonel?" he remarked when he recalled the offer years later. I asked him who he *would* have taken orders from. A general, maybe? "Depends on the general," he said.

The Graphite Reactor is still down there in Tennessee—the oldest reactor in the world, and, since 1996, a national historic landmark. The world's first radioactive isotope for medical use was also produced in the building, in August 1946. Still, in the many years since it was built, I've had misgivings about our company's participation in building the birthplace of the atomic bomb. I've regretted the loss of all those thousands of lives, though I realized that it probably saved countless others, Americans, maybe even my uncles'. To say nothing of the mutual deterrence our nuclear weapons permitted during the Cold War. Of course, we weren't Einsteins or Tellers or Oppenheimers. And if we hadn't done the steel work in Oak Ridge, another erector would have. Dad was just the low bidder. But still, we built them.

WHILE DAD WAS away aiding the war effort, I was making life difficult for my mother on the home front. I just had a knack for risky and less-than-responsible behavior, and in the years after the war ended I gave my parents little peace. Looking for excitement when I was fourteen, I rounded up five kids on the beach on Little Neck Bay and opened an umbrella in the bow of a rowboat. We let the wind pull us offshore until we were floating halfway across Long Island Sound, at which point the sky was getting dark—and the water rough. Time to turn around and go back. A second later, a wave crashed over us and flooded the boat. We were all hanging on the sides, floating in the darkness, about to drown because of my stupidity.

Finally, we saw the light of a boat coming toward us. Ecstatic, we had a girl in our group stand on the seat, and I gave her my T-shirt to wave. The boat got closer, and we could make out the letters on its bow: US COAST GUARD. Somebody on shore who had seen us push off had reported us missing. When my father found out about it, he took me to my room, had me lay on my side, gave me a single whack with a folded belt, told me to never do something like that again, and left. He was a man of few words and controlled temperament. He never cursed or screamed. And it took an act of incredible recklessness on my part for him to strike me. It was the only time he ever did. But I didn't press my luck. It didn't seem the right time to confess that I was running midnight cruises to Rye Playland, an amusement park across the Sound in Westchester, with his twenty-six-foot cabin cruiser, the *Joyce E.*

Even when he wasn't out of town on business, my father rarely came home much before we were all in bed. Trying to compensate, he would sit me in the chair next to him and, holding my hand, stare intently at me, and try to make an impression: "How is school? Are you studying hard? I'm depending on you to do well." But I was a miserable student. My worst subject was attendance. I would meet the gang at our bus stop on Northern Boulevard, and before the bus arrived somehow we would come to the conclusion that our interests would be better served by going to the Roxy or the Paramount in Manhattan to catch the latest movie and stage show. I usually sat in the balcony with a truant cheerleader, cheering and kissing through the whole show.

By the time I was a teenager, my mother had pretty much given up on any possibility of her oldest son being a good example for his younger brothers and sisters. On weekends and vacations, she assigned me to my father. "I can't handle him—take him with you," she demanded. I would travel with him when he went on the road negotiating jobs, getting my first real taste of the steel business beyond the yard in the Bronx. Though the company always had jobs going all over New York, I was fourteen before I saw ironworkers at work for the first time. My father took me with him one day when he went out to check on a building he was erecting for Con Edison, the New York City utility company. We parked the car in a field a few hundred yards from the building but never got out. There were a couple of cranes with long booms setting steel, and I could see ironworkers walking effortlessly across the beams high up on the peak of the building. "Look, Dad," I said, pointing nervously to the man nearest us walking on the ridge. "He's gonna fall."

"No, he won't," my father said matter-of-factly. "He's an ironworker. That's his job."

A beam was hooked to the crane, which swung it to about where the ironworker was standing. A second man crouched on a beam already set some distance away. The new beam was swung into a position so that both men eventually held onto it, easing it into position. "Wow," I said. "Did you see that?" Dad said: "Yes, I did." He looked over his shoulder and swung the car back to turn around and get back on the road to go home.

ONE DAY WHEN I was fourteen, my father told me, "Go put some clean underwear in a paper bag and get in the car." He told me to get behind the wheel and start driving.

I drove nonstop from our house in Douglaston, New York, to Jacksonville, Florida, while Dad filled my right ear with stories of his youth, of Grandpa working on the Manhattan Bridge, of erecting the Hotel Pierre and the Supreme Court building. He told me about the men he met through his work, especially in Washington. Men like Oliver Gasch, a lawyer in the Justice Department who would take Dad to the FBI building and let him shoot a Tommy gun at a target in the firing range in the basement. He'd bring the targets home, and I'd hang them on my bedroom wall and count the bullet holes. Gasch later became a United States attorney, a federal circuit judge, and a footnote to history as the man who signed the documents certifying Richard Nixon's resignation. But to my father, he was a friend and frequent fishing companion. For a man who was not considered gregarious, Dad had a lot to say on the road. When I started to fall asleep, he rolled down his window. We stayed in Jacksonville for a night, and in the morning drove on to the Keys. Then he put me on a train for home, and stayed in Florida with the car.

Despite my father's desire that I be a devoted student, the truth was that I spent as much time in the gym in the basement of P.S. 98, learning to box, as I did in class at St. Anastasia. There was a makeshift fight gym down there, and I caught the eye of the coach, a former pro trainer named Freddy Brown. He had trained Lou Nova, who eventually went far enough to lose a bout to Joe Louis. Mr. Brown taught me to throw a great right hook, and I started winning fights in the gym. I thought I was good enough to be an amateur boxer and fight in the Golden Gloves. But at fifteen I was a year too young, so I got my friend Steven Nolan to lend me his birth certificate. I went down to the Ridgewood Golden Glove Arena, signed up as Nolan, had my physical, and waited to be notified of my first fight.

A few weeks later, my father sat me down, looked me in the eyes, and said, "You missed your fight, Steven." He had intercepted the mail and demanded to know what was going on. I told him I wanted to be a boxer—told him all about my great punch, how I could smash a door with one blow. "I've won all my fights," I told him. "I'm twenty-one-and-oh."

Dad was unimpressed. He said I needed to devote my energies to school. I was never to fight again, he told me.

Two nights later, with everyone asleep, I got out of bed and packed some clothes and sixty dollars I had earned working on weekends at the yard. I went outside, quietly rolled his Pontiac into the street, and headed in the direction of Texas. I had it all planned out. I would get a job as a ranch hand and become a professional boxer. It always worked in the movies. Driving across the Hudson as the sun was rising over the George Washington Bridge, I glanced down and saw my father's panama hat. I put it on.

My adventure got off to a rough start. I picked up a hitchhiker in South Carolina who robbed me. And then, in Georgia, a state trooper saw a fifteen-year-old in a big car with New York plates, wearing his father's panama hat, and brought him into the station house. The trooper called my father in New York, who said he would fly down in the morning.

I spent the night in jail talking to a character named Speck. He was short and fat and seemed to know everything. "I thought you were about twenty-five when they brought you in," he said. "Then you took your hat off and I said, 'Shit, he's just a kid.'" I told him I had to escape. "I can't face my father. He's coming to pick me up tomorrow."

Speck said it wasn't such a big deal. "A lotta kids run away," he said. Though, for that matter, breaking out of jail wasn't such a big deal either. He walked across the cell to a pair of pipes that went through the wall. He snaked a short piece of wire from his belt, and used it to remove two hacksaw blades from the tiny space between the pipe and the wall. "I could get you outta here in a couple hours if I wanted to. It would be easy," he said. "But it wouldn't be any good. They'd pick you up on the street tomorrow and you'd be back here before noon. Then you'd end up in a chain gang instead of your old man's car."

He had a better idea. I should go home, Speck said, go back to school, and "lay low." He was getting out in six months and he'd come up to New York to get me. He was a safecracker, he explained, and he could use a driver, someone who knew the city. "You got real easy pickins' up there in New York," he said. I just nodded, too scared to say no to this ridiculous scheme. A captive audience, I listened to this jailhouse wizard long into the night, until he was suddenly interrupted by a commotion outside the cell. A sheriff's deputy was shoving two black men upstairs, clubbing them as they went, the bright red blood shimmering on their dark skin. "That's where they keep the niggers," Speck said. The thudding sound of billy club on flesh and bone continued on the second floor. I heard groans and finally words. *No more, boss, please no more.* I was stunned that this seemed to be normal business down here.

The next morning, the jailer slid a tin plate filled with mush under the steel door. I was sitting on the edge of my bunk with the plate bridging my knees when the door opened and the sheriff stepped into the cell. He pointed at me, then motioned with his billy club to follow him. I trailed him through several doorways to the kitchen of his private quarters. He told me to sit at the table. His wife served me grits and scrambled eggs, and the first cup of coffee I ever drank. A little while later, we went into the sheriff's office. My father was sitting in a chair. He was dressed in a white shirt opened at the collar. There was a small puddle of sweat resting in the hollow of his throat. He looked uncharacteristically worried. His lips were pressed in a tight smile.

"Ready to go home?" he asked.

"Yes," I said softly, avoiding eye contact.

The sheriff had him sign some papers. "I don't want the boy to have a record," he said.

"He won't," the sheriff assured him.

We got in the Pontiac and began the trip home in silence. That night, we stopped at a hotel near Washington. We dropped his suitcases off in the room and went down to the dining room. "See what my father wants," he joked with the waitress. I was baffled by his good humor. Later, back in the room, he sat in a chair, leaning back until it touched the radiator behind him. I sat on the edge of one of the two twin beds, the one farthest from him, studying the tufts on the bedspread as we spoke. I told him about the hitchhiker who robbed me.

"That's the kind of gang you were heading to get mixed up with," he said. "What did you have in mind?"

"I wanted to get away from school and be a boxer."

He stood and hitched up his pants. Then he dug his hands deep into his pockets. "I guess I haven't been a good enough father to cause you to steal my car and run away." He started to cry, and then so did I. "I'm willing to start all over, if you are," he said.

"I am," I said.

"There are two conditions," he said. "First, no more boxing; no more Mr. Brown. You've got to promise me you'll never see him again." I promised.

"Second. Back to school. No more cutting class. Work hard—I'll give you a hand, get you a tutor. Agreed?"

On the way home, we stopped in Washington, where the company was replacing the roof of the Senate chamber on the U.S. Capitol building. We stopped in front of the Capitol, and Dad tooted the horn. Grandpa came down to the car window and peered in. "I see you've escaped from the Georgia chain gang," he said.

I KEPT MY word when we got home. I quit boxing, and for the first time in my life began studying hard and working diligently. Meanwhile, Dad took to heart the responsibility he accepted for my errant ways, blaming himself and his endless absences for my years of rebelliousness and my ultimate flight of fantasy. He wasn't going to stop traveling, because that was the business, and the business was his lifeblood. Instead, he was going to bring *me* into *his* world. He made me his constant companion, taking me with him whether he was going three blocks or three states away. We traveled the country during school vacations, and he indoctrinated me in the Koch Rules of Life, bonding us in a way we never had been before.

The conversations in the car were strings of Dad's bromides: Family comes first. Always pay your bills. Your credit is your most important asset. My word is my bond. My signature is a handshake. Never give your word unless you intend to keep it. Always hire someone smarter than you are—if you're the smartest guy in the company you're in big trouble because you'll be doing everything and everything won't get done. His favorite prayer was: "Lord, protect me from my friends. My enemies I'll take care of myself." He was very generous with family but would never loan anyone money. Giving it away was okay, but not lending it. "I made a deal with the bank," he said. "I won't lend money if they don't erect steel." He pulled out a card he kept in his wallet. "Yours is the saddest story I've ever heard. Please accept this card as a token of my sympathy." Though he was a hard drinker, he told me, "I don't want you drinking. But if you decide you're going to drink, buy the best, the most expensive. With what I'm paying you, you won't get very drunk." We usually skipped lunch but toward the end of the day, Dad would start looking out for a roadside cafe that had a lot of trucks parked in front of it. "Truckers always know the places where you won't get poisoned," he said.

If we were on the road on a Sunday, Dad would drive far out of our way to find a Catholic church, which was odd because he refused to go to church himself. He would drive up to the church, tell me to go in to Mass, and give me two dollars for the plate. Then he would sit outside in the car and wait. When I asked him why he never came inside, he explained that it all stemmed from something that had happened to him years before. He'd gotten in a wreck, and an ambulance had taken him to a Catholic hospital in Queens. But when the nun in charge saw this unconscious man smelling of alcohol, she snapped, "We don't take drunks here," and refused to treat him. He may have been drunk, but his biggest problem at the moment was a concussion. The ambulance driver took him to Queens General, where the staff was merciful but incompetent. They pronounced him dead. At some point later, Dad came to, sat up in the gurney, and found himself surrounded by corpses. He was in the morgue.

That this sort of thing seemed to be a regular occurrence in the family— there was that time he hitched a ride on a truck that collided with a hearse, and the time two private hospitals refused to take Grandpa after he fell off the Manhattan Bridge—was no consolation. Dad never forgave the Church for this particular horror, and he never went to Mass again. But apparently he didn't want to pass his antagonism on to his children, and still sent them to Catholic school. And when we were on the road on a Sunday, he made sure to find a church and send me in to receive the sacraments and to put two dollars in the plate—one for him. It was typical of his sometimes-enigmatic way of thinking. But I tend to believe his thoughts about religion were more complicated than simple wrath against some wicked nun. Maybe it was a rebellion against his Catholic mother's extreme religiosity, or the influence of his Lutheran father's anti-Catholic sentiment. But his problem was with the church, not with God. He was a lapsed Catholic, but not a lapsed believer. So maybe the dollar was his way of hedging his bets.

Spending all this time with my father, I realized that he was very carefully giving me an education as valuable as anything I learned at Bayside High. At every stop, there would be a lesson. One day, I chauffeured him first to the tailor—he waited pantless in a booth while his suit was pressed— then to the shoemaker to have his shoes shined, before heading into the city. We drove to Wall Street, and I parked in front of a bank. He got out of the car and told me to wait. "How do I look?" he asked before going inside to meet one of his "best friends"—his banker.

When he came back downstairs, we headed upstate and made a stop at

Utica Structural Steel. Dad went into the office, leaving me to wander around the plant. There were fabricators, specializing in tanks, and there were giant rollers that bent flat plates into round, sphere-shaped forms. I rejoined Dad in the office, where he was talking with the operations manager, explaining his position on some long-forgotten issue. The man seemed to have trouble grasping the point Dad was trying to make. As we walked back to the car, I made an unflattering comment about the manager's intelligence. Then I felt a presence behind my shoulder. It was the manager, who had forgotten to tell my father something. They had a brief coda to their conversation, while I slinked into the car. "Here's a little secret," Dad said a minute later, driving past the plant gate. "When you leave a meeting, always count to ten before saying anything." When I asked him why he hadn't taken the time to explain the problem to the man, he said, "If he isn't bright enough to understand it, then it's not worth explaining it to him." He hated frittering away words and was impatient with what he considered needless illumination. If you couldn't read between the lines, you were apt to spend a lot of time around him being confused.

As a counter to men like the manager at Utica Steel, my father always made a point of identifying the few he thought were something special. One day we drove into the city to see Morris Shapiro at his office on Fourteenth Street. Morris was a steel detailer, the best one in town, according to my father. A detailer's work was a critical link in the chain of tasks that went into erecting a building. It was his job to produce plans that included a drawing of every single piece of steel to be erected on the job, and to enter its dimensions, specifications, and—most important—its number. The fabricator relied on the precision of the detailer's drawings to manufacture and mark each piece of steel correctly so that it not only connected properly once it was on the site, but also was strong enough to support the loads that would be imposed on the structure. "You can't pay too much attention to the importance of the detailer making neat and accurate drawings," Dad said. "And Morris is the best detail man there is. He's a master teacher."

One of Shapiro's students was a draftsman named John Loverde, a brilliant man who saw steel detailing as something more than a tedious chore. He was that rare combination of creator and marketer; if it were possible to be the Henry Ford of steel detailing, John was it. He eventually left Morris to start his own detailing shop on Long Island, and in the early 1960s he began renting the room-sized computers at the Grumman Aerospace Corporation several nights a week. By day, Grumman's computers were helping engineers build the lunar landing module from which Neil Armstrong would take his giant leap for mankind in 1969. By night, John Loverde was using them to make calculations for steel jobs, mostly bridges, which required extensive and laborious detailing by highly experienced and intelligent draftsmen. Loverde predicted that some day all of this painstaking work would be done by computer. And, of course, he was right. His work was the precursor to the Computer-Assisted Design (CAD) system, introduced in 1963 and the prototype that would revolutionize the industry twenty years later. Now it's used all over the world, not only for steel but for everything from plastic molds to bicycles. So Henry Ford wasn't such a far-fetched analogy. John eventually capped his career by detailing—the old-fashioned way—one tower of what is still the largest steel-erection job in the history of the world: the World Trade Center. He was there on the morning of August 6, 1968, as the first piece of steel was set.

Dad took me up to meet Marvin Goldstein, the owner of a small steel shop down the block from our office in the Bronx. Dad would use him to fabricate small jobs, usually urgently needed steel that was omitted by another fabricator on a job underway. Mr. Goldstein was a little, old man, gray haired and round shouldered. Whenever I saw him, he would grasp my hands and not let go until he was sure I understood him. Like so many other business associates, he felt compelled to tell me how smart my father was. "He knows what he wants," Mr. Goldstein said. "He sees problems before they happen. And he discounts his bills."

"He used to push a cart up and down the street, collecting scrap," Dad told me when we left Goldstein Steel one day. He wanted me to know that just about all the successful men in the steel business had come from humble beginnings, that it was hard work, determination, and smarts—as opposed to slacking off, fooling around, and being thick-headed—that got them where they were. A prime example: Dad himself.

Though he knew his share of big shots, my father was always interested in the opinions of everyday people. Supermarket clerks, hat salesmen, shoe shiners, the gardener—he was always asking them their thoughts about the stock market, the war, whatever the events of the day. He wasn't just making chit-chat. That wasn't his style. He was really interested in what they thought, and respected their opinions. "It sure gives you a feel for what's going on," he told me as we drove away after a gas station attendant told him how great he thought Levittown was going to be. "Pretty soon that man's opinion is gonna reach Wall Street."

✴ ✴

WE FLEW UP to Hartford to look over a big crawler crane Dad was interested in buying. It was my first time in a plane, and my father asked me if I had a penknife. "We'll need it to cut ourselves out of the plane if it crashes." I must have looked terrified. He laughed and said it wasn't true—but that it was when he flew in the Thirties, when planes were made out of canvas.

We arrived in Hartford, and a taxi took us to a country club where we met a fellow named Mr. Harlan. He owned both the country club and the crawler crane. We sat at a table from three in the afternoon till three in the morning as Dad negotiated the purchase. Finally, my father made his last offer. He took out his checkbook and wrote a check for $30,000. Harlan refused it. He wanted five thousand more, and my father wouldn't budge. On the way to the hotel that night, I asked why Harlan turned down the offer. It sounded like a good deal. "He didn't own the crane," Dad said. "I finally figured that out."

"Who owns it?" I asked.

"The bank," he said. "And he owes them a lot more than thirty thousand."

IN THE SPRING of my senior year at Bayside High School, there was a teachers' strike. That meant the school was closed for extracurricular activities, and that included the senior prom. My friend John McDermott and I sprang into action. We rented the Bayside Yacht Club, ordered the food and organized the music, printed up tickets, and sold them at a table in the school lunchroom. We didn't get dates, figuring we'd be too busy running the show.

The day of the prom, my father told me, "Go pack, we're going out of town."

"But, Dad, I've got the prom tonight," I told him.

"Sorry, I need you to drive me," he said. "Get your gear." I don't think he would have insisted if I'd had a date, but to him this was a choice between prom business and family business, and as he always said, family comes first. I shrugged and went up to pack. Oh, hell, I thought, I'll go to my college prom.

My father's close friend and sometime lawyer, Walter Weiss, was always trying to get him to expand his horizons. The post-war boom was going full bore, and Walter always seemed to be tuned into the next big thing. He and his brothers, Al and Joe, who were also lawyers, were constantly coming up with can't-miss business opportunities for my father to invest in, often pitching partnerships while out on the boat on a Sunday afternoon. *A smart guy like you? You should be doing more than putting up steel.* Even on a Sunday sail on the *Joyce E.*, the talk was all business, one reason my mother rarely came (that and seasickness). Dad would even go fishing on the boat dressed in a suit. To him, leisure clothes meant suit pants and a starched white shirt, without the tie. I bought him a sport shirt for Christmas only once. It never left his drawer.

Walter Weiss thought Dad should invest in a grocery company called King Kullen, which had opened the first American supermarket before the war. But Dad didn't think supermarkets would be that big. Investing in racetracks? Not for him. One summer day on Long Island Sound, Walter and his brothers tried to interest Dad in soda-vending machines. They had sprung up on military bases during the war, and Walter was convinced they were going to sweep America. "You can put them at gas stations, grocery stores. If you bought a thousand of them, you'd make a fortune." This was one idea that Dad thought was worth considering. He did some quick math, as if doing a takeoff on a steel job: how many bottles a machine held, how much he'd make on every bottle sold. He figured you'd have to sell a million bottles to make $50,000. Finally, he shook his head. The problem, as he saw it, was that half the population was women. "I can't picture a woman putting a nickel in a machine and drinking a soda from a bottle," he said. "Just not ladylike. It'll never be successful."

But the true reason Dad never went for any of the Weiss brothers' ideas was that he had no desire to venture from his trade. "Shoemaker, stick to your last," was this steel man's motto.

A Good Name

A good name is more to be desired than great riches;
esteem is better than silver or gold.
Rich and poor have this in common,
the Lord made them both.
A shrewd person sees trouble coming and lies low;
the simpleton walks right into it and pays the penalty.

—THE BOOK OF PROVERBS 1:3

5

THE
UNCLES

WHEN MY FATHER and I pulled up to the Capitol building in Washington on the way home from Georgia, I saw what I had been foolishly running away from. I gazed up at the regal white dome, whose iconic image I had seen only in my history books. Running up in front of the Capitol at a forty-five-degree angle was a long derrick boom with KOCH spelled out vertically in block letters. It was a stirring sight—our family was putting a new roof over the heads of the United States Senate—and only then did I realize that this was my future.

My father had mixed feelings about putting our name on our equipment, or allowing it to be displayed on the big sign at every job site that listed the architects, engineers, and contractors responsible for the building going up behind it. "When things happen on a job, people look around for people to sue," he explained. (This was one case where he did have his finger on the pulse of the future.) He thought that keeping a low profile until we broke down our cranes and derricks and left the site kept our family out of trouble, as if not having our name on display made our participation a secret. But as was often the case, there was a visceral feeling behind his pragmatism. He just didn't feel right about taking credit before the job was finished. He thought it was pretentious.

Despite the company's work on so many prominent structures in the Twenties, Thirties, and Forties, Koch Erecting was still very much a mom-and-pop operation—or rather a pop-and-pop one. The only salaried employees were the yard men in the Bronx and Aunt Julia, my father's baby sister, who worked in the office. Foremen like Charlie Ruddy and Jack Finnel were virtual employees, but the union ironworkers who made up the heart of the labor force were employed on a job-by-job basis. After the war, though, the company payroll had a growth spurt, mainly because Grandpa had three sons coming home from battle and wanted them to work in the family business. My father resisted the idea of bringing in Bob, Jerome, and Dan. He didn't find the prospect of being his brothers' boss appealing, and he was skeptical of the abilities of the younger two. But Grandpa insisted, and apart from their battle over partnership a decade earlier, Dad always honored his father. So now, suddenly, there were five Koch men working in the business.

All three of my uncles had come home from the war unscathed, which Grandma attributed to all the praying she had done. That especially went for Daniel, the one among them who had really wanted to see action, but never fulfilled his desire to fly combat missions because of the injuries he had sustained from his mishap at the Ping Pong table during flight training. On the other end of the gung ho scale was Jerome, who had left for the Army at the start of the war with a lot of trepidation. He worried about having to kill men, and thought that even in a just war it was "plain murder." But he was promoted to sergeant, and when the rest of his company was sent overseas, he remained stateside to train new men. When he came home, he was proud to report that he had made it through the war without shooting anyone, though presumably some of the men he had trained did.

Uncle Bob didn't shoot anyone, either. Early in the war, Dad had arranged for him to get a leave from the Navy to help work on the blimp hangars our company was building for the military in Georgia. With that and some earlier experience, Bob was recruited for the Navy construction battalion—the Seabees—that had been established in December of 1941 by the chief of the Navy's Bureau of Yards and Docks. Bob was one of 325,000 men who served in the new outfit in World War II. They built airstrips, bridges, roads, warehouses, hospitals, and housing all over the world, but mostly in the Pacific. At twenty-three, Bob was one of the junior men. The Navy wanted men with experience and skill, so in the early days of the war the average age of Seabees was thirty-seven. "We build, we fight," was their motto. Bob came out of the service quite conversant with heavy construction, and he had the Seabee hustle in his demeanor. That let him fit right into the family business, which my father ran with a firmness that would be familiar to any returning veteran.

Uncle Bob, thirteen years my father's junior, was a compact man with broad shoulders. He had a wide forehead topped by jet black hair, a long, thin nose, and a Kennedyesque smile. He was one of the better looking of the Koch brothers, and the most aggressive. He had started out wanting to

be a priest. After graduating from Cathedral High School, a kind of prepara-
tory academy for boys with priestly aspirations, he went to Georgetown
University but lost interest in the collar before freshman year was out. Given
a taste of the family business, he decided he wanted to follow in his big
brother's footsteps and erect steel.

Of the three of his brothers that Grandpa invited into the business,
Uncle Bob was the kind of man Dad might have hired eventually anyway.
He was self-assured and able, a grease-up-to-the-elbows worker who was
always jumping in to get the job done. He was a good planner—a good steel
erector. With Grandpa slowing down, Dad needed exactly that sort of hands-
on man to manage jobs in the field. But it didn't mean he would make it
easy for him.

Jerome, two years younger than Bob, was put to work in the office, where
he immediately lightened the mood. Jerome was affable and funny, the most
relaxed of all the Koch brothers. At Christmas, he came through the door of
Grandma and Grandpa's house in Scarsdale singing "Home for the
Holidays" and wearing a garish sport coat made of patched-together, multi-
colored swatches. Though he had been terrified of having to shoot anyone
in the war, Jerome had gone to Officers Candidate School, and after
Hiroshima was sent to Japan to take part in the destruction of Japanese military equipment. He came home with a few swords and grenades, and married a flaming redhead beauty named Mary O'Brien. They spent their snowy
wedding night in intensive care after Jerome crashed their car into a tree as
he drove away from the Westchester Country Club. They wore the scars of
their wedding night the rest of their lives.

Uncle Dan was the caboose of the family, born when Dad was eighteen
and already bidding on his first big job, the Biltmore in Coral Gables. Dan
had straight black hair and inherited his mother's dark, Indianesque looks.
He was only eight years older than me, so a visit to Grandma and Grandpa's
house in Scarsdale when I was a teenager meant a chance to hang out with
my cool uncle. His room was like a bachelor's paradise. He had flashy sports
jackets and an elegant tuxedo hanging in his closet. His shoes were all highly
polished, neatly treed and at parade-rest on his closet floor. A score of
vibrant neckties hung like banners from the rack above. Burl and meer-
schaum pipes stood in their holder on the bureau among scattered glistening gold and silver tie clips and cuff links. Dan had a serious record
collection. He would play "Sing Sing Sing" by Benny Goodman and tell me
how great it was. "Listen to those tom-toms!" he would say. "That's Gene
Krupa, from Chicago. The greatest drummer around." He would read the

names of the musicians off the record label, and tell me something about each of them. Then he would shoo me out of his room. "Got a hot date, kid, gotta get dressed." Where you going? I'd ask. "Night clubbing, my boy, night clubbing." A couple of years after the war, Dan married a Radio City Music Hall Rockette.

Coming into the business, Dan was put in charge of the equipment and its maintenance. When Dad bought three deck-mounted cranes at a government auction, Dan went to get them and bring them back to New York. Dan was ready for that assignment: The cranes were in Hawaii.

In addition to his brothers, Dad began hiring his brothers-in-law. He brought in his sister Gladys' husband, Joe Brown, as an estimator. And Tom Bracken, who was married to his sister Pat, worked as an operating engineer, starting with the blimp hangars. Meanwhile, he looked forward to having me around for the summer. The only man Dad hired who wasn't a relative would turn out to last the longest.

Rudy Loffredo was mild mannered and rail thin, a judicious, reliable company man to the core. He had grown up in the Bronx, gotten his engineering degree from City College, and gone into the Navy in 1944. Unlike the Koch brothers, he saw plenty of action, serving on the U.S.S. *Pittsburgh,* a heavy cruiser, in the Pacific off Japan. His ship lost 110 feet of bow to a typhoon. It was a toss-up whether it was that catastrophe or the time he and his shipmates shot down a kamikaze, that was his most intense moment of the war. "I was twenty-one," he recalled. "You fear nothing when you're twenty-one."

Rudy left the service in 1945, a member of the "52-20 club," so named for returning veterans whom the government paid twenty dollars a week for a year, or until they found a job. Rudy didn't even get his first week's check when he got a call telling him there was a job for him with the Port of New York Authority. They were building the Brooklyn Battery Tunnel, and needed civil engineers to work as inspectors. One of Rudy's jobs was to make sure the bolts fastening the steel that ringed the tunnel tubes were tight. So here was this skinny kid checking on the work of these big, burly ironworkers. Sometimes when Rudy asked them to show him that a bolt was tight, they would strain against their four-foot-long hand wrenches, groaning. It took Rudy a while to figure out they were pulling his leg. To really make sure the bolts were tight enough, he held a quarter against the head of the bolt, then had one of the men hit the other side with a hammer. If he felt any vibration in the quarter, it meant the bolt wasn't tight enough. The work took Rudy deep into the dark tunnel, where the air pressure caused men to get the bends if they stayed too long. So they would work inside for only an hour, then stay out for three before going back in for another hour.

Rudy had been working for the Port for about a year when he heard about a job opening through his wife's cousin, who was a secretary for our company. Joe Brown had decided to quit. Apparently he didn't feel he had much of a future as an estimator under my father, though Dad clearly depended on him and was very upset when he left. But when Rudy applied for the job, Dad cheered up, realizing he could replace Joe with a civil engineer for the same money. It wasn't essential for a steel erector to have an engineer on the payroll, but his knowledge wouldn't hurt. Rudy did takeoffs and became my father's right hand on bids. He was a man who was as finely calibrated as his calculations. He arrived in the office exactly at eight every morning and left exactly at five. He ate his lunch at his desk, precisely at noon and always the same ham and cheese on rye with mustard, a slice of apple pie, a cup of coffee with milk and one sugar. The menu never varied, not even for a day. In his entire career, Rudy never once asked for a raise. He waited for my father to say, "Rudy, I'm giving you a raise," and those days came often enough for him.

Rudy's agreeable presence in the office was ballast for the uneven relationship my father had with his younger brothers. Dad ran the business autocratically, as if he wanted to disabuse Bob and Jerome, especially, of any thought that they had a claim to the company simply because it was owned by their father and brother. Grandpa made it clear that when he was gone, his three younger sons would inherit equally his 50 percent ownership of the company. (The girls would get the real estate in Scarsdale and Florida, which meant they would have to wait until both Grandma and Grandpa passed on.) Dad would always be the biggest single stockholder and be the company's president, but he didn't like that his younger brothers would simply be *given* half of what he and Grandpa had built. He would make them earn it.

By 1950, Grandpa was starting to take a step back and regard his accomplishments. This is in the literal sense. He liked to find a spot away from a job and watch the progress. An ironworker named Sonny Rice told me he once found Grandpa in a grassy area a bit away from a racetrack they were building in New Jersey. "He was half-reclining, leaning on his elbow," Sonny said. "He called me over and said, 'Sonny, let me give you some advice. Change your name. Otherwise, they'll be calling you Sonny when you're an old man like me.'" In 1951, Grandpa went to Mexico City to supervise the erection of an office building. One day he found a park bench across the street and sat there looking the job over, paying no attention to the drunks loitering in the park. Suddenly, *la policia* swarmed in, rounded everyone up, and hauled them all to the station, Grandpa included. He went along peacefully, waiting till they got to the police station to explain that he was a sober man whose means of support were steel beams and columns and rivets.

Grandpa came home from Mexico City and announced he had run his last job. He was sixty-nine and had spent half a century walking steel. Dad did the math and figured Grandpa had erected, on average, about three hundred tons of steel every week for every one of those fifty years. He could retire in good conscience. Grandpa retained his financial and surely his emotional interest in the company, but as a practical matter Karl Koch Erecting Company was now all Dad's.

FOR YEARS, MY father had been fuming about the unfair advantage American Bridge and Bethlehem Steel had over the small erecting and fabricating companies. By the early fifties, he was boiling over. The big rolling mills sold their steel to fabrication shops that were their wholly owned subsidiaries. So nobody knew how much the steel really cost. And when the companies put in their bids to furnish and erect a job, they knew their only competitors were each other. To my father and his fellow independent erectors, it seemed that these two "competitors" were curiously not very competitive. Did they have an *understanding* that kept the prices high? You couldn't convince my father they didn't.

Dad's friend and lawyer Grant Horner thought he was right that Big Steel's ability to submit furnish-and-erect bids probably constituted a restraint of trade, but that he shouldn't give much thought to mounting a David-versus-Goliath lawsuit. The giants had an army of attorneys; Dad's lawyer didn't even have a secretary. And after all, it wasn't as though we were starving.

But it was not in my father's character to abide such a monumental insult to the love of his life—his work and his company. He was like so many other American dynasty builders, large and small, who worked too hard and worried too much and allowed themselves too little contentment. The struggle against the big companies went to the heart of my father's being. He wouldn't sue them, but neither would he disregard them. He turned his irritation into a personal crusade. He had a lot of contacts in Washington, and not a single one of them escaped his complaints.

With private companies, Dad's argument was all practical: If you insist on separate prices for furnishing the steel and erecting it, he told them, you are going to get a less expensive job because it will make the bidding on the erection portion more competitive. With public work, though, he argued on moral grounds as well: that it was unconscionable for the government—on the backs of taxpayers—to operate under a policy that gave giant companies even more advantage than they already had over smaller ones.

Dad didn't just harangue all those people who worked behind desks in buildings he built and some that he would have liked to. He wrote letters to the presidents of the companies themselves. And one year, he bought a few shares of stock in United States Steel, American Bridge's parent company, so he could go to the company's annual meeting. When it came time for comments from shareholders, he stood up and asked why the company's annual report didn't show a profit-and-loss statement for American Bridge. They looked at him blankly, told him it wasn't their policy, and asked for the next shareholder comment.

But back in Washington, the word slowly got through that American Bridge was just a sales arm—you could even call it a front—for U.S. Steel. They made their money at the rolling mills, and the general contractors and ultimately the building owners who were their customers—including the government—never really knew whether they were paying a fair price for the steel they were buying. Eventually, Dad's campaign paid off. Late in the administration of President Harry S. Truman, government contracts officials decided that henceforth bids for steel work on major federal projects would be broken in two—one for fabricating the steel, another for erecting it. The victory meant that Dad would no longer have to team up with one of the other fabricators to try to underbid Bethlehem or American Bridge on government work. It meant that—as had happened on a few jobs over the years—we would very likely be erecting steel from American Bridge and Bethlehem Steel on a regular basis. And it meant that, from that day forward and until the day he died, my father thought Harry S. Truman—who probably never even knew about this arcane change in government policy—was the greatest American president who ever lived.

BETTER LATE THAN NEVER, I discovered after my Georgia sojourn that I wasn't such a bad student after all. I was capable of bursts of intensive concentration and study, which produced suddenly high marks. In fact, when the results of the Regents exams came back during my senior year of high school in 1951, the dean of mathematics called me in with my father, laid the tests on his desk, and said it was obvious I had cheated. He asked Dad to persuade me to confess.

"We have nothing to confess," said my father, who knew how much I had studied. One of his charms was his telling use of the collective "we" when he spoke of my successes or failures.

"The only thing I can do is prove my ability," I said to the dean. "Give me a test right now—on any subject."

Without a word, the dean took a Regents book off his shelf and opened to a two-year-old math exam. "I'll sit here while you do it," he said. He turned to my father. "Do you want to leave, Mr. Koch?"

"No, this looks interesting," Dad said. "I think I'll stay."

I zipped through fifty multiple-choice questions, then solved the first bunch of equations. "Can I borrow your slide rule?" I asked. The dean pursed his lips and snatched the answer sheets impatiently. He put my test next to the answers in the book and checked each question, shaking his head as he went. He finally looked up and said, "You got them all right. Karl, we've never seen this kind of performance from you before. I'm truly amazed."

"We studied hard," my father said proudly, giving no hint that, truth be told, he was just as amazed. I had been such a hellion that he was taking no chances with my younger brother Donald. "I'm not going through *that* again," he said, referring either to my stealing away in the middle of the night or to the first sixteen years of my life in general. Ironically, Dad responded to his own guilt about having been away from home so much when I was growing up by spending even less time with Donald. Hedging his bets—and perhaps concluding that there wasn't much he could do to be around more—Dad packed Donald off to Cardinal Farley's Military Academy when he reached high school. The last thing he said to him when he left him in upstate Rhinebeck was: No boxing.

Dad and I stood up to leave the inquisition. The dean said he was sorry he had accused me of cheating. "We don't want an apology, Dean," my father told him. "We just want our diploma."

We got our diploma, but *I* still had a major problem. Though I'd mastered science and math, I had always been spectacularly awful with foreign languages. I had tried them all—Latin, French, Spanish—and had failed them all. I had to add more science and math courses to graduate, but without a single language credit I couldn't go to college. Uncle Jerome knew the dean at Manhattan College, an engineering school founded by the DeLaSalle

Christian Brothers that was actually in the Bronx. Dad asked Jerome to arrange an appointment, and I went up to see the dean. He told me he would be happy to accept me, as long as I could pass their entrance exam in math. "Don't worry," he said, "there's not a word of Latin or French in it."

ONE SATURDAY THAT spring, Dad took me for a drive out to Long Island. We headed east, then north up into the posh community of Sands Point, smelling the salt air as we neared Manhasset Bay. "Where're we going?" I asked.

"We're going to look at a house," he said, turning onto West Creek Farms Road.

"What for?"

We rolled down the road and Dad pulled into a long driveway that approached the left side of a sprawling brick ranch with a slate roof. It sat majestically on a huge piece of land—two acres, Dad said—with a woodsy, rolling grade in the back. We walked up to the house, and a big, blonde, square-jawed man came out with his right hand extended. "Hello, Mr. Koch, glad to see you."

My father introduced me to Mr. Wesley Copp. "He built the houses up here," he said.

"Yes, and this is the last one, the pick of the litter," Copp said, leading us inside. "And you and I have to talk your father into buying it."

There was a gigantic living room with a fireplace and a great bay window that looked over the rear gardens. The kitchen was out of a magazine. Dad told me to go into the bedrooms and jump on the floors as hard as I could. He and Copp went outside while I roamed the house stomping on the floors. I emerged and reported that the house appeared solid to me.

"I'd like to buy it, Wesley," Dad said. "Are you a gambling man?"

"Of sorts," Copp said quizzically.

They had already negotiated the price to a little over $50,000, but were still a couple of thousand dollars apart. "I'm not going to bother you by bargaining," Dad said. "How about we toss a coin? I flip, you call. You win, I give you fifty-three thousand. I win, it's fifty thousand." I couldn't believe this. Back then, three thousand dollars could just about buy an entire house, if only one in a more humble neighborhood. But Copp was game and called tails. Dad tossed the coin and it flipped in the air and hit the deck—heads. "How do you like your new house?" Dad asked me. Later in the car, I asked him how he could gamble so much money on the flip of a coin, and he couldn't have been more nonchalant. "Thought I would win," he said. "I lost the last three flips. I was due."

We were a long way from the little apartment in Jamaica from which we had moved only a dozen years earlier. The North Shore of Long Island was one of the most exclusive areas in the burgeoning New York suburbs, and Sands Point was one of the gems. It was very diverse—all kinds of rich people lived there. Since the early years of the century, there had been Goulds and Guggenheims and their reclusive guest Charles Lindbergh. There were Averill Harriman and Bill Macy, John Philip Sousa and Perry Como and the Mafia boss Frank Costello.

Two of Dad's many lawyer friends, Leo Dorsey and the extremely well-connected Bill Shea (for whom a stadium would be named a decade later), sponsored him for membership in the Sands Point Golf Club, where the club pro sold him a beautiful set of Ben Hogan woods and irons. Further down Barkers Point Road, on a spit of land jutting into the bay, was the Sands Point Bath and Racquet Club, which became my mother's haunt. It had a sprawling, wood-frame clubhouse with a postcard view of the sailboats bobbing in the bay. Individual beach cabanas lined the shore, set apart from the de rigueur pool and tennis courts.

Mother gathered us all up one evening, everyone dressed to the nines for a night at The Club. As we entered, I was stopped by the head waiter and then by the club manager, who barred me because I wasn't wearing a tie and refused to put on their emergency tie.

"I'm sorry, they are club rules," the manager said. "Absolutely no exceptions."

"How the hell do you wear a tie with a turtleneck?" I asked.

"Club rules, sir. I'm sorry."

My mother, mortified, fussed and fumed until I acquiesced. I wrapped the emergency tie around my turtleneck. We were escorted to our table, passing the head waiter on the way. "Shithead," I muttered.

Our conversion to post-war privilege was complete when, on one more Saturday morning, Dad took me to a shipyard on City Island and told a man named Ray, "Let's show the boy the boat." He'd bought a forty-foot Wheeler Sun Lounge, an honest-to-goodness yacht. "You're gonna have to learn how to drive that thing," Dad said as we drove way. "I'll be too damn busy."

As would I. The first and second Karl W. Koches were now ensconced in two of the toniest communities in the New York area, but the third one was knee-deep in calculus at DeLaSalle Hall, a dormitory on the campus of Manhattan College.

I don't know if the fix was in—knowing my father, it wasn't an accident—but I was assigned to a roommate, Nick Matich, who was a superb student and an intensely hard worker. Determined to get an engineering degree, I followed his example and did little but study. On weekends, the dorm was deserted except for Nick and me and the head prefect. One of the few times I went out, I put on a tie, using the traditional four-in-hand knot my father had taught me when I was younger. Nick taught me the Windsor. The next time I went home, I demonstrated it for Dad and suggested he try it. He just smiled and said, "That's kind of complicated. Me and my knot have traveled too many miles together to be separated now by that Windsor knot of yours." I used the Windsor for a few years but eventually went back to the old four-in-hand.

I got top grades in most of my courses that first year—I was especially partial to surveying—but flunked calculus and had to go to summer school at City College. This was a big disappointment to my dad, not just that I had failed the course but that it meant I couldn't work for the company out in the field.

By the end of my second year of engineering school, I was burnt out. I didn't work so hard because I loved to study. I had to work like a madman, especially in calculus, just to get it. My father told me, "If you need a break, take it. You can work for me for the year and go back next year. The school's not going away." I took him up on it—mostly because I wanted to be part of a project our company had begun working on earlier that year. I wanted to go to Oak Ridge, Tennessee.

It had been ten years since the company had worked on the first Oak Ridge plant, and eight years since the bomb that had been conceived there was dropped over Japan. Now there was a new arms race, and it was our one-time ally, the Soviet Union, that we were worried about. The next generation of nuclear weapon, the hydrogen bomb, would be developed at a new complex on the western edge of the reserve at Oak Ridge called K-33. The main building, called the gaseous diffusion plant, or K-902, would be a half mile long and eighty-two feet high, and house forty-two acres under one roof. It would cover more area than any structure ever built, and at more than 35,000 tons would be the third heaviest steel job (after the 44,000 tons in the Empire State Building and the 41,000 erected for the Chicago Merchandising Mart). It was also the first major government project put out for bid under the new procurement procedures.

American Bridge and Bethlehem Steel had to submit one price for fabricating and delivering the steel and another for erecting it. Dad worked the numbers over. Nothing was more important to him than underbidding American Bridge and Bethlehem Steel on this job. His final number to the general contractor, Maxon Construction, was $1.6 million—to Bethlehem's $2.6 million. He was so determined to get this job that he left *a million dollars* on the table. The guys from Bethlehem told him he was a fool for bidding so low—that it would be the end of our company.

Dad promised the Atomic Energy Commission, which had been created after the war and now oversaw operations at Oak Ridge, that all the steel would be up in less than a year. That timetable, though, was not entirely in our hands. It would require round-the-clock fabrication and delivery of steel by Bethlehem, which had been low bidder on the furnishing contract.

I arrived at Oak Ridge for a three-day trip in April to get my security clearance. The reserve was much more developed since the government took over these 59,000 remote acres a decade before and hastily built a research reserve and a town to go with it. Now there was even an Oak Ridge Golf and Country Club, where, a few weeks after my visit, all the construction companies were having a huge employee dance featuring the crowning of "Miss K-33."

My uncles Bob and Dan had been at Oak Ridge for three months, and the erection was more than halfway complete. Though this was the company's biggest and most important and time-pressured job, it had begun when we had several other large jobs already in progress, in Boston, Pennsylvania, and in Paducah, Kentucky, at a smaller gaseous-diffusion plant the Atomic Energy Commission was building. Dad shuttled among all the jobs and put Bob in charge of Oak Ridge as project manager, with Dan working under him supervising the equipment. Dan and his wife, Pat, were living in an apartment on the second floor of a dormitory building, and they invited me to stay with them for the summer. Pat was the former Rockette, a beautiful, joyous woman who was easily my favorite aunt. Oak Ridge was a spartan existence for them. After dinner, Dan rubbed his hands together and said, "How about a Dr. Pepper?" "Oh, goody!" Pat said. "How about you, Karl?" It seemed like the highlight of the day.

Dan took me over to the administration building to get me fingerprinted and photographed. I pinned my ID badge onto my lapel, and planted an aluminum hat on my head. He took me out to the K-902 site and showed me the cranes he had rented, eight of them lined up like soldiers, each one erecting a section of the building within its operating radius. The steel came from five different Bethlehem plants and arrived at the Oak Ridge rail yard exactly when it was needed. It was unloaded by crane and set on wooden pallets. A lumber carrier rode up to the pallet, slid its fingers underneath it and raised it off the ground, then took off down the gravel road to the building site. The driver would feed the load of steel to the crane operator, then scoot back to the rail yard to get another load. Around each crane were sections of discarded steel—misfabricated pieces that Uncle Bob directed the foreman not to bother trying to use. "Don't lose time with it," he said. "Just drop it and keep moving."

Time was what this job was all about, and it would turn out to trigger the beginning of an epic change in the way steel was erected. In getting ready for the job, my father discovered a serious problem that would make it virtually impossible to put up the building in the time promised: They couldn't find enough men. With many ironworkers in the service in Korea or already working at Paducah and other jobs, it would be nearly impossible to hire enough experienced rivet gangs to put such an enormous building up with any kind of speed. The plans called for more than a million rivets to be bolted up. Dad had an idea.

The previous summer, I had sat with him in his office in the Bronx as he told me about a development in steel construction that he said was going to revolutionize the industry. He held a rivet in his hands. It had served us well over the last seventy years or so, but it had a certain inevitable limitation. A rivet's job was to resist "shearing stress"—what happens when two contacting objects slide against each other and move apart in opposite directions. Engineers could calculate a rivet's clamping force when it was pounded hot and then allowed to cool. But they didn't use that calculation in their designs because that force couldn't be counted on long-term. Rivets eventually loosened. Even an infinitesimal slackening reduced the rivet's resistance to shear. That's what the engineer used in deciding how many rivets a joint needed: enough to resist the total shear at the joint, plus a safety factor.

"But this," Dad said, holding up an unfamiliar steel fastener, "is a different matter."

He held in his hand a high-tensile bolt. Someday soon, he explained, it was going to replace the beloved rivet. The new bolt created a friction between the two surfaces that gave it a clamping force so great that it theoretically never went into shear. Dad had heard about the new bolts from salesman for the companies that were starting to make them. They were trying to get steel erectors to start using them, but hadn't had any success to speak of, mainly because nobody seemed to want to be the first to put up a building or bridge without rivets.

Dad was so excited about the innovation that when I returned to school after that summer, I decided to look into it further. I gathered all the literature I could find and took it to Brother Aloysius Joseph, who was the technical adviser to *The Manhattan Engineer,* the official publication of the engineering school. Brother Joseph spent several evenings helping me research and write an article for the magazine on the experimental work on high-strength bolts being carried out by the Research Council on Riveted and Bolted Structural Joints. Their studies had found that high-strength bolts were more than four times more resistant to shearing stress than rivets. A hot driven rivet could withstand a clamping stress of 12,000 pounds per square inch. But a high-strength bolt of equal dimensions and tested under identical conditions produced a clamping stress of *50,000* PSI. It seemed that connections made with high-tensile steel bolts really did resist shear.

When my article was published in *The Manhattan Engineer* in January of 1953, I brought my father a tall stack of copies, which he began to pass out to business associates. He started with the owners and architects of buildings he was erecting. He hoped to persuade them to use the new bolts. The advantages were undeniable. Bolts didn't require the highly specialized four-man riveting crews that had been the heart and soul of ironworking since steel took over heavy construction seventy-five years earlier. The bolts needed no heaters with their portable forges and perfect tossing technique, no stickers-in or bolters-up. They only required two strong-armed men: one to hold the air-driven impact wrench that slugged and turned the nut and the other to "hold the roll," or stop the bolt from rotating while the nut was being impacted. By substituting a rivet that required the work of four men with a bolt that needed only two, contractors could double their labor efficiency, and of course, lower the customer's ultimate costs. And because the bolts resisted shear, fewer of them would be needed than rivets.

It was easier to persuade a private company to use the new technology than the government. Commercial corporations were a little more open to ideas that might save them money, and you only had to sell one or two people, not an entire bureaucracy. The first company that Dad convinced to go with bolts over rivets was Lederle Laboratories, a big pharmaceutical company most famous for making polio vaccines, which was building its new headquarters in Pearl River, New York. It would be one of the first major constructions in the United States to use high-strength bolts instead of rivets. So when our company was awarded the job of constructing the mammoth K-902 plant at Oak Ridge that same year, Dad had his ammunition ready. He arranged a meeting in Washington with the Atomic Energy Commission.

"I'd like a change in the job specifications," he told the commissioners, as representatives of Bethlehem Steel looked on. "There aren't enough riveters available to do the job. Most of them are in Korea, shooting M-1s instead of rivet guns."

"What do you propose?" he was asked.

"I'd like to use high-tensile bolts instead of rivets." He explained the research—my article was a handy source of information, though he didn't dare cite his twenty-one-year-old son as a reference—and said he had just used bolts with great success in the Lederle Laboratories building.

The boys from Bethlehem looked at Dad as though he were crazy. "You're going to need a *million* fasteners," one of them said. "Who're you going to get them from?"

"From *you*," Dad replied. "I'm going to buy them from *you*."

The fellows from Bethlehem conferred, then told the commissioners that their company had no objections to using high-strength bolts.

Uncle Dan was assigned the task of recruiting ironworkers in Tennessee. He went to the diner up the road and passed the word that men were needed for the K-902 plant. Those who came down were baffled by the new fasteners. *You mean you're not using rivets?* Dan showed them the impact wrench they would use to place the bolts. "It's just like using a pneumatic wrench to take the lugs off a truck tire," he explained.

I arrived at Oak Ridge the day after classes ended in June, by which point the impact wrenches had tightened more than half a million bolts. The building was being erected with terrific urgency, and the men were moving at a dead heat, busy as hell. Uncle Bob had us *ahead* of schedule, a shining moment for him in his big brother's eyes. With all that was going on, though, nobody knew anything about the work that would be done under this endless roof, other than that it was part of the development of the H-bomb. The size of the place was mind-boggling and only added to the aura of jittery mystery about the Red Menace. Only later did we learn that when completed, the plant was used for separating uranium-235 from uranium-238 for both atomic weapons and nuclear energy. A gigantic plant was necessary because the process required several thousand successive stages. Dad got a "Q" security clearance, the highest one possible, as did Grandpa, who just wanted to come to Oak Ridge to hang around and see what was going on. To get him in, Dad listed Grandpa as the company's comptroller.

I was listed as timekeeper, which wasn't my job, either. More accurately,

I was the bolt counter. Uncle Bob wanted me to go around the job and keep a daily count of how many bolts were being put in by the various crews. After a couple of days of walking around with a clipboard, I noticed bolts, maybe one an hour, whizzing by my head and thudding to the ground. I thought it was weird that these Tennessee ironworkers were so careless that they were dropping so many bolts. Then I realized they weren't dropping them. They were *throwing* them—at me. It was a lesson I would never forget. Ironworkers do *not* want someone watching them work. Especially someone with a clipboard, keeping track of their production from down there on the ground. Uncle Dan suggested I approach my work more like a fellow worker and less like a Communist spy. Of course, there was a definite line between the ironworkers and we in the company. Grandpa was the only Koch who was ever really a part of the brotherhood. But one thing you didn't want to do was stand beneath an irritated ironworker, so Dan taught me to approach the points and have as much face-to-face contact as possible before angling off to the next team.

This meant, of course, going *up there.* In the years since I'd started going around with my father, this was something I had assiduously avoided. Grandpa fell off the Manhattan Bridge, and I had no interest in making this a family tradition. I'd had my share of missteps, for sure, but they'd all been at sea level. It seemed, though, the time had come to make this rite of passage. I walked up to the K-902 plant, looked up for a second or two, then climbed a ladder eighteen feet to the first beam.

I held onto the column, and waited until there was little traffic around me. I took one step, then another, then another. Hell, I was walking a beam! It was a cakewalk. But halfway across, I somehow got myself into the wrong position. My left foot was too far behind my right and I couldn't swing it around in front to take the next step. Ever so gingerly, I dragged it up so that my two feet were together. But they were still twisted. I froze, and dared not look any place other than at the beam directly in front of my feet. It was a trick to see the beam but not the gigantic empty space beneath it. An ironworker up ahead called out, "*You okay, son? You want me to come out and get you?*"

"No, I'm okay," I lied.

He waited ten or fifteen seconds. I hadn't moved. "You okay?" he asked again.

"Yeah, I'm okay."

"Okay," he said, and walked off onto another beam.

This is the end, I thought. What do I do now? The last time I'd been so scared was when I'd tried to sail a rowboat with an umbrella across Long Island Sound and almost drowned myself and half the neighborhood. Who knows what impulses take over in situations like this, but I suddenly found myself singing. Very softly, the words to an old folk song, "The Old Oaken Bucket," started coming out of my mouth. When I got to the end of the first stanza, I said to myself, I'm going to take a step.

> *How dear to the heart*
> *Are the scenes of my childhood,*
> *When fond recollection*
> *Presents them to view!*

I slowly swung my left foot around my right, and to my absolute relief it landed on the beam. I sang another verse. I took another step. A third verse. A third step. One more to go, one verse away from the column.

> *The old oaken bucket,*
> *The ironbound bucket,*
> *The moss-covered bucket*
> *That hung in the well.*

I took a nice, long step, reached out, and touched the column. Talk about a long day's journey. Talk about reaching the Promised Land. I spent the rest of the day on Cloud Nine. I was like a troubadour inside, silently singing my heart out and walking all over the job. Eventually I learned the instinct of letting my big toe lead and using the base of my spine for balance. I walked steel the rest of the summer and in every season for the next four decades. Half a century after that day, I can still do it if I have to.

THE USE OF high-strength bolts at Oak Ridge was a phenomenal success in terms of both time and money. We erected 35,266 tons of steel in just eight months, which Dad claimed was a new national record. It inspired his new company slogan: "Karl Koch Speed-Ability Cuts Costs." He fairly gloated when he recalled the man from Bethlehem's prediction that his bid would sink the company. In fact, Dad told me, the government almost exercised a clause in the contract that limited excess profits.

Oak Ridge began the conversion of the world standard from the venerable rivet to the avant-garde high-strength bolt. As Dad predicted, the bolts revolutionized the industry, and within the decade, rivets would all but disappear, taking the timeless ballet of the rivet gangs with them. We did our last riveted job in 1960—a repair of the Manhattan Bridge, the span that had brought Grandpa to New York in 1908. We replaced the rivets he and his brother ironworkers pounded, and never used them again.

6

THE
EXPEDITOR

WHEN GRANDPA GOT tired of hanging around Oak Ridge, I drove him to Florida in my father's old gray Cadillac, which Dad had put Tennessee tags on and given me to get around the reserve. Grandma and Grandpa had a house in the sleepy coastal community of Surfside, midway between Miami and Fort Lauderdale, an area that had been their second home since they'd arrived to put up the Biltmore in 1925.

Grandpa was glad for the ride and the company, but didn't see what the hurry was. "If I don't hold onto my hat it'll be in the backseat, the way you drive," he said, clutching his gray fedora as we blew past the Great Smoky Mountains. It was a different story when he drove. Rolling at a leisurely pace down a narrow country road, he ignored the honking horn behind us. Finally, he slowed to a dead stop, right there on the road without pulling over. He ambled out of the car and walked back to the woman behind the wheel, took off his hat, and politely said, "If you're having trouble, lady, maybe I can help you."

"You're driving too slow," she said.

"Oh," he said. "In that case, I'll speed up." He got back in the car, and increased his speed a mile or two an hour.

I planned to stay with Grandpa in Florida for about a week, until some friends he was expecting arrived for a visit. Dad didn't like him staying alone, and Grandma wasn't coming down until the end of the fall. At seventy-one, Grandpa was still in good health, but was having a hard time with his eyes. Actually, the trouble was with his eyelids. They would close involuntarily. One morning at breakfast, he patted the newspaper on the table and gleefully told me, "I sneaked up on the paper last night and read the whole thing. Somehow or other my eyes didn't know what I was doing and didn't close on me. That's the secret—get up at two o'clock in the morning and read the newspaper." He asked me to leave the paper by his bed before I went to bed, so he could "sneak up on it in the middle of the night and read the whole damn thing" before his eyes realized what was going on.

Grandpa's doctor couldn't tell him why his eyelids were closing on their own or what he could do about it. At one point some of his children thought the problem was in his head and made an appointment with a psychiatrist. "So I went to see the psychiatrist in his big fancy office," Grandpa told me. "He talked to me for a while, asking me questions about my job and what I did. About Mrs. K. And tried to go digging into my childhood. After an hour, he said: 'Well, Mr. Koch, it will take a lot of sessions to get to the bottom of this. Meanwhile, let me give you a suggestion. You worked in construction with your hands your whole life, and you're not doing that now. That could be the cause. Since you have that nice work area in your basement that you told me about, go out and buy some power tools: a drill, a saw, a lathe, and make furniture for your wife. You can make some beautiful legs for chairs with that lathe.' " Grandpa said he stood up, took out his wallet, and handed the doctor fifty dollars. "Here ya are, Doc," he told him. "This pays for my session. I won't be coming back, and I'll tell you why. You got me going out and buying all them machines and sitting down in the basement, standing at the saw, cutting some wood for those legs you talked about. My eyes will close. I'll cut off my fingers, and then I'll really be in a fix. And besides that, if I manage to make any furniture, Mrs. K would throw it into the fireplace. She only collects antiques."

While I was in Florida, Dad called and told me that as soon as Grandpa's friends arrived, he wanted me to go to North Carolina. "I've got a job for you," he said.

A couple of weeks earlier, Dad had gotten the drawings for another secret project at Oak Ridge. It wasn't a building, but an arrangement of steel towers to be erected in a remote area of the reserve. It was cryptically named the Tower Shielding Facility, or TSF, and, as with everything else we did at Oak Ridge, we had no idea what its function would be. On every other structure we built, whether it was the Proctor & Gamble headquarters in Cincinnati or the Juilliard School of Music in New York or the Broad Causeway in Miami, there was no mystery about the purpose it would serve. But at Oak Ridge, it was *all* mystery. It would be years before we would learn what went on after we left. And the TSF was the most enigmatic of all. The only thing we knew was that it consisted of four 315-foot towers with cable strung between them and guy wires holding them in place. And, even more than usual, that we had to build it lickety split.

Dad was fond of telling customers and contractors alike that our company was "organized for speed." What he meant by that was erecting the steel quickly once it arrived from the fabricator. But in this case, the speed he needed was in *finding* a fabricator. It would be unusual for any of his usual shops to have an immediate slot in their schedules, and indeed when he called them, they were all booked up with jobs that couldn't be stopped or delayed. Unless he found someone fast, Dad couldn't make a bid. His buddy Jim Tilley at Bristol Steel said he wished he could help him out, but he just didn't have any floor space. Dad asked him if he had any ideas. "I know a fella in Greensboro, North Carolina," he said. "W.B. Truitt, Truitt Manufacturing. Perfect guy for you—he makes structural steel towers and steel assemblies. I'll give you his number. He might have an opening, but you'll have to make it worth his while to get it done fast. He'll need some inducements."

I had often seen Dad roll up a set of drawings and shoot off someplace, but never this hastily. As Grandpa and I were heading off for Florida, Dad hopped a plane to North Carolina and was spreading the drawings out on a table in front of Bill Truitt and his two sons by late afternoon. "I normally wouldn't be rushing you like this," he told them (a lie—he was *always* rushing someone) "but we need to do this posthaste." Truitt was a thin and somewhat bowed elderly gentleman with wisps of gray hair and wire-framed spectacles perched on the edge of his nose. The office was a large room where he worked behind a big desk and his sons sat at drafting tables, with their secretary, Betty, near the door. Truitt leafed through the drawings, studying how the members were welded to each other, as Bill Junior and Wallace looked on. He walked behind his desk and sat down, and his sons returned to their drafting stools.

"We're interested in the job, Mr. Koch, and we certainly can do it," Truitt said. "We'll get back to you with a price."

Not good enough. Dad remembered Jim Tilley's advice. "Mr. Truitt," Dad said, "if we get together on this job, we'll pay you as you complete and deliver each tower. You won't have to wait until the whole job is finished. And we'll pay you within seven days after you submit your invoice. But I need a price. I'll stay in town if you need a couple of days."

"No, no," Truitt replied. "We'll be ready tomorrow morning. We have to get some material quotes and I want to talk to my shop foreman, and shock him with the schedule you're talking about. But my floor is open, so if we agree on a price I can start as soon as I get my material."

They shook hands, and Truitt escorted Dad out to a taxi that would take him to the hotel in town. Dad saw some men loading boxes onto a van from a shed beside the main fabricating plant. "What's that they're loading?" he asked.

"Ironing boards," Truitt said. "We manufacture them as a side line. You know steel jobs get hot and cold." He smiled. "The ironing board business always stays hot."

They signed a contract the next morning, and before the day was out Dad submitted the winning bid to the Atomic Energy Commission. When he got back to New York, Dad called me at Grandpa's house and told me to come home to New York as soon as Grandpa's visitors arrived. When I got home to Sands Point, he told me about the project and said: "You have a new title: Expeditor."

"What the hell is that?" I asked.

"We need these towers fast," he said. "I need someone down there to make sure they don't switch men off our job and start making ironing boards."

I drove down to Greensboro expeditiously, got a room at the Y, and headed over to the Truitt plant. It seemed to me the Truitts were well aware of the importance of the Oak Ridge towers: The ironing-board operation was shut down. They put Bobby Hayes, their brightest and most conscientious foreman, in charge of laying out and fabricating the sections for the towers. Bobby was meticulous, constantly checking the layout and accuracy of the jig and the templates. But his diligence came in a relaxed, Southern manner, as opposed to the tense New York style with which I reciprocated. I took my father's orders and trust very seriously. I wanted to be the best damn expeditor in the steel business—and for all I knew, the fate of the free world rested on my shoulders. It must have been with an elbow to the ribs that everywhere I went, people saw my license plate and called me "Tennessee."

The Truitts thought I was making a Yankee pain in the ass of myself in the shop, and suggested I get myself a date and go out to the Plantation Supper Club, the finest dinner and dance place around. "You're all uptight out there on the floor, Karl," Bill Junior said. "Quite frankly, you're bustin' our balls. You ought to relax. On us." That sounded pretty good to me, and Betty, sitting over in the corner, overheard us. "How about you, Betty?" I asked. "You want to get out of your boss's hair?" She turned in her chair and looked at me wide-eyed. "Would you like to date a Yankee?" She turned to Bill and asked if it would be all right. "Your nights are your own," he said.

For his part, Bobby, a patient and even-keeled man, endured my expediting with grace. He had been a bomber pilot in the war, and even after his twentieth raid over Germany, he just kept flying, as if it was a job assignment no different from KP duty. Bobby and I got to be chums, and he invited me out to his farm for dinner. He introduced me to black-eyed peas and collard greens, and to his livestock. He took me out to meet the cows—a couple of whoops and yaws were enough to get Old Bossy to come running up to the gate to meet the stressed-out New Yorker. As for Betty, we went out to the Plantation Supper Club quite a few times. Sometimes, we would go up to the mountains and picnic beside a gurgling mountain stream.

The Truitts managed to get me to relax and still finish the components for the four towers on time and measurement-perfect. They delivered them to Oak Ridge, where we designed special basket booms to erect them. The towers, 315 feet high, were placed at four corners, two of them connected by cross beams so they looked like two enormous staples sticking in the ground. The story I heard was that they would be used to study the effects of radiation on pilots who flew through atomic clouds. Rumor had it that planes would fly right between the towers. Only years later, when the government declassified the material, did we see photos of the TSF facility in operation and learn the real story. It turned out to be not that much different from what I'd heard.

The Department of Defense had been trying to develop a nuclear-powered airplane and needed to design compact, lightweight shielding to protect such a plane's flight crew and their instruments from reactor radiation. The towers were designed to test different kinds of potential shields. A vat shaped like a witch's cauldron, containing a radioactive cylinder, was set on the ground. From a lead-sealed underground control room, technicians released the vat's latches with remote controls. The radioactive material entombed in the vat was lifted out with cables and moved into position high above the ground and suspended between the four towers. A caboose was suspended by moveable cables inside the grid formed by the four towers. To simulate a cockpit, instruments and controls were installed in the caboose, cloaked in a changing variety of shielding materials. The technicians moved the cables up and down and side to side to test the shields at different elevations and angles and distances from the radiation source. They recorded thousands of readings of radioactivity.

The nuclear-powered planes were never built, though submarines were.

The Tower Shielding Facility produced a wealth of useful technology for both military and civil use. In one test, a Pratt and Whitney J-57 jet engine was mounted between the towers to see how its operation would be affected by being in the proximity of intensive radiation. (Contrary to the rumor we heard, no plane every flew between the towers.) In another experiment, the results of which were included in a major safety report by the Atomic Energy Commission, a twenty-three-ton nuclear containment package was dropped thirty feet to test its integrity.

In December 1953, the government, apparently unimpressed with my contribution to national defense, drafted me into the Army. I went to Greensboro to say good-bye to Betty, then hurried home to Sands Point to prepare to leave for Fort Dix, New Jersey. Dad and I gave each other a firm but matter-of-fact handshake—we weren't a family whose men did a lot of hugging—and my mother drove me to the train station in Port Washington. I kissed her good-bye and climbed up to the coach to find a seat. "Good-bye! Good-bye!" I heard her calling. I took a window seat and saw her on the platform with a pensive expression on her face. As the train pulled out, she began running down the platform, just like in the movies. "Good-bye! Good-bye!" she called out, waving. It reminded me of my first day of kindergarten.

Troops were still being sent overseas six months after the end of the Korean War, and the Cold War was just heating up. But it was a peacetime army I was called to join. After basic training at Fort Dix, six months of radio schooling in Georgia, and a hitch with the signal corps at Fort Knox, Kentucky, where tending bar in the officers' club was as about as exciting as it got, I came home to Sands Point on a warm June night in 1955. I was ready to resume my apprenticeship and then to finally start my third year of engineering school. I spent a good deal of the summer with Rudy Loffredo, our company engineer, checking anchor bolts for a series of high-rise apartment houses we were building up and down Third Avenue. In September, I returned to Manhattan College.

It felt strange being back in the classroom, living in the dorm. My sabbatical had lasted twice as long as planned, and the transition wasn't smooth. I was a twenty-three-year-old junior. Not long into the term, I was sitting in a hydraulics class when Brother Austin said, "Okay, boys, let's design a dam." And it hit me: *I'm in the wrong place.* I don't want to design a damn dam.

I had been away too long. A couple of years earlier, nothing had been more important to me than getting an engineering degree. School was a grind, but I loved that it brought me closer to my father's world, and that I would learn so much that would impress him and make him proud. Indeed, my paper on high-tensile bolts had been my shining moment. After it was published, Brother Leo, the dean of the engineering school, asked me to organize what was to be an annual dinner for the American Institute of Steel Construction, a plum assignment for a second-year man. He suggested I try to get Emil H. Praeger as the guest of honor. Praeger was a magic name in American civil engineering, best known among his brethren for his vital role in the invasion of Normandy at the end of World War II. As a captain in the Navy, he had designed rectangular floating concrete breakwaters, known as Mulberries and code named Phoenix, which were constructed in England and floated across the English Channel to form a protected harbor for the invasion. Normandy never would have been chosen for the D-Day landing had it not been for Praeger's Mulberries. I contacted Praeger, and to my delight, he accepted. I was never more proud than when I introduced him to the gathering, and he regaled us with stories about his most recent design, the Tappan Zee Bridge, which would span the widest part of the Hudson River.

But now, sitting in my hydraulics class two years later, I wanted to be out there, not in here. I didn't want to design a dam. I would like to *build* a dam, but I'd just as soon let all these smart guys surrounding me in this classroom handle the paperwork. I didn't want to be like old Bill Truitt's sons in Greensboro, sitting on a drafting stool all day long under their father's watchful eyes. And I sure as hell was not interested in struggling again with calculus.

I went home and headed straight for my parents' bedroom. My father, just home from work, was reclining on the bed reading the *Wall Street Journal*. He was in his undershorts but still had his white shirt on. His pants were neatly hung over a chair. I stood at the foot of the bed and told him I wanted to quit school. "I want to work for the company, Dad," I announced. He laid the newspaper in his lap and stared at me over the top of his glasses. He studied me for a good long moment, as if considering whether or not to employ me.

"Are you sure it's what you want?" he said finally.

In fact, I hadn't even considered anything else. I had grown up in the company. Pete the yard foreman had called me "Boss" since I was six. I had spent school vacations getting greasy and sweaty loading and unloading trucks at the yard. For twelve years, over thousands of miles, I had sat side-by-side with my father, talking about the art of the steel and soaking up his unique wisdom. My mother told me he cried when he discovered I had taken his Pontiac and driven away. And I'd turned myself around, literally and figuratively. *Of course* he was going to give me a job. He gave me his name—how could he deny me a place in the company?

But to Dad, asking if I was sure was a serious question. He had been training me hard for years, but the fact was that I still didn't know a whole hell of a lot. Compared to him when he was my age, I was practically a ne'er-do-well—Christ, he had already built the Pierre and the New Yorker and was about to put in a bid for the goddamn *Empire State Building*. I hadn't even done a takeoff yet. Working in the yard, being his sidekick, parachuting in to jobs and acting like the boss's son—none of this was the same as making a lifetime commitment to carrying on the company. "I always wanted it, Dad," I said.

"Okay, I'm glad," he said. "Wake me up in the morning, we'll go in together."

DAD THREW ME into the business headfirst. Up until my last job before leaving for the Army, expediting the work for the Tower Shielding Facility at the Truitt plant, everything had been a matter of helping out and doing what I was told, but mostly watching, listening, learning. It wasn't until my father sent me to Greensboro that I had any real responsibility. Now, two years later, he sent me into the field, either as timekeeper or assistant superintendent. If I went out with Uncle Bob, and he left toward the end of the job to get another one going, he would leave me in charge. If a job ended and another wasn't starting right away, I went to the office and helped do takeoffs with my father's right-hand man, company engineer Rudy Loffredo.

The two of them would compute the bid, using a formula that was part basic math, part instinct, and part a reflection of personality. Invariably, Dad would ask Rudy what his number was and then say, "Add fifty thousand." It wasn't an especially audacious add-on. Though he was a gambler and anything but timid, Dad could be curiously conservative when it came to bidding. Maybe it was something that had stayed with him from the early days, when he just wanted to get jobs and establish the company and didn't care about making a big profit, but Dad felt that our ability to offer lean bids was what separated us from our lumbering, big-time competitors.

I was eager to learn everything there was to know about the business, but as much as I admired how my father had built the company, I was less interested in his end, bids and Christmas bonuses and other executive matters, than in what had been *his* father's—putting up the buildings. They say some things skip a generation. I wanted to be out there, up there, building the jobs alongside the ironworkers themselves. I knew I was a boss, not a union man as Grandpa had been when he started out, but I was out to prove I was one of them at heart because that's how I felt. I wanted to be as much a part of the action on high steel over New York as Uncle Dan wanted to fly combat missions over Europe.

I started at the bottom. Rudy taught me how to check the bolts for the steel base plates that anchored every erection. We used a surveying instrument to level the plates, which numbered fifty or sixty. Then we left the general contractor with the work of adjusting the anchor bolts by bending them—it was called hickeying—within the beer cans they were set in to get them plumb. Four or five days later, I went back to the job and checked to see if they were all adjusted and it was time to bolt down the base plates and begin the erection. There was continuous arguing and threatening—"If they're not right, we're not starting," I would tell the general contractor's superintendent, who would reply that, Jesus Christ, they *are* right—and I was constantly on the phone with Rudy, telling him what was going on and asking his advice. Finally, when we agreed that all the bolts were on-line, a crane set the plates and we leveled each one with carefully placed shims. Then the ironworkers tightened the nuts, locking the plates into perfect alignment and elevation. Now we were ready to receive the first load of columns and beams.

These jobs in the city always started in a deep hole in the ground. It meant we had to roll a truck crane down a long, steep ramp to get it into position to set the steel. On Day One, a man stood on the ramp motioning right and left to guide the truck crane driver from the street onto the ramp. I was sometimes that man. In one instance, the driver was fully on the ramp when he tried to mesh the gears and couldn't get the truck into low gear. Stuck in neutral, he began riding down the ramp standing up on the brakes, panic creeping across his face as he descended. It was too much weight and too much momentum for the brakes to stop—I saw the crane coming at me. I leaped out of the way, tumbling down the slope, just as the terrified driver whizzed by me and saw the hundred-foot boom heading straight for the adjacent building. The driver finally managed to slow down the runaway crane as he bottomed out, but couldn't stop before the head of the boom poked a hole through a bathroom window in the next building. The guy was so shook up it took us ten minutes to get him to drive the crane back up the slope to pull the boom out of the broken window before a crowd gathered and a photographer from the *Daily News* showed up.

We tried again. I got back on the ramp, and the operator, sweating in December, got back in the cab. With the ironworkers watching a little more closely than usual, he rolled the crane down and reached the bottom of the ramp uneventfully. Then a truck loaded with 40,000 pounds of steel chained to its deck lumbered down the ramp creaking and groaning. When this first load reached the bottom of the hole, the raising gang—the hooker-on, the signal man, the tag-line man, and the elite of the raising-gang, the connectors—began the erection process.

THE FIRST REAL moment of potential danger of any steel construction—assuming there are no runaway cranes—came at the instant when two connectors released the chains binding the first twenty-ton load of steel. The chains slid to the ground, and the loads began to be picked off the truck by the crane in bundles, and sent upstairs. The men were beginning the process of "shaking out the load"—unbundling and sorting the steel. This marked the arrival on the job of the ironworker's nemesis—gravity.

The connectors on the ground performed the task of hooking the line from the derrick to the bundles of steel on the truck. Later on, they would be hundreds of feet in the air, connecting beams to columns, but they had to be no less careful down here on the truck, or on the lower floors. Gravity can be duplicitous that way. It can get you at any elevation. No longer bound, a beam plucked from the top of the stack could cause the others to roll over, tumble, or crash—not good news for an inattentive or merely unlucky ironworker. A beam could shift a few inches or a few feet or not at all, but an ironworker who wanted to play Russian roulette was better off at Bugsy Siegel's new casino in the Nevada desert. Men who didn't respect the steel and stand clear were apt to have their legs broken, their feet smashed, their arms pinned. It was not unusual for ironworkers to perform a controlled crash—forcing a pile of steel to collapse just to make it safe. The foreman—also known as the pusher on big jobs—shouted *Stand clear!* before permitting the signal to be given. It was carefully planned and executed, but the controlled crash was nearly as blood-chilling a sight as an unexpected one.

The connectors developed their own cautionary styles when they were shaking out a load—whatever it took to keep their bodies and feet as far removed from the bundle as possible and still hook the beam. Each man stood at one end of the bundle, and carefully wrapped the beam in heavy slings with loops called eyes. The main load line came down from the derrick with spreader hooks at the end of it, and the men slipped the hooks through the eyes of the slings. They stood back as the signal man motioned to the hoist operator, and the piece was jerked free of the bundle and swung into the air. Up on the highest deck, right below the area where the beam would be erected, the hooker-on and the tag-line man caught the piece as it came in, guiding it to a free spot on the plank floor, landed it, and unhooked it.

The point of shaking out was to get every piece of steel in position for an efficient erection. The foreman directed the operation. Holding drawings in one hand, he pointed with the other, yelling out numbers and instructions. The building plans were divided into "derrick sections," and the steel was delivered and then sorted accordingly. At the huge Oak Ridge plant, there was so much steel being delivered so continuously that there were literally acres of beams and columns spread out around the site, all exactly where they needed to be.

"I'm looking for piece one-four-six," the foreman announced amid the Manhattan traffic. One of the connecters spotted it. "Okay," the foreman said. "That's next." He yelled up and gestured to the receiving connectors. *"Put it up in the north corner. It's a fascia beam, so lay it down parallel to the street."*

When the sorting was finished, when all the steel for the first derrick section of the building was spread out and ready to be erected, the raising gang went into action, actually building the building. First, they erected two-story columns around the perimeter. Then they put up the interior columns, which looked strangely like tall steel soldiers surrounding the scurrying ironworkers. Now the horizontal framing beams were connected to those columns.

The foreman directed the hooker-on to send up beam number B-122. "Use half-inch," he said, and the man grabbed a choker, a wire rope with eyes spliced in both ends, and one half an inch in diameter to carry a beam a little heavier than the rest. Like every other man, the hooker-on had to be highly proficient at his own arcane aspect of the operation. His particular skill was in finding the precise center of gravity of a beam, no matter what its configuration. He stood back, glanced at both ends of the piece, stepped forward, and slid the choker underneath, bringing one eye through the other, pulling the wire tight—"snugging it up"—and hitting the eye tight with his spud wrench. He looped the other eye over the hook, giving a slight motion of his hand so the crane operator took some strain. The connector stepped back again, signaled the crane to start the lift, and son of a bitch if that thing didn't go up level, in perfect balance and harmony with the universe.

I once saw an ironworker rigger named Bud Simmons hook on a thirty-ton, fifty-foot section of tower and make an impossible lift. A stiff-leg derrick set way up on top of the building, three-hundred-fifty feet high, brought the tower section up from the street and had to swing it into position to land on top of the hundred-foot section of tower already erected. The lifting block of the main hoist line was within inches of reaching "two-block condition," meaning it couldn't go any farther. And that last section of tower swung within a hair's clearance and was safely bolted in place. What made it work—what made it an incredible feat—was that Simmons had placed the lifting slings at exactly the right place on the section. He added shackles, tying the various slings together, adding a few more inches to their length, then stood across the street and telephoned the operator to take a strain. He went back to the section, unhooked everything, and took one turn of the cable around the picking point, then went back across the street and sighted it again. "That's good, he said, "take it away."

When it was finally swung into position, it was like a machine part being fitted into place. Blind luck or sheer, mysterious talent, it was the kind of thing that would put Bud Simmons in the ironworker hall of fame if there was one. He had not taken a single measurement.

Simmons couldn't have done it without his tag-line man. If the hooker-on was critical to the beam's launch, the tag-line man was vital to its safe arrival. It was almost as if he were taking the trip up with the steel. He took a long manila line with a hook at its end and tied it on or attached it to a hole in a lug at the end of the beam. When the signal-man motioned to the hoist operator to begin raising the piece, the tag-line man held onto the manila line, controlling the beam. Without that line and the man holding it, the piece would be spinning around, swinging with the wind. Finally, when the beam neared its destination, the tag-line man pulled the line to maneuver the piece into the hands of the connectors, who guided the beam into position and secured it with erection bolts, temporary fasteners that would be replaced by permanent high-strength bolts once the raising gang left that area and the bolting-up gang moved in.

While the connectors were up "making their piece," the foreman and the other two men down below were getting ready to hook on to the next beam. "Piece one-fifty-nine," the foreman said. The hooker-on spotted the member, but saw that a short connective piece was laying across the top of it. "This diaphragm has to be moved first," he yelled over to the foreman. But the derrick was busy at the moment, still hooked onto the fascia beam above. "Well, goddammit," the foreman yelled back, "*move* the fuckin' thing, or do you want me to get my wife up here and *she'll* move it?" The diaphragm weighed about two hundred pounds, a relative feather. The men humped it out of the way.

THE CRANE IN the hole erected the steel up to about the fifth floor before climbing out and standing in the street on its outriggers to continue the job. When the crane had set steel as far as its boom could reach from there, it was time for the derrick. This was when the ironworkers might as well have been at sea. They truly became riggers, raising and assembling the derrick for the upper floors. The guy derrick, the most often used in those days, was composed of a mast and a boom, delivered in sections. They were raised up and bolted together to their full length while lying on the setting floor. Down on the first floor, meanwhile, a hoist was pushed on rollers and finally lashed to the building structure near the elevator shaft. The hoist had two or three drums, powered by a gasoline or a diesel engine. Cables ran from the drums, up the elevator shaft, and then to the derrick, which sat on a pair of forty-foot beams spanning the shaft. This allowed the operator of the hoist to control the derrick's boom and the main load.

The mast and boom were mounted on a ball-and-socket joint that gave the mast the ability to lean in the direction of loading. On top of the mast there was a gudgeon, a pin around which rotated a large circular plate—called a spider—with three-inch Swiss cheese holes around its perimeter. Six or eight heavy steel cables, or guys, radiated in a horizontal circle from the spider and were lashed to structural steel members already in place around the perimeter of the building. A heavy-duty turnbuckle at the lashed end of each guy was used to adjust the tension in the guys to keep the mast plumb. After all this, the derrick, weighing a bit over twenty-one tons, was ready to set steel.

From now until the building was finished, the derrick's boom reached out to the street and unloaded the steel delivered to the job by a continuous flow of flatbed trailers. The steel was picked off the trucks in bundles, raised to the top of the building, swung in, and landed on the planked floor that the derrick was operating from. (Starting with the second story, every other floor was planked over to prevent ironworkers from falling more than twenty feet.) Then the shaking-out procedure would be repeated for each load of steel. The derrick pusher constantly peered off the top of the building—whatever floor that was at the moment—looking down into the street for the latest truckload of steel pulling up. He called to the nearest connector. "Hey, kid, get your partner and go on down and unload the steel. I'm sending the main load block down now."

The guy derrick was rigged to erect steel higher and higher. Every two floors, a painstaking maneuver called jumping the derrick was put into operation. The boom was brought up against the mast, detached, then raised to its new operating position two floors above, with temporary guys used to hold it in place. Then the boom, in turn, pulled the mast up. The mast guys were then reattached to the steel beams and columns on the new floor, and the derrick was ready to go to work again. The process was repeated until the building was topped out thirty or forty or fifty floors later.

All these operations occurred in a highly orchestrated sequence whose components appeared to be independent of one another. In fact, they were all connected, which meant that communication between the ironworkers was vital—and it had to be accomplished without a word being uttered. With noise in the air and distance between them, shouting didn't work. Twenty-first century telecommunications might have helped, but this was 1955. Hand-held wired telephone systems were just starting to come into use. So the men had their own language—part sign language, part gesture, part primal sound. It could be a monosyllabic shout—*Yo!* or *Ho!*—or a whistle. There were hand signals and bells.

The key to fluency in this language was not accent but instinct. I was on a bridge once when an ironworker's whistle saved me from an unplanned amputation. I had noticed that a barge carrying material was poorly lashed to the pier. I hopped a Bridge Builder service boat and told the captain to bring me out to the barge. But as we approached, I saw that the barge had now broken free and was starting to drift downriver. I instructed the captain to bring me up to an adjoining material barge, and when he pulled alongside, I leaped onto its narrow catwalk. I ran down the catwalk toward the escaping barge, my right arm hugging the parapet to keep me balanced. What I didn't see was that a short distance away, ironworkers sorting steel on a crane barge were hooking onto a forty-foot floor beam and about to flip it over to get it into position for setting. The signal was given, the crane put a strain on the lifting cables, and the beam's flange rose up. An ironworker named Harry Lynch saw that it was about to slap with tons of force against the inside of the bulkhead—at a point where my arm would be in a second or two. Seeing the impending disaster, all he could do was send a piercing whistle through the air. Still running, paying no attention to anything but the escaping barge, I heard that whistle. Without breaking stride, I yanked my arm up in the air almost at the instant that the girder smacked the bulkhead. I didn't see it coming, and I didn't see Harry Lynch. I don't know whether it was reflex or intuition that caused my brain to connect that whistle to my arm.

Everyone instantly knew what had occurred. I stopped, turned my head back, and saw Harry gazing at me with a hard stare. I gave him a bent smile and a nod of my head, and continued running. I caught the barge. Years later, when Harry visited me on a job after he had become business agent for Local 361 in Brooklyn, I reminded him of that moment. I thanked him feverishly for saving me from becoming a one-armed steel man. As he had years before, he just smiled. Sometimes, ironworkers just don't need words to communicate.

I WORKED UNDER Uncle Bob on a few jobs until my father put me in charge of my first one, a high-rise apartment tower in Midtown Manhattan. Everything was going smoothly. The derrick had made nearly a dozen two-story jumps and we were about two thirds of the way up when Charlie Ruddy came by. Charlie was the company's best and most safety-conscious foreman. He was the first foreman my father ever hired, back in the Twenties, before I was born. Dad sent him over to the job to see how I was doing.

Charlie sat on a keg of bolts near the perimeter of the floor as I darted around, showing off my acquired talents, aware that Old Man was watching. I went from shinning up columns to helping the men get set up in their various activities: hanging floats, impacting bolts, plumbing up columns, locating the right beams from the pile on deck. I was sure Charlie would be impressed by how active I was and how much I knew. Finally, near quitting time, he motioned for me to come over to where he was sitting. "Roll a keg over here, Karl," he said. "Sit with me for a while." I pulled up next to him and he asked me how the day had gone. Great, I said. Then he waved his hand at the various work stations. "From here, you can see the whole job and everyone on it," he said. "When you were up on that column over there for half an hour this morning, you missed seeing what was going on everyplace else. When you're running a job, you're not being paid to help out. You're being paid to see trouble before it starts. You're being paid to fix it once it happens." I started getting the feeling he wasn't so impressed with my work. "Karl, your father sent me out here to keep an eye on you. You'll always be alone on these jobs. Your job is to stay out of harm's way. You've got to change what I've seen today. I can't tell your father what I saw."

I went home deflated, but realized that Charlie was right. Running a job wasn't about me getting into the action and feeling all pumped up about myself. It was about taking responsibility for the whole thing—especially for making sure there weren't any big mistakes that jeopardized the job or the men. I was joining the business at a transitional time for job safety, when there were plenty of men who had started out in the days when their only head protection was an old, gray fedora. Hard hats had since become commonplace, but were still optional. It would be years before the arrival of OSHA and its strict rules requiring men to wear construction helmets and safety harnesses, and before every job was carefully watched by a full-time safety officer and occasionally subject to visits by an OSHA inspector. In those days much more than these, safety was an individual responsibility, not a government one, and it was up to the foreman and ultimately the superintendent to finish the job with the same number of men they had started with.

One day I was standing on a sidewalk bridge, talking to Bobby Hayes, a foreman, when, *swish-whomp*, a claw hammer sailed right between us. The claw embedded itself two inches into the timber deck, exactly in the middle of the two feet of space that separated us. We looked up, and couldn't see a soul anywhere on the thirty-five stories above. We quickly evacuated. Bobby had a hard hat on. I didn't. A few days later, I was standing with another foreman, Frank Higgins. Frank's specialty was detail work; nobody could read difficult architectural and mechanical drawings better, and he was known for making the most precise measurements so that pieces fit exactly. We were going over a drawing when a two-by-three-foot piece of plywood hit Frank squarely on the head, driving him to his knees. The paper went flying as Frank grasped his hard hat, now firmly clamped down on his head. "Holy shit!" he exclaimed as he spit out a mouthful of grit. "There's sand in my mouth!"

It was a moment before we realized it was his *teeth*—they had been pulverized. I had to wonder if it wasn't dangerous to stand near a foreman, or if it was just me who was unpopular. It reminded me of the old ironworker who said he'd rather work way up top than *anyplace* underneath. But the truth was that *anyplace* was where accidents happened. A steel erection site was a minefield, one freak accident after another waiting to happen, until you couldn't call it a freak anymore.

A good ironworker searched his work area for traps: someplace where a man might fall through. It could be as simple as a slightly cracked plank. Twenty men could walk back and forth on it all day long and not even notice it. But one man carrying a bucket of bolts could break the load and fall through. A trap could be a piece of plank that wasn't properly supported on one end, or a ladder that wasn't tied off. An open area that wasn't covered safely was a death chute. Oil spilled on a beam, an overloaded sling, a strained choker—all were deadly hazards. A hand-spliced sling could catch on an unwary ironworker's gloved hand, lifting him off his feet as the load was being hoisted. Slipping through, he could lose his footing and tumble to his death. A suddenly rolled beam or a slipped jack could take the fingers off an ironworker. A crushing fall or a hand or leg caught in a turning drum on a crane could cause years of agonizing pain or leave amputation as the only option. A man might leave a bolt, a steel wedge, or some other metal object on an item to be hoisted. Unseen, it would be lifted into the air, be jarred loose, and sail toward the ground, the ending of the story a matter of fate. It was not unusual to be on a job site and hear the *woomph* of death's door slamming as something crashed to the ground nearby. All heads turned tentatively and eyes shot glances full of anxiety and dread.

These were not like your mother's fretful warnings—*you'll poke your eye out if you do that!* They weren't even hypotheticals or worse-case scenarios. They were almost routine occurrences. An inattentive oiler on one of our cranes once got his head caught between a swinging counterweight and the cab of a crane and was decapitated. Three laborers walking and holding onto a crane as it was slowly moving down the street were electrocuted when the boom hit high-tension wires. The only men who were safe were the two who were actually on the crane, the driver and the operator. The rubber tires saved them. An electric transmission man on a rail bridge job, a marvelous technician and a gracious gentleman, slipped off a beam, fell to the tracks, and fried on the third rail. Years later, a lady ironworker who fashioned herself to be equal to any man proved to be no more invincible. She fell six feet onto her head and joined the ranks of all the men killed in action on high steel. Evident on every construction job are the reinforcing rods used in concrete pours. They are left protruding well over a foot until the next pour, looking like spears in the bottom of a tiger trap dug into the jungle floor. For too many men, they are just that—traps. Many have fallen and been impaled. I know of one incident too horrible to write about even here.

For years before I went to work for my family's company, I had heard stories like these. The mishaps were extremely painful for my father, who helped the workers' families as much as he could. "For three days after each event, your Dad was just destroyed," my mother said. That many men died in this business was a given, but I didn't dwell on it. Some people are just stoic about it. For me, it was something else. Sometimes a truth is so intolerable that denial is the only possible response. It takes a personal experience to hit you over the head with reality. It wasn't until the claw hammer fell between Bobby Hayes and me, and then I saw Frank Higgins get popped on the head and lose his teeth, that I came to the earth-shattering realization that *I could get killed out here.* The least I could do was wear a hard hat. And I did from that point on. Years later, it would save my life.

The back-to-back close calls also gave meaning to Charlie Ruddy's lecture up on the twenty-sixth floor of that high-rise in midtown, and explained why he made safety both a science and a religion. The peril of the work couldn't be an afterthought. Any man could make a mistake at any time that could cost him or someone else. Even a man as cautious as Charlie. On a job years later, two men asked him to come onto a float to examine a misfit of the steel. Charlie pivoted on one hand down to the float, as if jumping over a fence. His added weight caused the whole platform and all three men to fall twelve feet. Charlie badly injured his back and legs and was never the same again. He knew better, he taught me better, yet somehow if you were in this business long enough the tricks of fate could tumble your way.

Still, I heeded Charlie's admonition only to a point. Later, after the completion of the Marine Midland Building, a unique steel core structure at 110 William Street in downtown Manhattan, the bank discovered that the walls in the fan room on the thirty-fifth floor were moving every time the massive air-conditioning unit was turned on. The walls had to be braced with steel. We unloaded the supports in the street and raised them to the roof with a Chicago boom fastened to a column. We humped the steel into the fan room, stood it up, and bolted it into place to brace and reinforce the wall. Then we had to tie the wall to the steel by poking eighteen-inch bolts through stainless steel plates, through the brick, and into three bracing columns. It was easy drilling the holes through the brick wall—we went inside out, using the holes in the columns as guides. The tricky part was putting the bolts in. It meant going *outside* the building, thirty-five stories off the ground.

Whoever went would work from a bosun's chair, a small wooden seat that would be hung from lines attached to a block and tackle and suspended from a steel member on the roof. It would allow the worker to lower himself against the outside sheer wall of the building. Like a lot of the equipment used in steel rigging, the bosun's chair is derived from merchant sailing. A "bosun" is slang for a "boatswain," the foreman in charge of the deck crew on a ship. Bosun's chairs are used to hang shipmates from masts or over the side to enable them to paint, untangle line, or check for hull damage in hard-to-reach places.

John DeSmidt, a cowboy of a foreman with a broad southern twang, got into the bosun's chair on the roof of the building on William Street and merrily climbed over the parapet wall to show the ironworkers how to bolt the first column. He left them with the job of taking measurements and going to our inventory of bolts and selecting the right lengths. John lowered himself using a set of falls—a pair of wood blocks with manila line laced through the sheaves—and even rappelled off the wall two or three times, like a rock climber, to get to the lowest hole. But when the men began passing down the bolts and plates, John found that they were getting him the wrong size bolts and that even the right ones didn't go in easily. The situation brought out John's cantankerous side, which some men thought was his only side. *Goddammit, this bolt is too short. . . . Ream that hole, I can't get this fuckin' bolt through. . . . Goddammit, knock some of that brick away.* He was trying to direct men working above him without seeing what they were doing. He knew he had to be up on top and someone else should be in the chair.

John finally got all the bolts through the holes and the men tightened the nuts from the inside. When he finished the first column, he pulled himself up to the roof and told one of the ironworkers to take his turn in the chair. The man refused. He asked the second man, and he wouldn't go either. Neither would the third. "Hell, John," I said, "I'll go." The men were only too happy to let me go, and John—a different kind of foreman from Charlie Ruddy, to be sure—said okay, why the hell not. He fastened me into the bosun's chair and helped me over the parapet wall. There I sat, three-hundred-fifty feet above the street—and froze. I was afraid to go up or down. "Let the line slip through your hands," John yelled down. He had laced the rope so that it came up between my legs, which would let me slip through as slowly or rapidly as I wanted. "Just slip an inch or two, that's all. Get the feel of it." I had a death grip on the line, and looked up and saw four sets of helmets and eyes peering down, like four Kilroys.

I took a deep breath and let a couple inches of the rope go through my hands, then a few more. I descended to the first set of holes, securing my position by putting a half hitch over the hook that swallowed the shackle. John passed down the bolts and plates and I entered the first one, elated and trembling—as if I had just withdrawn Excalibur from the stone. I finished the column and returned over the parapet. We ate our lunches sitting on kegs and I declared how easy the job was, hoping to persuade another man to go overboard. There were still no takers. After lunch, I went down in the chair again for the remaining two columns, descending like an expert rapeller in the Grand Canyon.

7

GRAVITY

O F ALL THE foremen who worked for our company, it was the youngest of them, John DeSmidt, who took me under his wing the most. At thirty-five, he was only nine years older than me, an ironworker in the middle of a career that would have only three employers but eventually bring him to thirty-nine states. John was born in Humboldt, Iowa, and moved down to Louisiana as a kid—"Ioway" and "Looziana," as he pronounced them. His father gave up the farm life to become a crane operator with the Pittsburgh–Des Moines Steel Company, and at sixteen, John joined the company himself, working sixty hours a week at thirty cents an hour, riveting water tanks. He later went to work as a foreman for the John A. Beasley Company, a steel erector, and in 1955 found himself in Cleveland, building a bridge over the Cuyahoga River that was in shouting distance of a rail bridge our company was building for the New York–Chicago–St. Louis Railroad Company.

"Well, winter came and they was gonna shut down," John told me. "Every winter, they sent me down to Muskogee, Oklahoma, and I'd make chokers. I had a family; my daughter was born in Cleveland. So that year, I told them, 'I'm not goin' down to Oklahoma with you guys. I'll be here when you get back.' Well, that last Friday, I go over to the Koch job, the Nickel Plate Bridge, and say, 'I'm lookin' for a job, I'll do any goddamn thing you got.'" Uncle Bob was running the job, and he already had a foreman, a local guy by the name of Marshall. He didn't have anything for John. But then he changed his mind and sent someone over at eleven o'clock that night to tell John to show up in the morning. "I said, 'Tomorrow's Saturday.' He says, 'Ya gotta come in tomorrow, we need you.' So I went in tomorrow and they're boomin' up a damn truss. It's cold and it's raining. I said, 'This ain't gonna work.' The damn truss was loose. I guess they decided I might know what I was talking about, because three days later I've got Marshall's job. Turns out he didn't know shit."

The Nickel Plate Bridge, originally built in 1906, was no job for a foreman who didn't know shit. A new span had to be erected and the old one removed without interrupting train traffic, and the new structure had to be built in exactly the same alignment as the original. In essence, a bridge had to be built over a bridge under a bridge. It was very complicated and took nearly two years to complete. John stayed with it even when the Beasley men came back to Cleveland in the spring, and greatly impressed Bob as an industrious, workwise man. When the job was over, Bob invited him to come to New York, promising that the Koch Company would keep him plenty busy. "I decided, shit, I've never been back east and I always wanted to go," John recalled.

John arrived in the big city on a cold winter day when we were preparing to put up the Marine Midland Building. He drove a rented car to the job site and waited. I pulled next to him, and he got out and asked if I was Karl. Yes, I said, and told him how glad I was to meet him. Bob had lauded him so enthusiastically that I could hardly wait to shake his hand. "Let me buy you breakfast," he said, beating me to the punch.

We went to the diner two corners away and sat at the counter. "Your Uncle Bob told me you'd be out here, and what I get is that this is one of your first times runnin' a job." I nodded. "Well, that's good 'cause nobody had a chance to teach you a lot of bad habits. You and I are gonna be close, and I'm gonna make a good hand atta ya, 'cause we're gonna have to depend on each other. Now, if you're gonna be workin' in the field, you've got to have a good breakfast that will keep you warm and carry you until lunch time." He told the buxom waitress, "Give me and this young buck a couple of big bowls of hot oatmeal and some buttered toast and orange juice and a big mug of black coffee for each of us, and give me the ticket." He turned to me and winked. "Now that'll hold ya."

He was a big man, six or six-one and solidly built. He wasn't the most muscular ironworker I'd met, but he was strong and agile and could climb like a mountain goat. He was demanding as a foreman, impatient with men who were stupid or just didn't hold up their end, but he gave everyone a fair shot. He was gregarious and raucous and smiled more than your average foreman. At one point when we were heading out for a job in New Jersey, my father warned us that the union business agent, Wes Hanson, wasn't called the hammer for nothing. The first day, we walked up to the five-man gang the hall had sent down. John flashed his wide, infectious grin and drawled, "Hi, boys, I'm John DeSmidt," and stuck out his hand. There were no takers.

John, totally unfazed and not missing a beat, pointed to an overhead conveyer truss damaged by fire. "We have to take that ugly brute down, boys, and I'm gonna need all the good ideas I can get, and we want to do it so none of us get hurt."

"Who's this little fella with you?" one of the men asked. This guy was so enormous—seven feet easily—that it seemed as though *he* had been erected. Naturally, his name was Tiny Salinski. At five-eight I was a fireplug next to him.

"That's the guy that's gonna pay us," John said. Tiny walked over to me, put his hands under my arms, and hoisted me in the air high over his head. "I'll bet you don't weigh a hundred pounds soaking wet," he said.

"Now, don't you drop him," John said. "'Cause then, you'll have to pick *me* up." By the end of the day, he had them eating out of his hands.

Though I was the boss's son, I didn't see the barrier between union men and management that my uncles and father did. I ate with the ironworkers and drank with them. I went hunting and fishing with them, visited their homes, and invited them to mine. I found a place to live for John and his family, close to the ocean in Long Beach, near where my family had spent summers when I was a kid.

One weekend, John invited me to go bear hunting up near his in-laws' house in Bangor, Maine. Being a city kid, I had never hunted before, but I was game. On the drive up, John gave me some instructions. "If you get lost, whatever the hell you do, don't run," he said. "There're stories about people runnin' themselves to death in the woods we're headin' for." John tells a good story, I thought. How would anyone know if a dead man had been running?

We pulled up to a barn, and his father in-law walked out to greet us. At six-four, he towered over me almost as much as Tiny Salinski. "This is Karl Koch, my friend from New York," John said. The old man sized me up. "Built kinda close to the axle, ain't he?"

"Maybe," I said with a smile, "but did you ever see a sledge hammer with a six-foot handle?" He was unimpressed, probably thinking the only way I was six feet was if I stood on a milk crate.

"We're going hunting," John said.

The old man looked at me and said, "There's bears in them woods, boy."

"I know," I said, trying to match wits. "That's why John brought me up here—to get him one."

The next morning, John took me to the edge of the pine-tree forest and gave me a 30-30 Winchester and two shells. "How come only two?" I asked, loading the rifle.

"If you miss with your first shot, you gotta get him with the second one," John said. "You'll never have time for a third shot."

"Well, maybe you ought to give me another bullet in case I run into two bears."

"Not likely," John said, sounding like John Wayne.

We began walking a long path where the underbrush was beat down and small trees had been cut away. Soon the path divided. "You take the left fork, I'll go right," John said. "When you get to a big clearing in about fifteen or twenty minutes, you'll find me waiting for you." He took a few steps and disappeared among the black trunks of the tall pines. He left me with no instructions about what to do should I encounter a bear, other than to shoot him. He didn't tell me, and I neglected to ask, *where* I should shoot the bear—in the heart or between the eyes? Or once in each? Both shots in his chest, I decided as I walked.

I checked my watch at fifteen minutes. No clearing yet. Checked it again five minutes later. There was no clearing at twenty-five minutes, and none at thirty. Shit, I thought, I must have gotten off the path. It wasn't that well defined. I went ahead for another five minutes, but still no clearing, no sign of John. I came to a tree that was snapped off about thirty feet high—the remaining trunk had a lightning scar running down to the ground. Okay, time to turn back. I started retracing my steps. A compass would be nice. I walked for a half hour and started hollering for John. I learned two things about the woods: Even in broad daylight, it was dark; you couldn't even see the sky through the pine umbrella. And sound sure didn't travel.

Suddenly, I saw a patch of blue sky over a broken pine. It looked familiar. Son of a bitch—there was the lightning-bolt scar. Shit. I started running. I ran faster and faster, and then remembered John's warning. And he was right. What an overwhelming instinct it is to run when you're lost. I stopped and rested against a tree. The woods were deadly silent. I decided to use one of my rounds, hoping John would hear it. The rifle shot echoed, and I called John's name. Silence. I started walking.

Three hours later, I finally came to a clearing, but it hardly matched John's description. There were half a dozen foot-high piles of what looked like blueberries scattered around. Bear shit. All the leaves on the lower branches of the trees in this area were stripped away. And me with one bul-let to defend myself, never mind shoot a bear. I got out of there before the bears came home and found me in their bathroom.

I kept walking and heard a stream gurgling through the trees. I stood at its edge and finally used my Boy Scout training and followed it down the hills. Eventually, I heard a god-awful swishing sound through the trees. My gun was cocked and ready. It got louder. *Swishhh. Swishhhh.* I was lost and scared and only had one round, but I was going down fighting. Suddenly I broke out into the open, and found myself beside a highway with trucks rushing by. *Swishhh. Swishhhh.* The barn was just around the bend.

I walked up the driveway. John's father-in-law came out. "Boy," he said, "there's a posse out there lookin' for you." He went into the barn and came out with a horse collar with a bell attached. "Put this on for the rest of your huntin' trip." I asked him why he wasn't out there with the "posse." "I stayed behind to stop you from goin' back in again," he said.

"Knew where I was every minute," I said, and went inside for a cold beer.

THE JOB WAS more my element, and being up there with the men, I devel-oped an appreciation for those with exquisite skills, talents so special that they became their identity. Johnny No-Slag could burn metal with an oxy-gen-acetylene torch so it looked like a hot knife running through butter, the metal as slick and smooth as you could have it—no slag. Johnny, a welder, carried special burning tips in a leather case, and selected them as carefully as a surgeon would choose his scalpel.

According to ironworker rules, management men were supposed to man-age. They weren't allowed to do union labor. But as the adventure on the bosun's chair showed, there was a certain gray area on this question. Some ironworkers were completely fearless and game for improvisation. Others were wary as cats about maneuvers they didn't teach in apprentice school. So the line between management and labor could at times be fuzzy, at least in my mind. If I had to do something a little crazy to get the job done—now *that* was good management. If I got a thrill out of it, what was wrong with a fringe benefit now and then for management?

I was working with Johnny Hayes one day on an overpass of the East River Drive. The last task to be done was to tighten a few bolts below. Johnny bent down and tried to reach them with his spud wrench. "Can't get 'em," he groaned, strained to the limit.

"No problem," I said. "I'll hold your feet and you can hang over."

Johnny looked down at the whizzing traffic. "Not me," he said. "I got six kids to feed. You're single—I'll hold *your* feet." I was delighted. Johnny held my feet and I dropped down and tightened the bolts. I've never felt more secure than that day when Johnny hung me over the Drive. At that moment, I felt a part of the brotherhood. It was only a month later when Johnny had a heart attack on the job. He died in my arms as I whispered the Act of Contrition in his ear. And then Frank Higgins and I went to Johnny's house to break the news to his wife while her six children sat around her, hushed and stunned. Frank and I left Johnny's house and went to a tavern to anesthetize our sorrow. That Christmas and for several more, I went to Johnny's house and left a box full of children's clothes on his doorstep.

ON OR OFF the job, the conversation among a group of ironworkers invariably revolved around the work. A veteran journeyman's war stories could sustain a weekend hunting trip, and even the least verbal among them was capable of articulating his sense of wonderment about this work we did. Even the men for whom the work was virtually genetic—like me, many were second- and third-generation steel men whose lives were inextricable from the culture—never took it for granted. An ironworker never went through the motions. "It's a different world up there," I heard more than once, and time after time I saw that an ironworker was a different *man* up there. It didn't matter if he was up in some loan officer's future office forty stories above the cacophony of a hundred honking taxicabs, or on a half-built bridge watching a tugboat slicing through the churning waters of the icy river below. Something changed him when he went to work. He might have been drinking and laughing and carousing last night, but today, right now, everything was serious, every step a mortal matter.

An ironworker never took his eyes off the steel from the time he punched in until the four-thirty whistle blew. This was especially true for the men with the most perilous specialty: the connectors, the elite and absolutely critical men who caught the steel in the air and put beam to column. Before any job was started, one of the first questions we asked was: Who are our connectors going to be? Against union rules, some contractors paid connectors more than other ironworkers.

A connector had a special confidence and pride in his art. He was always teamed up with another man, and through most of his career his name would be attached to his partner's when anyone spoke of him. Ianelli and Glouster. Wangh and Kenny. Jimmy Coyle and Bobby Caneron. While riveting gangs usually stuck to their own ethnic group, connectors couldn't afford to base their partnerships on something so arbitrary. A man's alertness and agility were far more important than the language his parents spoke when they came through Ellis Island. Their bond equaled the sanctity of a partnership of policemen, with the longevity and comfort of a good marriage. It was a matter of one extremely able man recognizing another, and deciding that he was someone he could trust with his life on every job from this day forward, till death—preferably of natural causes—or retirement did they part.

Each man knew exactly the moves he should make to put him in the most wise position to connect a beam, and he knew exactly where his partner would be. Their every movement was prudent and measured. They took no unnecessary steps and wasted no motion. A pair of cops had to be ready to protect each other at any moment, but steel-connecting partners literally held each other's lives in their hands every hour, every day, with every thirty-foot beam they reached for. There couldn't be a stronger bond between two men.

The connectors were at the receiving end of an intricate sequence of events initiated by the other members of their raising gang. As the hooker-on, the tag-line man, and the signal man played out their own precisely calibrated choreography, the connectors sat on a beam, wiggled their feet, and gazed out as if they had nothing to do. If they were lucky, there might be some pretty girls to watch, and if they were really lucky and high up, one of them might spot a naked woman through the window of the next building, and whistle and nod in that direction to his partner. But even that momentary diversion couldn't distract them from the ton of steel floating up toward them. As it began its ascent, they walked out onto a previously set beam, with only the plank floor twenty feet below to catch them if they fell. That was if they fell the *right* way. If they were on an exterior beam, falling the wrong way meant curtains, unless they could fly. The only things between a man's safety and his death were his own sense of balance and agility, and his good sense. Years later, all ironworkers working more than six feet off the ground would be required by law to be "tied off," which actually means tied *on* to the building. The only exception was connectors when they were connecting.

Bobby Taylor, one of four brothers who were great connectors, stood ready as a beam swung into its final approach. The signal man watched closely, guiding the last few inches of the hoist operator's delivery as he relayed Bobby's directions. *Go ahead, Charlie. Hold it. Okay. Easy. Go ahead.*

Hold it. Finally, Bobby pulled the beam to line up the holes at his end with the column he was clamping it to. It was very near where he wanted it, and at this point only he knew what the derrick would have to do. "Raise it a fraction," he called out to the signal man. The holes were nearly in line. "I just need a short-hair up." The signal man relayed the instruction and the hoist operator made the delicate adjustment. Taylor speared the hole with the tapered end of his spud wrench, and now all the holes were in line. He forced the wrench tight, then let go. He grabbed an erecting bolt from the bolt bag hanging off his belt. He pushed the bolt through the adjacent hole, wedging and clamping his body against the steel to free up both hands and reach around the column to put a nut around the erection bolt. He spun the nut home, then scampered onto the beam and hollered to his partner, his brother Rodney, "I got my end!"

Rodney didn't have to go through the same gyrations because he could support himself on the newly placed beam. He speared the holes with his spud wrench and grabbed two erection bolts, not from his bolt bag but from the surface of the beam itself, which served as a handy tabletop when it came up. He put his bolts through, tightened them, and yelled, "I got my end!" Now Bobby climbed up on the beam and walked the flange, which was only twelve inches wide, for half the length of the thirty-foot beam. As he approached the choker, the signal man waved his hand in a down motion, indicating to the hoist operator that he should give the line enough slack to allow Bobby to pull the choker off the hook. Bobby bent down, letting one eye of the choker slip through the other, and then gently swung it out and let it drop safely on the deck below. The sound of the choker whapping against the timber floor signaled the erection of one more piece of the building. Later on, when the derrick was working on another section and out of the way, the bolter-ups would come in and replace the erection bolts with rivets.

The most daring maneuver for an erector was connecting the fascia beams, those on the extreme outside of the building, to the columns. The connector climbed up the columns without ladders or ropes, spider-like. He grabbed the near flange in his gloved hands and placed his feet on the inside of the far flange. He needed to be simultaneously dexterous and powerful to support his bodyweight and keep going. He had to repeatedly grab a handhold above his head with one arm, take a new grip with one foot, throw the other arm up over his head, grasping the steel, and then move the other foot for a new grip. The good ones—and only the good ones did this job—climbed faster than a man could walk up a ladder. Once he reached the top, the con-

My mother at age eighteen, about to leave show business. She married my father *(right)* in 1930. *(Courtesy of the author)*

Christmas in Scarsdale, New York, with my father's family in the 1940s.
(Back row, left to right) Jerome, Pat, Julia, Bob. *(Front row, left to right)* Delores, Dad, Grandma, Grandpa, Gladys, Cornelia, Danny. *(Courtesy of the author)*

(Opposite, top) U.S. Department of Commerce, Washington, D.C., December 1929. *(Courtesy of the author)*

(Opposite, bottom) U.S. Supreme Court Building, Washington, D.C., May 1932. *("Commercial Photo Company" Reproduced from the records of the Architect of the Capitol)*

(Right) The "Statue of Freedom" on top of the U.S. Capitol Dome, as viewed through the newly installed beams of the North Wing Senate Chamber Building in 1949. *(Courtesy of the author)*

(Below) Library of Congress, 1936. *("Commercial Photo Company" Reproduced from the records of the Architect of the Capitol)*

Dirigible hangars built by my father and grandfather during World War II in the United States and Panama.
(Courtesy of the author)

A typical Koch crane. After World War II, surplus stationary cranes were mounted on truck chassis by our master mechanic, Tony Frandina, to serve into the 1950s as mobile cranes.
(Courtesy of the author)

My boxing career over, I posed with my two brothers: Donald *(left)* and Roger on Dad's 40-foot Wheeler Sunlounge in the summer of 1949.
(Courtesy of the author)

I am observing the impacting of bolts on the Robert Moses Bridge with ironworker connector Harry Lynch *(middle)* and foreman Dick Wiggins *(right)* in 1962. Harry saved my arm from being crushed.
(Courtesy of the author)

Andover-Methuen Bridge, 1958. I was proud of the bridges we built. I worked on this job with John DeSmidt and Bob Koch. *(Courtesy of the author)*

My father's security badge from the Manhattan Project in Oak Ridge, Tennessee, during World War II. *(Courtesy of the author)*

Oak Ridge K-33 hydrogen bomb plant, where I first learned to walk the iron. *(Department of Energy, photograph by Ed Westcott)*

Our next door neighbor and the award-winning bridge spanning the horizon were both named Robert Moses, seen at the top looking at his namesake bridge. *(Courtesy of Robert Moses Papers, Manuscripts and Archives Division, The New York Public Library, Astor Lenox and Tilden Foundations)*

My father *(below)* overlooking construction of the Robert Moses Bridge in September 1962. My wife, Vivian, and me *(right)*. *(Courtesy of the author)*

AISC convention in 1950. *(Seated, left to right)* Jerome Koch, Karl Koch Sr., Bob Koch, and Karl Koch Jr. (with unidentified guests). *(Courtesy of the author)*

Four generations of Karls. *(Left to right)* Karl Jr., Karl Sr., Karl III, and baby Karl IV during Christmas in Scarsdale in 1962. *(Courtesy of the author)*

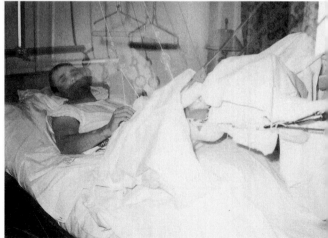

Uncle Bob's Polaroid of me, taken on Christmas morning. I would spend one year after the accident in and out of the hospital. *(Courtesy of the author)*

nector either perched on another beam—if one was there—or, if not, clamped his body into a scissors-grip position with his legs, supporting himself with one arm as he placed and bolted the new beam.

The senior connectors were methodical and quiet as they walked the steel—you almost didn't notice them. If you were on the ground watching them getting ready to receive a beam, and you were distracted even momentarily, by the time you looked back the beam would be connected and the men would be onto the next point. The younger teams were more conspicuous. It wasn't exactly showmanship—unless there were attractive women in sight—but the younger connectors were more likely to work at a strut, if such a thing was possible on high steel. When they walked out onto that long beam to disconnect the choker around the middle, their steps were quicker and more assured than the older men's. The young connectors were also quicker to ask for extra money because, after all, they were *connectors*. They knew that the real measure of how well a job was going—the only way to judge whether it had been a good day or a bad day, other than whether everyone who went up in the morning came down in the afternoon under his own power—was how many pieces were set. How many *they* set, and what hairy situations they had triumphed over in the process. Maybe it was just the way things were in general, but veteran connectors seemed to be less bigheaded about it than the younger guys.

One morning on a job in Port Chester, New York, we were about to start the day when one of the veteran connectors was missing. "Where's Shine?" I asked his partner. He said he didn't know, but was sure Shine would show up—he always did. The crane was started up, the men took up their various stations, and the lone connector went up on the beam and sat there as if his partner was on the other end. The men on the ground were busy moving the steel from the bundles that were unloaded from the trucks the previous day, getting ready to pick the next beam to be erected. Just then, Shine pulled up in his car and parked it next to his partner's car. When he stepped out, there was a roar of laughter. Shine was fully dressed in a tuxedo. He kicked off his patent leather shoes and laced up his boots. He gently laid his tuxedo jacket on the backseat of the car. He flipped off his clip-on bow tie and tossed it through the window. He walked over to the job, scurried up a ladder, walked a beam to his position, and stood there—black pants, cummerbund, white shirt—clapping his hands together and calling out: "Let's go, boys."

"See how much I love you, Karl?" Shine said at the coffee break before changing into more formal ironworker attire. Shine was outlandish.

✖   ✖

I HAD GROWN up hearing stories about the Caughnawaga Indians, but it wasn't until 1960 that I worked with any of their members. We had gotten a three-million-dollar contract from New York City's transportation department for a major repair on the Manhattan Bridge. The day I set foot on the bridge, I became the third Karl Koch to work on the span.

One day early in the job, I was standing on the deck looking down on four Caughnawagas who were removing rivets in preparation for replacing old plates with new steel. Knocking out fifty-year-old rivets was a grueling, time-consuming process. As Grandpa had said before we started, "Watch out for those rivets, they're all nickel alloy, and we had a hell of a time driving them." When it came time to knock out those rivets, we had a hell of a job driving them back out. Over the years, dynamic forces on the structure moved the steel plates infinitesimally, making it impossible for the rivet to slip out the way it had slipped in decades before. And when you came to a place where rivets joined three or four or even five layers of plates—adding up to as much as four inches in thickness—you had to drill them out, a long and costly procedure.

I stood there watching the men, keeping track of how many they were replacing. But what I was really doing was imagining Grandpa up here on this bridge, wondering whether he had banged any of these very rivets back in 1908—maybe even driving some of them with just one blow. And I looked down into the river. I tried to imagine what it must have been like to fall into these frigid waters in February, and how the hell he had survived. I wondered where on the bridge he had lost his footing, and why.

Years earlier, when bolts came raining down on me that day at Oak Ridge, I had learned that ironworkers didn't like to be watched. But I had a habit of staring when I was deep in thought. One of the Caughnawagas, Roy Diabo—a relative of John Diabo, the first Caughnawaga ironworker in New York—saw me looking down and edged closer to where I was standing. He motioned for me to bend down, as if he wanted to tell me something. I stooped to hear him, and he put the tip of an unlit burning torch near my ear and pressed the trigger lever. A burst of compressed oxygen penetrated my eardrum. "*Are you fuckin' crazy?*" I shouted. He returned to his position, laughing. "Just playing game with you," he called back, unsmiling. John DeSmidt advised me to be careful with the Indians. "They like to play," he said. "But playing with them can get you killed."

Maybe the Indians could fool around because they were so at ease up there. But every ironworker is part of a brotherhood whose history is steeped in danger and death. One day, Roy invited me onto a float, a four-by-five-foot plywood deck that served as the work platform. The float was tied off to the structural members with heavy manila hemp line, sturdy enough but precarious. I jumped lightly to the float. One of the men lost his balance for a moment, then braced himself and straightened. "Never jump on a float," he barked, poking me in the chest with his finger. "Everybody can go down."

Still, for the most part, of all the ethnic groups, the Indians were the most stoic about injury, among other things. They tended to be rather cheerless and not very talkative. One night on the bridge, I was temporarily blinded by welding flashes while I was holding two pieces of mating iron together for the welder. I caught a flash smack in the face. Both eyes were in searing pain that night, relieved only by the thin slices of cucumber I placed over them. Later, I described the accident to one of my Caughnawaga friends, Mike Montour, whom I called Chief. "You learn," he said simply. Mike taught me a few things himself. It was common for a sliver of rust, paint, dirt, or even steel to fly into an ironworker's eye. Mike showed me how to remove it with a matchstick softened by saliva. The first time I tried it, I had the ironworker press on the matchstick lightly with his teeth to get it just a little bit moist. Then I instructed the patient to pull his eyelid up while I held his cheekbone with one hand and dabbed at the speck with the matchstick. The victim thanked me and said, "You do good," and word spread that this was my particular specialty. After that, I would routinely be called by an Indian to come sit on a beam facing him. He would point to one of his eyes and say, "Take out chip." It became part of the ritual for both of us to examine the particle in the sunlight after it was out. Years later when I offered this service to a young ironworker, he said, "Are you fucking kidding me?"

I loved the Indian ironworkers' little tricks of the trade, and they got a kick out of sharing them with the boss's son. Mike was a master at removing the old rivets. He drilled into the shaft, then used a punch on a small jackhammer to thump the rivet out. His technique stretched the rivet so it could come out of the hole. "I bet they never teach you that in school," Mike said. "Show this to your daddy. Tell him I teach you the Indian way."

My father always had tremendous respect for the Caughnawagas. He was in awe of their sense of balance, of how they practically danced on the steel. Some of them seemed to float. What my father appreciated less was how they tended to float off to another job without notice. Though dozens of Caughnawagas belonged to the Manhattan and Brooklyn locals, and a Caughnawaga community was long established in the unassuming Brooklyn neighborhood of North Gowanus, most worked in the city only sporadically. The New York jobs tended not to be on such tight schedules that steel erectors had to offer a lot of overtime pay, which could keep good men. Many Caughnawaga rivet gangs preferred to chase the more lucrative rush jobs that popped up around the country, and they didn't think twice about leaving a job, piling into a car, and driving hundreds or even thousands of miles to double their pay. It wasn't unusual for a Caughnawaga gang to work in five or six cities all over the country in the course of a year. A few brought their families if they were working far from home, but most stayed on the road and returned to Brooklyn on weekends. Some didn't see their families for months.

But maybe there was more to their peripatetic ways than money. A foreman for American Bridge offered the *New Yorker* writer Joseph Mitchell the observation that the search for overtime was only an excuse, that it was restlessness that kept them on the move. "Everything will be going along fine on a job," he said in 1949. "Good conditions. Plenty of overtime. A nice city. Then the news will come over the grapevine about some big new job opening up somewhere. It might be a thousand miles away. That kind of news always causes a lot of talk, what we call water-bucket talk, but the Indians don't talk. They know what's in each other's mind. For a couple of days, they're tensed up and edgy. They've heard the call. Then, all of a sudden, they turn in their tools, and they're gone. Can't wait another minute. They'll quit at lunchtime, in the middle of the week. They won't even wait for their pay. Some other gang will collect their money and hold it until a postcard comes back telling where to send it."

The flight of a Caughnawaga rivet gang was unpredictable, other than the relative certainty that its next job would not be in the same state. Mitchell spoke to the manager of erection for Bethlehem Steel, George Lane, who recalled a time in 1936 when the company was finishing a job in New York and was starting another one only three blocks away the very next day. Lane saw one of his foreman trying to persuade a Caughnawaga gang to work on the new job. But they had heard about a job in Hartford. The foreman explained the advantages of staying: They'd make the same money, and no more overtime, in Hartford as they would here. But they'd have traveling expenses and have to leave their families and find lodging. But the men couldn't be persuaded. "A year or so later, I ran into this gang on a job in Newark," Lane said, "and I asked the heater how they made out in Hartford. He said they didn't go to Hartford. He said, 'We went to San Francisco, California. We went out and worked on the Golden Gate Bridge.'"

✹   ✹

I DIDN'T WORK outside New York for three years. Partly it was because my father wanted to keep me close at hand. But it was also because he deliberately kept our company nearly as contained. The big Pennsylvania corporations—U.S. Steel's American Bridge, Bethlehem Steel, and a third firm, Lehigh Structural Steel—were considered the major national companies because they both furnished and erected and had the resources to build jobs all over the country. We operated mostly around New York and on the East Coast, doing a few jobs in the Midwest and some farther west only occasionally. The post-war boom was still in full force, but my father chose not to chase a lot of jobs that would have changed the nature of our company. We would have had to expand our management and labor force, buy more equipment, and open more offices. In the process, we would have sacrificed the competitive edge we had in the New York and Northeast markets.

It was unusual for us not to get a job we bid against the bigger companies because we were much more efficient than they were. We had a well-trained, tightly controlled, and very loyal labor force. We had minimal overhead. And we had Dad's contentment with modest profit margins. The big companies had to have more contingency money in their bids for their labor costs because their workers were far removed from management control. They didn't have the ability, as we did, to make decisions instantly in the field, by the highest authority in the company. Union business agents and contractors liked that they could deal directly with the head of the company.

Nobody was more willing to work cheap than my father, and he took tremendous, vengeful pleasure in undercutting the big companies and having them deliver their steel to our cranes. Once when my father and I walked into the Alfred E. Smith Hotel in Baltimore to bid on a bridge job, I saw that his entrance was noted by the men from American Bridge. Later, a friend of his came up to our room and told him he had been standing with the American Bridge people before our arrival. They had been discussing whether Koch would be bidding on the job. "They took one look at you," my father's friend said, "and one of them said, 'The party's over, boys. Here comes the old bastard now.'" My father absolutely beamed when he heard the story, as if he had just been given his greatest accolade.

He was an impossible act to follow. We were together in Pittsburgh, getting a job going, when he had to leave town unexpectedly and sent me to meet a business agent at a hotel. I sidled up to the bar and announced to the bartender that my name was Karl Koch and I was there to meet the business agent for the ironworkers local. A couple of men at the bar, apparently the BA's associates, looked me over skeptically and left the room.

A few minutes later, the agent paraded into the room with his cadre about him. He brusquely bellied up to the rail, pounded his fist on the bar, and said, "Where's Karl Koch?"

I swiveled in my chair and said, "I'm Karl Koch."

"Horseshit!" he said drunkenly.

"I'm his son," I answered quickly before he decided to push me off my barstool.

His demeanor changed instantly. He encircled my head in a friendly head lock, painfully bending my ear against my head. "Son of a bitch, I'm gettin' old," he said. The grip on my head indicated that he had many good years left. "Where's your old man? I thought I was going to see him."

"Had to leave town," I said, then explained, "I'm just here to clarify the union's position on bringing in men from out of town."

"He'll do all the clarifying," the business agent said, pointing to his assistant—obviously interested only in clarifying his position on hierarchy. To him and a lot of people, Karl Koch II *was* Koch Erecting. The business agent turned and walked out of the bar with a grunt.

ONE DAY EARLY in 1955, Dad got a phone call from my sister Roberta and her boyfriend, Jack Daly. They had eloped, which usually meant only one thing in those days, and were getting married in Maryland.

Now my father had an unexpected responsibility for his second daughter. Jack was my age, a horse trainer's son just out of Iona College. He had no experience in construction. But under the circumstances—ours being a Catholic family in 1955—Dad thought it best to keep some control over the situation by giving his new son-in-law a job and sending his expectant daughter out of town. He put Jack to work under Bob on the Proctor & Gamble general office building in Cincinnati. Under the circumstances, Dad was relatively matter-of-fact. The only remark he ever made to me about it was a one-liner: "If he wanted to work for the company so badly, he should have put in an application." My uncle didn't make it easy for Jack. "Bob really busted my balls in Cincinnati," he later told me.

Jack established himself as a quick study, and moved into the business more smoothly than Dad might have thought he would. From Cincinnati, he went with Bob to Cleveland to work on the Nickel Plate Bridge. It was he who knocked on John DeSmidt's door late one Friday night after Bob decided the foreman he'd hired didn't know shit and that he might do better with Beasley's.

Jack, like me, worked under Bob on several jobs, and then was given greater responsibility for running jobs himself. As far as work in the field went, neither my father nor uncle made any distinction between Jack and me: "Just get the job done." If someone was needed—to move the men, work with the inspector, meet a truckload or boatload of steel—whichever one of us was free would do it. Jack and I became close friends, and he eventually joined my brother Donald and me to make a merry threesome.

If my father favored me over Jack, he was not obvious about it, and did it privately, with money. Not so much in salary, but in the annual Christmas bonus that was his favorite executive privilege. Bonus Time was Judgment Day in our company, a moment as weighty in Dad's mind as a hook block. He took great pleasure in using the extra check at Christmas to show his gratitude for work well done. He gave extremely careful thought to who got what, and in a rare instance of consultation, gave serious credence to Bob's opinions. At Christmas in 1955, my first year working for him full-time, my father had called me into his office and wrote a check out for the princely sum of $1,000. "Here's your first bonus," he said, pushing the check across the big oak desk. "You're doing a good job and this shows you our appreciation." I looked at the check and it startled me. I pushed it back to him. "Dad, I don't deserve it. I've only been here six months. People have been here longer who don't get a bonus like this." (I was there every Christmas when he wrote bonus checks, so I knew.) My father smiled, took the check, folded it, and put it in the top drawer of his desk. "But I really appreciate it, Dad," I said. He smiled and said, "Go on back and finish what you're doing. I'll see you later."

Six months later, I wanted to get a new car. I went to Dad and told him I could really use that bonus check now. "What bonus check?" he asked. I reminded him. He looked at me in bewilderment. "I don't remember," he said.

"Don't you remember?" I persisted, not catching on. "You folded it and put it in the top drawer."

He looked down at his desk and said, "Here?"

"Yes!" I said.

He opened the drawer and peered inside. "It's not here," he said, closing the drawer. I knew it was a lost cause and turned to walk out of the office.

"That's a thousand-dollar lesson for you," he said just as I reached the door. "If someone offers you money for a good job, then take it."

✖   ✖

A FEW YEARS earlier, around the time Grandpa retired, Dad had appointed my uncle Bob vice president of the company. But the title was inconsequential. Dad was the only one whose decisions and opinions counted, and besides, Bob, like Grandpa, was a field man, not an office man or a guy who liked to spend his time working union officials over drinks. He slid right into Grandpa's role as the chief project superintendent—and out in the field, it didn't matter what corporate title he had. He was The Boss. He traveled from job to job with terrific energy and efficiency, which explained his rousing success at Oak Ridge and perhaps his facility at being on the road constantly and still managing to start a family that would eventually number twelve children.

Bob might have learned a thing or two about being a hard-driving boss from *his* boss. From the day they joined the company after the war, Bob—and to a lesser extent, Jerome—just about tolerated their older brother. Dad ran his steel business with an iron hand, and at fifty, he was showing no signs of softening. "When I was your age, I thought a man at fifty was at the end of the road," he told me that year. "But I'm in the prime of my life." I was in the office one day when Bob came in from a job, his fingers covered in bloody mud. "We set fifty pieces today," he said with weary satisfaction. And my father looked at him and asked flatly, "What did you do in the afternoon?"

At the end of each work day, Monday through Saturday, after Rudy, Aunt Julia, Elsie the bookkeeper, and the yard crew had gone home, Dad held his brothers and me for a meeting that ran until seven or eight o'clock. He conducted business from behind his massive desk, a dark oak antique that was six feet long and three feet wide, with capacious cabinets on either side—one for liquor—a pull-out tray, and bookshelves. It was complemented by a brass spittoon I had emptied when I was nine. Separated from the rest of us by his oak garrison, Dad led the discussion of jobs in progress, others we were bidding, cranes we were buying, trucks that were broken down. He was relentless about making sure all the bases were covered on every project, every day—that his brothers were doing their jobs. *And by the way, who's car was that parked in front of the gas pump today? That guy, when we get to bonus time, we're going to remember that.* (He never did.)

My uncles sat sullen and obedient before him, like hostages, reporting on the day's events and taking orders for the next one while their wives waited and their children sat around fatherless dinner tables. The instructions were unquestionable, the questions unremitting, and my uncles' opinions invariably judged parochial or superfluous. Dad was never harsh or abusive, just stern and unequivocal. He almost always had a cigarette dangling from his lips, the ash growing longer and longer as the smoke swirled to the ceiling and my uncles and me sat entranced by the suspense. Somehow he always managed to flick it into his crystal ashtray just in time, much to everyone's disappointment. I didn't realize until much later that my uncles were smoldering as well. To this day, I can't say what they resented more: their brother's ownership of the company, or the way he exercised his power. They must have felt as feeble as the ashes on his cigarette.

A man of idiosyncratic ritual, my father signaled the end of the meeting by reaching into the cabinet under his desktop and bringing out a bottle of Haig & Haig Pinch scotch and one shot glass. He filled the glass and carefully lifted it to his lips, catching sight of the group staring at him over the top of the glass. "Would you boys like a drink?" he asked. My uncles always declined, as if accepting this afterthought would have been an acknowledgment that they didn't resent the hell out of being here.

Bob, who escaped many of the daily meetings by being on jobs out of town, took the most umbrage among the three younger brothers, but he never expressed it openly to my father. Comments out of earshot or under his breath—or the occasional cutting remark to me—were his manner of expressing hostility. Nowadays there are a couple of common phrases that describe the way my father and uncle behaved. Dad was a control freak. Bob was passive-aggressive.

Bob chose as his biggest ongoing grumble Dad's conservative business impulses. Bob groused that with Dad's bids, we were working too cheap— committing the cardinal sin of leaving money on the table. But more than that, he found it infuriating that Dad refused to go after lucrative jobs that could put us into Big Steel territory. As far as Uncle Bob was concerned, his big brother thought too small. It was as if they came from different generations (which, with thirteen years between them, they virtually did). They could have been mistaken for a father and son with "issues": the older man set in his ways and autocratic, his values and attitudes established during the decade of the Great Depression, dismissive of the younger man's abilities and ideas. And the younger man inheriting the benefits of his elder's accomplishments while impatiently disparaging him as old-fashioned and too easily satisfied. "We're putting food on the table," was Dad's standard, enough-said understatement. But the way Bob saw it, his table was just a little more crowded and a little less full. With a dozen kids, Bob and his wife, Evelyn, served dinner in shifts. They didn't have a sprawling house in Sands Point with the club memberships and the forty-foot yacht. Bob didn't own half the company.

In small ways at first, Bob extended his antipathy toward his brother to his brother's eldest son. He was not overly warm to me. Until I went to college, Bob had been just one of my many uncles, and not an especially close one. The extended family got together only a couple of times a year in Scarsdale, and it was anything but intimate. At Christmas, Grandma and Grandpa's house was filled with dozens of my aunts and uncles and cousins, the crowd getting bigger each year—the pregnant aunt in last year's photo holding her newborn baby on her lap in this year's, as Uncle Dan posed in his Santa Claus costume. The first time I ever spent any time with Uncle Bob was the summer before I started engineering school, when Dad had put me to work as a timekeeper at the construction of the Sayreville powerhouse in New Jersey. I was excited: It would be my first real experience on a job, and I was eager to get a taste of the intricacies of the work from Uncle Bob. My father ran the business, but I thought Uncle Bob had the best job. You would never find Bob going fishing in a pressed suit.

Dad directed me to go down to Sayreville, get myself a room, and report to Uncle Bob. I did everything he said in that order, but as soon as I showed up at the job, it was obvious Bob didn't want me there. He spoke to me minimally, and quickly clarified any notion that he would take me under his wing. His orders were perfunctory: "Make a plan rack. Hang the drawings in the rack. Here's a time book. Keep the time of the men on the job. Wait in the shanty." I learned by observing and talking to the foremen. At night, Bob went home and I went to the rooming house. We never ate together in a restaurant. Anybody who happened onto the job would never know we spent Christmases together.

I didn't see Bob's manner as anything remarkable or especially offensive. I just figured this was Bob, and this was what life was like in a family business, one as rough-and-tumble as steel erecting. Looking back, I realize that Bob kept his festering bitterness well enough under wraps that at the time I didn't connect the distance he put between us with his feelings toward my father. Anyway, to me his frosty attitude was secondary to the command he had for the work. By the time I went to work for the company five years later, I wanted nothing more than to emulate him. Bob was a great steel erector. I wanted *to be* a great steel erector. I could tolerate his surliness if I could learn from him what I really wanted to know and what my father couldn't teach me. So I jumped at the chance to go out on jobs with him.

In the spring of 1958, my father sent me on the road for the first time since I had officially joined the company three years earlier. The job was in northern Massachusetts. We were building a bridge across the Shawsee River, a tributary of the Merrimack near the New Hampshire border. I arrived in Andover on the first day of the job, and met Bob at the site. He took me to a rooming house and told me we were going to share a room, which I found encouraging. We retired in silence that night, and got up in the morning and went directly to the job the same way. He went off to breakfast on his own an hour or so later.

The piers were already cast and in the water when we arrived. Our trucks delivered the steel pontoons that would support the cranes in the water, and we put them in the river and bolted them together. As we built the bridge over the next few months, Bob and my relationship was as it had been in Sayreville. We roomed together but I was all but invisible to him. Virtually the only words spoken were in Bob's head. The onetime aspiring priest knelt beside his bed each night praying silently.

His manner toward me wasn't much different during the day. His orders on the job were cryptic, delivered staccato. Teaching me the trade was not on his to-do list. I was anxious to please him, though, and made myself a model subordinate, carrying out his orders quietly and efficiently. I accepted everything he threw at me, including the unspoken but plain fact that he was jealous of my father and didn't like me. I suspected he was disappointed by my performance: He expected me to fuck up.

I considered it a matter of both character and pragmatism to ignore the personal slights. I was a steel man, and a steel man did his job and didn't whine about his feelings being hurt. But mostly, I didn't want to cause trouble for my father by complaining about his brother, and I didn't want to imperil my career by battling Bob. I was hell-bent on learning from him, even if I had to do it without him knowing. "How's Uncle Bob treating you?" Dad asked me constantly. I would tell him, "Okay, fine."

Forty-four years later, I visited John DeSmidt at his retirement home, a small, working ranch on the west coast of Florida where he seemed content and mellow. At one point during our reminiscence, he remarked, unprovoked, "It was a shame how Bob used to treat you on the job." I was startled by the remark, because I truly didn't think it had showed. I must have been like the little kid who covers his eyes and thinks nobody can see him. "Oh, Jesus, Karl," John said. "If you didn't know that . . . Oh, shit, I wanted to give him hell about that, but that was when I first went to work for him. If I'd been crazier I'd've given him hell. I had great respect and love for that man, but he treated you like dirt."

I remember only one real conversation with Uncle Bob during the bridge construction in Massachusetts. One night after he said his prayers, he got up off his knees and sat on his bed. I sat on mine, facing him. I tried to start a conversation. I wanted him to say something nice about my father, about his accomplishment in building the company that kept us all gainfully employed. "He built magnificent structures in the early history of the company," I said awkwardly, and mentioned some of the jobs I knew my father was most proud of—the Pierre, the Supreme Court, the first Oak Ridge building during the war.

"Don't keep saying your father," he said. "Your grandfather built those jobs." Bob hated hearing about the early work—the Pierre, especially. Later on, in fact, whenever my father talked about the Pierre, apropos of something we were currently working on or just reminiscing, Bob would leave the room. "Your father didn't erect anything," Bob said to me.

"But he *got* the jobs," I protested.

"Your father always bid jobs too cheap," Bob countered. "We never made big money. We're still not. The company's not going anywhere." It was the first time he had ever shared an opinion with me—much less one so openly scornful of my father. I pointed out that we had all the work we could handle. Bob said we could handle a lot more. There were jobs out there that we could be bidding on, should be bidding on. This bridge we were building in the New England hinterlands—small potatoes.

"I have a goal," Bob said. "I want to make a million dollars. And I'm going to reach that goal."

8

PEARLS

ONE NIGHT IN 1958—January thirty-first, to be precise about it—
I spied a beautiful girl at a Young Republicans dance at the Riviera Club in
Port Washington. She was perched daintily on a stool at the bar, surrounded
by five or six guys who saw what I saw: a blonde beauty with sparkling blue
eyes, wearing a scoop-necked black velvet-and-taffeta dress, with a pearl
punctuating each ear and a string of them draped around her neck. She
glanced away for a moment, probably sensing suitor number seven staring
at her from a distance, and I caught a fleeting gaze. My God, I thought, she
winked at me. I turned away, wondering if it was my imagination. Only one
way to find out.

I waded through the crowd, probably a little too quickly to maintain any
airs of Cary Grant suave. I pushed my hand through her court and invited
her to dance. Anxious to make an impression in the face of so much competition, I whirled her around the ballroom, even cutting between tables
filled with people dining. My audacity seemed to delight her. But she
refused to allow me to drive her home. "I don't know you," she explained.
At nineteen, she was six years younger than me.

I went home, and my little brother Donald, a freshman at Villanova
rooming with me for the weekend, woke up as I was getting ready for bed.
He asked me if I'd had a good time. "The best," I said, splashing my face
with water. "Tonight I met the woman I'm going to marry."

I knew I was going to marry Vivian Sullivan, but the object of my
attention wasn't exactly leaping into my arms. The problem was an over-
abundance of contenders. She would only see me in the daytime, reserving
the nights for her regular boyfriends. But I made the most of my first oppor-

tunity. I drove her far into New Jersey on the pretext of visiting a job, and plotted to use the ride back to entice her into whatever adventures appeared along the way. We passed a small airport. "Would you like to fly?" I asked, and she said, "Oh, yes," and I went off to find Sky King and his little Cessna. A few minutes later, we were up in the air, over the Hudson, looping around Manhattan and buzzing the Statue of Liberty. Back on the ground, we resumed the trip home and passed a horse stable. "Do you want to go horseback riding?" "Oh, yes." And down the bridle path we went. It was getting late, and Vivian said no more detours. I was hoping all the fun would lead to a date after dark, but her evening schedule was still booked solid.

I picked her up at her home in Oyster Bay one snowy Saturday afternoon and drove to a popular hill nearby. I gave a couple of kids a dollar to borrow their sled for one ride. We took it up to the top of the hill. "You go first," Vivian said. I said, "No, no, you go first, then I'll go." She laid on the sled and I pushed it. While it was running I jumped on top of her, and she screamed all the way to the bottom of the hill. I lost ground with that move. I needed a dramatic comeback.

"Would you like to go to the opera next Saturday night?" I blurted.

"Oh, yes," she said happily. "I've never been to the opera." *Madame Butterfly* was playing at the Met, but when I took a break from work on Monday morning to get tickets, the only seats left were boxes priced to raise money for charity. The two seats cost two-hundred-fifty dollars, an exorbitant cost for pretty much anyone but the people who owned the buildings we erected. Definitely a stretch for what my father was paying me, but a smart investment nonetheless. I picked Vivian up in Oyster Bay, and handed her a nosegay of fragrant violets, à la Oscar Wilde, which I had carefully selected to match her eyes. Vivian thanked me politely, held them to her nose briefly, then tossed them carelessly into the backseat. When we arrived at the Metropolitan Opera House, the man taking tickets examined ours and informed us the date was for next week's performance. Vivian wasn't overly impressed with me at this point—I found out later she had bought an expensive blue velvet dress for the occasion—but agreed to come back with me.

A week later, she put the blue velvet dress on again, and we watched the opera from our private box. It was a magical evening. Vivian looked like a princess. Afterward, I took her to the top of Beekman Towers, and when we stood out in the cold air on the balcony overlooking the East River, we shared our first kiss. After that, Vivian's calendar seemed to open up.

Vivian was the descendent of immigrants new and old. Her father,

Everett Sullivan, was the first-generation son of Irish parents. Her mother, Vivian Royce, was a direct descendent of Thomas Wicks, who left Plymouth Colony to come to Long Island, where he was one of the founders of the town of Huntington in 1653. His grandson, Alexander Wicks, was a noted patriot who fought the British on Long Island. We had an old-fashioned courtship that lasted a month short of two years. On Christmas Eve, 1959, Vivian and I went to midnight mass at St. Dominic's Church in Oyster Bay, then went to a little restaurant for a bite to eat. It was four-thirty in the morning when I took the ring out of my pocket and proposed. We woke her parents with the news, and in the morning went to Scarsdale for the annual Koch Christmas gathering. Vivian was overwhelmed by the sheer enormity of the crowd, but also got her first taste of the chill in the air. She was deliriously happy and couldn't wait to meet everyone and show off her ring, but nobody seemed particularly interested. Least of all Grandma, who was standing by the fireplace when I introduced Vivian. "Grandma, this is Vivian, the girl I'm going to marry," I said. "We got engaged this morning." She offered a soft "Hummph" and turned her back and went to her chair. Vivian looked at me wide-eyed. "She treats all her grandchildren that way," I said, only a slight exaggeration.

We were married in May. My father asked me where we were going on our honeymoon, and I said we would take a week in Florida. "I've rented a cabin for you up in Buzzard's Bay, Cape Cod," he said. "Why don't you go up there after Florida and take the summer off?" What an amazing coincidence—Buzzard's Bay was where we had a job starting up. To Dad, romance meant massaging a bid number and doing the traditional minuet with the general contractor, followed by courting the union business agent. What better way for me to spend the first couple months of my marriage than replacing the cable on the Buzzard's Bay Bridge?

After returning from Florida, Vivian and I left New York at two in the morning and got to Cape Cod at seven. I checked my bride into a motel and told her I was going down to our job and that I'd be back soon. But when I got to the bridge, I got involved with Uncle Bob and John DeSmidt unloading the trucks and preparing for our work. I didn't get back to the motel until six in the evening. I knocked on our door, but there was no answer. I went to the desk. "Check-out time is ten o'clock," the woman told me coolly, apparently meaning three hours after we checked in. "Your wife didn't have any money so I kicked her out."

"You kicked her *out*?" I said. "Where'd she go?"

"I saw her walking down the road with her suitcases."

I found Vivian in a restaurant half a mile away, sitting at a table, her eyes swollen from crying, and profusely thanked the owner for taking care of her. I might have told her that this was just a tradition among Koch men, abandoning our brides to tend to business.

We found the cabin and spent the summer on the Cape, me working on the bridge, Vivian fighting crickets. The job was a vertical-lift railroad bridge that stayed in the up position about twenty-three-and-a-half hours a day to allow boat traffic to pass in the Cape Cod Canal below. The trains came through twice daily, and that's the only time the bridge came down to join the tracks. Our contract was to replace all the cables connecting the counterweight to the lifting girders on the main span without interrupting the rail traffic. The procedure was to remove and replace a cable at a time—two, if there was enough time—between the two scheduled trains. The early and late hours were used for releasing and attaching. John DeSmidt laughs to this day at the memory of the two of us sitting on the pier at three in the morning fishing for striped bass—on my honeymoon.

After we installed all the cables, we had to equalize the tension between each of them. A senior engineer for John A. Roebling Company, the builders of the Brooklyn Bridge, advised us on how to tension the cables. "Just hit the cable with a baseball bat," he said. "Not a steel mallet because you don't want to damage the cable. Hit the cable, then set the bat down. Hold a stopwatch in one hand and the cable with the other. You'll feel the vibrations as they run up and down the cable. Count them and time them. You want the vibrations to be the same in all the cables." All we had to do to adjust a cable that was too tight or too loose was to tighten or loosen the oversized nut that attached the cable to the lifting girder. That is, that's all a two-man crew had to do with an impact wrench that was as big as I was. *Bam Bam Bam Bam.* We hit the cables with the baseball bat, felt for the vibrations, then made the adjustments, tightening and loosening the nuts as if we were tuning a harp. (Years later, when I explained the technique to the head of a major contracting company, he thought I was either an idiot or a liar. He brought me to his mentor, a bridge expert in his eighties, and had me repeat my explanation. "Of all things," the head of the company said, looking for support from his mentor, "hitting it with a baseball bat!" The old man looked at him and said, "Goddammit, you've got to hit it with *something.*")

✖   ✖

IN THE FALL, we were back home working on a slightly bigger bridge in more familiar territory. We had won a contract to renovate the Williamsburg Bridge's center roadway. One of the first things we needed to do was sub out a piece of the work, filling potholes with new cement that would dry quickly. We were working overnight, and the cement had to be dry in time for the morning traffic. We hired a small driveway contractor from New Jersey. Every night, two men pulled up to the job in a van, leaped out, and ran their hoses and jackhammers out fifty feet. The driver was a guy named Ray Donovan. The owner of the little company, Ronnie Schiavone, rode shotgun. They started the compressor and began chopping out the spalled concrete around the various potholes, then filled them with the new cement. We had three dollars a square foot for this work in our bid, and paid them two. We had a man watching carefully to see that they weren't turning two-square-foot holes into four-square-foot holes.

At coffee break one of the first few nights, we were standing around the fire we made in an empty fifty-gallon drum filled with broken wood cartons. "When are you going home?" one of the men, Donovan, asked me. "You're not gonna stand out here every night, are you?"

"I never go home," I said, somewhat suspicious of the question. "There's always been a Koch on a Koch job, ever since the company was founded. That's why we've been so successful all these years. Why do you ask?"

"No reason," he said, shrugging his shoulders.

Before the year was out, we noticed the name Schiavone appearing on the bidding lists for city and state bridge work. They started winning work, and over the next twenty years, Schiavone Construction Company, that small New Jersey "driveway contractor," would become one of the nation's largest heavy-construction companies. Ray Donovan would become its president, and in 1981 he would be named Secretary of Labor by the new president, Ronald Reagan. (Unfortunately, Donovan's tenure was to be best known for his trial on charges that, prior to leaving for Washington, he had sanctioned a $2,000 bribe to an official of the union representing the men who blast out pavement. His accuser was a blasters' union official of dubious credibility, and Donovan was acquitted. To some, he became a symbol of over-zealous prosecution of government officials. As Donovan famously asked after his acquittal, "Where do I go to get my reputation back?")

Donovan returned to Schiavone after leaving the Cabinet, and one day in the mid-1980s, I was in the bathroom at the company's headquarters—Ronnie Schiavone had hired me as a consultant to help the company get bridge work—and I heard a quizzical voice from the urinal to my left: "Karl?" I turned and saw Ray Donovan.

"Hi, Ray," I said. Back in his office over coffee, he asked me if I remembered that night on the Williamsburg Bridge. "We were standing by the fire," he reminded me, "and I asked you if you were ever going to leave the job."

"Yes," I said, "I remember that."

"Well, that night, when Ronnie and I drove home, we talked about you, and we decided: 'If that little shit can run a job, so can we. There's no magic to it. It just takes balls and hard work.' "

THE EARLY SIXTIES were fast times for Vivian and me. She was having babies and I was erecting steel. Expecting our first child in 1961, it was a foregone conclusion that if it was a boy he would be named Karl William Koch IV. But it was a girl. Fair enough—we made her the second Vivian Koch (and the third successive Vivian on her mother's side). Karl IV made his entrance a year later. We moved into larger quarters, a house in Port Washington, not far from my parents in Sands Point.

Meanwhile, I was going hither and yon working on bridges and buildings and powerhouses, on cranes and trucks, boats and barges. From summers of dust-choked, sweating ironworkers climbing toward the sun to do their work to winters of iceberg rivers and grumpy engines and men freezing in their boots. To me, the official arrival of winter wasn't December 21 or the first snow, but when an ironworker asked, as the wind whipped us on top of some high-rise, "Hey, Junior, your daddy got any work in Florida this winter?"

We installed an electrified mobile platform beneath the Brooklyn Bridge, the first of its kind. It allowed the bridge's underbelly to be exposed for inspection for the first time since the famous span was opened in 1883. Belmont Race Track's original grandstand, built by August Belmont, was razed, and we put up a new one. We built a terminal for Braniff Airlines at Idlewild Airport, later to be named John F. Kennedy International. We went up to Pittsfield, Massachusetts, and erected a building for General Electric, the first fully welded structure in the country.

Despite some interesting and prominent projects, highway-overpass-type work was our bread-and-butter. But the profits were razor-thin on these jobs because the bids were so competitive, and Dad knew that we couldn't continue relying on them. "The foremen make as much on a job as the company does," he said, only a bit of an exaggeration. Yet, he didn't seem able to find a better way for us. As long as we had a job underway and another in the pipeline, he wasn't in a great hurry to get another one, unless he had a kicker—a creative idea unique to a project that would save time and labor—or saw room for a lot of money.

Uncle Bob, of course, was much more ambitious, and had much more of a gambling instinct than Dad. Watching his big brother playing it safe had made Bob increasingly frustrated, even more impatient to go after bigger work, make more money, stop fooling around. He had a lot of pent-up resentment about his role in the business, or lack of it, and about the direction, or lack of it, he saw the company taking. In many ways, it all came down to his own sense of self-worth. He thought that his great experience and stellar reputation in the industry—both of which were undeniable—were being wasted on viaducts and overpasses and jobs with microscopic profit margins.

The other brothers were squarely on Bob's side, though less like pressure cookers than him, and less hung up on Dad's business philosophy. More fundamentally, they were jealous of his monopoly on power and his greater wealth. Jerome was content to tend to the company books and let Bob ruminate and boil over. Dan, meanwhile, had already up and left. He quit to start his own construction company in Puerto Rico.

The resentment was like a slowly spreading virus that had been germinating for years. I remember a night as far back as World War II, when Grandma said the rosary and asked the family to pray for Grandpa and Dad. Aunt Patty objected. "I'm not praying for these millionaires anymore," she said. "They're better off than all of us." A decade later, the atmosphere was so poisonous that when Dad followed his axiom Family First and paid off some of his sisters' mortgages, Patty's husband, the crane operator Tom Bracken, was angry. At a family gathering, he came up to Dad and said, "You have no right paying off my mortgage. It's every man's dream to pay his own mortgage off, and you took that away from me." Dad didn't know how to respond. He simply lowered his eyes.

By 1962, Dad finally started to loosen his iron grip on the company. It was not voluntary. He was having some problems with his health, and for the first time, wasn't adhering to a strict twelve-hour, six-day schedule. The trouble actually went back five years—to a point only months after Dad, at fifty, told me that he wasn't over the hill but in the prime of life. We were in his office with the door closed and he held his hands out, palms down and fingers extended at eye level. "See that little finger twitch?" he asked.

"Yeah," I said. "How come?"

"Guess I'm getting old." Over the next few years, he did this self-examination more often. Sometimes when we were in a meeting or just talking in his office, I would look at his hands and see the slight tremor. Eventually, I noticed he no longer held his hands up, because he knew they would shake. When he was around other people, he would keep his hands in his pockets or below the top of his desk, in his lap. One day I saw him take a pill and asked him what it was. A sedative, he said. He had seen a doctor who gave him a prescription. "It's for these damn tremors." He would stop more frequently to drink a few beers so the tremors were less noticeable—to him, anyway.

It seemed that both Dad and Grandpa were growing old together. In 1961, we were all at the annual convention of the American Institute of Steel Construction in Florida—"the steel convention," as it was always referred to—and after dinner one night Dad asked me to escort Grandpa back to his hotel room.

We went upstairs, and Grandpa sat on his bed and motioned for me to sit on the adjacent twin bed facing him. He slowly untied his shoes and removed his socks. Then he carefully placed his shoes under the bed with the socks tucked in. He folded his hands in his lap and said, "Karlie"—he was the only person who ever called me Karlie, and I kind of liked it—"I've run my race, and I'm coming to the end of the road. I've left a lot of nice monuments behind me, and I hope when you look at them you'll think of me. Now it's your turn. Try to remember what I've taught you."

When I thought of Grandpa, I thought of his simple, uncompromising sense of integrity. In an industry, a world, filled with corner cutters, Grandpa just wouldn't do it. And after he retired, if there was one thing he wanted our company to maintain, it was its virtue. On the Andover-Methuen Bridge in Massachusetts in 1958, we had a particularly irritating inspector, and I was anxious to finish the job and get rid of him. His job was to go out on the wooden float that was tied off to the steel and inspect the bolts. When the ironworkers did the final tightening of the nuts with their torque wrenches, he was supposed to be with them and make sure the bolts were fixed to a specific tension. But the inspector was rarely ready when they were, and it seemed to me that all he was doing was delaying us. He was anything but conscientious. I noticed that if the float was removed, he wouldn't bother to test the bolts at that spot. Toward the end of the job, I told the ironworkers to torque the bolts and remove the platform as quickly as possible. We inspected the bolts ourselves, and the job went quickly. One day when we were close to packing up, I went back to New York for a day to take care of a few things. I saw my grandfather, and he asked how the job was going. "Great, Grandpa," I said. "We have a few more points to do and a lot of bolts to inspect." He asked how the inspector was. "He's a lazy son of a bitch, Grandpa. The men are always standing around waiting for him." Grandpa said that I had to stay on top of him. "I know the type," he said. "He probably doesn't want the job to end. But you make sure that he tests every point, and signs off on them. Those fellas up there paid us good money for that job, and we want to make sure that we give them a good job. That's your job, Karlie."

Grandpa had been retired for years by then, but it wouldn't stop being his company until the day he died and his stock was passed on to my uncles. His principles were enmeshed in the soul of our company.

"I've tried to teach you the right way," Grandpa said now, in the hotel room in Florida. "I hope you'll remember the lessons and take good care of your father. He has always taken such good care of us. Now it's our turn to take care of him."

I nodded. There was a long silence. The only thing I could say was: "I'm proud of you, Grandpa."

Grandpa stood up and said, "Now, I think I'll head for the bathroom." I reached out to hold his arm. "Wait a minute, I can't move yet," he said. "I gotta build up a head of steam." It was the ironworker's legacy: The arthritis from the cold steel had caught up to him. It made him feel closer to the end than he actually was. He would live another decade, long enough to see his name atop the world.

THE SIGHT OF Karl Koch I and II now toiling against enemies much more powerful than United States Steel gave our company an air of inevitable transition and—to me, anyway—unsteadiness. The beginning of my father's long, slow decline gave Uncle Bob his opening. With Dad's increasing absences, Bob began to assert his power as vice president of the company. After seventeen years in the field, he took it upon himself to come into the office and run more of the operation. At forty-four, Bob's black hair was now starting to turn white-gray. He liked to refer to this as "getting snow on the roof," and said it almost boastfully, apparently relishing the effect his maturity might have on his business stature. Dad was still in charge and nothing left the office without his approval, but Bob, for the first time, was a force in deciding what jobs we would bid and for how much—involvement he had long yearned for but which his brother had denied him.

To do this, Bob needed Rudy Loffredo. For the same seventeen years that Bob had been working out in the field, Rudy had been Dad's faithful right-hand man in the office, doing all his takeoffs and absorbing his business principles as if by osmosis. Bob knew that Rudy was an honest, unassuming, and extremely loyal assistant to my father, and that his own relationship with the company engineer was more casual—the product of hundreds of phone conversations between the office and the field but relatively little personal contact. Bob knew that he would have to bring Rudy into his way of thinking.

Dad was famous for figuring bids in his head. My youngest sister, Pamela, born nineteen years after me, in 1951, remembers seeing Dad laying in bed in his room, the television on, staring up at the ceiling. "Mom would find me in there and shoo me out," Pamela recalled. "She said he was figuring a job—no pencil or paper, just figuring a job in his head. Mom said he did that their whole married life. His mind was always a sea of numbers."

When Bob and Rudy began doing bids together, they worked the numbers so long and hard that they might have thrown in an add-on to cover the cost of the pencils. When they were finished, Dad would walk in and ask, "What's your price?" Bob would give him the number, and Dad would say, "Let's add more money to it," or "Let's put more contingencies in," or even, "Let's not bid that job." *Whatever* Dad said would aggravate Bob, but he waited until his big brother left the room before saying, "*God!*" with terrific frustration, or making an exasperated sound like *Ccchhheesh*. Before long, Bob seemed to think the less Dad knew, the better, especially about jobs that had complicated work. And now he could get away with it, up to a point. "You know, let's not worry Karl about all this goddamn piling," he said to Rudy one day. And then Rudy, uncomfortable about keeping Dad in the dark, would feel obliged to worry him about the goddamn piling. "Christ," Bob said when he found out, "why'd you have to tell him that?"

Rudy was in an awful position, and he may have been less able than some to withstand the pressures Bob exerted. The less Dad showed up at the office, the harder it was for Rudy to resist Bob, and the easier it was to withhold information. Rudy began to capitulate. I noticed that when Rudy spoke to Dad—and me—about jobs being bid, he seemed curiously circumspect. This man of detail was now vague and general in his descriptions. That left it to me to keep my father informed. I did what I could, but I was most often in the field; besides, if Bob was keeping things from Dad, he certainly wasn't going to share them with *me*.

Early in 1962, New York State announced it would build a bridge to connect Fire Island National Seashore to the mainland of Long Island, and invited bids from major contractors. Established in 1908, the western end of Fire Island was the first oceanfront state park in New York, and the only one until Robert Moses, the fabled power broker of public works in New York, created Jones Beach twenty years later. After a devastating hurricane in 1938 that virtually eliminated the beach, Moses chose a stretch of sand two and a half miles west of the Fire Island Lighthouse as a new site, and built a bath-house and other amenities. Ferries brought visitors over from the mainland. In 1954, Moses added a five-mile causeway across Great South Bay, con-necting the mainland to Captree State Park, which sat at the easternmost end of a narrow barrier island that ended twenty-five miles to the west at Jones Beach. But there was yet another body of water, the Fire Island Inlet, sepa-rating Captree from the state park on Fire Island. To get to the park, beach-goers had to take a water shuttle. But the new bridge, a lovely 600-foot, cantilevered-arch span that would be named the Robert Moses Bridge, would make it possible to drive there. The state park would be the only part of Fire Island accessible by car.

The Moses bridge was the kind of job Bob had in mind when he said we should be doing bigger, more lucrative projects. His idea was to bid the bridge not as a steel erector for a larger general contractor, but as *the* general contractor, hiring subcontractors to do the concrete, electrical, and paint work. Despite all the famous buildings we erected, in the history of the com-pany we had never had the ultimate, overall responsibility for a single one, other than the many bridge projects we did that were pure rehabilitations. For that matter, we had never erected the steel for a bridge this big, or one with material delivered by ocean barge and sunk into nothing but sand on either side of a channel fed by strong ocean currents. Getting Dad's approval for such a bold venture was no easy feat. This was a man who was too used to the way he tied his tie to change his knot. But he agreed that this was a good job to bid.

Bob and Rudy worked their tails off, took bids from steel fabricators and other subs, and spread the numbers out before them. They chose Fort Pitt Ironworks to furnish the steel, the same outfit Dad had worked with since the Washington work in the 1930s, and ended up with a bid of three million dollars and change. When they were done, Dad came into the office and flipped through the bid as someone might page through the magazine sec-tion of the *New York Times*. And all he said when he finished was: "Add fifty thousand." It was his standard response, adding to the add-on for unknown contingencies. And all Bob said—when Dad left the office—was *Ccchhheesh*.

Ccchhheesh. And slammed around the room. You would think Dad had asked him a million questions and then told him to rip it up and not even bid the job. But Bob was so used to being pissed off that he didn't know enough to be relieved—didn't know a victory when he saw one. Dad was still the president of the company, but Bob clearly dreamed of the day when he didn't have to add a goddamn fifty thousand if he didn't want to. He added it, and we were low bidder—by $130,000. Bob and Rudy's bid would have left $180,000 on the table. Dad picked up an extra $50,000 just by flipping through the pages, and Bob hated that. But the real news was that Dad was loosening the leash on Bob and Rudy. He was testing their ability because he knew the time had come when he had to think about passing the torch. And he felt they had passed the first test. It was a good job, and a good bid.

On a warm day in July of 1962, a truck with a police escort crossed the Fire Island Causeway and delivered a Manitowoc crawler crane and pontoons to the southern edge of Captree State Park. We set the pontoons in the bay and connected them to form a rigid, floating platform. The crane propelled itself across a ramp and onto the pontoons, and we were ready to go. We hired a local tugboat captain, Stan Stevens, and his boat, *The Wrestler,* to do the heavy towing, and bought and converted a military surplus boat into a towboat, commonly called a bridge builder, to pull the lighter loads. Thirty approach spans would be erected on either side of the main span, and they were easy to pick off the transport barge chugged in from the Atlantic and snaked between the two barrier islands. We drove piles into the sandy-bottomed bed of the inlet and set cages over the piles to bolt them into place. The ironworkers wore hardhats and bathing suits to duck underwater to bolt up the lowest holes. Some of them simply stripped down and jumped in in their underwear. Bob went in with them. Once all the piles were driven and the cages securely attached, we added sections of towers, and the bridge began to take shape.

That September, when the rental rates came down, Vivian and I found a beachfront house on Captree with a perfect view of the gestating bridge from the rear deck, virtually in our backyard. Cynthia had been born only weeks earlier, our third child in three years, and it was an idyllic place for our young family to spend the last weeks of summer and the early fall. Every morning when I left the house, Vivian gave me a brown bag packed the night before. Invariably, I would open the bag at lunchtime and find apples and peaches with tiny bites taken from them, peanut butter and jelly that had been munched on, cupcakes with the icing licked off. And there was always a little love note from Vivian floating around the bag.

Everyone had his lunch specialty as the men gathered on the barge or in the shanty each noon. John DeSmidt, as tough an ironworker as there was, would remove his hard hat and spread a white linen napkin across an over-turned bolt keg, and beautifully arrange his three-course meal. There would be radishes and celery, a hearty sandwich, and a sealed container of dessert. He even had a salt shaker. I half-expected him to pull a bottle of Chianti from his metal lunch box.

One lunchtime in the shanty, I took a peak into my brown bag and saw that it was half-devoured. A little embarrassed, I got up and went outside to eat in peace and read my love note. Roy Diabo followed me out with half a sandwich. "Karl," he said, "you like venison?" I lied and said I did. "You take this. This one I shot myself." He put the sandwich in my hand and stood there waiting for me to take a bite. Not a very adventurous eater, I really would have preferred my pathetic little peanut butter and jelly, but I couldn't insult my Caughnawaga friend by refusing a sandwich he had bagged himself. I took a vigorous bite and told him how it good it was. It tasted like any other meat to me, but with a powder keg of seasoning.

Sometimes I didn't bother coming down from the bridge to join the men. I kept that brown paper bag in the side pocket of my fatigue jacket, and sat up on the bridge with my feet dangling above the channel, high enough to see over the width of Fire Island and out to the infinite indigo ocean. Perched on the crisscrossing girders, I munched on my precious half-eaten apples and read my love notes. Food for the soul.

At the end of the day, after the men had gone home, it pleased me to retreat to the beach instead of the parking lot and sit alone, leaning against a sand dune, looking at the bridge taking form. There had been opposition by local people who thought it an intrusion on the natural setting, and maybe have the disastrous effect of opening the entire Fire Island National Seashore to traffic. (It didn't; there are still no roads on Fire Island proper.) But I thought she was beautiful, with her smooth, flowing lines, the steel gently crossing the inlet. One day when the blushing evening sky gave it a stunning backdrop, I looked self-consciously around the deserted beach, left then right, to make sure I was alone. "Hello, Bridge," I said. "You're mine— I'm the one building you. You're gorgeous. Wait'll you're finished." I thought the raw red oxide gave the bridge a perfect complexion. I wish we didn't have to paint over it. At moments like these, I felt washed over by a lightness and peace, a counterweight to the heavy air of hostility surround-ing my uncle.

By this point, Dad was not well. His gait was stiff and his face seemed at times almost frozen. That fixed stare of his, what we always thought was his gaze of concentration when he was calculating a bid, came more and more often, when he wasn't bidding a job. Pamela said that Dad was often so focused on a particular job that "you never knew where in the country his mind was at any given moment." Now it was even harder to tell. "I think we'd better see Doctor Mountain," I told my father.

Dr. John David Mountain had been our family doctor since a close friend of his married my father's cousin Grace. But that's a modest way to describe him. He was a man who was well on his way to becoming a legend in the Long Island medical community. He was instrumental in creating one of the New York area's leading teaching hospitals, North Shore University Hospital on Long Island, and in creating its first-rate surgical center and emergency room. He used his irresistible personality and considerable powers of persuasion to bring leading doctors to North Shore, and to get some of the most financially and socially influential citizens of Long Island's Gold Coast to join in building the hospital into a leading institution.

I once had Dr. Mountain in my car when we stopped at a service station for gas, and he spied a jalopy with an "NSH" parking sticker on its bumper up on the lift. "Who's car is that, Rudy?" he asked the owner. Rudy mentioned the owner's name, and it was a hospital employee. "Put four new tires on it and charge it to me," Dr. Mountain said. "She's got kids and she shouldn't be driving around on those bald tires. Don't tell her it's from me—just say she won 'em 'cause she was the one-thousandth car to go up on the lift or something." We got back in the car and he brushed off my questions. Dr. Mountain was a mentor to countless young doctors. Any time I was in his office, he would have a stack of letters neatly piled on his desk, all from graduates and mailed from points around the globe. "These are my men," he said, then described the work they were doing, the hospitals and departments they headed, the people they were helping. "Not half-bad, huh? This is what it's all about. This is why I'm in medicine."

When we went to see him, Dr. Mountain examined Dad and talked to him about his symptoms, then insisted he see a neurologist. He sent us to one of the best in the business, Dr. Melvin Yahr at the Neurological Institute at Columbia-Presbyterian Hospital. Dr. Mountain suspected Dad had Parkinson's disease. Dr. Yahr was the head of the Parkinson's Disease Foundation Institute.

Dr. Yahr put Dad in the hospital for a week or so of tests. When the results came back, he bluntly told us, "You're about to go through the horrors of Parkinson's." He said that the symptoms so far—the fixed stare and frozen face, the stiff walk and hand tremors—were still relatively mild. But he thought they would be alleviated somewhat by a new drug called levodopa. "I need you and your nearest relative to sign a consent form," he said. "Who in your family will be taking care of your medical regimen?"

"My son," Dad said, pointing to me.

We both signed the form, and the next day my old friend Joe Sherry and I went to pick up the prescription. I held the bottle in my hand and began to worry. Dr. Yahr said the medicine would reduce some of the more pronounced symptoms of Parkinson's, though he might experience nausea or dizziness as side effects. The question was which was worse? I decided to take the drug myself before giving it to my father. "I'll take one, too," Joe said. We each took half a pill and waited for the side effects. We had none. A few hours later, I took a full pill—still no ill effects. I gave Dad the medicine, and for the first week matched him pill for pill. Neither of us had anything worse than some occasional mild dizziness, and the medicine did, as promised, relieve his symptoms to a degree. Dad took his illness in stride. He was a little embarrassed about the hand-shaking, but didn't complain or feel sorry for himself. But I lived in dread of the disease's inexorable progress—the "horrors of Parkinson's." And I knew that nothing would ever be the same again.

THE FIRE ISLAND BRIDGE marked the real transition of power and spirit of our company. It was to be our last job under my father's active management. Dad and I spoke every night and saw each other every weekend, always discussing the progress and the problems of the job. We had brought all our company's resources and experience to bear, and he was engaged, astute, and proud of what he saw unfolding. It was the highlight of my career, the job on which I felt I was finally proving myself and on which I most felt my father's pride in me. Yet, at the same time, there was a distance between him and the job that was symbolic. White-haired and fighting Parkinson's, he sat on our deck in his suit and tie, gazing across at the bridge. He had never been a familiar face on any project we were building, too busy getting our next job and running the show from the office in the Bronx. But here he was, watching, not up close, but detached.

One of the few times he ventured onto the span itself was near its completion, when he drove up with Pamela, the baby of the family who was twelve at the time, and let her write her name in the wet concrete with her finger. When she wrote her initials, he told her, "No, no, write your whole name," and she did. One day, I snapped some pictures of Dad on the deck, with the sand dunes and the half-built bridge in the background. When I look at the pictures now, he seems proud but wistful, and not quite the iron-fisted, self-assured man we all knew. The lion in winter.

Bob sensed that this was his moment. It was because of his ambition that we were general contractors on this job, not just steel erectors, and he took an ownership of this project and asserted himself in ways he never had before. Most notably, he no longer kept his disrespect for Dad bottled up. After years of muttering under his breath, he criticized him openly now, in one instance dismissing Dad's decision to tow a giant derrick boat out to the job as a precaution, should the crane that was set on pontoons be insufficient. Bob was a master rigger—really, a master beyond the usual sense of the word—and he considered the derrick boat an insult. He didn't think it was necessary, and refused to use it.

Feeling emboldened almost by the day, Bob pushed the envelope. He used the crane beyond its safe operating radius, a risk that was compounded by the fact that we were maneuvering from a floating barge, so its operation was controlled not only by its rated load limits, but also by the list of the barge. When a crawler crane is lifting loads beyond its capacity, it goes up on its toes, and eventually starts to tip over. The solution is to land the load, move the crane closer to it, then pick the load again. We couldn't do that here because we had the crane as close to the edge of the pontoons as we could get it without causing too much list. We would have to move the barge closer to the work—a time-consuming and costly procedure. This was just the kind of situation my father had in mind when he bought the derrick boat and directed Bob to take it out to the job.

Bob had another idea, and it was brilliant but risky. Welded to the deck of the pontoons were lifting eyes that were used for dropping the pontoons into the water at the beginning of a job or lifting them out at the end. When the rear end of the crane began to lift up off the deck, Bob had the men tie the crane to the barge. Like just about everything else Bob improvised on this job, it worked. The twenty-five-ton girder was lifted and set without trouble. The derrick boat Dad ordered sat silently moored until the end of the construction, never used.

We added sections to the bridge until it finally rested on the two towers. The men worked until the snows came and the huge chunks of ice that filled the inlet made further work impossible. Before heading back to the reservation, the Caughnawagas took the barges to a safe harbor and battened down the equipment on the bridge. We came back in May of 1963. The final top-cord closing piece was set amid banners and tooting boat horns, along with some surreptitious jacking which allowed for an exact fit. Bob Moses watched proudly from a boat in the inlet. The bridge—along with the causeway connected to it and the state park that was the object of it all—would all be named for him.

After the structure truss was completed in September, Uncle Bob left me in charge of the subcontractors who would finish the job the rest of the fall. As the electrical wires were pulled and the painters touched up, four iron-workers aligned the handrails. Then, after the deck was poured, we strung timber barricades across the roadway to prevent anyone from using the unopened bridge to get to Fire Island. One day, Sid Shapiro, the state super-intendent of parks for Long Island, drove up alone in a black limousine and parked near the barricade. He got out of the car and started walking out on the bridge, and I hurried over to greet him.

"Hi, Karl," he said. "Is it safe to use the bridge to go over to the island?"

"Sure," I said, "but be aware that I'm still putting hand rails up over there." I gestured toward the Fire Island side of the bridge.

"Would it be too much trouble for you to move a section of barricade so Mr. Moses can use the bridge to get over to the island?"

"Sure," I said. "So Mr. Moses is a fisherman?"

"Oh, no, there are some houses over there that the park owns and Mr. Moses uses one of them for a summer house. Now Bob doesn't have to use the ferry from Bay Shore."

I made sure to keep the bridge clear of obstructions, and Moses started using the bridge, mostly at night or early in the morning when we were off-shift. Late one afternoon, I was alone on the main span checking the hand rail with a level when I noticed the limousine enter and slowly cross the bridge. I intended to stop my measurements momentarily and wave at the dark tinted glass as the car passed, but it stopped just shy of the truss, about a hundred feet away. Sid got out and walked up, smiling. "Karl, Mr. Moses would like a word with you," he said. "Come on, let's say hello."

Robert Moses was never elected to a single public office, but he was the most powerful man in twentieth-century New York City and State. Turning the public authorities he created and headed into nearly omnipotent political machines, he was personally responsible for completing public projects costing $27 billion, back when a billion dollars was worth something. All the city's toll bridges, every Long Island parkway, Lincoln Center and the

United Nations headquarters, Jones Beach, Shea Stadium, and both the 1939–40 and 1964–65 World's Fairs—Moses built them all and scores more projects. It's no exaggeration to call him the greatest builder the world has ever seen. Nor is it an overstatement to call him one of the most arrogant public figures of the twentieth century. Even his critics would agree that he was a genius of politics and public works, and his champions would concede that he didn't accomplish all he did by being respectful of much of anything but himself and his unchecked power.

As Shapiro and I approached the limo's rear door, the window's whining motor slid the glass down, revealing Moses' familiar piercing eyes and wide smile. "I want to congratulate you on the fine job you've done on this bridge," Moses said.

"Thank you, sir," I said.

"You're ahead of schedule and I want you to know we appreciate it." He settled back in his seat muttering something about wishing he had us working on the World's Fair, which was scheduled to open the following spring but was, as Moses' legion of critics noted in the press almost daily, mired in debt and disorganization. Full of pride, and I suppose at that moment full of myself, I boldly announced: "The Fair's all fucked up, Mr. Moses." I then informed him: "You've got to unscramble it."

An angry frown wrinkled Moses' famous brow. "Open the door and get in here," he commanded. As I reached for the handle, Sid Shapiro, his eyes bugged out, stepped back as if he had been punched in the nose. I pulled the door open and Moses pointed to the jump seat. "Pull that seat down and get in here and close the door."

All I knew about the World's Fair being "fucked up," as I put it so eloquently, was what I had read in the newspapers and what Uncle Bob had told me. Always an expert on any subject, Bob one day at lunch in Rudy's office had hammered away at what a mess the construction of the fair was. Moses' strength had always been his organization, but this World's Fair was a muddle from the start, and it ended his decades-long honeymoon with the press. As Robert A. Caro explained in *The Power Broker,* his classic, Pulitzer prize–winning 1974 biography, Moses exercised his usual control, insisting on having everything his way, even though he knew little about World's Fairs and, in fact, had little interest in them. The fair would be a hodgepodge of temporary structures, and if there was something the monument maker cared nothing about, it was temporary structures. What he cared about was the park that would be left behind in Flushing Meadows.

From a construction man's point of view, the biggest problem with the

World's Fair was that there was no equivalent to a general contractor. Each country came with its own architectural renderings for its pavilion, for which it had to hire an American firm to make sure it complied with local building codes and structural design standards. Each country then had to hire a general contractor who in turn had to hire subs, who in turn directed material, equipment, and union labor to the site. Instead of one construction project with labor and material and schedule problems to deal with, there were two hundred—each one owned by a different foreign country with no experience with the ways of American construction. And all of this on the tightest of schedules. It would have made a hell of a lot more sense, Uncle Bob said, to have one company, an American firm, running the whole show.

While Bob was holding forth, Dad left the room. World's Fairs were a sore subject for him. Back in 1939, he had had a contract with the Soviet Union to erect a seventy-five-foot statue, of a worker holding a red star, at the Soviet pavilion at the first New York World's Fair at Flushing Meadows. After the statue went up, public indignation about the communistic symbolism forced Moses' World's Fair corporation to tell the Russians to take the statue down. After erecting *and* removing the statue, Dad was refused payment by the Russians and by the World's Fair Authority. He hated the Russians and World's Fairs ever since.

"Now tell me why you think the fair is all fucked up," Moses asked inside his limousine. I repeated Bob's discourse the best I could, explaining to the most powerful man in New York State where he had gone wrong. "And how do I unscramble it?" he asked, seemingly interested in what I had to say about it. I explained with great fervor how the construction should be centralized, even throwing in some wild hand gestures to make a closing point. Moses never said a word, keeping his hands folded on his lap and just staring at me as I made my case. Just as I had uttered my last sentence, and while my hand was still in the air, he said, "Okay, get out." Snapped back to reality, I fumbled for the door handle and pushed it open and stepped outside in one disordered motion. Sid Shapiro closed the door, then got back behind the wheel and drove over the bridge. I watched them cross, thinking maybe I should have ended the encounter by saying "Thank you, Mr. Moses," back when he complimented our work on his bridge.

Three days later, Harold Ekoff, the project manager for the bridge designer Majesky and Masters, came rushing up to the bridge from his field office. "Karl," he said, "come on back to the office, your father wants you to call him." My father never called me on the job. I followed Ekoff back to his office and called my father in the Bronx.

"Hi, Dad," I said. "What's up?"

"Listen," he said, "stop politicking and finish that bridge. You just got Bob Moses all riled up that you're going to solve all his problems at the World's Fair." I swallowed slowly and waited for the rest. "Now he wants us to meet General Potter at the fairgrounds next Tuesday."

"Who's General Potter?" I asked.

"He's running the whole show for Moses."

"He wants us there at nine A.M. So don't go to the bridge on Tuesday. Put on a suit and meet us at the office at seven. We'll drive to Queens from there. Bob and Rudy are coming, too."

Tuesday morning, we drove down Moses' Bruckner Expressway, across his Triborough Bridge and onto his Grand Central Parkway, passed his half-completed Shea Stadium, and walked into the administration office of his World's Fair. A secretary escorted us into a room with a conference table that had to be thirty feet long. Bob, Rudy, and I sat down near the middle, but Dad hesitated, hat in hand.

"Can I help you, Mr. Koch?" the secretary asked.

"Oh, I'm just looking for a place to hang my hat."

"Here, let me take it. We have a coat tree in the next room."

Dad surrendered his hat and sat down. We sat in silence for ten minutes. Dad didn't like to be kept waiting, especially at the World's Fair. He was just about to get up and leave, when William Potter walked in and stood at the head of the table. He was a big man about my father's age. He wore a dark suit and walked with military bearing, tall and straight.

"Gentlemen," he said, "I would like to make a statement before I begin." He paused, looking straight at me. "I'm here because Bob Moses ordered me to be here. I want you to know I never married contractors on a job and I'm not going to start now. Now what do you have to say?"

Dad smiled. "I have two things to say. The first is to remind you that the last time we met, General Potter, you were *Major* Potter. That was in Panama when I put up that one-thousand-foot dirigible hanger. You were the battalion commander, as I recall."

"I certainly do remember you, Karl," Potter said. "You put on a little weight since then."

"You're getting there yourself, General."

"Your company is quite well known, Karl. You are to be congratulated." He paused. "What was the second thing you wanted to say?"

"Where is my hat?" Dad said. "I came in with a hat. I want to leave with a hat."

The secretary who was taking notes jumped up and went into the next room for Dad's hat. Dad fixed his fedora on his head, smiled at the General, and said, "So long, Major." We all followed him out.

Bob and Rudy were silent at the meeting and on the trip back to the office. Bob never took credit—or the blame—for the views I had so brazenly thrown at Moses. But he was right. The World's Fair was a bust. It left a trail of debt, and it destroyed Moses' reputation. As for me, my father had some simple instructions when we got outside after the one-minute meeting with Potter. "Your job is to put that damn bridge up," he said. "Don't go politicking. Get your suit off and get out there in your work clothes." He pretended to be stern, but I could tell he was proud that I'd had the guts to tell Bob Moses what I thought.

We went back to work on his bridge to Fire Island. The subcontractors finished their work in December, and the finishing touches by other contractors were done in the spring of 1964. The first cars crossed the bridge on June 13, 1964, just two months after the World's Fair opened. The bridge was a bigger success. It turned Robert Moses State Park into one of the most popular ocean beaches on the East Coast, and did it in style. The bridge, the first one ever built entirely by the Koch company, won the 1965 Prize Bridge Award from the American Institute of Steel Construction, an annual award given to the project judged to have employed the most "imaginative and aesthetic use of fabricated structural steel in bridges."

The bridge accomplished one more thing: It turned Bob Koch into the new power broker of the Karl Koch Erecting Company.

9

LEGS

THE 1964 STEEL convention was in Boca Raton, and we were all there—Dad, Grandpa, Bob and Jerome, and me, along with our wives. It was an opportunity for the men in the steel industry to meet and talk about jobs and equipment and tell war stories, and for the women to wear formal clothes.

A new addition was my younger brother Donald, who had graduated from Villanova in 1960 and replaced me as my father's driver, receiver of wisdom, and confidant. Just as I took after Grandpa in my preference for working in the field, Donald seemed to inherit our father's business and financial talents. Dad had sent him to military school as a teenager out of fear that he might roll his car into the street in the middle of the night and run off like me, but Donald didn't have that in him. A year after graduating college, a year of work under his belt, Donald married Mary Ann Barretta, who, by strange coincidence, was the daughter of the chauffeur who had driven Vivian and me to our wedding. For the first year of their marriage, Donald and Mary Ann lived on the second floor of Vivian and my two-family house in Flushing. Living and working together, Donald and I, seven years apart in age, grew closer than we had ever been. We played golf at Sands Point Golf Club, went skeet-shooting, sailed, and hunted together. Eventually, we became advisers to our youngest brother, Roger, and expected that one day he would join us at our banquet table at the annual steel convention.

My father told me that he never came home from a convention without a job. In Boca Raton, I decided that it was time for me to make some effort to excel in my father's area and try my hand at selling the Koch Company and its "speed-ability." Uncle Bob wasn't the only one thinking about filling the void that would be created by my father's inevitable retirement. I didn't know how I was going to do it—romancing other contractors and doing the company's bidding didn't come naturally for me—but somehow I was going to bring home a job.

I met Jack Busch, whose family business, the Haven-Busch Company, was a fabricator in Michigan. When I said I was from New York he asked if we would be interested in a job they were fabricating for Korvette's, a major discount department store chain in the metropolitan area. Putting my best sales foot forward, I said we'd be very interested and exchanged business cards with him. I came home pretty sure my first sales pitch had been a winner, and I was right. Bob and Rudy put the proposal together and by the fall we were building a department store in the Westchester County community of Port Chester, just south of the Connecticut border.

One afternoon as the job was winding down in early December, I went to the office to pick up the cash payroll and get it to the job site in time to hand out at quitting time. It was the end of a cool day and the sky was the color of lead. Headlights were already passing by on Boston Post Road. The men were working on the last section of the store, the patio shop, which would be filled with redwood picnic tables, barbecue grills, and chaise longues come spring.

The men were connecting beams about fifteen feet off the ground when I pulled up. But as I looked in from the road, something didn't look right. A young ironworker was sitting sidesaddle on a beam that was to be double-connected, meaning that it and another beam would be joined to the same column with shared bolts. One beam was up and the crane had positioned the second one. The connector was pushing against the cinderblock wall that was already in place, trying to open the tight space between the column and the wall so he could put a nut on the bolt on the double connection. But behind the connector was real trouble: The roof trusses were already landed across the beams, even though the beam connections hadn't been made. *Christ,* I thought, still sitting behind the wheel, *what the hell are they doing? That's too much weight on those beams.* They were trying to fix a misalignment to make the connection, but they had the trusses bearing down on the flimsiest of links. The foreman, a veteran named Earle, was studying the blueprints and didn't see what was going on. I reached for my hard hat, got out of the car, and started walking double-time toward the work.

I knew that one of two things had to happen to prevent a disaster. Either the crane had to simultaneously boom up and slack down on the load line to keep the beam level and the load line plumb—a very difficult maneuver in this situation for an obviously inept crew. Or they had to block the column against the cinderblock wall so that the connector could get his hand in there and put the nut on. As I passed the foreman, I called out, "You've got a dangerous situation here! Come on over where the work is." He lowered the blueprints and didn't respond. I called up to the connector, "Hold everything, don't move! That beam can come down!"

"I know what the fuck I'm doing," the connector snarled.

"There's no nut on that bolt!" I shot back. "That son of a bitch can come down!" I turned to the hooker-on, who seemed to know what was going on. "Let's block that column," I told him, and he moved quickly to pick up a five-foot length of two-by-four. We both walked over to the column as the connector turned away.

"Chii—rist, I know what I'm doin'," I heard him say—and then the sudden roar of disengaging, crashing steel and a massive thud that reverberated across the construction site, a collision of sounds that I can still hear in my head thirty-eight years later. It was the moment of terror that every construction man keeps buried in his subconscious—the accident, the maiming, the fatal slip of fate that is a daily threat but which always happens to someone else.

I couldn't have been unconscious for more than a minute or two. When I opened my eyes, the horrific, thumping jangle that was the last sound I had registered had been replaced by an eerie silence, except for the coughing of the crane's diesel. I was down. I could feel my left cheek pressed into the cold earth and both arms spread-eagled in front of me. The men who had been up on the beam were now down here with me. The kid who *knew what the fuck he was doing* was splayed out, unconscious. My hard hat was four feet away, flattened, the back of it sheared off. *How bad am I hit?* I thought, like a soldier at the front the second he realizes he's taken flak from somewhere.

I clenched my fists. I could feel my forearms and biceps tighten. *So far so good.* I flexed my arms and felt movement in the shoulders. *Good.* I slowly raised my head and shifted my neck and torso—all okay, all still moving. *Hot shit, I'm okay.* I lengthened my back muscles clear down to my hips like a stretching dog. I was conscious of the frosted earth bracing the warmth of my groin. *I still have my balls. My hips and my back are okay. I'm thinking clearly. Thank God my head isn't split open .*

Now, the legs. I tested them, trying to move my toes, my ankles, my knees—nothing worked. *Okay, don't panic.* I thought my legs were just broken, and I'd done that before, once when I tripped while trying to snatch the Sunday funnies from my sister Marie when I was five, and then when I'd fractured a femur while playing football as a teenager. So another broken leg or two—I could handle that. I'd get to take my first vacation since I started working.

I slipped in and out of consciousness as it got darker and colder, and five bodies strained to lift the steel off me. "Get that damn twelve-by-twelve under here!" yelled the old foreman, then turned to me. "How ya doin', kid?"

"Okay, but get that stuff off my legs."

"It's off, it's off. We're waiting for the ambulance."

I fought unconsciousness. *I can't keep blacking out.* I looked up and saw one of the laborers, a black man named George who was a jack-of-all-trades for the general contractor. "Hold my hand, George. That's it. Tighter! Tighter, George!" George and I were locked that way until the ambulance and police came rushing into the project.

"The ambulance is here, Karl," Earle said. "We're taking you first."

I saw the paramedics with a canvas stretcher, the same kind that had painfully rolled my broken bones together when I was taken from the football field years before. "Take the other men first," I said.

"Nothing doin', Karl, you're hurt worse than they are. You go first."

"Not a chance. The others have head injuries. I'm still running this job. They go first." I turned to George. "I need you to do exactly what I tell you, George. Will you?"

"Okay, kid, whatever I can," he said, staring at the sight of my crazily skewed limbs, bones and flesh mashed in blood-sodden khaki slacks. I told him to get a full sheet of three-quarter-inch plywood and place me upon it. The ironworkers didn't want to move me, but I told them I had to go to the hospital on a board, not a canvas hammock. I knew it would prevent a lot of muscles and veins from being torn. These men of steel gently lifted me as two others slipped the plywood under my body. All of them lifted the plywood together. The ambulance attendants, not to be undone, slipped their canvas stretcher underneath the plywood, muttering something about regulations. They put me in the back of the ambulance for what had to be the world's shortest emergency trip: The hospital was right across the street.

The cash bag with the week's payroll never got delivered. It stayed where I had left it, on the front seat of my car.

✳   ✳

A NURSE IN the emergency room at United Hospital gave me a shot of morphine, the first of hundreds, as it would turn out. It kept me drifting in and out of consciousness. I asked for a phone but didn't get it. *Where the fuck is that phone? I need to call Vivian.* I called the nurse and told her I needed a damn phone, where is the damn phone? My wife is seven-and-a-half months pregnant. I've got to talk to her before anyone else does. Christ knows what they'll tell her. The nurse brought the phone. "Hi, honey," I said as brightly as I could manage through the stupor. "I'm in the emergency room in Port Chester. A steamroller ran over my foot, and they think I might have a couple of broken toes. They'll probably keep me overnight. I'll call you later."

A doctor came over and looked me over. "You did yourself a very big favor," he said. "Instructing your people to put that plywood under you was very smart. Your legs would have been mangled worse if they had moved you in a stretcher. You have some severe fractures, and we have to pull these bones back into shape before we take you into the operating room."

"That's okay, Doc," I said. "Just give me a shot before you start."

"We already have. We've given you all the shots you can take. We can't give you any more."

"Oh boy, I guess I'm in trouble. Okay." I raised my eyes toward the nurse and asked her to hold my hand. She reached down and clasped my hand in both of hers.

The doctor moved to the foot of the stretcher. The only thing I could hear was a terrible screaming coming from the next berth, the scream of a man trying to use every gasp of air in his lungs to blow away the pain. Poor bastard, I thought, he's really going through hell. And then I was out of air and the screaming stopped. *My God,* I realized, *that was me screaming.* And then I passed out.

When I came to, I had huge casts on my legs and my brother Donald was standing at my bedside. "God, you got clobbered," he said.

"What happened?" I asked. The last thing I remembered was the kid saying he knew what he was doing. My back was turned when he struck the blow that sent the steel and everyone on it hurtling toward me. I was looking at the hooker-on who was going to block out the beam when all hell broke loose.

"The stupid son of a bitch hit the drift pin," Donald said. "There was so much load on it that it squirted out the hole. There were five tons of joist on the beams in that bay and just the pin to hold it. No nut on it, just the bolt." Donald told me that the first joist hit me on the back of my hard hat, destroying it and knocking me flat. Some more joists piled up on my legs, along with the rest of the pile that had been carelessly and precariously placed on top of the unbolted beams. But Donald said it could have been even worse—and there was only one result that could have been worse. An air-conditioning unit nearby shielded me from getting the full brunt of the falling steel, he said. I wasn't hit by either of the beams that fell.

"It's just my legs, though," I said, looking for assurance.

"Yeah, just your legs."

"But I can't feel a thing. I can't move my toes. You're sure it's just my legs?"

"It's just your legs. That's what they said."

VIVIAN HAD JUST returned from a walk with the kids and was getting the house ready for Christmas when I called her. A few minutes later, Donald and three men she didn't know were at the door. They came inside, and Donald asked Vivian to sit down. He told her the accident was more serious than a couple of broken toes, though he couldn't bring himself to tell her *how* serious. "Something didn't look right to Karl, and he ran in to warn the men up on the steel," Donald said. "It came down on him." Since she had known me, Vivian had always had a small fear that I might fall off a bridge or a building. She never imagined that the *steel* would fall on *me*. Years later, unbeknownst to me, she put her memories of the accident on paper and sent them to my writing collaborator. She wrote some things I never knew. "Every day, I would walk my three children," she recalled. "Vivi was three, Karlie two, and Cynthia, my baby, was eighteen months. We were a busy convoy. Two in the carriage and one holding on to the side. I was almost eight months pregnant with our fourth child, John. Dressing my babies was at least a ten-minute operation. Gloves, scarves, hats. But it was worth it to go outside and see their little rosy cheeks in the crisp air and then come home to settle in for the evening. But for some reason, that day I was restless. Not my usual happy self. I've never been able to explain that feeling, and never since have I had the sense of apprehension I felt that day. Years later, I knew it was some kind of intuition."

Vivian called her mother and father, who rushed over to stay with the children, and Donald and the other men took her to the hospital. Vivian was in a fog. "I was twenty-six, a girl. The hospital was a place to have babies or tonsils out," she wrote. "If there is a time when you know that youth is over, this was it for us. The hospital was a dirty, dingy, ugly place. I remember being ushered into a large waiting room. People were crying. They were ironworkers' wives and mothers. Two other men had been hurt, fractures to the shoulder and hip. All I had been told was that Karl had broken his legs."

No one wanted to tell a woman nearly eight months pregnant that her husband's legs were not merely broken but shattered, in all likelihood beyond repair. Vivian got the first inkling of the magnitude of the accident when someone handed her a bag. Inside was a torn shirt, one leg of a pair of ripped, blood-stained trousers, and one boot. And then she was guided into an office to sign a consent form. She read the words:

Both legs crushed, compound fracture, no circulation, shock.

"Oh, God!" she screamed. "God help Karl." She was trembling, dizzy. *"What does this mean? Oh, God."*

A doctor appeared and casually told her, "We're going to have to amputate both his legs."

Vivian's knees buckled. Donald caught her. She managed to draw herself up, and demanded to see the chief surgeon.

"I am the chief," the doctor said. He told her that I had no femoral pulse, which meant I had no circulation in either leg, which meant gangrene would set in.

I had once seen a man in the hospital with gangrene that got worse and worse until he begged the doctors to take his leg off, which they did. But I wasn't there yet, and if there was ever a time to get a second opinion, this was it, laying here in some crummy local hospital where the chief surgeon could tell a pregnant woman that he was going to cut the legs off her thirty-two-year-old husband, and tell her this as casually as if he was ordering lunch.

"Don't let them take my legs," I told Vivian—an instinctive thing to say because the doctor hadn't told me what he had told her.

I turned to Donald. "Look, I think I've got a problem," I said. "I think you'd better call Dr. Mountain. He's the only straight guy I know, and if these guys are screwing around with me he'll protect me."

"I'll call him now," Donald said, and started out of the room.

"Ask him to come up here, Donald!"

An hour later, Dr. John Mountain was at my bedside, his lips forming a stiff half-smile. "How're you doing, young fella?" he asked.

"Gee, fine, Doc. God, it was nice of you to come up here. You didn't have to do that, but I'm sure glad you did." He was accompanied by Jack Gallagher, a friend of mine since we were teenagers, who was now working as an administrator at North Shore Hospital (and would go on to run virtually the entire Long Island hospital system). Dr. Mountain had grabbed him on his way out the door when Donald called.

"How do your legs feel?" Dr. Mountain asked.

"I don't have any feeling. I can't move my toes."

He quickly pulled down the cover sheet and slipped his probing fingers between my hipbone and the top of the cast, silently feeling for the femoral pulse. He withdrew his hand, spun on his heels, and rushed from the room. His shadow was hardly through the door when he returned, carrying an electric vibrating cast-cutter. He put the vibrating blade on the thigh of the cast and started a rocking motion, splitting the plaster encasement. The dust flew, and like fine snow soon covered the blue overcoat the good doctor had never paused to take off.

A nurse came in the room, saw this bizarre sight of a stranger in an overcoat cutting away at a gravely injured patient, and started screaming frantically. *"Who are you? Who are you? Whatayou think you're doing? Get away from the patient!"* She leapt on Dr. Mountain's back and tried to pin his arms. "Get her off me!" Mountain cried to Jack, who pulled the nurse off, carried her out of the room, and held the door shut. The ridiculous scene would have played like screwball comedy were it not for the very real possibility that I would be wheeling myself around the rest of my life.

The orthopedic resident and a security guard came next. Dr. Mountain, for the first time, took his eyes from his work and fixed them on the resident. "I am a surgeon," Mountain said before the startled young doctor could say a word. "My name is John Mountain and I am this boy's personal physician. He is in shock. The edema in his legs is severely compromising his circulation. Continuing like this, the only option will be to amputate. Go get a cast spreader and help me open these casts. Or this boy is going to own this hospital!"

The resident whirled, forced the security guard from the room, and began assisting Dr. Mountain, who finished traveling the full length of the cast, splitting it from hip to toe. Taking the spreader from the resident, he opened the right cast while the resident worked on the left one.

"How does that feel?"

"Better," I lied.

Mountain spread the cast further. "How does that feel now?"

"Better," another lie. And then slowly I could feel a breeze on my legs, slipping in like a cold fog. "That feels better, Doc. I can feel it. It's cool. That does feel better."

Dr. Mountain gently slipped some pillows beneath my legs. "I'm glad you're here," I said before drifting off under the influence of the morphine.

While I was off somewhere, the situation got even more tense. Dr. Mountain wanted to move me to Columbia-Presbyterian Hospital and put me under the care of a top surgeon, just as he had sent my father to a leading Parkinson's expert. But the surgical chief in Port Chester—who was enraged when he found out about Dr. Mountain and what he had done—told my family that a move now would kill me. Dr. Mountain thought the opposite was true, and in a contest of credibility, there *was* no contest. It was Vivian's call, and she made it without hesitation. She reached the surgical chief and told him an ambulance was on its way to move me to Columbia. "You can't do that!" the doctor screamed into the phone. "Any move will kill him! He's in critical condition. He'll never make it!" When he finished his tirade, Vivian calmly informed him that it was her wish that I be moved. That was the kind of trust we had in Dr. Mountain.

I DON'T REMEMBER actually being transferred to Columbia. I awoke there, surrounded by a battalion of people in white and so much equipment that it precluded any possibility of being in the regular intensive care unit. I had to have a large, private room in the Harkness Pavilion, on a VIP floor whose patients had included the Duchess of Windsor, who brought her own towels and sheets.

I was receiving blood and clear fluid intravenously. There was a nurse on each of my arms watching a blood pressure apparatus and constantly pumping her little rubber ball and relaying numbers to the doctors around my bed. Every time one of them gave a reading, a doctor muttered. I could feel the vibrations run through my legs and up my whole body from the clanking of metal pipes and rods that technicians were assembling around my bed. I noticed that both of my legs were slung and hanging from the contraption.

"How are you doing, fellas?" I asked groggily.

A redheaded doctor with a plaid bow tie stood at the foot of the bed. He raised his eyes and met my stare. "Good, you're awake," he said. "Don't be frightened."

"I'm not frightened," I said. "It looks like you fellas are putting some traction bars together."

"Oh," the doctor said, "you know what this is."

"Traction. I've been in traction before. I broke my left mid-femur back in high school. I was in traction for three months."

"How did you break it?"

"Playing football."

My stoic good humor notwithstanding, I was of course frightened—terrified. The doctors were constantly whispering to one another. One would rush from the room; another would come in with X rays they all gathered around to read. I glanced up at my elevated left leg. Between the blood and the gauze, I could see a long silver pin, about three-sixteenths of an inch around. It had been driven neatly through my shinbone below the knee. One of the doctors was attaching an apparatus to each side of the pin. From this, I knew, they would hang some weights, probably sandbags, through a system of pulleys. How ironic, I thought. I've got a bunch of riggers taking care of me. I resisted my professional curiosity. I tried not to look too closely at the gear. I would rather not look and I would rather not know. Not now, anyway.

The sounds in the room were all I could handle. There were the incessant chanting of the blood-pressure readings and the hammering and tinkering with the traction apparatus. "There, that's good," one of them would say in a husky voice. "I've got it here," I'd hear from the other side of the bed. What scared me most was *their* concern—their intensity. I wanted to see doctors confidently going about routine work. But I couldn't tell from the disjointed conversation what they were doing, or even if *they* knew. I wanted to feel gratitude about being in the care of the best hospital in New York, and optimistic that after a few uncomfortable days I would be free of pain and on the road to going home. But I took a look around and knew I must be dreaming.

THE NURSE ON my left says, "No pressure, Doctor."

I tell him I want to see the boss.

He ignores me. The stress in the room is as heavy as the beam that put me here. I have an impulse to break the tension. I start groping at my chest.

"What are you doing?" the doctor says, alarmed, pulling my arm down forcefully. "Keep your arm down. It's very important that you keep still. We're giving you a transfusion."

I keep trying to grab my chest. "Are you troubled?" the doctor asks. "Do you have pain? Is there a pain in your chest?"

"No, no," I tell him, "I feel great. I was just trying to check my pocket. I had a key there, and I was just trying to make sure it was still there."

"There aren't any pockets in these gowns. What are you talking about?"

"Well, I had a key there when they undressed me at the other hospital, and I made sure that I kept the key with me. And, as I recall, I had a pocket in that gown, and I kept the key in the pocket. What time is it, Doc?"

"It's two-thirty in the morning."

"Nuts!"

"What's wrong?"

"I had a ten-thirty date at the Playboy Club and now I missed it. Hey, Doc! One of your interns stole my key. You guys stop everything you're doing and empty your pockets on the bed."

After a beat, a wave of relieved chuckles washes over the room. The only one not laughing is the doctor in charge, the one with the red hair and the bow tie. He frowns sternly, but then says, "Hey, listen, just relax, will you, Karl? If you don't keep quiet, I'll have one of my boys level you with one of these sandbags."

"Okay, Doc," I reply. "Just thought I'd break the tension."

Someone slips a mask over my face, and I lapse into unconsciousness.

THE DOCTOR'S NAME was Keith McElroy, and he was the chief of orthopedic surgery. Much later, Dr. McElroy told me he hadn't laughed because my vital statistics were plummeting. There were brief moments when I had *no* blood pressure. "You were dead, Karl," he said.

"How could that be?" I asked. I didn't have one of those near-death experiences. I saw no white light. No tunnels, or bridges. I was conscious, joking around.

"The last thing to go is one's sense of humor," Dr. McElroy said.

Over the next two years, Dr. McElroy led a team of doctors in a massive reconstruction project. The steel had crushed, mangled, and broken virtually every bone in both legs, from the hips to the ankles—everything but the one bone I had broken in high school, the femur. Dr. McElroy told me my knee was smashed in fifty places, that it looked like a "shattered mirror" on X ray. Twenty-five years later, he presented a lecture about my case at a medical meeting. After describing the injuries I presented when I first got to the hospital, Dr. McElroy asked: "What steps would you take next?" Every doctor in the room said he would perform a bilateral amputation at the hip. "No,"

Dr. McElroy said. "This patient has been walking since nineteen sixty-seven, and I'll tell you how we did it."

From the day of the accident, on December 10, 1964, I spent a full year in the hospital, and over those twelve months I had eighteen operations to repair my legs. I became a man of steel of a different sort. The surgeons used staples, pins, and screws, seemingly everything but a high-tensile bolt, to hold scores of bone fragments together. In one of the operations, the doctors cut three inches from my left shinbone so it would match the length of the right leg, which had fewer bits of bone for them to use when they rebuilt it. I was never Tiny Salinski, but the accident cost me three inches of height I could hardly spare, bringing me down to five-foot-five. But it didn't matter how short my legs were, so long as they were attached to the rest of me. It wasn't until a month after the accident that I found out—or that it registered, because I was so out of it the first few days—how close I had come to having my legs amputated.

One day Dr. McElroy moved to the foot of the bed and removed the coverings from my legs, slung in traction. Several times he sank his fingers into the swollen flesh and as the dimple became smooth, he observed the color. He removed the gauze from the right ankle. "We'll change this dressing every hour and keep these pads moist with distilled water," he said, accustomed by now to a patient who appreciated the details.

When he lifted the gauze, he exposed a jagged, tooth-like material sticking out of the ankle. "What's that, Doc?" I asked.

"That? That's your bone."

"Couldn't get it all back in, huh Doc?"

"Not yet anyway. We'll have to watch this." He replaced the moist gauze and said he'd be back later. "You'll be here, won't you?" he asked with a wink.

"I haven't checked my calendar yet," I said.

I was in critical condition for the first four weeks, and only Vivian could visit me for the first two. She recognized that my sense of humor kept me going, but she wasn't fooled by my bravado. "Everyone thinks your jokes are great," she said, "but I know what you're doing. Keep it up, darling, tell your jokes, but don't tell them to me. I know."

Dr. Mountain prescribed some tranquilizers for Vivian, but she didn't take them—"even though my friends popped them like candy," she later told me—and eventually she flushed them down the toilet. She prayed instead, and, on her mother's Yankee advice, stayed busy with the babies. My mother-in-law stayed with the children, often accompanied by my father-in-law, an emergency service man for the Long Island Lighting Company who was used to twenty-four-hour shifts. Vivian came to the hospital every day, and called the nursing station from home at three every morning, like clockwork. I was allowed morphine every three hours, and always arranged my shot to coincide with her visits.

Though the visitor list was restricted to my wife, one day Donald and our brother-in-law Jack climbed the back stairs and slipped into my room. I was so happy to see them. When the restrictions were loosened slightly, Donald brought my mother and father up for a sorrowful five-minute visit. Dad could hardly manage any words. In his first conversation with Vivian right after the accident, he had said the only helpful thing he could think of: Don't worry, you will never have to worry about money. You will get Karl's check every week.

On Christmas morning, Uncle Bob stepped into the room. He was dressed in his holiday best. "They have you rigged up for slaughter," he opened. "But you look pretty good." He had a brown leather case in his hands, and pulled a Polaroid camera out of it. How nice, I thought—a Christmas present. "I'd like to take your picture and show the gang up in Scarsdale," Bob said, quickly scuttling that possibility. "They're all moaning and groaning about how you're down here dying. You sure don't look like you're dying to me. You'll be out of here in no time." He raised his camera and told me to smile.

It was very soon after the accident, the beginning of a long ordeal, and my body didn't have the wherewithal to summon the anger that would boil up later. Yes, the accident was the result of incompetence on the part of the ironworkers and bad timing on mine. If I'd arrived even a minute later, the steel would have fallen before I got there. And yes, I put myself in harm's way. I should have been more careful. But the fact was that the calamity was not just the fault of the young connector, or the old foreman, or of simple fate. It was, to me, a disastrous lapse by Bob and Rudy that allowed the ironworker's error to become my ruination.

On every job my father ever bid, he made sure that any column with double-connected beams had "beam seats"—small ridges that were, in effect, safety nets. Since making double connections could be a tricky act of coordination and strength, each of these columns had a four-inch shelf welded onto it so that if the connector had an alignment or bolting problem and one or both of the beams came loose, they couldn't go anywhere. They simply rested on the beam seat. Not only was it infinitely safer, it also made connecting much easier. But for some reason, beam seats were recommended but not required. The erector had to specify them in his contract with the fabricator, who was apt to charge more for them. Dad always insisted on beam seats, and he refused to pay a penny extra for them. To him, beam seats on double connections were as optional as brakes on a car. The Korvette's job was the first one he wasn't involved with. If I allowed myself one sorrow, it was that he had been unable to stay actively involved in the company, if only for just one more job. This was the first job I ever brought in, and the first one in which our proposal had not passed before my father's eyes before leaving the office. If it had, there is no question that those columns would have had beam seats, and the steel never would have fallen. But Bob and Rudy never even had a conversation about them with Haven-Busch, the fabricator.

"Smile," Bob said. "We don't want everyone to think you're unhappy."

I smiled, but the flash failed. "We'll have to take another one," Bob said. "Let's have another smile." This time, I could only manage half a smile, but the flash popped and we waited for the instant picture to magically appear. So that's what I look like, I thought as the picture materialized. My face looked haggard as hell. Vivian told me I was gray—not pale but literally gray.

"There—you look great," Bob said. "That's really fine." It was the most good-natured he had been to me in years. "Listen, I have a long day ahead of me and I have to go," he said only two or three minutes after he arrived. "Best of luck." He scooped up his Polaroid and threw his coat over his shoulder on his way out the door, headed for another Christmas gathering of the Koches in Scarsdale. He never visited me in the hospital again.

Donald brought Dad up about once a month, and my father would gamely try to keep my humor up. After the surgery to equalize the lengths of my legs, he joked that it was a good thing: Otherwise, I would look like I was raised on the side of a mountain. "You'd always be walking clockwise around the mountain." But he had a very hard time coming to see me. There wasn't much he could say about the accident, but did lay some of the responsibility at Uncle Bob's feet for not making sure the columns came with beam seats. "I forgot more about the steel business than Bob ever learned," he said softly, shaking his head. "I'm sorry you had to take a lickin'." Once when Donald visited, he told me that Dad had come with him but was sitting out in the solarium. "He was crying," Donald said. "He didn't want you to see him."

Mike Montour, the Mohawk ironworker whom I liked to called Chief, came one day with a bottle of Scotch in one pocket and a pint of Hennessy in the other. He put the Johnny Walker in the closet and sat on the chair beside my bed. He poured a stiff belt into my water glass, but I couldn't drink so I just left it on the table. Then he started to pour his own. For the next two hours, he just kept pouring cognac down his throat, until tears were running down his cheeks. The only thing he said to me for the whole time was, "You're a good man. You shouldn't have got hurt." He'd have another drink and his deep voice would roll again. "You're a good man. You shouldn't have got hurt." Finally, he stood up, threw the empty bottle into the trash, and walked out.

A day or two later, Donald came to visit and poured himself a Scotch. Donald had taken my place in the field, starting with the Korvette's shopping center. I told him about Mike's strange but very much appreciated visit, the only one by an ironworker. "Well, Karl," Donald said, bringing up a familiar rub, "you know you're not a brother to the ironworkers."

"Yeah, but I work just as hard as they do, I get just as dirty," I said, adding, superfluously, "I take the same risks."

"You're in management," Donald said, "and never the twain shall meet."

IN FEBRUARY, VIVIAN called me from the delivery room at North Shore Hospital to tell me our second son was born. We named him John David Mountain Koch, after the doctor who saved my life, and my legs.

For that whole year, Vivian was a single mom. It was as if I was off at war, or in prison. I settled into my home on the eleventh floor of the Harkness Pavilion, along with a few other long-termers. There was the owner of the Four Seasons restaurant, who checked in only after his statues and potted plants arrived. There was a fellow on the floor who was visited occasionally by a belly dancer. When his wife visited, his private nurse hid the belly dancer in my room, where she visited me until she got the all-clear to go back. And there was Tony Roig, who was there almost as long as I was. He was a wealthy Puerto Rican sugar plantation owner who was one of the first liver shunt patients. He discovered one day that there was a direct line of sight from my window to the building across the street where student nurses were housed. He had his wife bring his binoculars from Puerto Rico, and started dropping by my room each afternoon at five, pulling my bed up to the window. For easier spotting, we devised a grid system, 1 to 20 for the vertical floors, A to J horizontally. "E-10 with the pink curtains," he would say, then hand me the binoculars.

I'd hold onto the monkey bar with my left hand while Tony stood behind, pushing me up to a sitting position, as I struggled to hold the binoculars steady with my right hand and catch a quick glimpse of a young nurse walking around in her bra before collapsing back onto the bed, exhausted. "Oh, thank you, Tony," I gasped, "that was great." One a night was all I could handle. Then Tony would wheel my bed back to its position. This went on for several weeks until Head Nurse Haulk, a former Army captain, burst into the room, chasing Tony back to his room and shaming me. After that, we confined our activities to placing bets on horse races with Tony's bookie, who visited every day.

I was in for the long haul as surgery became as regular as a car wash. I couldn't be taken out of the canopy of steel and cable around my bed, and the surgical team couldn't move everything to the operating room. So they came to *me*. My room became my personal O.R., as well as my private recovery room—a room in which recovery never ended. Every few weeks, Dr. McElroy would pay me a visit, tell me I was strong enough for the next procedure, and the following morning the room would fill once again with doctors and nurses and carts of supplies and equipment. A Chinese doctor rattled bottles at the foot of the bed and quietly advised me that he would put me to sleep. I emerged half a day later with more hardware in my legs, another layer of pain to deal with.

The surgery usually lasted all day—eight, ten, twelve hours. No sooner would I recover from one operation when Dr. McElroy would tell me it was time for another. He and all the doctors and nurses became like my Dr. Frankensteins. Dr. George Crickelair, Columbia's chief of plastic surgery, did all the skin grafting. Dr. Ferdinand McAllistair, a world-renowned vascular surgeon, repaired my blood vessels and stood by ready to put plastic veins in my right leg, a procedure he had originated. I had a bond with these doctors unlike any I can imagine. They were my saviors, gifted and heroic, and yet they were also my tormentors. There were moments when I might have decided to be done with it—to go back to the hospital in Port Chester, find that first doctor with his iciness and impatience, and tell him that I'd thought about it and decided I wanted him to cut my legs off after all.

But I wanted my legs, in whatever condition. So what I felt for the doctors at Columbia was boundless gratitude. Years later, George Crickelair, the plastic surgery chief, invited me to his lakefront house in the mountains of New Jersey to go fishing. He told me to drive to the dock and call from a pay phone. A few minutes later, he came around the bend, put-putting in his outboard, and picked me up. We spent the day fishing for trout, and later sat on the dock, fishing and chatting. I went up to the house to get a beer, and when I got to the kitchen, there was a four-foot snake curled up in front of the refrigerator. I went back to the dock and said, "George, we have company." He looked at me quizzically, waiting for more. "A big black snake," I said. "In the kitchen." He smiled. "Oh, him. He knows he's not supposed to play in the kitchen." He went up and threw the snake into the brush beside the house. "Good thing Eleanor wasn't here," he said.

"Karl, do you know why I've always liked you?" Crickelair said as we sat on the dock. "Surgeons spend hours planning their procedures, learned over a lifetime. Finally they stand over a table repairing wounds for hours and hours. Sometimes twelve hours, and they can't leave. They defecate in their pants if they have to"—one of the trade secrets I learned from my surgical marathon was that surgeons sometimes wear diapers—"all for the sake of getting their patients back to their families. And how often these patients forget. I like you because you never forgot." If I felt close to ironworkers, it couldn't begin to compare to the affection, the love, I felt for my doctors.

The doctors performed an open reduction of both ankles, reworking the twisted bones into a better position and fusing them together with staples. Then Dr. McElroy was back at my bedside a few weeks later announcing another procedure. There was a tibia flap in my left leg, a pedicle flap in my right ankle. He reset multiple fractures in my right knee. One surgery was devoted to removing the screws from my right ankle. And always, skin grafts from my stomach.

A few weeks after one surgery, McElroy proudly marched a group of residents and attending physicians into my room. "Show them how you can move your knee," he instructed me. I could move it about thirty degrees, about 20 percent of normal range, which was 20 percent more than what the doctors in Port Chester expected.

I lived for any good news. One morning, on a rare occasion when there were no medical personnel in my room and I was alone, I felt free to let go for a second. I burst out crying. Then the door suddenly opened, and in walked Dr. McAllistair. Embarrassed, I shut it down and apologized. "I never did that before," I told him, which was the truth.

"Nothing to be embarrassed about," he said. "There are people on this floor who cry every time they look at you. You're entitled."

He went to the foot of the bed and placed his long fingers on the top of my right foot. He stared at me, then broke out into a big smile. "A hearty, bounding pulse," he said. He came back to the head of the bed and shook my hand heartily. "Well, Karl, you won't see me again, and I couldn't be happier for you."

"Where are you going?" I asked.

"Sailing up the Hudson—now that I don't have to change the veins in your legs." It was a great victory.

I WAS RELEASED from the hospital at the end of April, nearly five months after I'd come in. To say it was great to go home would be ridiculous. It was surreal. But leaving the hospital was hardly the end. I knew I would be back for more surgery, and that rehabilitation would become as much a part of my life as eating and sleeping. I was to have three more stays in the hospital that year, two of them a month long each. The operations would continue for years.

When I got into my bed at home for the first time and Vivian opened the bedroom door, I could feel the painful vibration in my legs. The door had to be opened and closely gingerly, as if I were a sleeping baby. In the hospital, I had been allowed morphine every three hours, but I didn't want to become addicted so I was determined to add a minute a day between shots: three hours, then three hours and one minute, two minutes, three, ten, fifteen, until I couldn't stand it anymore. When the pain became so unbearable that my body arched and only my shoulders touched the mattress and my head was pressed into the pillow, I knew it was time to tell the nurse I was ready for another shot. I sweated so much that the orderlies had to change my sheets three times a night. So many times I felt like taking one of John DeSmidt's shotguns and blowing my foot off. But when I finally got home, I laid in bed and refused to take anything stronger than Bufferin. My children may get a cripple for a father, I thought, but never a drug addict.

I couldn't walk without crutches, but eventually I could ride a bicycle. I started on a stationary bike next to my bed, then took Vivian's three-speed around town. Then off to visit Jack and Roberta. Then to my parents' house in Sands Point. With each mile, my legs got stronger. But I still couldn't walk without crutches. In June, angry and frustrated, I asked Vivian to give me a hundred dollars, I put my underwear in a paper bag, and told her I wouldn't be back until I could walk. I hopped on the bike wearing a protective pneumatic cast below the knee on my right leg, kind of like an airbag with a plastic shell. And off I rode for Montauk Point, the farthest point on eastern Long Island, a hundred miles from home.

I rode thirty miles a day, stopping each night at a different motel, first making sure there was a bar next door. I persuaded the owner to let me ride the bike into my room, then rode over to the tavern and told the bartender from the door, "I can't walk, so I've got to ride the bike to the bar." Everyone seemed glad to oblige, and was probably happy for the entertainment. I got pretty drunk, the only thing that deadened the pain. Morphine was a narcotic and Bufferin was like candy. Alcohol worked. Eventually, I wobbled back to the motel and went to bed and watched the ceiling turn around. In the morning, I rode some more. Each day, I got farther away from suburbia and deeper into the pastoral countryside of Long Island's East End. It was June, strawberry season, and every couple of miles there would be a U-PICK-EM sign and a clot of cars parked at the foot of the fields. On the third day, nearing Montauk, a car filled with kids sped by, and I felt a thump on my chest. I looked down and saw blood spilling. *Oh my God, now I've been shot.* Then I realized I'd been hit all right—hit by a strawberry.

It took me four days to get to Montauk, three to get home. The last two were the hardest, and I didn't call Vivian either day as I had the first five. When I finally arrived back in Port Washington, she had the police out looking for me. "Okay, wise guy," she said when I showed up, "let me see you walk."

"All right," I said, and a mere ten minutes later, I had made it from the garage all the way up to our bedroom, leaning on every wall, door jamb, table, and chair along the way.

I couldn't walk, but I could work. For the rest of the summer, I rode my bike from Port Washington to the office in the Bronx, not exactly a Sunday jaunt. Making it over the Whitestone Bridge twice a day was my cross to bear. My old pal Bob Moses hadn't put in a bike path, surely an oversight on his part, so it was just me and the trucks and cars fighting for road. Truck drivers began to recognize me and started picking me up on the approach, dropping me on the other side. I resumed the trip on two wheels, eventually arriving at my drawing board to work on estimates with Rudy.

I hated crutches—to me they said "cripple"—and was determined to find a better way to walk. I saw a John Wayne movie on TV. He played a wounded soldier who managed to walk with the aid of a pair of canes. If it was good enough for the Duke . . . So from then on, I adopted the two-cane method. Later, I bought myself a Ferrari and wore an ascot, figuring that as long as I was a cripple, why not be a dashing one? And maybe people would stare at the car instead of at me.

In the fall of 1966, I was back at Columbia, another three-week stay for another operation. One day, a nurse wheeled me down to the solarium at the end of the hallway. It was dusk, and I looked out at the lights twinkling on the George Washington Bridge. The elevator bell rang, and Donald stepped onto the floor and walked into my room, backpedaling when he realized my bed was empty. He turned and saw me in the solarium, and whistled. My legs were straight out in front of me, wrapped from toe to hip in casts. We went through the ritual, him asking how I was doing, me filling him in on the latest news of my legs. Then Donald said he had some news of his own.

"We're bidding on the World Trade Center."

Donald watched me take in the information. "You're kidding," I said after a beat.

"We're getting the drawings in. We're putting a bid in."

"The *Trade Center?*"

Like most New Yorkers, we had followed the development of this mammoth public project since it first started popping up in the newspapers five or six years earlier. What it would be, where it would be built, what it would look like, and how tall it would be—and of course, how many hundreds of millions of dollars it would cost—had been the subject of years of public discussion and work. But it was obvious this was a job only the boys of Big Steel could handle. We had never even considered trying to get in on it. So Donald's news floored me. I knew I had been out of things for more than a year, but at what point did we become the new U.S. Steel?

"The Port Authority asked us to bid," Donald said. "They had some problems with Bethlehem and American Bridge. Austin Tobin got pissed off at them and now they're asking us for a bid."

"How much tonnage are we talking about?" I asked Donald.

"About a hundred-ninety-thousand in the whole project, both towers," Donald said.

"Oh, man." That was three times more than the Empire State Building. "It's kind of over our head, isn't it? What does Dad think about it?"

"I told him about it, but he's been pretty bad lately."

Donald and I discussed the project until after midnight, when the nurses kicked him out. He turned me around and began wheeling me back to my room, and I thought of the night in the rooming house in Massachusetts eight years earlier, when Uncle Bob told me he was determined to be a millionaire. Now the powerful Port of New York Authority was inviting our family company into the biggest steel job in the history of the world. And Dad was out of little brother's way.

"What colossal balls Bob has," I said to Donald as he rolled me back to my room.

Center of the Universe

Beyond the compelling need to make this a
monument to world peace, the World Trade Center
should, because of its importance, become a
representation of man's belief in humanity,
his need for individual dignity, his beliefs in the
cooperation of men, and through cooperation,
his ability to find greatness.

—MINORU YAMASAKI

10

STIRRING
THE
BLOOD

In 1958, a thoroughly modern skyscraper began to rise amid a collection of aging and unremarkable commercial buildings in Lower Manhattan. It was sixty stories of glass and aluminum, the new home of Chase Manhattan Bank. The design by the top-notch architectural firm of Skidmore, Owings & Merrill was befitting of the power and prestige of its owner, but the location chosen by David Rockefeller, the co-chairman of the bank, was not a little audacious. For at that time, in the scheme of things, the southern tip of Manhattan was Nowheresville. It was old, it was stodgy, it was all business. And it wasn't about to change. That it was considered bold for a bank to build in the financial district is all you need to know about the appeal of the neighborhood.

Lower Manhattan was the only significant commercial area of the city largely left out of the economic-boom party of the post-war decade. There was some new building downtown—the Marine Midland Bank, for one, which we erected on William Street in 1958—but to the consternation of government and business leaders in the city, there was too big a concentration of cranes and derricks toiling in Midtown. Downtown had City Hall and building after building housing investment firms, banks, and insurance companies. There were blocks that had almost nothing but stores that sold TV tubes and transistors. Compared to the electricity uptown, the borough's bottom was lifeless, at least by New York standards.

David Rockefeller, of course, was wired for power. Besides heading one of the country's largest banks, he was the grandson of the first American billionaire, Standard Oil founder John D. Rockefeller. His brother, Nelson, was the new governor of New York. Building downtown was daring, but calculated to start something. Even before the excavation for his new headquarters began on the block bordered by Pine, Liberty, William, and Nassau streets, he founded a corporate civic association called the Downtown–Lower Manhattan Association, and recruited the heads of virtually every major company with a presence in the area to push for redevelopment. The Downtown Association was not your typical civic association. Among its members were the chief executives of American Express, W.R. Grace, The Wall Street Journal, banks and investment houses from Lehman Brothers to Morgan Guaranty Trust, and the presidents of both the American and New York stock exchanges. One of Rockefeller's first moves as the group's chairman was to hire Skidmore, Owings & Merrill to come up with some ideas for reinvigorating the area.

Daniel H. Burnham, the architect of the Flatiron Building, New York's first skyscraper, once said: "Make no small plans, for they have no power to stir the blood." The Skidmore firm and the Downtown Association took this dictum to heart, and came up with a blood-stirring plan that called for spending the staggering sum of one *billion* dollars to virtually tear down and rebuild the financial center of the world. It was a massive proposal of urban renewal that called for razing scores of buildings, closing or widening streets, and turning some of the East River piers into a heliport and a marina. The centerpiece of the entire 564-acre overhaul was a major building devoted to world trade. A World Trade Center.

The idea for a trade center was not new. It went back more than a decade, all the way to 1946, when anyone in the business of economics and commerce could see that the war had left the world smaller. A wall would later go up in Berlin, but everywhere else it seemed fences were coming down. The developed world was becoming one huge shipping lane. To a large extent, the success of American commerce would be tied to the reconstruction of Europe, and to trade with our recent archenemy, Japan. Recognizing New York City's place, front and center, in the national and world economy, the state legislature voted to establish a World Trade Corporation to explore the possibility of creating a center for global commerce—a building in Manhattan, or a group of them, where companies engaged in importing and exporting could conduct the business of the world.

The World Trade Corporation came up with a plan to build not one building but *twenty*-one—exhibition halls and offices totaling five million square feet, filling ten city blocks, and with a price tag of $140 million. It was a grand plan—much too grand. Even though some fifty-six million tons of goods were exported and imported through New York each year, chances were extremely remote that there would be enough demand for space to allow the state to recoup its investment. Instead of scaling back, the state packed up the plans and locked them away in storage, not to be heard from again.

When David Rockefeller started his Downtown Association twelve years later, he thought a center like the one discussed years earlier was exactly the kind of thing that could ignite the commercial gentrification he envisioned for Lower Manhattan. This was not a concept unfamiliar to him: The building of Rockefeller Center in the 1930s had a similar effect on the Midtown area. After its initial proposal in 1958, the Skidmore firm completed a detailed plan that called for a trade center to be built on a thirteen-acre site at the far eastern end of Wall Street, along the East River (about where the South Street Seaport would eventually be located). The plan called for a nine-hundred-foot-long exhibition hall with a pair of interior courtyards, to be called the World Trade Mart; a building to house all the security exchanges; and a fifty- to seventy-story tower, reminiscent of the United Nations building sixty blocks upriver, for trade commissions, banks, brokerages, and corporations both foreign and domestic. There would be a World Trade Hotel and a restaurant called the World Trade Club.

In January of 1960, Rockefeller published an impressive, bound proposal, eighteen pages long and seventeen inches wide, and addressed it to his brother, along with New Jersey's governor, Robert Meyner, and New York City Mayor Robert Wagner. Rockefeller told the press that he expected most of the $250 million cost to be borne by private investment, and that he hoped that the Trade Center could start taking leases when foreign visitors arrived in four years for the New York World's Fair. Rockefeller saved his hardest pitch for his choice to build the project, the only public agency he believed had the financial clout, the political muscle, and the public charter to get it done. In a bit of none-too-subtle sweet talk, Rockefeller named the entire project the Port of New York World Trade Center. He wanted the Port of New York Authority to build it.

ROBERT MOSES HAD no peers as a master builder, but if there was anyone who could even be considered a close second—a man capable of standing up to the Power Broker himself—it was Austin Tobin. As executive director of the Port Authority for thirty years starting in 1942, Tobin, like Moses, ran a public agency with the autonomy and ruthless efficiency of a private enterprise and assembled an empire of bridges, tunnels, and shipping and transportation terminals, including the three airports serving the vast tri-state metropolis collectively known as New York.

If Moses was the single most powerful non-elected individual in the United States in the decades before and after World War II, it was Tobin who ran the most powerful agency—a government organization that was so far beyond the reach of public scrutiny and control that a new term had to be invented. The Port Authority, it was said, was a "quasi-government" agency. It was conceived in 1918 by the legislatures of New York and New Jersey, ostensibly to build and operate a rail tunnel beneath Upper New York Bay linking New Jersey and an expanded commercial port in Brooklyn. The tunnel was never built, but the charter written by the two legislatures in 1921— and approved by Congress, the first time an interstate agency was created under a section in the Constitution—did ease (if not end) two centuries of border disputes and power struggles between the two states. It gave the Port Authority the "full power and authority to purchase, construct, lease and operate terminal, transportation and other facilities of commerce."

With virtual carte blanche from the legislatures, with its commissioners appointed by the governors of the two states rather than elected by their voters, and with the legal authority to finance projects through bond issues, the Port had raw, potentially unchecked power. A decade after its formation, it was the model for the mighty Tennessee Valley Authority, created in 1933 by President Franklin D. Roosevelt and Congress as "a corporation clothed with the power of government but possessed of the flexibility and initiative of a private enterprise" to help lift the country out of the Depression. The Port Authority was unencumbered by civil service laws, so it was able to build a staff of talented, well-paid engineers, lawyers, and accountants who were recruited young and rose through the ranks. It was every bit like a blue-chip company with a swaggering, can-do corporate culture. And its CEO, Austin Tobin, was every bit the mover and shaker of post-war urban America. The Port Authority's commissioners may have benefited from patronage, but Tobin made sure his permanent staff was a pure meritocracy.

Tobin, an attorney by trade who put in fifteen years in the Port Authority's law department before heading the agency, didn't have the over-sized public image that Moses did. He didn't need his picture in the paper, preferring that the commissioners he theoretically reported to, and who renewed his appointment every year for three decades, be the public face of the PA. But Tobin was most definitely in charge, and he was as big a thinker as Moses. A literate man who wrote poetry and loved the opera, he liked to quote Daniel H. Burnham's "make no small plans" saying on the rare occasions when he spoke publicly. And he matched Moses bridge for bridge, tunnel for tunnel. Moses had the Triborough, Tobin the George Washington. Moses tunneled under the East River, opening the Midtown and Brooklyn-Battery tunnels. Tobin's agency had the west side, crossing the Hudson to New Jersey with the Holland and Lincoln tunnels. Tobin didn't build the ribbons and cloverleaves of parkway that Moses rolled out across New York and Long Island, but he made up for it by cornering the market on all the region's airports and marine terminals. By the time the World Trade Center was being considered, Tobin's PA had raised more than two billion dollars on its own credit to build and operate twenty-four facilities. But there was nothing very exciting on the drawing board. There were no more bridges to build, no more tunnels to drill.

If the Port Authority was a quasi-government agency, it could be said that the Downtown–Lower Manhattan Association became a virtual quasi-government agency. Such was the Rockefeller crowd's cumulative clout and effectiveness—and perhaps arrogance—that a group made up entirely of corporate executives could commission detailed plans for a massive public development project and then presume to hand it over to an elite government-sponsored agency and say: "Here, build this." But that's what they did, and perhaps only an outfit as like-minded and autonomous as the Port Authority—and one run by a man eager for a big project—would have been so willing to run with the ball. Austin Tobin jumped on the idea. He assembled a panel of distinguished architects to study the proposal, and assigned people throughout the PA to work on developing it. Engineering, finance, law, port development—virtually every department had a piece of the World Trade Center to explore. In March of 1961, only fourteen months after the Downtown Association's report, the Port Authority announced its intention to build the World Trade Center. Let the political games begin.

New Jersey was always wary of anything the Port did that favored New York. After all, it was the Port of *New York* Authority. New Jersey wouldn't even be acknowledged in the agency's name until 1972, at Tobin's retirement. For years, New Jerseyans had complained about the sorry state of the Hudson and Manhattan Railroad. Now it was bankrupt. To many in New Jersey, it was partly Tobin's fault: His well-traveled bridges and tunnels had killed the railroad, they said. Still, Tobin steadfastly refused to bail out the Hudson and Manhattan. But now New Jersey had some leverage: the project that was quickly becoming Tobin's baby, perhaps his last hurrah.

The World Trade Center idea was widely lauded by editorial writers and trade groups on both sides of the Hudson, but New Jersey Governor

Meyner—who could stall or even scuttle the project—was noncommittal. At the very least, he could certainly make trouble if he wanted to, more trouble than it was worth to the Port. Tobin decided that taking over and resuscitating the railroad was a fair price to pay to get the Trade Center built. But he wasn't home-free yet. The haggling continued, the two governors began bickering in the press—Meyner complained that Rockefeller didn't return his calls—and before long, it was 1962. New Jersey's election of a new governor, Richard J. Hughes, was good news for Tobin, but more than gubernatorial politics, it was dumb luck and astute improvisation on the part of the Port Authority that finally got things unstuck. All it involved was moving the entire World Trade Center project to a completely new location.

Along with old trains and an empty bank account, the Port Authority acquired a pair of dilapidated office buildings when it agreed to take over the Hudson and Manhattan Railroad. The buildings were above the line's Lower Manhattan terminal on Church Street. Tobin and his staff didn't think the buildings were worth fixing up, but if they tore them down, what then? One of those talented people Tobin kept around had a bright idea: Why not raze the buildings and build the Trade Center *there*? The fifteen-acre site was only seven blocks east of the proposed location—there were only ten blocks river to river at the tapered tip of Lower Manhattan—but more important was what was underneath: tubes and tracks. Moving the Trade Center to the west side from the east would afford much better subway connections—and a direct path to New Jersey. It was almost too perfect. Tobin got along better with the new governor of New Jersey than the old one, and the proposed move sealed the deal. Newspaper editorialists, for whom the nearly two years of fits and starts and cross-Hudson Ping-Pong had become a staple, pronounced the arrangement a winner—not in the least, a face-saver for New Jersey's politicians, who could finally declare victory while delivering something real to their constituents. "The beauty of the compromise," said the *Newark Sunday News*, "is that while substantially meeting New Jersey's objections, it gives New York all it really wanted in the first place."

WITH THE TRADE CENTER having cleared the hurdle of the Hudson River and looking more like a viable project, Austin Tobin in February of 1962 created a new operating unit of the Port Authority called the World Trade Office and promoted a fifteen-year veteran of the engineering department to be its head. Guy Tozzoli had a lot of experience and a passion for his work that made him a favorite of Tobin's. With degrees in analytic mechanics and physics, Tozzoli's credits included supervising construction of Newark Airport and several of the Port's marine terminal facilities. He had been a pioneer in building ports for the large containers used to transport goods. He was also given an additional part-time responsibility, directing the transportation section of the World's Fair. Anybody complaining about being under too much pressure at work would get no sympathy from Tozzoli. He had the privilege of working for both Austin Tobin *and* Robert Moses.

A technical man, Tozzoli had proved himself an able problem solver on his previous projects. But those obstacles were all about engineering and construction management. The World Trade Center was to be something else again. He found that the problems across the Hudson were less than half the battle—a mere warmup for the obstacles thrown down by the New York side that would take years to navigate. Though both state legislatures approved bills authorizing the Port Authority to build the Trade Center and take over the Hudson and Manhattan tubes, and both governors signed the bills, there were many people yet to be heard from.

First, there was the mayor, Robert Wagner, and his apparently bruised feelings. After all the attention paid to New Jersey, he was shocked—*shocked*—that the city had not been at the center of the negotiations and that the interests of the very home of the World Trade Center were not being given "paramount consideration." Wagner's astonishment and indignation were big-league posturing. The Trade Center was a no-lose situation for the city—an important area would be given an exciting facelift that would enhance further the city's world-class status, and the city barely had to lift a finger. The burdens were the Port's; the payoffs, the city's. All Wagner really wanted was the best deal he could get for the city in the form of payment from the tax-exempt Port Authority to cover lost tax revenue. Like New Jersey, the city had all the leverage it needed in a single jurisdictional weapon. The project could not proceed without the city's approval of street closings and construction permits. Once again, to Tobin it was a small price to pay, and as soon as Wagner got what he wanted, he was onboard.

The mounting support from the legislature, the governor, and now the mayor, felt like a railroading to the people most affected by the change of venue to the west side. Building the Trade Center would mean razing thirteen square blocks worth of buildings housing some three thousand small businesses, factories, offices, and a few dozen furnished rooms. The owners of the small businesses, especially the little mom-and-pop electronics shops that made up "Radio Row," were ready to make a fight of it. Their protests came screaming from the daily newspapers, where they were portrayed as victims in a David-versus-Goliath battle that went to the heart of democracy. "It's just as though we were living in Russia or Cuba, where a man doesn't have anything to say about what happens to him," Oscar Nadel told Woody Klein, a reporter for the *World-Telegram*. Nadel had a little radio shop on Greenwich Street, and at fifty-seven, he was looking toward retirement, not to starting over. "If it were for the betterment of the city, that would be one thing. But this is simply big business running over us." There was the lament of one of the owners of Bob & Walter's flower shop, Bob Miller: "This is a rotten deal. This is the garden center of the city. Everybody comes to me for special plants. I'm washed up after this."

The Port Authority responded to a barrage of bad press by taking the position that the occupants were better off elsewhere anyway. The Port released a study saying that most of the 158 buildings to be torn down were more than a hundred years old, and 89 percent of them were not fireproof. And the rest were in bad shape. Tozzoli set up a storefront to help people find places nearby to move to, and offered each of them up to $3,000 for moving expenses. But to most it was a lame gesture. "This is the same as Castro taking over," complained Leo Marks, the unhappy owner of World Happiness Products on Greenwich Street. One day a group of merchants built a coffin containing the body of "Mr. Small Businessman" and conducted a mock funeral procession along Church Street.

The opposition spent more than a year in court battling the Port Authority, which was harder to fight than City Hall, and actually won a battle that threw the entire project into doubt for a few weeks in the late winter of 1963. In February, a state appeals court ruled that the Port Authority's plan was unconstitutional because it amounted to a public agency taking land by eminent domain for a project that would be for the primary benefit of private enterprise. But five weeks later, the Court of Appeals, the state's highest, reversed the decision, and later that year, the U.S. Supreme Court declined to take the case. This fight was over, but it would hardly be the last one for the Port Authority. For there is a fitting parallel in two American quests that spanned one end of the decade of the 1960s to the other. One was the pursuit of landing a man on the moon. The other was building the World Trade Center.

11

FEAR
OF
HEIGHTS

To Austin Tobin and Guy Tozzoli, there was no doubt that the Trade Center would be built. It was only a question of when. So even as the Port Authority's legal department was trying to shake off the people biting at the agency's heels, Tobin and Tozzoli were marching ahead. Lost amidst all the controversies was that the design that the Skidmore firm came up with for the Downtown Association was a non-starter. It was now four years since the day that proposal was released with great fanfare, and in that time Tobin had become much less enamored of it. A man of cultured tastes, Tobin was determined that the World Trade Center be an architectural gem. The last major Port Authority construction, the PA's bus terminal on the west side of Manhattan built in 1950, had received a rude reception from critics, and Tobin and Tozzoli resolved to come back strong. They wanted nothing less than a "shattering breakthrough" that would "influence the course of world architecture," in the words of staff members in one internal Port Authority report.

Tozzoli began looking for the right architect to achieve such heights, and decided he found him in a small office in the suburbs of Michigan. Minoru Yamasaki was an architect of note, but not the kind of first-tier designer who might be expected to be chosen to conceive such a significant project as the World Trade Center. Not too long before, Yamasaki's office had been housed in a loft above a suburban Detroit sporting goods store whose rear faced the tracks of the Grand Trunk Railroad. Yamasaki once recalled talking to a prominent interior designer on the phone when their conversation was interrupted mid-sentence by the shrill whistle of a passing train. "Where the hell are you, Yama?" the designer asked when it stopped. "In a train station?"

But more than the trappings of his office, it was his controversial place in American architecture that made his selection a surprising and even baffling choice to some people, especially those at the Skidmore firm whose work would be replaced by his like so much urban renewal.

Yamasaki, a diminutive man of 130 pounds who was known affectionately as Yama to clients and colleagues, had designed a building in Seattle for IBM, an airport terminal for St. Louis, and a consulate office in Kobe, Japan, for the State Department. Though born in the United States, he was a world traveler and his work reflected both his Japanese roots and the serene elements he drew from the cultures of the places he visited. His buildings featured Japanese-style pools, Italian sculpture, light building materials, and a devotion to the calming qualities of space. He was certainly an intriguing choice to design the World Trade Center.

Yamasaki was born in 1912 to Japanese immigrant parents who had settled in Seattle a decade earlier. He was a "nisei," a Japanese-American. His father had come from a well-off family whose rice farm was one of the largest on the western shore of the main island of Honshu. It was customary in rural Japan for the eldest son to inherit the entire estate, and Yamasaki's father was the third son, destined to work on the farm without any chance of owning it. Shortly after the turn of the century, he decided to join his brother, the second son, who had already left for the United States several years earlier. In Seattle, he was introduced to a tailor's daughter in a traditional marriage arrangement.

When Yamasaki was young, his family lived in a hillside tenement in Seattle that seemed in danger of sliding down to the street at any moment. There was an outhouse, only cold running water, and a tub in the kitchen. Yamasaki's father had an American immigrant's determination to work hard and make the most of his opportunity in America for his children. He cleaned the floors of a chocolate factory and always worked another job or two, and eventually he was able to move the family to a flat with a bathroom and hot water. Like the other young nisei in their immigrant community, Minoru grew up bilingual, with one foot in traditional Japanese culture and the other stepping into an American future. He helped his father clean the factory on Sunday mornings, scraping the caked pieces of chocolate off the floor, but forbidden to take even a single piece off the shelf.

When he was a senior in high school, Yamasaki was the only student in all of Seattle to score a perfect grade on a citywide math test. Ironically, though, he had little interest in languages and geography, and his mediocre grades in these subjects kept him from graduating near the top of his class.

One day, Yamasaki's uncle Koken, his mother's brother, stopped in on his way to Chicago, where he had been offered a job. With some financial help from Yamasaki's father, Koken had graduated from the University of California with a degree in architecture. During his visit, he unrolled the drawings he had made in college, and when Yamasaki saw them he saw his life's work in front of him. "I almost exploded with excitement," he once wrote. But when he reached the University of Washington, he found he had a problem: He couldn't draw. He worked hard to improve, spending all his free time sketching with a pencil and watercolors. That released an untapped artistic expression and turned him into an able painter.

Still, Yamasaki struggled in his architecture courses, and even more with his confidence. With his math abilities, he got better grades in engineering, and wondered if he might be better off going in that direction, even though, he said, "I so enjoyed the experience of drawing and painting, and I found myself deeply attracted to these more emotional arts." He asked for some advice from one of the school's most respected architects, Lionel Pries, who was becoming a mentor to him. The professor pulled out some drawings he had made when he was in school, and Yamasaki was shocked to see how amateurish they were. The professor told Yamasaki to stay with architecture—that he was destined to become not a good architect but a great one.

It was the Depression, and the only way Yamasaki could stay in school was to work summers. For a nisei, the options were limited. The best he could do was to work in the salmon canneries in Alaska, which were full of "Orientals" willing to work in despicable conditions for low pay: about sixteen dollars for a hard and hazardous 126-hour week, bunking with a hundred men in one room sleeping on straw mattresses. His first night, he recalled, everyone was up with flashlights at three in the morning, trying to kill the bedbugs. Finally, they poured kerosene over the bunks, which eliminated the bugs but left a stench for a week. Many of the workers had beriberi; others lost fingers and arms in the canning machines that were derisively dubbed Iron Chinks. Yamasaki spent three summers working in the canneries, and they left an indelible mark. "While I had been raised in a family where hard work was the rule and luxuries the occasional reward," Yamasaki wrote, "still I was motivated by a clear understanding that life could be lived more beautifully—not solely a material life, but one in which aesthetics and gentility were much more involved, no matter at how fundamental a level."

After his graduation with honors, Yamasaki, who had made his first visit to Japan the summer before, had an opportunity to go to Tokyo to work for his uncle Koken, who had moved back after finding that non-citizens in the United States couldn't become licensed architects. But Yamasaki was a citizen. He decided to go to New York and see if he could find a job as a junior architect. He went from office to office, but found many of them either shut down or about to be, and wound up getting a job wrapping dishes for a Japanese import company and enrolling in night school at New York University for a master's degree in architecture. Two years later, in 1936, he turned down an offer by his employer to go to Japan and learn to be a china designer. Instead, he took his first professional job, as a designer-draftsman for a small architectural firm in New York. It was a decision that probably saved him from being conscripted into the Japanese army a few years later. After a year in his first job, his employer ran out of work and joined the ranks of firms closed down by bad times. But Yamasaki was talented enough to be hired by one of the few architectural firms in New York with work. It was Shreve, Lamb, and Harmon, architects of the Empire State Building.

On December 5, 1941, Yamasaki married a nisei who was a Juilliard piano student. Two days later, Pearl Harbor was attacked, and Yamasaki, with good reason, thought he would be in serious trouble as a man of Japanese descent. A member of his draft board, in fact, accused him of knowing about the attack in advance—why else would he have gotten married just two days before? Among the projects he had worked on for the Shreve firm were defense buildings for the government. With the United States at war with Japan, Yamasaki was investigated carefully, but any worries about security risks were apparently outweighed by the need for his skills. With his employer's help, Yamasaki was permitted to continue to work on defense projects, and was put in charge of constructing a number of buildings at a huge $50 million naval station at Lake Seneca, New York, that, like every other war-related construction, had to be done in record time.

In the very same months in 1942 when my father was rushing to build the first Oak Ridge plant in Tennessee, Minoru Yamasaki was driving hard to finish ten buildings at the Sampson Naval Training Station in upstate New York. But the feeling of being watched was always there. One Sunday, Yamasaki and his wife, Teruko, were taking a walk at a beautiful state park called Watkins Glen when a practice air-raid alarm sounded and they were herded with everyone else into a shelter. They noticed a woman staring at them intently, and when the drill was over she ran out to a policeman, who came up to them and said, with some embarrassment, "I know you wouldn't be in this public area if you were, but that woman insists that I find out whether or not you're spies." Yamasaki showed his War Department identification.

Back in New York, Yamasaki had his share of incidents that reminded him of the racial attitudes he grew up with in Seattle. He worked on an apartment project complex for three years, only to be told by the rental agent when they were finished that he couldn't rent one. A man on the subway asked him one day, "What are you, Chinese or Jap?" Yamasaki was on his way to Columbia University to take a voluntary class in how to build air-raid shelters.

Later in the war, worked slowed at the Shreve firm, and Yamasaki was furloughed. But he wasn't out of work for long. He was recommended to Wallace Harrison, the chief architect of Rockefeller Center, to do a rendering for a large house that his firm, Harrison, Fouilhoux and Abramovitz, had been hired to design. Yamasaki had long admired Harrison's work—besides Rockefeller Center, he had designed the United Nations Secretariat—and, hoping to impress him, Yamasaki spent a week on the rendering, rather than the day or two he would normally put in. Harrison was so impressed that he offered Yamasaki a job with a substantial raise over what he had been earning, and a week later handed him a Christmas bonus of twenty-five dollars and a glass of straight Scotch. After his second drink, Yamasaki boldly asked Harrison if he could buy *him* a drink, and the two of them repaired to the Mayan Room in Rockefeller Center. Drunk and ecstatic at his sudden good fortune, Yamasaki smiled and greeted everyone who boarded his bus, and barely managed the block-long walk from his stop and the three-flight climb to his apartment. He opened the door, shouted, "Merry Christmas, everyone!" and then promptly crawled under the piano and fell asleep.

At the end of the war, Yamasaki moved to Detroit as the chief of design for an architectural firm, and four years later he and two other members of the firm, George Hellmuth and Joseph Leinweber, left to form a bi-city partnership, in Detroit and St. Louis. Yamasaki ran the Detroit office and spent the next few years designing schools, houses, urban development plans, and some corporate buildings. He was a great admirer and disciple of Ludwig Mies van der Rohe, the German-born Chicago architect who coined the term "less is more" to describe the philosophy he embraced in projects that became icons of contemporary architecture: from the Barcelona Pavilion at the 1928–29 World's Fair to the Seagram Building in New York, whose unbroken height of bronze and glass rose on Park Avenue in 1958. Mies was a minimalist in every way. He refused to engage in idle conversation, and was even less fond of public speaking. Invited once to be the main speaker at a dedication of one of his buildings in Detroit, he followed the mayor, members of the City Council, and then the developer to the podium. He smiled, said, "The many speakers have said everything, so I have nothing to add," and sat down. He received a standing ovation.

Yamasaki combined van der Rohe's influence with his own notions of grace. His buildings were notable for their lightness, as if he had jewelry in mind when he drew them. "When people go into good buildings, there should be serenity and delight," he once said. During a month-long visit to Japan in 1955, in preparation for designing the American consulate in Kobe, Yamasaki was captivated by the concept of the *tokonoma*, an alcove that is a spiritual and artistic focal point of a Japanese home and is often adorned with flowers, pieces of art, and religious objects. Coming home to Michigan, Yamasaki built a *tokonoma* in his own house, and he and his wife put a vase and a collection of Japanese dolls in it. As his workload expanded, he was in great need of the tranquility with which he sought to imbue his buildings.

Yamasaki was consumed with his work, even when he slept. He recalled once getting out of bed at three in the morning and sketching the new concept for a group of towers in California that he had just seen in his dreams. There were ups and downs in his career: His Lambert–St. Louis airport terminal in 1956 was a trendsetter, but the Pruitt-Igoe housing project in the same city a year before—a project that was lauded in the architectural world and which made Yamasaki's reputation—turned out to be such a functional failure that it was eventually imploded, as were hundreds of others around the country modeled after it. Yamasaki's intensity ultimately brought on ulcers that became so severe that they nearly killed him. He spent a long period in the hospital and then in convalescence.

In the late 1950s, Yamasaki stepped back and reappraised his work. He decided that many of his projects were "shallow imitations" of the designs of Mies van der Rohe. He spent a lot of time in Europe and the Far East, especially India, looking for inspiration for a new direction in his work, away from modern minimalism and toward a new style that conveyed softness and aesthetics. He also wanted to move away from large urban projects. "As I grow older in life I find that it is really best to concentrate on a smaller area," he said at the time. Other areas of his life were also contracting. In 1961 he and his wife of twenty years, Teruko, divorced. (Yamasaki later married and divorced twice more, and eventually remarried Teruko.) His firm divorced, too, with the St. Louis office splitting off and becoming Hellmuth, Obata + Kassabaum. That agency would move to Kansas City and go on to become the second largest architectural firm in the world, perhaps best known for the revolution in classic retro baseball parks it created around the country in the 1990s. Yamasaki, meanwhile, stayed in Detroit and formed

Yamasaki & Associates, which began attracting many young and talented architects who helped him pursue his new direction in design.

In 1959, Yamasaki won the second of his three First Honor Awards from the American Institute of Architects for his design of the McGregor Memorial Conference Center on the campus of Wayne State University in Detroit. It was a simple two-story building but for a dramatic atrium with a huge skylight and fine landscaping including a reflecting pool with sculptured islands. Yamasaki said he was concerned with "what happens to a human being as he goes from space to space" and that he sought to give the visitor "the delight of change and surprise." Some critics, though, thought the building looked like a cake.

Others, including some fellow architects, considered his work too delicate—"dainty," in the words of one—with its preoccupation with adornments such as pools and courts, plants, canopies, colonnades, domes, and other flourishes that pleased his aesthetic senses. But Yamasaki was impatient with the idea that the human drive for inner peace couldn't be reflected even in major urban architecture. "There are a very few influential architects who sincerely believe that all buildings must be 'strong,'" he once said, words that would one day feel uncomfortable to read. "The word 'strong' in this context seems to connote 'powerful'—that is, each building should be a monument to the virility of our society. These architects look with derision upon attempts to build a friendly, more gentle kind of building."

SOON AFTER DECIDING he wanted to build the World Trade Center in 1960, Austin Tobin had assembled three of the most prominent architects in the nation—a "genius committee"—to come up with a basic conceptual plan. They included Wallace Harrison, the architect of Rockefeller Center who had once employed Yamasaki; Gordon Bunshaft of the Skidmore firm, who had designed Lever House, the first innovative skyscraper built in New York after World War II; and Edward Durrell Stone, whose work included the Museum of Modern Art and the U.S. Embassy in New Delhi, India. They were heavyweights, to be sure, but Tobin was unimpressed with what they came up with. The biggest problem was that it was impossible to design this project by committee—especially when the committee was composed of such accomplished and strong-minded men, each with his own idea of what the World Trade Center should be.

In the summer of 1962, Guy Tozzoli turned his deputy, Richard Sullivan, and his chief of planning and construction, Malcolm Levy, into a search committee. "I said, 'I want you to find me a great architect—one great architect,'" Tozzoli told me. "And I told them that when they recommended someone to me I hoped it would be someone who would live more than twenty years, because this project was going to take that long."

Minoru Yamasaki hadn't designed a single high-rise building. He worked in a small office in a Midwestern suburb. But Sullivan included him on the list of forty or so significant architects to whom he wrote asking if they were interested in the project. The letter offered the most basic details—the location and size of the site, the office space requirements, and the estimated cost of the plan. When Yamasaki read that the Trade Center was expected to cost $280,000,000, he thought it was a mistake—Sullivan must have inadvertently added an extra zero. He considered a $280 million project much too big an undertaking for his office, whose staff numbered fifty-five people, a virtual boutique compared with the major firms.

Intrigued, Yamasaki's colleagues insisted he call Sullivan. No, Sullivan told him, there was no mistake. It's a $280-million project—nearly twice that if you count the trains and tubes. Yamasaki said he appreciated being considered but that his office wasn't equipped to handle it—the Port Authority needed a firm with several hundred people, not several dozen. Sullivan said it didn't matter and asked Yamasaki if he would at least come to New York for an interview. Yamasaki figured it would be a waste of time, but flew to New York and met with Sullivan and Levy, and later with Tozzoli and Tobin. They told Yamasaki that they were searching for a chief architect—one right person. How many people he had working for him was irrelevant. Whomever was chosen could augment his staff with a design group of architects and engineers from around the country. This stirred Yamasaki's blood indeed.

Tozzoli studied Yamasaki's work and listened to him explain his philosophy. He and others on the Port Authority staff especially liked Yamasaki's McGregor Conference Center in Detroit, with its skylight-illuminated atrium and unique sense of both interior and exterior space. They were also impressed with his willingness to set himself apart from the architectural mainstream, which was holding onto Mies van der Rohe's "international style" as a Holy Grail. Yamasaki was bored with the architectural uniform of the day, all flat glass and no texture. Contemporary building design, he felt, literally needed a facelift. Many in his field considered Yamasaki a sellout—a "kitsch monger," in the words of one detractor—for supposedly abandoning his principles in favor of making some kind of personal artistic statement.

All of this was so much professional sniping to Tozzoli. He liked Yamasaki and his work, and thought he might be the architect they were looking for. After all, if you wanted something unexpected, you had to look beyond the faces in the first row. "There wasn't a major architect in the world that we didn't speak to," Tozzoli recalled. Among those who submitted ideas were Philip Johnson and I. M. Pei. "And I kept coming back to Yamasaki." But Tozzoli figured he'd better hedge his bets: He'd give Yamasaki some help. "I was competing against all the other people who were developing buildings around us in New York City," he said. "We're going to have ten or twelve million square feet of space, and I have to fill it or I get fired."

He decided to team Yamasaki up with Emery Roth and Sons, a venerable New York firm that had built more office buildings after the war than any other architectural agency. Roth was considered tops in the field for designing buildings that made the best use of space. In late August, Tobin called Yamasaki to say that he was going to recommend to the board of commissioners of the Port Authority that he be named the chief architect of the World Trade Center. The board's approval, of course, was a rubber stamp. In Michigan, Yamasaki's office erupted in glorious celebration. His desire to work on smaller projects was now officially over.

The Port Authority gave Yamasaki its basic order: We need twelve million square feet of floor area and accommodations for the Hudson tubes and subway connections. We have sixteen acres and $500 million. Yamasaki flew to New York to see what he had to work with, and to feel it. He walked the fourteen-square-block site from Vesey Street south to Liberty Street, from Church Street over to West Street. He walked for days, looking at every street and every building, breathing in the fumes of the traffic that choked the narrow streets. To his eye, it was one big blight, a community of dilapidated old buildings housing businesses that could be relocated "without much anguish." He concluded that—from an architectural point of view—there was not a single building worth saving. "Let me go home and do my models," he told Tozzoli.

Back in Michigan, Yamasaki's first task was to consider what to do with all those streets and all that traffic. Lower Manhattan was a network of narrow passageways originally designed for horse and carriage. He wanted to get rid of them and turn the entire site into one "super block." That, of course, was much easier said than done. An architect's bright idea can be everyone else's bad headache—especially in New York, where construction bureaucracy is a blood sport. "De-mapping" streets would mean months of nego-

tiation with the city for the Port Authority. But to Yamasaki, it was necessary. To come up with a unified plan, he needed a clean canvas.

The earlier concept by the Skidmore firm envisioned one medium–sized
office tower and everything else long and low. But from the beginning,
Yamasaki was thinking tall. With the square footage the Port Authority
wanted, he believed the only way to build was up. And one tower almost
certainly wouldn't do it, unless you wanted the top to be in the strato-
sphere—something he considered briefly with a model of a single 150–story
tower. On principle, Yamasaki believed strongly that in a city such as New
York, tall buildings had to be separated by short ones, and that there needed
to be enough ground space, free of traffic, so that the people who worked in
these buildings could go outside and not feel overrun by them—so that even
in downtown New York, a person could find serenity. In the Trade Center,
Yamasaki saw a great opportunity to create a large open space in one of the
most congested urban areas on the planet—and still provide an enormous
amount of floor space. To him, it was architectural nirvana. All he needed to
do was make the buildings tall enough. He felt that in Manhattan it didn't
really matter how high you went up. What counted more was how the scale
of the buildings felt at ground level.

To test this premise, Yamasaki headed uptown and spent days studying
the queen of the skyscrapers, the Empire State Building. He walked around
it over and over, looking at it from different points and angles, taking in the
spatial sensations. He concluded that people feel as comfortable standing
next to an eighty-story building as a forty-story one—and if the bases of the
towers he had in mind had an open feeling, the issue would be diminished
that much more. In his office in Michigan, there was some skepticism about
Yamasaki's idea to go straight up, rather than to take advantage of all that
prime Manhattan real estate to construct a group of stunning lower buildings, sacrificing, of course, the open plaza concept that was central to
Yamasaki's conception. "A couple of them went to stand next to and walk
around the Empire State Building, as I had," Yamasaki later wrote. "They
came back convinced, as I was, that there was no diminution of the soul, no
antlike feelings in the face of such a large object. Man had made it and could
comprehend it . . . There was a wish and a need to be able to stand back
from it, to see and comprehend its height." That's what Yamasaki wanted to
do with the Trade Center.

So how many buildings, and how big should they be? Yamasaki considered every idea that popped into his or anyone else's head. His staff built
models of all of them, nearly a hundred all together. He experimented with

shapes and sizes and numbers. He tried three towers, then four. But that started to make the Trade Center look like a housing complex—frighteningly so, in light of Yama's Pruitt-Igoe debacle. Eventually, he decided on a pair of towers, each about eighty stories high, with a few low buildings and a large open plaza with sculptures, a reflecting pool, and places for people to sit. The plaza would be at the towers' mezzanine level, overlooking the main concourse and its restaurants and stores.

The only problem was that even 160 floors would fall two million square feet short of the twelve million the Port Authority wanted. And going any higher would mean adding more elevators to accommodate the increased traffic. And that meant less floor space. The generally accepted principal was that the loss of floor space became a critical economic issue after the eightieth floor. And there was some thought given to whether tenants would even want to rent offices so high up. The views would be spectacular, but it would turn their trip from the street to their desks into a second commute. Not to mention the fear factor.

Yamasaki wasn't the only one thinking about the people who would one day occupy these buildings. While he was imagining the World Trade Center, the Port Authority was already selling space in it. In fact, the question of who the tenants would be had been a preoccupation since the earliest days of the project, which was conceived on the premise that New York needed a central place to facilitate world trade. That meant that the tenants had to be *engaged* in world trade. In fact, the legislation authorizing the development and construction of the Trade Center required that at least 75 percent of the tenants had to be involved in international trade.

The first to be recruited, and the first to lease space, was an obvious one: the U.S. Customs Service, whose nearby Customs House headquarters was a landmark—designed by Cass Gilbert (of Supreme Court and Woolworth Building fame) and built in 1907—but woefully inadequate for the needs of the modern Customs Service. But getting Customs was easy, and not a very good indication of the market. The problem for Tozzoli was that private companies, the real targets, were not lining up to rent space in what so far had been a largely hypothetical building complex. Between the political jockeying, the legal battles, and the fact that there was not even an illustration of the Trade Center to look at, a lot of people were not convinced the thing would ever be built. Tozzoli was well aware that upon its opening in 1931, the Empire State Building was a virtual ghost town—80 percent vacant, one of its financiers on the eightieth floor, thirty-nine stories from his nearest neighbor, and New Yorkers ridiculing it as the Empty State Building.

Tozzoli needed a hook, and he found one in a comment by a colleague named Lee Jaffe that he had never forgotten. Jaffe, a former newspaper reporter, was a pioneer in her field, one of the early government public relations officers. Austin Tobin had hired her in 1944 to improve the Port Authority's public image, and she had since become one of his closest staff members. She was an astute promoter of the Port Authority's interests, and her high status at such a powerful agency made her perhaps the most influential publicist in the city. In 1960, when the Port was first considering the Downtown Association's entreaty to build the Trade Center, Jaffe had written an internal memo in which she had said, almost in passing, that if the Port was going to build a great project, it should build the world's tallest building. That sentence had stuck in Tozzoli's mind. Now, three years later, and getting nervous about filling all that space, he decided that Jaffe was absolutely right. If anything would make the Trade Center more marketable, it was offering companies the chance to do business from what would instantly become one of the world's most famous addresses. So the paradoxical solution to filling two huge buildings, Tozzoli concluded, was to make them even bigger. Tobin was more than amenable to raising the stature of the Trade Center to epic proportions. As far as the cost was concerned, to Tobin the sky was not the limit. The Port Authority had money piling up from its airports, tunnels, bridges, and other enterprises, and rather than leave it sitting on the shelf to tempt the politicians to grab it for mass transit, why not combine it with the usual PA bonds to crown his tenure with a monument that even Bob Moses would envy?

Tozzoli flew out to Detroit twice a month to see how Yamasaki was coming, and on one of these trips, Yamasaki showed him his first sketch of the Twin Towers. Tozzoli thought it was beautiful, but asked if it fulfilled the floor-space requirements. Yamasaki told him that was the only problem: It was two million square feet short. He would have to figure out a way to put that space in another building. Tozzoli was confused: Why didn't Yamasaki simply make the towers taller? Yamasaki told him that he'd reached the limit, that going any higher would be trouble.

"Yama," Tozzoli said with his ready smile, "President Kennedy is going to put a man on the moon. I want you to build me the tallest buildings in the world."

Elevators opened the door to skyscrapers toward the end of the nineteenth century, and a century later they were limiting them. If the towers of the World Trade Center were going to be more than a hundred floors high—which they would have to be to surpass the Empire State Building—Yamasaki and his colleagues had to conceive a new elevator system. For a while, this became the most pressing preoccupation at Yamasaki & Associates, at Emery Roth and Sons, and at the Port of New York Authority. And it made Austin Tobin nervous—not just about the elevators but about the engineering complications that seemed to be surfacing around every phase of the project. He already knew that excavating the site for the foundation was going to be massively complicated. At one time, these sixteen acres had been part of the Hudson River. And somehow they were going to have to excavate without interrupting the train lines that ran right through the site.

The person he had in charge, Guy Tozzoli, though a man who knew how to solve problems and get big things done, was certainly a bit out of his element. He had never supervised the development and construction of a high-rise building, let alone one that was being conceived as a landmark for the ages. So Tobin decided to give him a safety net: an advisory committee of seven experts in real estate, banking, and construction. Tozzoli would meet with them monthly, and they would offer their opinions and guidance. Tozzoli, no fan of committees, was naturally wary. But he had no choice. And maybe these people could help.

The solution to the height problem turned out to be in the very analogy that illustrated one of the problems: that forcing tenants to take elevators to the ninetieth or hundredth floor, or beyond, was like adding another leg to their commute to work. One day, a Port Authority architect named Herb Tessler came to Mal Levy with an idea: designing the elevator system like the subways. "Say you take the Eighth Avenue, and you want to go to Fiftieth Street," he told Levy and then Tozzoli. "Well, you go from 125th Street to 59th Street, then you get off and cross the platform to another train that takes you to the local stop." Tessler's notion was to divide each tower into zones, and to have express and local elevators. The elevators would be huge, the biggest ever made, capable indeed of holding as many people as a subway car. The twelve local elevators would be fed at two express levels—"sky lobbies," as these transfer points would later be called. And twelve elevators didn't have to mean twelve space-taking shafts. With three zones, they could share four shafts. That would eliminate the problem of losing too much rentable floor space in the service of building to the sky.

Tozzoli thought Tessler's inspiration might very well be the great idea that would make Lee Jaffe's suggestion feasible. But, of course, he had to see if it could be done. He called Otis Elevators, the pioneering concern that had sparked the skyscraper revolution in the first place. The company responded enthusiastically. Its engineers had no doubt they could make it work. If the buildings were 110 stories—which would make the World Trade Center the new World's Tallest Building by eight stories and a hundred feet—sky lobbies could be located on floors 44 and 78. When they ran the numbers through their room-sized computers, the engineers found that the plan was a winner. It would leave 75 percent of the total floor area available for renting, rather than the 50 percent that would have come with a conventional elevator system—and even at that it would provide *more* elevators than was necessary to carry the 50,000 people who might work in or visit the towers each day. And there was a bonus: Not only could the Otis people engineer the express elevators to hold fifty-five people and 10,000 pounds, but they could design them so that there were doors on both sides, allowing the first passenger in to be the first out. That would be another first in a building that was starting to become full of them.

But to Tozzoli's dismay, when he presented the idea to the advisory committee, the experts were unanimously against it. They were sure that people would not accept the notion of subway-like transfers on elevators. They told Tozzoli and Levy that the second and third zones would be nearly impossible to rent.

Levy was shaken when the meeting ended, but Tozzoli told him, "They're wrong." What if they're right? Levy asked. "Then we'll have an empty tower."

Of course, getting the idea past Austin Tobin was now more complicated than it had been an hour before. Tozzoli went up to Tobin's office and informed him that "your committee" had shot down a great idea that was going to allow them to erect a building for the ages. He explained how Otis was prepared to design and install a revolutionary elevator system, with high-speed express cars that could carry big crowds of people from the lobby to the 110th floor in under a minute. He told him the great news that the computers showed that the building would actually be "over-elevatored"—a fine thing, Tozzoli said, because "people hate to wait." With 104 passenger elevators, including 23 of the mammoth express "shuttle" cars, in each tower, the Trade Center would have what amounted to its own subway line. Tozzoli told Tobin, "We have to do this. If we're going to build something great, we have to take a risk."

Tobin weighed Tozzoli's pitch against the committee's nay-saying, and decided to give him the green light. Yamasaki could now proceed to figure out how to build the world's tallest building, times two.

Since his commission by the Port Authority, he had gotten some practice, designing the first two high-rises of his career, a headquarters for

Michigan Consolidated Gas Company in Detroit and the IBM Building in his hometown of Seattle. On the latter project, which he designed after getting the Trade Center commission, he worked with a Seattle engineering partnership called Worthington, Skilling, Helle and Jackson. When the Port Authority put out a call to engineering firms interested in the job of carrying out Yamasaki's design plans for the World Trade Center, the Seattle engineers were one of eight firms asked to submit proposals. The others were large New York firms, all of which had worked on many high-rise buildings. The Seattle firm's tallest was twenty-two stories. But what it had, aside from the priceless benefit of being favored by Yamasaki, was John Skilling, a partner "who had that wonderful rolling tongue of salesmanship," in the words of one of the up-and-coming engineers on his staff, Leslie Robertson.

Skilling assigned Robertson to help him prepare a proposal and took him to New York when he presented it to the Port Authority's board. Skilling kept the presentation simple, so simple that it belied all the work that had gone into it. He used a large drawing pad and a marker to explain the work his firm had done with Yamasaki on the IBM Building, and how its key elements might be incorporated into the architect's design for the Trade Center. Both called for heavy structural steel on the perimeter, and half as much glass as was common in the skyscrapers that were starting to sprout up around Manhattan and across the country. But there was more than form, and even more than function, at play in Yamasaki's leap to tall buildings. When it came to skyscrapers, his abandonment of the International Style was personal: The architect who was designing the tallest buildings on earth was afraid of heights.

When he stood in front of a glass wall from any kind of height in one of the newer skyscrapers, Yamasaki became weak in the knees, overwhelmed by the sensation that he could fall right out. In the IBM Building, he and Skilling's firm had designed exterior walls made of closely spaced steel pipes. Yamasaki felt secure looking out from this building, no matter how high he was. He applied the same concept to his design for the World Trade Center, calling for windows that went floor to ceiling but were spaced at shoulder-width—Yamasaki's shoulders, which were narrow as a schoolboy's. This would give even someone with acrophobia something solid to look out through, even lean on, without fear. It was not false security: Unlike virtually every other tall building of the twentieth century, the World Trade Center would draw its strength largely from its outer walls.

The earliest skyscrapers were designed with a lot of caution and even more steel. Their structural support, jungles of riveted beams and columns, made them extremely strong, if not very conducive to dividing up into appealing spaces. The Empire State Building, for instance, is dense with steel framing, and inside it tends to feel like a catacomb. Such older buildings were said to be of "curtain-wall" construction because their exterior walls didn't do much more than keep the rain out and people in. All the structural support was inside. By the 1960s, skyscraper design had evolved into what became known as "tube structure," in which the load was shared by heavy steel exterior columns and a central core made of some combination of steel and concrete. This central tube provided both structural support and a place to put elevators, stairwells, and bathrooms. These newer buildings were less expensive to put up because they required less of everything: Modern structural steel was stronger, so a building could do with less of it. Less steel meant less riveting, bolting, and on-site welding. The expensive and dangerous labor of on-site ironwork could be reduced in favor of more efficient and cost-effective off-site prefabrication. And because the tube construction shifted more of the load to the exterior walls, making them something more than skin, it reduced the need for interior support columns, freeing up more useable space for tenants. The result of all this was a boom in the construction of high-rise buildings in New York during the Sixties and Seventies.

When John Skilling and his young associate, Leslie Robertson, studied Yamasaki's conception for the World Trade Center in 1963, the engineer's challenge was clear to them. They had to come up with a way to help Yamasaki meet the Port Authority's prodigious floor-space requirements while making the building strong enough, particularly to withstand the high winds that whipped off New York Harbor. By virtue of their work together on the IBM Building, Skilling had a clear advantage over the other engineering firms being considered. In fact, once Yamasaki was selected, it was virtually a foregone conclusion that the Skilling engineers would be among the first people he would want on the team he was told he could assemble. He told Skilling something that an engineer never hears from an architect: "I want your structure to be part of my architecture."

The job went to Robertson, then thirty-four, the son of an underachieving inventer from California. Robertson had dropped out of high school and joined the Navy at sixteen, eventually returning home and going to college at Berkeley. He turned the training he'd received in electronics in the service into an early career designing electrical systems for factories. Then he advanced to structural engineering and spent some time designing offshore oil-drilling rigs before returning to the West Coast and joining the Skilling firm in 1958. "Then John Skilling, almost beyond belief, was willing to entrust the design for the World Trade Center to me, when no one in their right mind would entrust a thirty-four-year-old engineer with it." Not to mention a thirty-four-year-old who had no degree in engineering, structural or otherwise. Robertson had gotten a bachelor's degree in science and everything else was on-the-job training.

Robertson worked up a tube structure not unlike the conventional designs of the time in concept, but which pushed the envelope, with even more of the load on the exterior walls. If some buildings had a curtain wall, the Trade Center's would be an iron curtain. Where supporting columns in most buildings were spaced fifteen or even thirty feet apart, the Trade Center's fourteen-inch perimeter columns would be less than four feet apart. And where the exterior columns in most skyscrapers were concealed behind glass or concrete facades, like underwear, the Trade Center towers' structural steel would *be* their facade, though dressed smartly in stainless steel, or if that turned out to be too pricey, in Alcoa aluminum. There were two reasons the outer walls had to provide most of the towers' strength. First, they had to compensate for the unique elevator system. In tube constructions, the elevator core took on a large percentage of the building's load-bearing function. But here, the clever and critical express-and-local elevator system was designed specifically to save space by *eliminating* shafts that spanned the entire height of the building. So the buildings would have to draw strength elsewhere—from the outside walls. The second reason for the heavy exterior was a version of the first: Besides compensating for the loss of support in the elevator core, it had to take up the slack created by another feature designed to maximize the amount of rentable floor space. A flooring system without columns.

The unusual number of load-bearing columns on the 208-foot exterior walls was almost a throwback a hundred years to the earliest use of steel over wood in heavy construction. Those 1880s-era buildings, the forebears of the first skyscrapers that came twenty years later, were held up by cast iron closely packed around the perimeter. But if the Trade Center's outer limits were from bygone times, the insides were as modern as color TV. With floor panels reinforced by prefabricated trusses, the floors spanned up to sixty feet without support from interior columns. It was as if the tower were made up of 110 cigar boxes stacked on top of one another. Employing a design that virtually eliminated interior columns, Yamasaki and Robertson gave Tozzoli and the Port Authority something that no other developer could offer prospective tenants: on every one of the 220 floors, the largest stretches of unobstructed office space in Manhattan.

All this was done, of course, behind the thick walls of the Port Authority offices on Eighth Avenue, Yamasaki's scale model kept tightly under wraps. The last public display of the proposed Trade Center had been the comparatively conventional Skidmore design for the east side four years and thousands of newspaper articles earlier. So it was that on January 18, 1964, a throng of officials including Austin Tobin, Governors Rockefeller and Hughes, and Mayor Wagner, and a serene-looking Minoru Yamasaki, stood before a model of gargantuan proportions and made the stunning announcement that by the end of the decade the Empire State Building would lose its crown. Upon the graveyard of World Happiness Products and Heins and Bolet Electric Appliances & Radio-TV, Nussbaum's Liquors, Johnny the Chef's, and Cantor the Cabinet King, would rise the tallest buildings on earth.

12

400 MILLION POUNDS OF STEEL

THE 1,350-FOOT OBLONG boxes already dubbed the Twin Towers were unveiled in the form of a gleaming model that Wilt Chamberlain would have had to crane his neck to see. Eight feet tall and set on a platform, they reached for the ceiling of the ballroom of the New York Hilton as politicians and reporters peered up in awe. Minoru Yamasaki assured everyone that even the acrophobic had nothing to worry about. "People are not afraid of height when the width of the window is not much more than that of their shoulders," explained Yama, whose own shoulders came up to about the tenth floor of the models. He left unsaid that he could attest to this personally.

There was other important news that day—President Johnson meeting with Martin Luther King, Jr., about the civil rights bill about to reach Congress and the Federal Trade Commission proposing that a health warning from the Surgeon General be required on every cigarette box and advertisement—but the lead story in the *New York Times* the next morning was the stunning news that BIGGEST BUILDINGS IN WORLD TO RISE AT TRADE CENTER. The photo of the model next to the story left no doubt: It could barely fit above the fold. The coverage was enthusiastic and admiring—as was most reporting on the Port Authority in those days—if a little oblivious. Little noted was that some people found the towers as appealing as a pair of sore thumbs. The objections weren't on aesthetic grounds; not yet anyway. They were about money.

There were protests outside the announcement by a few dozen diehard downtown business owners and their families who were determined to go kicking and screaming. GOV ROCKEFELLER DO YOU WANT MY DADDY TO LOSE

HIS JOB? asked a sign carried by a young boy and girl, the children of Radio Row. Austin Tobin told the press that of course the Port Authority was concerned about these folks, and would do everything it could to help them. But it really wasn't them he was concerned about. These powerless people soon had some powerful allies. For the first time in its four-decade history, the Port Authority was being challenged by a potent segment of the New York business community: the leading players in the commercial real estate industry who saw the world's biggest buildings as their world's biggest threat. They could cause a lot of trouble for Tobin.

They contended that the Trade Center was four times too big for the market and nothing but an ego trip for Tobin. They dismissed the possibility that the Port Authority, a bridge-and-tunnel outfit, could find enough importer-exporters to fill two Pan Am Buildings worth of space. "And when they find they can't, they're going to dump the space on the open market at reduced rents," complained a jittery Harold Uris, whose company was one of the city's most prolific developers of office buildings. Real estate men like Uris feared—no, they were terrified—that the Twin Towers would puncture the entire market for office space in Manhattan. And they had the wherewithal to throw yet another roadblock in front of this long-suffering project.

The opponents, savvy enough to realize they weren't going to stop the project altogether, formed a group called the Committee for a Reasonable World Trade Center, with the more moderate goal of knocking it down a few dozen stories so it was just another high-rise in a city of them. Perhaps it was no coincidence that the Reasonable committee's leader was Lawrence Wien, the managing partner of the syndicate that owned the Empire State Building. Tobin couldn't resist the easy dig at Wien's self-interest, if not his manhood. "Wien is causing all this commotion because he doesn't want his building to be the third tallest in the city," Tobin told R. W. Apple of the *Times*.

But Wien wasn't the only one causing the commotion. He was joined by his partner in the Empire State Building, Harry Helmsley, along with several other heavyweight developers, including Laurence Tisch and Harold Uris, all of whom would lose tenants to the Trade Center. But these were shrewd men who knew there were few things more galling to the public than the spectacle of megamillionaires whining about not making enough money. To give their protest some credence, they had to deflect the attention to a notion some might find nearly as irksome: the heavy-handed Port Authority, a powerful, tax-exempt public agency, going into the commercial real-estate business. As much of a stretch of credulity it would be, they had to portray themselves as David to the PA's Goliath. And Goliath came in the person of Austin Tobin.

The Reasonable committee presented the amusingly incongruous image of rich and powerful men, the ultimate insiders, playing the role of gadflies. They didn't bother lobbying Governor Rockefeller, who had just capped his long support of his brother's concept by announcing that the state would lease two million square feet of space in the Trade Center—nearly half of one tower—to centralize the downstate offices of some forty state agencies. Instead, they did an end-around to City Hall. Robert Wagner had appointed a Mayor's Coordinating Committee on the Trade Center, and the developers hoped to convince a majority of its sixteen members that the Port Authority was about to drive New York City into economic disaster. And that the only way to avert such a catastrophe was for the city to step in and use the one weapon at its disposal—its power to withhold approval of the Port Authority's plan to eliminate four streets that cut through the site of the Trade Center—to force Tobin to scale back the project.

At one point, Guy Tozzoli met with Helmsley and Wien and asked, "Can you please tell me what a 'reasonable' World Trade Center is?"

"A hundred floors high," Helmsley said.

"A hundred floors high when the Empire State Building is a hundred-and-two floors," Tozzoli said.

If you counted its 222-foot television antenna, the Empire State Building would still be champion, 122 feet taller than the Twin Towers. But that would require some kind of asterisk in the Guinness record book. Besides, the Trade Center would eventually have its own antenna.

It wasn't surprising that Helmsley and Wien really cared about the World's Tallest crown. They had a lot of ego and a lot of money wrapped up in the honor. "They were really concerned with losing their income from the observation deck," Tozzoli recalled. "I told them I was going to put an observation deck on one building and I was going to put a restaurant-club on the other. And I said to them, 'I don't know what you're all excited about. You're in Mid Manhattan. I'm going to have a bunch of different customers from you. Yours are up where all the hotels are. It's like two different cities.'"

Wien and Helmsley were not the least bit soothed. To make their case to the public, they hired Robert Kopple, a lawyer of local repute. Kopple was pugnacious even by New York standards. He delighted in taunting Tobin in the press. He referred to the Trade Center as "this bloated project—these Tobin Towers" and objected even to the Port Authority's plans to move its own offices into the Trade Center. To which Tobin, lunging for the bait, replied: "We'll have our offices anywhere we damned well please!" Proving that New York was just a big small town, Kopple was the originator of the idea for the World's Fair that was about to open. He'd been forced out when Robert Moses took over.

Moses supported the Trade Center, even if it was the only major public project in memory that didn't have his name on it. Also lining up behind the Trade Center, apparently not sharing in the panic of their peers, were the top executives of two of the most prominent real-estate concerns in the city, Tishman Realty & Construction and Rudin Management. (Tishman's support wasn't surprising. It was one of four high-rise contractors the PA had hired to advise on preliminary construction issues.) Meanwhile, many brokers—eyeing the big commissions that would be generated by a major turnover among tenants—thought the Trade Center was just what the city needed. So, of course, did my brethren in the construction industry. What we had here was a slight case of civil war in the New York City real estate industry.

As the politics of business and the business of politics played out, people unburdened by self-interest judged the Trade Center somewhat more objectively. When Ada Louise Huxtable, the esteemed *Times* architecture critic, looked the models over at the announcement at the Hilton, she was jubilant. Taking note of the protesters outside, she wrote, "What they were picketing may turn out to be New York's dominating landmark. . . . Seen from any angle, they would overshadow all of Manhattan's celebrated skyscrapers and become the new focus of the city's famous skyline. The controversial elements of the scheme are human, not architectural. From the design aspect this is not only the biggest but the best new building project that New York has seen in a long time. It represents a level of taste and thought that has been distressingly rare in the city's mass of nondescript postwar commercial construction."

As the image of the towers sank into public consciousness, they began to imbue New York with a feeling of anticipation, as if the big city had suddenly come upon a way to get even bigger. It was said that the towers would afford a forty-five-mile panoramic view from a quarter-mile up in the sky— which PA publicist Lee Jaffe pointed out was twenty miles farther than the view from the observation level of Larry Wien's Empire State Building. On a clear day you might not be able to see forever, but you could see all the way down to Trenton. The opponents groused. Why would anyone in New York want to see Trenton?

✳   ✳

BY 1965, THE World Trade Center project was beginning its sixth year of ges-
tation—eighth if you counted the two when David Rockefeller's Downtown
Association was planting the seeds. Radio Row was on Death Row, but for
now all those little electronics stores and other mom-and-pop shops were
still in business, and there wasn't a backhoe or bulldozer in sight. But the
project finally was in full swing, at least as far as it could be from behind
desks and in front of drafting tables. Tozzoli was working on acquiring prop-
erties, trolling for tenants, and preparing to put out the first bid calls for
work that would eventually require the material and services of some forty-
seven "principal contractors" and more than two hundred secondary ones.
Yamasaki and Skilling and their staffs were refining the architectural plans
and resolving engineering issues, which were relentless. The PA's own engineers were trying to figure out what to do about soil that was more conducive to sifting for archeological treasures than for digging a foundation for
the world's tallest buildings. The finance department was doling out the proceeds of the first $75-million bond sale, mostly for professional and admin-
istrative costs and land acquisition, and readying the next one.

And Austin Tobin was on the phone. He was politicking, assuring everyone that the Trade Center was *not* bloated, that it would *not* be half-empty,
that it would *not* wreak havoc on the real estate market. Tobin made it clear
that he had no intention of scaling it back, and so far, Mayor Wagner was
holding firm, giving no indication that the Reasonable committee was sway-
ing him. But by now that didn't mean much: Wagner was a lame duck, having decided not to run for a fourth term. Tobin would have to start over with
the next mayor—either Democratic City Comptroller Abe Beame or
Republican Congressman John Lindsay (the Conservative Party candidate,
William F. Buckley, would almost certainly be back to full-time commentat-
ing after the election). Tobin betrayed no worry, but behind his public
resolve was an uncharacteristically apprehensive Port Authority, an agency
unaccustomed to having to convince anybody of anything. It was hard to
say who was working under more pressure: the Trade Center's design and
engineering team or those on Tozzoli's staff charged with finding prospective tenants and signing them up. The biggest lease so far, the state's two million feet, hardly counted. It was considered a gimme from the governor, like
a wealthy dad writing a check for the down payment on his newlywed daughter's house. The second-biggest was the Port Authority itself. What the PA
needed was a steady stream of commitments from good-sized private companies somehow engaged in foreign trade.

The PA's PR could have done without the announcement later in the

202 | Karl Koch III

year that the estimated cost of the project was now $525 million, up from $350 million. The earlier figure was only for construction, the Port explained, and didn't include the costs of land acquisition, architecture and engineering fees, administration, or financing. For that matter, it was no help to the credibility of the Port Authority or the project that so many different figures had been quoted over the past couple of years that it was impossible for even someone following the developments closely to figure out how much the Trade Center was really going to cost. The only thing that was clear was that this was a project destined for delays worse than any to be found on Tobin's bridges. The first major bid calls, for demolition, excavation, foundation work, and structural steel, were to go out late in 1965. Then it was the spring of 1966. Politics would push it back once more.

In November, New York City elected John V. Lindsay, a dashing, liberal Republican whose freshness and iconoclasm—*John V. Lindsay is Supercalifragilisticexpialidocious* was his campaign theme—catapulted him to victory in an overwhelmingly Democratic city that had become tired and tarnished, in the dumps over white flight and urban blight. Lindsay offered renewal. But if Tobin thought this meant clear sailing for a project that offered nothing if not renewal, he was wrong. Lindsay was as staunch an advocate for the disadvantaged as there was in the Republican Party, and he was inheriting what an aide called "an almost bankrupt metropolis facing almost incurable problems." In the World Trade Center, he saw a project for the *advantaged* whose dividends needed to be shared uptown. Mayor Wagner's agreement on payments in lieu of taxes was only informal, and now all bets were off. The negotiations started the week Lindsay took office in January of 1966. Tobin offered the city $4 million a year. Lindsay wanted $27 million.

The talks went on futilely for seven months, even as the Port Authority was writing checks for millions of dollars on a weekly basis to buy up the plots of land that made up the sixteen acres in question. From his new office just a stroll away at City Hall, Lindsay found the Trade Center the first stubborn issue of his administration. He didn't want to stop the project—he had no objections to it in principle and it was too far along anyway—but he was more than willing to use his power to deny street closings as a cudgel to get a better deal for the city than Wagner had.

Meanwhile, Larry Wien and his Committee for a Reasonable World Trade Center were still very much in the picture. They, too, had renewed their lobbying when City Hall changed hands, and their lawyer and chief *antagoniste* Robert Kopple kept up his public relations campaign. Trying to compensate for the traditional gentle treatment of the Port Authority in the news columns, they reached into their deep pockets for what to them was practically spare change to run full-page ads in the *Times*. They found a few friends on the City Council, who realized that after six years of planning, negotiation, and litigation, after more than $60 million had been spent and the project was edging ever closer to fruition, there had never been a single public hearing on it. Such was the autonomy of the Port of New York Authority. So the Council called a public hearing, and invited Austin Tobin to be the star witness. It was May, and once again the bid calls would be delayed, at least until summer. Until the city and the Port agreed on a price, the vital permits to close streets, move utility lines, and bring in the cranes and derricks, for Tobin, the keys to the kingdom would stay locked in a drawer in some office in City Hall.

Tobin sat in the City Council chamber, which was packed with competitors out for blood and politicians hoping to land a few blows themselves, and assumed a combative stance that suggested he was itching for a fight himself. He offered his litany of reasons why the Trade Center was a good thing, a great thing, for New York: The city's position as the world's greatest trading center was threatened as never before by competition from other developing ports, he said, and now it was vital to act dramatically to create a "central marketplace" with the latest equipment to expedite foreign trade. With about two hundred members of construction unions picketing outside in support of the Trade Center, and the president of the Building and Construction Trades Council, Peter Brennan, waiting to speak for labor inside, Tobin said that the Trade Center would provide construction jobs for as many as eight thousand workmen earning $200 million over the life of the project, followed by employment for 50,000 in the completed towers. To the accusation that the Port Authority was some kind of "super government" virtually unaccountable to the city or state, Tobin clenched his fists and angrily pointed out that the legislatures and governors of both New York and New Jersey had authorized the Trade Center, and that Mayor Wagner had worked closely on the plans with the PA.

Now it was Larry Wien's turn. The World Trade Center, he said, was nothing more than a private real estate venture cloaked in the disguise of public interest. Yes, the city and state were supporting it, but all that proved was that Tobin was a powerful man and a good salesman. To date, Wien said, the Port Authority had commitments for only a quarter of the ten million square feet of space in the towers, and the PA itself, and the State of New York, its virtual partner, accounted for most of it. That meant that space would have to be rented "to practically anyone," whether or not they were involved in foreign trade. And if that were the case, what was the point? There was plenty of space available all over the city. Those involved in foreign trade didn't need these towers.

The hearing did little but give the two sides the chance to continue the longest running argument in New York since the question of who was the better centerfielder, Mantle or Mays. Things deteriorated from there. In July, Lindsay's seven-member negotiating team, frustrated by the deadlocked negotiations over the in-lieu-of-taxes payments, refused to grant the PA a permit to install some telephone cables at the site. It was a message, of course, and Tobin sent one right back: He refused to continue negotiations until he got the permit. And the city replied to his reply that the permit wouldn't be granted until Tobin resumed talks and softened his position. It got worse: Lindsay and Tobin argued in the press over whether Lindsay had given his personal assurance that the permit would be granted. "Austin Tobin must have misinterpreted what I said to him," Lindsay said at a news conference. "I've done everything in my power to reach agreement with them. Austin wants to build first and reach agreement later. Of course, if we were willing to give away Manhattan, they could start digging up the city any time. The door is open, wide open. The conference table is sitting there. All Austin has to do is come in and sit down."

Two weeks later, the two men were seen smiling broadly and shaking hands on the front page of every paper in town.

A deal had been made, but only after Lindsay and Tobin stepped out of the picture for a moment. Lindsay's top deputy, Robert Price, had accepted an offer by an old friend, George Shapiro, a lawyer who had once been counsel to Governor Thomas E. Dewey, to talk to Rosaleen Skehan, the Port Authority's general counsel. The two lawyers met quietly for days and hammered out a deal that called for the PA to make an annual payment to the city equal to the taxes that would be paid by a private developer, but only on the percentage of the buildings leased to private tenants. The PA projected that in the first year private tenants would account for only 40 percent of the leased space, the rest being federal and state agencies. That would make the payment about $6.2 million—much closer to Tobin's number than Lindsay's. But there was more for the city in the deal than that. The Port Authority agreed to make $146 million worth of improvements around the city, including some at the Trade Center that would have otherwise been the city's responsibility. And in the most creative and far-reaching part of the deal, the two sides agreed to a brilliant solution to a question PA engineers had been puzzling over.

Having concluded that the only way to safely anchor the towers in the mushy earth of Lower Manhattan was to dig a seventy-foot-deep hole and reach all the way to bedrock, the Port Authority had to figure out what to do with all that dirt. The solution: Give it to the city. They would actually create new land on Manhattan Island, twenty-eight acres of it, by trucking the excavated material to the site of a group of abandoned Hudson River piers just a couple of blocks away. The city could then sell the land to developers—appraisers figured it could be worth up to $90 million—and middle-income housing could be built. It was an inspired idea for both the city and the Port Authority, and it made perfect sense: the site was a landfill to begin with. Years later, after the excavators had built a perfect rectangle on the banks of the Hudson, an ambitious development called Battery Park City would sprout from the soil that once occupied the hole in the ground that became the basement of the World Trade Center.

DEWEY DIDN'T DEFEAT Truman but Dewey's lawyer defeated the opposition to the World Trade Center. The deal George Shapiro did with the Port Authority on the city's behalf ended, for all intents and purposes, the long battle over the Twin Towers. Wien's group and some last holdouts from Radio Row would hang on to watch for missteps and offer commentary every time a new cost overrun was announced. But the coveted city permits were Tobin's deliverance. Within days, the Port Authority began taking bids on more than $100 million worth of construction work. The first contract awarded was the only one that was never in doubt—for the work that was making this project what it was. Otis Elevator Company would be paid $35 million—the largest contract in the history of the elevator industry—to design, manufacture, and install 46 of the largest high-speed elevator cars ever built, plus 162 standard cars, and 49 high-speed escalators, half to serve the PATH rail service.

Earlier in the year, the PA had added two new levels of management to the project. First, Tozzoli brought in the agency's best on-site engineer, Ray Monti, to be construction manager. Monti had been the number two engineer on the expansion of the Port Authority bus terminal in 1959, and was most recently in charge of constructing a 120-foot-high heliport, the PA's exhibit for the World's Fair. Meanwhile, Tishman Realty & Construction, one of the four firms the Authority had hired to serve on its construction advisory committee (the others were the venerable Fuller, Turner, and Diesel companies) was promoted from the group to "consultant-contractor." Officially, the firm, headed by David Tishman and his son John, was given a sixteen-month contract for $250,000 to review bid documents before they went out and to advise the PA on cost estimates, construction timetables, and material-delivery schedules. But in fact, it was the prelude to something much bigger. Tozzoli planned to keep the management of the major contracts in-house, but eventually he wanted to have a general contractor to supervise the hundreds of specialized companies that would be streaming through the project down the line.

By the end of August, Tozzoli, Mal Levy, Ray Monti, and John Tishman were busy reviewing proposals for all the key early work: Demolition, the inevitable flattening of Radio Row. Excavation, a massive job that would be shared by five companies. And construction of the basement wall, a 3,100-foot enclosure as complicated as any part of the project. And then, the last bid taken in this first round: the steelwork. Erection was still a couple of years away, but in terms of labor, material, and logistics, no other piece of the construction was in greater need of planning. In fact, the process had begun two years earlier, in the spring of 1964, soon after the Twin Towers were introduced to the public.

Erecting the World Trade Center meant putting up more steel than went into the Golden Gate Bridge. More than the brand-new Verrazano Narrows, the world's longest suspension bridge, a two-mile span built with 135,000 tons of steel. And the Trade Center would use triple the amount used in the steel-heavy Empire State Building. But it wasn't just a big job; it was a hugely complicated one. This wouldn't just be an order for 190,000 tons of standard beams and columns and a few thousand kegs of bolts, to be connected and fastened like hundreds of buildings before. In his design, Yamasaki had married the architectural to the structural. So the job called for steel of dozens of different shapes, sizes, weights, strengths, and fabrication requirements. The exterior columns were made of high-strength structural steel and prefabricated welded plates. They would sit atop four-story columns that looked like tuning forks. The floors would be trusses, corrugated steel decks serving as the form for the concrete floor and the ducts to carry power and telephone lines. From the ninth floor to the roof there would be 32,000 tons of steel for 101 stories of core columns and box beams. All told, there would be twelve different kinds of steel, each with a different strength rating. All this was the result of an architect's vision and an engineer's innovation. It was a fabricator's nightmare.

To Tobin and Tozzoli and their construction team, the choice for steel was as obvious as the selection of Otis for the elevator contract. For the biggest steel job in history, they needed the biggest steel company. Or at the very least, the second biggest. It was either United States Steel's American Bridge division or Bethlehem Steel. So focused on the two companies was Tobin that he told Tozzoli to bring them in, give them an early look at the plans, and ask for preliminary prices. Don't even bother with anyone else. It was understood that since these weren't the final plans, and erection was still three years away at least, the companies would not be giving their official bids, only hard estimates that would help the Port Authority's budget planning. Since it was, to Tobin, a foregone conclusion that one of the two companies would get the steel contract, he saw no problem in departing from the customary bidding procedure and establishing an early and ongoing relationship with them. In fact, he later told his board of commissioners, given the size and nature of the job, it would have been "inappropriate" to put the steel contract up for bid in the usual way.

That summer, U.S. Steel and Bethlehem came in with their "estimates for budget purposes." The numbers were remarkably close: Bethlehem said it could furnish, fabricate, deliver, and erect the steel for $438 a ton—about $81 million for the whole job. U.S. Steel came in only $10 a ton higher, about $83 million. Based on these estimates—which were apparently solid enough that both companies drew up draft contracts—Tozzoli's construction consultants projected the total steel expense at $81.7 million, slightly more than Bethlehem's low bid. The companies included the caveat that there could be increases in labor and material costs by the time the contracts were actually signed, but agreed to cap them, so that their official bids would be no more than $20 a ton higher than these estimates. So even if the cap were reached, the cost would be at most $3 million over the amount budgeted, significant money but not disastrous for a project exceeding half a billion dollars.

Now it was a year and a half later, early in 1966. Negotiations on the in-lieu-of-taxes payments were underway with the new mayor, and as soon as a deal was struck, demolition would be underway and the countdown to construction would begin. The Tishman company had just been named consultant-contractor, and John Tishman's first major task was to get the steel bids in and the contract settled so there would be ample time for whichever company was selected to gear up. The Skilling engineers had detailed the job, and when they were finished, the bid set—the final plans and specifications the companies would use to calculate their proposals—weighed in at more than six hundred pounds. But there was really nothing new in them. The tonnage of steel and difficulty of the work were the same as when the companies submitted their preliminary numbers two years earlier. And PA staff engineers and construction experts had worked closely with the steel companies in these two years to keep the escalations to a minimum. So Tozzoli expected no surprises. This would be more or less a formality, a rare uncomplicated moment in the long prenatal life of the World Trade Center—to Tozzoli, the payoff of a standard bit of Port Authority savvy and foresight.

And then Tozzoli heard something very strange that made him very nervous. It was August. The final proposals were due in a few weeks. "And all of a sudden in a meeting with U.S. Steel, they tell me, 'The job is so big, why don't you give us each a tower?' I said, 'I don't understand, you've been talking to me for three years. Now you're telling me the job is too big, maybe we should split it up?" Tozzoli definitely did not like the sound of that. He had a feeling he knew what it meant. The next day he was flying to California to try to persuade Kaiser Steel to put in a bid. But the nation's third-largest steel company wasn't interested.

The sealed proposals from U.S. Steel and Bethlehem arrived in the Port Authority office on Wednesday, August 17, 1966. The envelopes sat on a table in the room Tozzoli used to display the model of the Trade Center. All his main people were there: Mal Levy and Ray Monti and John Tishman. Everyone present except the boss. Tobin was upstairs in his office. He told Tozzoli to call him when he had his steel contractor.

Tozzoli opened the envelope from Bethlehem, the original low bidder. He looked for a familiar number, something around $80 million. The one he saw drained the blood from his face. *$119 million.* "I slit the second envelope open," Tozzoli said. "We are in deep shit."

U.S. Steel's bid was $122 million. The prices didn't just break the supposed 20 percent escalation cap, which was never guaranteed in writing. They shattered them. The bids were nearly half again higher than the original estimates. The four men sat in stunned silence, as silent and despairing as the eight-foot model of the Twin Towers staring down at them. The towers that at that instant were in actual danger of never being built. When the man from Bethlehem called and asked when they could start negotiations, Tozzoli told him not to hold his breath.

Exactly what Austin Tobin thought at the moment Tozzoli told him the numbers is impossible to know, but it's safe to assume that it was something along the lines of: *The sons of bitches fucked us.*

Tobin, enraged, could not believe that the steel companies had the gall to submit such bloated prices, without any warning, after working with his people so closely for two full years. And waiting to do it until the project was already under way. Even as the bids were being opened, buildings were being demolished and utility wires were being dug up downtown, Tobin could come to only one conclusion: They had played him. And it was impossible not to suspect that they had played him *together.* What else could explain it? Their original estimates were within a couple of percentage points of each other. That could happen, especially in an industry like steel that was dominated by a couple of giants. Then they both kept in close touch with the PA in the intervening two years, each acting as if they were already on the job. And now they both submitted inflated bids, both without warning, and with almost identically calibrated escalations. Bethlehem's bid was a $38 million increase over its original estimate. U.S. Steel's was $39 million higher. Both were 47 percent jumps over their first prices.

The bids seemed to help explain the cryptic remark Tozzoli heard in the weeks before they were delivered. *The job is too big for us. Maybe we should split it up.* "I knew what that meant," Tozzoli recalled. But even now, thirty-six years later, all he was willing to do was leave the implication hanging. Was it collusion? "I didn't say that. There's no way I would say that." But somebody did say something to the Justice Department, whose antitrust division went on to investigate whether the companies had engaged in price-fixing or any other "restrictive business practices." The investigation would pass from the Johnson to the Nixon administration, and no charges would ever be brought. But on the face of the circumstances, coincidence seems implausible. It would mean that after coming up with very close initial prices, both companies had determined, independently, that the job was more costly than they'd thought and that their original estimates were too low. It would mean that their reconsideration somehow yielded the exact same percentage increase. It would mean that both decided on their own not to give the Port Authority a head's up.

Perhaps Tobin had been naive in essentially announcing to the two companies back in 1964, "Gentlemen, we are going to forego the usual bidding procedures because you are the big boys, and we need you. So congratulations, you have no competition other than yourselves." And then trusting them to go home to Pennsylvania and spend the next two years not talking to each other—not seeing a golden opportunity to hustle the most powerful public works agency in the United States. Perhaps the best evidence of a setup was the passing comment whispered in Tozzoli's ear at the eleventh hour that, lo and behold, the job was just too big, even for them. *So why don't we split it up? We can each take a tower. What's their bid? Hey, how about that, almost the same as ours! We can just split the difference.* And the PA would have no choice because, after all, who but U.S. Steel and Bethlehem Steel could erect the World Trade Center? If they didn't do the job, the job wasn't getting done. It was not an unheard-of attitude in this industry.

If this was indeed the scenario, the steel companies made a miscalculation of their own. They underestimated the resolve and resourcefulness of the Port Authority. And they certainly underestimated the wrath of Austin Tobin.

A HEAVINESS HUNG over the emergency meeting Tobin called of the Port Authority Board of Commissioners. Tobin and his staff were on the defensive, having to explain to an angry and incredulous board how they could have gotten the agency in so terrible a jam that it could scuttle the entire project. With the Committee for a Reasonable World Trade Center taking out ads in the *Times* every time a cost overrun was disclosed—and sometimes when it was just a rumor floating around—the thought of admitting a $38 million blunder was unbearable to everyone in the room. Tobin and Tozzoli and everyone connected with them were in a hole so deep they needed excavation equipment to climb out of it.

To Tobin, the only good thing about this meeting was that nobody outside the room—in other words, the press and the Trade Center's opponents—would hear about it. All government bodies had a measure of privacy when it came to sensitive matters such as pending contracts, and the Port Authority's unique status allowed it more freedom than most to conduct its business largely out of public view and scrutiny. But that also meant that the commissioners didn't have to observe the usual decorum. They could get as angry as they wanted. And they were very angry.

First, Tobin had to explain his unconventional handling of the steel contract. He chose his words carefully, almost stammering to get them out. "The usual bidding procedure would be inappropriate for this work," he said in lawyerly fashion, "because of the work's complexity and the necessity of continuing interchange of information between the prospective contractors and the Port Authority." Then Tozzoli had to assure the commissioners that this was not just the tip of the iceberg. "Tozzoli, how do we know that your estimate for the whole project isn't all screwed up?" is how he sums up his recollection of the meeting.

"They were really upset," recalled John Tishman. "They were very concerned about the buildings really being too large. They were ready to redesign the project, or even abandon it."

But Tobin and his people were not about to let that happen. Shutting down the project was out of the question. Accepting the steel companies' per-ton prices and scaling back the towers was unacceptable. Negotiating with them would be fruitless; they were too far apart. Worst of all was the specter of conceding defeat to Wien's group. The stature of the Port Authority might never recover.

Tozzoli had an idea. He'd actually thought of it even before he and his team left the model room the day the bids were opened. He had turned to the mock-up of the Trade Center and said to Levy, Monti, and Tishman, "How many pieces of steel in those towers?" Nobody knew. "We knew how many tons," Tozzoli recalled, "but individual pieces, who the hell knew? And I thought of when I was young and my father bought me an erector set. It had a bunch of pieces in a box. And I could build anything I wanted. I could build a bridge, I could build a building. I said to Mal and Ray and John, 'Maybe we have to divide it up and go to small contractors. Small people who can afford to do the fabrication and ship it off.' "

Tobin thought it might work. It was a perfect 180-degree turn from his original idea, that only the big companies could build the Trade Center, but it was painful to think about how that had turned out. And what was the alternative? When the Port Authority commissioners asked what Tobin and his staff proposed to do about the debacle, Tobin asked Tozzoli to explain his idea. The commissioners were skeptical. It seemed counterintuitive that you'd get a better price by breaking up the job into who-knew-how-many little pieces. And how long would it take to get all the bids in, maybe dozens of them, before they would know whether the gamble had paid off? For that matter, where would the raw steel come from, if not the big rolling mills in Pennsylvania?

The commissioners wanted to know what John Tishman thought. He knew more than anyone in the room about subcontractors, and that's why they'd hired him. He told them he was confident they could pull it off with small contractors. "I didn't know that we could," Tishman admitted sheepishly years later, "but I swore we could."

✖   ✖

GIVEN THE GREEN LIGHT, Tobin's people attacked their mission with a sense of purpose that electrified the usually staid, quietly efficient Port Authority offices. A certain arrogance, a sense of invincibility, was almost part of the genetic makeup of the Port Authority, and if there was ever a time it needed to draw on its strength, this was it.

Led by John Tishman and Leslie Robertson, the Port Authority staff scrambled to break down the fabrication of these 400 million pounds of steel—the heart, bone, and muscle of the Twin Towers—into logical components, and then to match each package to a specialized shop. It would mean hiring a dozen or more contractors, all of them needing close supervision by a battalion of expeditors and inspectors, and devising a schedule and delivery system that somehow kept the entire enterprise from disintegrating into chaos. It was hard to imagine that only forty-eight hours earlier, it had been considered one of the few certainties of this project that all this work would be handled rather painlessly by a single, giant company.

The Port Authority group was out to rescue the World Trade Center, of course, and to save their own necks. But in the process, Tobin didn't mind at all demonstrating his contempt for the two big steel companies. Tozzoli let it be known in the industry that the Port Authority was slicing up the steelwork of the Trade Center—and that it would take no bids from U.S. Steel and Bethlehem. There was a bit of vengeance involved, but the more practical reason for freezing them out was to ensure that they didn't cause any further trouble by scaring off the smaller companies into whose hands the PA was now placing the destiny of the World Trade Center.

Over the five-year course of the construction, the Port Authority wouldn't have to leave the city to find the vast majority of its major contractors. But when it came to the steel, this would be America's job, and the world's. PA men fanned out across the country, plans in hand, to Pittsburgh, Houston, St. Louis, Los Angeles, and Seattle; to Lynchburg, Virginia, and Plainfield, New Jersey; to Granite City, Illinois. There was one package for the base plates, another for the steel that would be erected below street level, six stories down to bedrock. There were three packages for the exterior steel, two for the modular-floor system, one for the elevator shafts. A dozen packages in all, each to be completed in a different corner of the United States and then shipped by rail to a central receiving point across the Hudson in New Jersey. All told, more than 200,000 separate pieces of steel.

By the fall, the PA had invited bids from nearly thirty contractors. Some of them declined, suspecting, ironically, that the New York port agency wanted only to use them as pawns in an elaborate chess game with Bethlehem and U.S. Steel. They thought the entire process was a ruse to try to drive the big companies' prices back down. In fact, the opposite was true. Just as earlier it had openly and straightforwardly gone directly to the big companies and closed the door on everyone else, now the Port Authority was doing the same thing in reverse. "People thought we weren't doing this for real, that we were just fooling around," Tozzoli said. "I had to put a letter out there to everybody—'This is to advise you that U.S. Steel and Bethlehem cannot bid on these projects.' Tobin had the guts to let me burn that bridge, because there was no other way."

The bids started coming in, and they were reasonable enough to suggest that Tozzoli's idea might actually work. For the exterior bearing walls, the heavy welded columns and cross panels called spandrels that would fit together to form the main structural support of the towers, a low bid was received from Pacific Car & Foundry—a Seattle company that had started out making Pullman cars in the early 1900s and later manufactured everything from winches to Sherman tanks. The company would fabricate 5,828 of these units and ship them across the country by rail. At 55,000 tons and $21 million, this contract accounted for more than a quarter of the steel.

The floor trusses, the other crucial component of the design that would allow the building to go up without interior support columns, would be furnished by Laclede Steel Company of St. Louis, a truss specialist. From Pittsburgh would come the giant "trees" from which the exterior wall panels would grow, starting at the 9th floor and going all the way up to the 110th. The trees might look simple once they were delivered, but you couldn't tell that to the shop men at Pittsburgh–Des Moines Steel who had to assemble, blast clean, paint, and then weld together 152 units that had a variety of widths and grades of carbon, alloy and high-strength steels—a $3.2 million contract. When all the dozen contracts for fabricating and erecting the steel were ultimately added up, the tally would be $85.4 million—$33 million less than Bethlehem's bid and $37 million less than U.S. Steel's. And not much higher than what both companies had offered as their original prices two years earlier.

All the steel shops were responsible for acquiring their own raw steel, with the Port Authority sending out inspectors to their plants to approve the material before it was fabricated. They found it not only in the United States but in Britain and Japan. Pacific Car & Foundry, the exterior-wall fabricator, bought most of its steel, a fifth of the material for the entire project, from Yawata Iron and Steel, Japan's largest steel maker,.

IT IS A supreme irony to me that it was the business tactics of the big steel companies—the sort of big-footed, heavy-handed domination of the industry that drove my father to distraction and which he complained about for years—that wound up giving us the biggest erecting job in the history of the steel industry, only to hasten the dismantling of our company as a family enterprise.

Like most New Yorkers, we had followed the grinding development of the World Trade Center project for years. But unlike many in the city's construction industry, we had only a spectator's interest. The unsurprising word going around was that the Port Authority was already working with the big steel companies, and since the PA didn't have to follow the same public bidding procedures as the state or city governments, that was that. Not that this was a problem for us. Even if a general call had gone out for bids, we wouldn't have moved on it. This job—if you could call erecting nearly 200,000 tons of steel a *job*—was just too big for us, and, anyway, it wasn't really our province. The closest thing to the Trade Center ever erected by the Koch Company was the New Yorker Hotel, minuscule in comparison and built decades before. We had erected a handful of thirty- and forty-story buildings during the early years of New York's high-rise building boom of the Sixties. But we had generally avoided that work because it was too competitive, and if we happened to come in as the low bidder on a job, it usually meant our profit would be slim. We had found bridge repair a less crowded and more lucrative field. For one thing, the Big Two never touched that market. We made it our niche and did about 80 percent of the bridge repair work around New York in the Fifties and Sixties.

So when my brother Donald told me that night in the solarium at Columbia-Presbyterian Hospital that we were bidding on the World Trade Center, I was flabbergasted. The thought of us taking on such a project, with my father out of the picture and my uncles Bob and Jerome running the show, scared me. Yet it also stirred me. Whatever traits we didn't have in common, Bob and I did seem to share the gene that has to do with pride and ambition. "Wow, the Trade Center," I said. "Man, what a job. I didn't think Bob had the balls."

I asked Donald for some details. All I knew was that by weight it would easily be the biggest steel job in history. I had seen pictures of the model in the newspaper and had a sense of its unusual design from stories I had read in the *Engineering News-Record*, the weekly magazine for the construction industry. But what kind of steel would go into the job? Where was it coming from? Who was doing the fabricating? What was the timetable? What kind of manpower would we need? What kind of equipment?

Donald couldn't tell me much. "Bob and Jerome are burying all the information," he said. All he knew was that Bethlehem and U.S. Steel had the job, and now they didn't. Austin Tobin was said to be on a warpath and the Port Authority was divvying up the job to a slew of fabricators, and one erector. Amazingly, the two steel giants had been reduced to minor subcontractors, supplying raw steel to three of the smaller fabricators who were receiving Port Authority contracts instead of them.

"Who else is figuring the erection?" I asked. "Any of the fabricators?"

"I heard Dreier estimated the job," Donald said.

"That's not his kind of a job."

"I also heard that Beasley's bidding the job." They were erectors whose work was cutting-edge—I saw pictures of one of their jobs once that took my breath away—but they worked mainly in the west so rarely competed with us.

"What's our price?" I asked.

"Twenty million dollars."

I gave a long, low whistle. I had no idea if it was a lot or a little for this job. It just sounded like an ungodly amount of money for a little pea-shooter like us. "That's a lot of dough," I said.

From what Donald had managed to pull out of Bob and Jerome, they were figuring on three years of work and setting our labor and overhead cost at $12 million, with another $3 million for equipment. "They're not too clear about the remaining five million," Donald said. "I don't think they really know, but right now they're calling it profit. They seem to be leaving as wide a margin for error as they can. If the job overrun is a million or more, the company can still make a few million dollars."

"That's a hell of a way to figure a job," I said.

"Yeah, I know," said Donald, shaking his head. "Bob's like a cat on a hot tin roof. He's all over the place. He's out on the jobs; he's in the office. One day he wants this job; the next day he doesn't."

"What does Dad think about it?"

"I told him about it, but he's pretty sick and he's letting Bob run the show. If he was in any shape, he'd blow the whistle on it."

"How are things in the office?"

"I try to stay out of there. They make me feel like I was hired to sweep the floors. I'm better off out in the field."

Donald's real strength was his business acumen, but he couldn't stand the antagonism our uncles had for anything associated with our father. Even with Dad no longer in control, it only seemed to be getting worse. Or maybe that was actually the reason. After all these years, Bob and Jerome were flexing their muscles. Donald was an easygoing sort, and the coldness and the secrecy about the Trade Center really affected him. I urged him to get back into the office to keep an eye on things for us, but he didn't have the stomach for it. "Out in the field I'm my own boss and I don't have to put up with all the office bullshit—everybody talking behind closed doors, keeping me away from the bidding. To find out anything, I have to go to Bob and make a pain in the ass out of myself. You know, they don't want us around. Besides, right now I'm taking the deck off the Willis Avenue Bridge."

The next day the nurse wheeled me back down to the solarium. It was 180 degrees of windows, and looking south from 165th Street you had an unobstructed view of the entire borough of Manhattan, all the way down to Wall Street. One day, I thought, that skyline will be different. The World Trade Center will be standing there, the tallest buildings in the world. And if our bid is accepted, our family will build them. It was still an almost incomprehensible thought, that our little company, experienced and accomplished as it was, would be given the assignment of erecting these buildings that would be icons. And it was an uneasy thought. Minoru Yamasaki and Leslie Robertson had designed these twin buildings to reach the sky and stand tall and strong. But what about our company? With our foundation crumbling beneath us, we were already shaky at the core. Could we build these towers without toppling over ourselves?

Now more than at any moment since I'd been struck down by a ton of steel at the Korvette's patio shop eighteen months earlier, I felt an urgency to get back to work. I had to get out of that hospital and into the office in the Bronx that still contained my father's big, oak desk. I knew it was a critical moment, and I had to return a modicum of his presence to the company he built.

But things were moving more quickly on the Trade Center's skeleton than on mine. Before I could get out of the hospital, Donald was back with more news: We were low bidder.

13

KANGAROOS

CASANOVA STREET IN the South Bronx was in a neighborhood so chock full of steel businesses that old-timers called it Little Pittsburgh. The area sat at the bank of the Harlem River, block after block of small, mostly family-owned outfits: iron dealers, light structural steel suppliers, crane-rental companies, machine shops, and fabricators of everything from stair-ways to storefronts, all of it coexisting with the remnants of another era. When my father took my sister Marie and me to the office with him on Saturdays when we were young, we would sit in the front office and watch the goats walk by. As late as the Sixties, the neighbors across the street were a horse-feed and hay business and a pickle man.

My father bought the building at 362 Casanova Street just before the war, and it became a second home, a place that drew our extended family together like a net, whether we liked it or not. The building was divided into thirds, with offices and a small shop flanking a large garage where trucks stayed the night. The four offices on the left side of the building were laid out like a railroad flat, three of them open on one side to a narrow wain-scoted corridor. In the front office was the secretary and receptionist, Ed Walters, the only one in the company who carried an attaché case to and from work. It was for his lunch. The next office belonged to Elsie Breur, the long-time bookkeeper and my father's most fiercely loyal employee. Then came Jerome, the general administrator who took care of everything except bidding. The last and largest office, though not by much, was my father's. It was the only one in the building with total privacy.

My father's office, the scene of all those early-evening meetings, was filled with heavy, one-of-a-kind furniture. There was his big oak desk with its serious leather chair. Prominently displayed on the desk were the three famous see-hear-speak-no-evil monkeys. Donald and I used to guess who they represented. One whole wall was covered with blown-up photos of past jobs and letters of commendation, including the Henry Stimson "Thank you for keeping the secret" telegram. Along the near wall was an eight-foot-long conference table with bulky, hand-carved legs and a thick green glass top. And in the corner was a massive table made of three pieces of polished gray granite. During the lean years of the Depression, when he did small jobs and sometimes accepted payment in goods or services, Dad had erected a crane runway for a tombstone manufacturer. For part of his fee, he asked the owner to make him a granite table. The top was about the size of a family plot marker and its two legs were clearly headstones. Everyone wondered whether the table was an investment of sorts, but nobody dared ask.

By the fall of 1966, my father's office had been unoccupied for over a year, his working days clearly over. Bob rightly might have claimed the office, but he left it as it was, not out of respect, I strongly suspect, so much as a visceral aversion to that room. Though he was now for all practical purposes the chief executive of the company, Bob seemed satisfied camped out in the large room on the other side of the building, the engineering office where Rudy Loffredo had his desk and I had mine.

It was sad to me that my father's office was so still and drained of life at the very time when the building seemed as if it had suddenly become the center of the steel universe. It was here that we began mobilizing for the construction of the World Trade Center, preparing for a technical, logistical, and financial challenge unimaginable only a few months earlier. For me, there was the added burden of trying to hobble back to full-time work after two years of only sporadic appearances. But with all that was going on, I didn't have the luxury of easing into it.

I walked into the office on crutches my first day back after being released from my latest hospital stay in December. Rudy greeted me warmly. Bob and Jerome acted as if I were coming back from lunch. They were working on receivables at Jerome's desk when I came in to say hello. They raised their heads and looked at me for a second, then turned back to each other.

"I take that as a welcome, boys," I said.

"Oh, hi, Karl, sorry," Jerome said. "We're trying to collect money here."

Back in the engineering office, Rudy jumped up and got a chair to elevate my foot, and I claimed a desk across from the drafting table and tried to catch up to the quickened pace of life in the old office. The Port Authority's acceptance of our low bid had begun an arduous procedure, first to establish that we were competent and financially capable of the job at hand, and then to try to get us to make our low bid even lower. Banker's Trust, among others, offered a letter attesting to our long and favorable relationship over thirty-five years, stating that the company was "known and respected throughout the industry," and that it was pleased to reserve credit of up to a million dollars for this project. Satisfying the Port Authority that the Koch Company could do the job was easy. To my surprise and alarm, though, so, too, was Bob and Jerome's acceptance of the conditions the PA set down. Much too easy.

As Donald had told me, my uncles were not forthcoming with information. We didn't know much at all about our bid other than that it was four times our previous record, the $5 million renovation of the Manhattan Bridge six years earlier. And that was a bridge—we knew bridges. The Trade Center was much bigger than anything we had ever done, and we were so in the dark about how Bob and Rudy had arrived at our price, that it was impossible to tell whether we would make a ton of money on this massive job or lose our shirts. And then, early in 1967, a heavy package arrived from the Port Authority office. The contract.

It landed like an anvil on a table in the engineering office, near Bob's desk. It was thick as the proverbial Manhattan phone book, but nobody seemed very interested in it. I stared at it, wondering what we were getting ourselves into. I knew Bob would give me hell if he saw me with it, so I stayed late one night and went through it. I got home after midnight, unsettled as hell. The contract included provisions we'd never agreed to on any of our jobs, and excluded a crucial one that we'd never gone without.

Guy Tozzoli was under terrific pressure to make sure that the sum of these dozen steel contracts came nowhere near the $119 million that had been Bethlehem's low bid. That, of course, was the whole point of this exercise. It also seemed clear that to reach that goal and salvage the mess it found itself in, the Port would use the new state of affairs to its advantage. Tobin and Tozzoli and company had demonstrated quite clearly that they weren't afraid to mix it up with Big Steel, so they had not the slightest hesitation about bullying those of us in little steel who would be marshmallows in comparison.

The Port Authority people no doubt thought, not unreasonably, that if they were going to manage this unwieldy, coast-to-coast operation of steel fabrication and erection, they would have to keep tight reins on all these companies. They might have also assumed that we were so thrilled to have this job of a lifetime that we would agree to anything they put in front of us. And in our case, they were right.

Donald had told me in the hospital that Bob had gone back and forth about the Trade Center, wanting the job one day, not wanting it the next. But apparently he had worked things out. From the day I returned to the office, I didn't see a hint of hesitation. With each passing week, Bob became more and more seduced by the idea of leading our company to its greatest glory and making the millions he dreamed of. After all those years of sublimation, stifled by what he considered his big brother's pedestrian ambitions, the first thing Bob Koch found himself presented with as the practical head of the company was the opportunity to build the tallest buildings on earth. It was the answer to his prayers.

Even at that, I was astounded when I pored over the contract that Bob and Jerome had no plans for a lawyer to review it, let alone negotiate. In fact, they seemed to be totally indifferent to it. The contract included penalties for failing to finish certain work by certain dates—requirements whose satisfaction would depend as much on the fabricators' performance as on ours. Missing, meanwhile, was a standard provision to cover escalations in labor costs, something that would have been an automatic deal-breaker for my father.

Our work was always labor-intensive; 80 percent of the money we were paid went toward payroll and benefits. And since our three-year contracts with the ironworkers' locals were negotiated by a group representing all the contractors in the city, we had little control over increases in our labor costs. So our contracts always provided that any increase caused by collective-bargaining agreements would be covered by the building's owner or general contractor. This was *especially* important with the Trade Center contract. Because the project was of such magnitude that excavation and foundation work would take two years, we wouldn't begin the erection until August of 1968. That was only three months before the current union contract expired. The next contract would bind us for another three years, which almost exactly coincided with the time we expected to be building the Trade Center. There was no way to know today how big a raise the union might get.

The contract would leave us holding the bag, but nobody in the office even talked about it, not Bob or Jerome, not Rudy, not even my brother Donald or brother-in-law Jack Daly. I assumed my uncles must have had discussions with the Port Authority before my return to the office, but whatever they talked about, however hard they negotiated, the result was a lousy contract for us. It wasn't like my uncle Bob, who usually embraced the tradition that no contract should be signed before an appropriate period of serious haggling. But in this case, it was as if the deal were a fait accompli the moment we were told we were low bidder, and the contract was just a silly formality. Two 110-story towers, $20 million. Sold to the lowest bidder. Sign right here.

AS IF ERECTING half a mile of tower wasn't ambitious enough, out of nowhere came a second contract, for $2.5 million, to construct and deliver the Trade Center's 5,760 floor sections. Because the corrugated steel floor panels were so essential to the erection, as inextricable a part of the design as the beams and columns, the Port Authority had decided that whomever assembled them had to install them. Tying the work into a package this way was a smart move: The erector and floor assembler couldn't blame each other for delays if they were the same company. This was not another case of being strong-armed by the Port Authority. They told us they wanted us to do the job, asked us how much we wanted, and gave it to us. It would turn out to be the most profitable part of the job for us.

But it also meant that in addition to already having by far the biggest job in the company's history, we were now also in the pre-fab business. We would be assembling two components: thirty- and sixty-foot-long sections of flat corrugated steel from Illinois and cross-braced trusses, with utility ducts and outlet ports built into them, from St. Louis. And then we would deliver them to the site by barge. This meant we had to have a plant. The plant had to be on the water.

Like the erection contract, the floor-panel job was a done deal by the time I got back into action after my accident. The difference was in how long my uncles kept it a secret. Neither Donald nor I learned about it until we started hearing things about looking for waterfront property in Jersey. Now I understood what my brother had meant when he told me about all the mystery, the closed doors, the generally weird and unsettling atmosphere in the office ever since the Trade Center had come up. It was amazing to us the lengths to which they went to exclude us. All because we were our father's sons. The words "World Trade Center," it seemed, symbolized their emancipation.

THE MORNING AFTER I read the erection contract, I walked up to Bob's desk and plopped the document down in front of him. "Bob, are you running this company?" I asked. "Or are you going to let the Port stomp all over us?

If we don't make our points in this contract, they'll wipe us out. I want a joint contract reading with Donald, Rudy, Jerome, and Jack, and I want to hear what you have to say."

"All right, get everybody in here," Bob sneered. "We'll hold your séance right now."

For the next few hours, we went over everything I had marked in red. "How can we not have an escalation clause?" I asked. "If any contract needs one, it's this one."

"They told us to estimate our escalation and build it into our price when we bid," Jerome said. "They wanted our total number, no escalation."

"What did you figure?"

"Five percent."

"What if the union gets ten percent?"

"Over the last ten years they never got more than *three* percent," Rudy Loffredo said. "Wake up, Karl. If anything, we're going to *make* money on the union item."

"What happens if they win a seven-hour day?" I asked.

"Never happen!" Bob said. "I don't even want to discuss your crazy ideas."

"We *have* to talk about it," I said.

"Christ, Karl, we could argue like this all day long. Rudy's right, the union will never get more than a three or four percent increase and they'll never get a seven-hour day."

"How do you know that? Why are you so willing to gamble? I get the feeling the Port Authority has convinced you that we won't get this contract unless we waive escalation."

"That's right!" Bob snapped.

"That's bad business, and you ought to go to the next meeting and tell them we want escalation and we want to strike out this 'Penalty and Incentive' schedule. And how about this bond?" I flipped through the contract, jabbing my index finger at the clauses I had marked in red.

"We're on the hook for twenty million dollars to guarantee our performance?"

Our company's record was so strong that our bonding company, in response to a request from my father, no longer required personal guarantees from the owners of the company. A year earlier, knowing that he was in the process of handing the reins over to Bob, my father had decided that while he trusted Bob, he didn't trust him enough to pledge his own house and fortune if he screwed up. So now it was the *company's* assets, not his or anyone's personal property, that were on the line. It was after he received a letter from the bonding company, stating that personal guarantees were no longer required, that Dad stopped showing up at the office on a regular basis and let Bob have his head in running the company. But it meant that Bob was sitting at the crap table with our entire company on the line—and then some. We were committing to a $20 million bond, an amount that was four times the assets of the company. The bonding company apparently felt we had $15 million worth of experience, reputation, and good moral character.

"This whole conversation is a crock of shit," Bob said finally. "Listen, Karl, you asked for a review, and we reviewed it. We're all in agreement here. Even if we're not, I think this is the best contract we can get, and I think we're going to make a lot of money on this job."

"Come on, Bob," I said. "Let's get a lawyer to read this contract."

"A lawyer?" Bob said. "Hell, a lawyer would never let us sign a contract like this. We all know that." It was one of his favorite lines.

"If we don't sign, we don't do the job," Jerome said. "Don't you realize that any city authority or federal agency writes its contracts like this? Nobody ever enforces these terms. Nobody even thinks about them except some little bald-headed guy in the back room who fills in the blanks. The Port would never insist that they be fulfilled to the letter."

"Jerome," I said. "I can read. If we don't make these schedules, this contract could break us and we can lose our company. This contract states explicitly that we are accepting the responsibility for other contractors and their performance. Doesn't anybody see it? No one in his right mind would accept this kind of responsibility!"

All of this was on top of the fact that the more I thought about it, the more I was worried about our bid. The rumor was that Beasley had put in $30 million, a full 50 percent higher than us. What if that were true? Whoever heard of leaving *ten million dollars* on the table? What if the final bids from Bethlehem and U.S. Steel were actually the right ones? That labor escalation was built into our number meant that our base bid was not $20 million, but nearly a million dollars less. And I saw no contingency in the bid, money to cover the unknowns and to just make us feel better about putting the whole company on the block.

What had seemed at first blush like an ungodly amount of money was now making me wonder if we might be building these 110-story towers at a bargain price. Especially since my uncles never seemed to have the time to sit down with me and explain exactly how they had arrived at that price. The only thing they made clear was that whatever it took, whatever we had to agree to, the Koch Erecting Company was going to build the World Trade Center.

WHAT NONE OF us knew—what I didn't find out until thirty-six years later—was that we were actually in a powerful bargaining position. In fact, it wasn't the Port Authority who had *us* over a barrel. But Guy Tozzoli had the omnipotent aura of the Port Authority, and he was a much better poker player than Bob Koch. He managed to keep us from finding out that we weren't the low bidder. We were the *only* bidder.

I had always assumed that what we'd heard was true, that we were competing with at least one other erector, probably the Beasley people from Dallas, and maybe one other. This perception was based on guesses that became assumptions that became rumors that became perceived reality. Even all these years later, when I asked Tozzoli if he'd gotten bids from Beasley or any other erectors, he said, "Yes, I had estimates from others. You guys gave me the best bid."

It was a conspicuously unspecific answer, but it seemed impolite to cross-examine him, especially since he was just confirming the accepted truth anyway. It was only after I went to see John Tishman that I realized Tozzoli wasn't just being vague.

The bombshell came out casually enough, almost in passing, over lunch with Tishman in his thirtieth-floor office on Fifth Avenue. At seventy-four, still very fit, he was now chairman and chief executive officer of the city's preeminent construction company. He was reminiscing about those crazy few months in 1966, when all hell broke loose on the steel contract and the entire Trade Center project was in serious jeopardy of never being built—without the public even getting a whiff of it. I asked him at one point about our bid, trying to get a sense of whether we had priced ourselves too low.

"We had nothing to compare it to," Tishman said. "You were the only bidder."

It took me a moment to take those words in. With those five words, he took a wrecking ball to a vital piece of my personal history. What it meant was that just as it seemed the Big Steel companies had played the Port Authority, the Port Authority had played *us*. Not that I blame them. I wouldn't have expected them to tell us we had no competition. And, of course, we were ultimately responsible for our bid number, not Guy Tozzoli or John Tishman or anyone else. But it did put a different light on all those onerous contract provisions. And it meant I had to rewrite my perception of some of the most tense times of my life.

I asked Tishman how we came to be the only company in the United States willing to build the World Trade Center. He said that after the door was shut on the Big Two, the Port Authority turned its focus on the second tier: large national and regional companies such as Kaiser Steel in California and the Dallas-based Beasley firm. But none of the out-of-town firms could be persuaded to come to New York and take on such an enormous, and enormously complicated, project. Mostly, they were wary of the unions. The job would require an army of ironworkers and Teamsters, and those guys could be hard enough to handle for local builders who had long-standing relationships with them. There was also the notorious New York City construction bureaucracy. No surprise a company from Texas would decline an invitation to bid this job.

"Everybody was afraid to come into New York," Tishman said. "We were looking for independent steel erectors. You had a marvelous history, and you were very strong with the unions."

"Koch is the oldest union erecting company in the country," I said, proudly adding that my grandfather was a member of Local 35. I recounted my father's story about losing the Empire State Building to the non-union American Bridge Company.

Tishman told me he was the one who had suggested our company be recruited for the Trade Center, another thing I didn't know. "I found you," he said with delight, adding, "it was our idea to break the job out, and find great fabricating shops around the country that would each take a part of the job. And it worked." (I've discovered that when it comes to the World Trade Center—as in, probably, life in general—for every bright idea there are at least two claims of authorship, and the number grows as the years go by. John Skilling and Leslie Robertson argued bitterly after they split into two firms over who was more responsible for the Trade Center's unique engineering scheme, a question that would one day be turned on its head. Tozzoli and Tishman each feels responsible for coming up with the Idea that Saved the World Trade Center, but the moment of conception is long lost. No doubt the historical truth is that they both had a hand in it.)

Once it became clear that no major national erector was going to come to New York, the Trade Center team's pickings were slim. And with demolition already underway at the site, time was short. On his own projects, Tishman always hired Bethlehem or U.S. Steel. So he needed to find an independent erector. But the only major one around New York besides us was Harris Structural Steel, a New Jersey company that was really a bridge shop. They didn't do high-rises. There were a few other contractors—Atlas Steel Erectors, A.J. McNulty, Ermco, and the erection department of Grand Iron Works—but none was a viable contender. Ermco worked cheap but the owner was always fighting both with the union and his customers. McNulty was a good erector, but didn't do a lot of it. And Grand Iron—which was headed by Joe Brown, my aunt Gladys's husband, who had left my father years earlier when he decided there was no future for a brother-in-law in Karl Koch Erecting—was primarily a fabricator that only erected its own work. These were small, unbonded companies, with little to recommend them for such a major undertaking. And even if the Port Authority had asked, it's hard to imagine any of them even considering a job that was too big for U.S. Steel.

That left us. We weren't markedly bigger than the other concerns in town in terms of office space, but we were a company that could be said to have been born to build these towers. And one led by a man fueled by pent-up resentment who thrived on risk.

"We were lucky to find you," said John Tishman.

But back in 1966, they weren't acting so lucky. They were acting like they had other options, not an unwise thing to do when the alternative was letting us know they were dead in the water without us. Which is why Tozzoli, all these years later, was apparently still keeping up the ruse, at this point probably out of politeness, if not embarrassment. Considering how things played out, he didn't have the heart to tell me we had them by the balls and didn't even know it.

BOB SIGNED THE contract in February 1967. It called for us to start erecting the first tower on the fifteenth of July 1968. We had eighteen months to plan and organize the closest thing any of us would come to what Colonel William A. Starrett, one of the builders of the Empire State Building, compared to a military operation. "Building skyscrapers," he wrote timelessly in 1928, "is the nearest peace-time equivalent of war."

Around the city, the word in the trade was that we were out of our minds.

All that winter, messengers from the Port Authority arrived on Casanova Street with fifty-pound rolls of plans showing the details of every nook and cranny of the project. Sometimes, we would get two or three versions of the same floor; the slightest revision triggered a reprint and a new delivery. At first, Bob and Rudy faithfully opened every roll, and pored over every sheet. Soon, though, the volume was so great that they piled them on the plan desk and then allowed them to collect on the floor, unopened.

They didn't need to read every page to know that the first decision to be made was, very simply, how we were going to get all that heavy steel so high in the sky. It wasn't a complicated question on most jobs. Guy derricks—Yankee derricks, as they were known around the world—had built virtually every tall building in New York. And they could build the Twin Towers. But they would do it slowly and expensively. With the performance provisions put in the contract and the escalations left out, it wasn't long before we realized this would be the most daunting problem we would face, even tougher than recruiting and managing a force of ironworkers numbering in the hundreds. But even at that we didn't foresee just how consuming a question it would become, and we definitely couldn't have predicted the profound effect it would have on the entire heavy construction industry.

Bob and Rudy had bid the job based on the expectation that we would use standard guy derricks—six of them, rather than the usual four, because the center core columns were heavier and would be harder to reach than was typical. But it wasn't until later, after Bob had signed the contract and our engineers began preparing drawings to show the Port Authority, that anyone realized that this arrangement wouldn't work very well. The size of the towers and the weight of the cumbersome exterior columns would require much larger, stronger, and faster derricks.

Though the Twin Towers looked like a pair of toothpicks, that was because they were just so damned tall. In fact, at 209 feet square, they were also very broad—massively broad. In terms of cubic volume, each tower was half again as large as the Empire State Building. This wide girth meant there was a long distance between the corners of the elevator core, where the cranes would be placed, and the outer edges of the building. Between the dimensions of the towers and the girth of its steel members, we calculated that we needed a crane that could extend out fifty feet from the building, and be capable of lifting fifty tons at a time. Anything less would mean an inefficient operation and elaborate bracing to avoid making the building lean as it went up.

It was a tall order. Those were huge capacities, and we weren't going to find what we needed in a catalogue. I claimed the research job, and Jerome gave me a list of people to call at the major American crane manufacturers. Jerome headed up an offshoot of our erecting business called Koch Crane Company, which purchased repaired cranes, hoists, derricks, and water equipment, and rented them out. He was very interested in my search efforts, but was unsurprised when I told him that none of the American companies could offer us anything even remotely hopeful.

I looked to Europe. For years the French, Germans, Italians, and English had been using heavy-capacity equipment called tower cranes. These were so named because they sat on 120-foot-tall towers placed in the building's elevator core. The tower was braced by the core, and disengaged and then "jumped" every few floors. But the European cranes were geared to the world market, most of which didn't have the raw material and industrial capacity to build primarily with structural steel, as we did in the United States. Instead, these countries had to use poured concrete, carried in big ten-ton buckets.

The tower cranes of Europe handled concrete quite nicely, but because of the difference in density between concrete and steel they couldn't handle anything near the weight of steel we would be lifting. In addition, these cranes had a fixed horizontal boom. The physics of this arrangement made a building lean in the crane's direction when it carried a heavy weight at its extreme end, unless it was fully restrained by a bracing system. Picture yourself standing straight, feet together and arms extended straight out in front. Now imagine holding a ten-pound bag of potatoes in your hands. You'll feel the strain in every joint in your body and notice you're leaning forward. That's what happens to a building when the wrong crane is used.

One phone call gave me my first ray of hope. The Lieber Company in Germany offered to build a crane that could make all the picks and climbs we needed, though figuring out the bracing would be up to us. All excited, I raced back to Jerome's office to tell him about the hot lead. How much? he asked, sharing my excitement, if with a notch more caution. They're coming up with a price as we speak, I told him. When could they deliver them? That might be a problem. It sounded like they needed a long lead time. But that question became moot when the man from Lieber called back: $600,000 each, way beyond our budget. The schedule laid out by Malcolm Levy, the Port's chief of WTC planning, called for us to begin erecting the second tower when the first was less than a third of the way up. So we would need eight cranes, four for each tower. That put the cost of the German cranes at nearly $5 million. It wasn't even close to being affordable: it would eat up half our bid price—before a single payday.

Lieber's offer was the only one we got. Bob decided our only recourse was to design and build our own cranes. Now this was a frightening thought. It was an engineering art way beyond our capability. Our company engineer, Rudy Loffredo, certainly couldn't do it. So Bob hired a crane designer from American Bridge named Jim Markel. It was typical of Bob's sometimes wild improvisation on jobs, the kind of daring gamble that made everyone else jittery. Bob was a real idea man, and he was as brazen as they came. But this was like nothing else. The investment of time required would put us way out on a limb. And if it didn't work, we would be back to square one, late in the game. We would be back to using guy derricks, so many that the labor to man them could easily bankrupt us—even if the union got *no* raise.

SOON AFTER WE signed the contract, the Port Authority called us in to meet with its engineers and construction people, along with representatives from Yamasaki's office and engineers from the Seattle Skilling firm. Bob wouldn't let me come, but I got an earful about it from Jerome and Rudy. The trouble started right away, Jerome said, when Jack Kyle, the Port's chief engineer, asked Bob what kind of derricks we planned to use, and Bob said we were going to use European-type tower cranes.

"Which manufacturer?" Kyle asked.

"Actually, no manufacturer makes a crane big enough for this job," Bob told him. "So we plan to build our own cranes."

The room fell silent. "Do you have any experience in building cranes?" Kyle asked warily. "Have you ever built any kind of crane?"

"We've done repair work and constructed various components of all the major manufactured cranes that we've used."

"Do you have the personnel to design this crane for you, Mr. Koch?" someone else asked.

"Yes, we do. We have one of the finest crane engineers in the country working in our office."

"How long has he been with you?"

"About six weeks, but he has thirty years experience. His name is Jim Markel, maybe you've heard of him?"

"No, I haven't. You're aware that before you begin to manufacture your crane, we have the prerogative of checking all your calculations."

Planning chief Mal Levy asked how long it would take to build the crane. Bob hedged the question, pointing out that we had nearly a year and a half to deliver the first crane to the job. Levy let him off the hook with a gentle reminder that we wouldn't get very far with just one crane. But then Levy asked the question that must have set more than one person in the room to wondering what kind of cockamamie company the Port Authority had hired.

"Can we see the plans for this crane?"

"Well, right now," Bob said, "we don't have any drawings. We're still working on the calculations."

"No drawings yet! How far are you along with the calculations? When do you think you'll finish?"

"We're about forty percent completed and should finish the initial steps in six or eight weeks."

"I don't like this one bit!" interjected Ray Monti, the construction manager. "I think Koch should be forced to use the six derricks he originally anticipated in his bid. We can't trust the building of this project and all the schedules we have to maintain to cranes manufactured by someone who has never even built a crane before."

Levy felt there was enough time to wait and see what we came up with. "Let's give Jack a chance to review them and offer his comments," Levy said, nodding at Jack Kyle and then back to Bob. "We're not giving you a go-ahead or a refusal at this point, Mr. Koch, but I encourage you to speed up in whatever way you can getting these figures to us."

"Listen, gentlemen," Bob said, trying to regain control of the situation, "we don't intend to make these cranes in our backyard. A fabricating plant will manufacture the structural frame work, and major crane manufacturers will make the main component parts: Boyd's clyde hoists and drums, Cummings' diesels, and Westinghouse controls and safety devices. Our part is the design and assembly."

"I still don't like it," Monti said.

Back at the office, I grilled Jerome. *What did they say? Then what did Bob say? And then what did they say about that? And how did Bob respond to* that?

"What do you think, Jerome?" I asked finally.

"I think we're going to use derricks," he said.

But Bob was adamant. We would build the damn cranes ourselves.

THAT AFTERNOON, I drove up the long driveway to Mom and Dad's house in Sands Point. It was a sunny spring day, and Dad was on the patio, sunning himself on a chaise longue. My mother always encouraged him to "rest out back," then would leave him for a while with the nurse while she went shopping with any available daughter. At sixty-one, Dad was an old man before his time, a gladiator humbled and bent from disease, but still possessed of a great and giving brain.

"Hi, Pop, how're you doing?"

"Good, good," he said, squinting up at me. "What happened at the meeting downtown today?"

"Pop, I didn't go, but I heard all about it."

"Why didn't you go?"

"I hate to sound like a cry baby, but Uncle Bob wouldn't let me. He doesn't want me around."

"That sounds like him," Dad nodded. "Who told you about the meeting?"

"I got most of the information from Jerome and then I checked the highlights with Bob and Rudy. The Port wanted to know what kind of equipment we're going to use."

"Guy derricks, right?"

"No, that was the original thought, but now we're going with tower cranes that we're going to make ourselves."

"Oh, Christ! You're trusting the success of the job to homemade cranes?"

"Guy derricks are just too small and too slow," I said. "And there's nothing else out there."

"And what's this going to cost? They'll probably eat up whatever you save."

"If it works, we'll be ahead. We hired a crane designer from American Bridge, and I've seen his work. He's good."

"I don't like it. It will never work. You go into the office tomorrow and tell Bob to forget it. Use the guy derricks."

"Okay, Pop," I said, but knew I wouldn't.

Conversations with my father took on a certain convention. Donald or I would fill him in on events and developments, and then he would digest the information and offer them back the next time we spoke, almost like a mental game, just to confirm his memory and verify the accuracy of what he was saying. "Bob's thinking of building his own cranes for the job, is that right?" he might say. However sharp his memory, his judgment was still on the money.

"I don't know, Karl," Dad said, "this twenty million dollars of yours sounds pretty cheap."

"It's not mine, Dad, it's Bob and Rudy's." I could only imagine how the Master Bidder might have figured this job. He would have declined it, no doubt, for the same reason he avoided a lot of jobs: He could see it was a losing proposition. Even now, I could almost hear the beads sliding and clicking on his internal abacus.

"You have to build two one-hundred-ten-story buildings at ten million dollars each. What does the escalation clause read like?"

I hadn't told him about the details of the contract, not wanting to upset him, and hoped he wouldn't ask. But of course he asked. He always wanted details; that hadn't changed. I didn't want to lie to him, and I didn't want to get him riled up, so I found myself in the strange position of defending my uncles. "The Port won't allow escalation," I told him.

"You guys must be out of your cotton-pickin' minds!"

"They figured the union for four or five percent tops, and they allowed for that in the bid."

"So you guys are so smart you even know what the union is going to do two years before contract?"

"Not exactly, but the record is there for the past ten settlements."

My father rested his trembling hands on the blanket laid across his legs. "It sounds like you've been listening to your Uncle Jerome," he said, folding his arms against his body and tucking his hands into his armpits.

"Come to think of it, those were his words."

"It looks like you're not keeping your eyes open down there."

"I'm doing my best, Dad," I said. "I'm doing my level best."

He laid his head back, and we sat in silence for a few seconds, the only sounds the wind blowing through the trees and Dad's strained breathing.

"I don't think you guys are as crazy as the Port Authority," he said. "They have no damn business giving you this job. Thank God I got my name off that bond." He lifted his head off the pillow and stared into my eyes. "You're not signing any bonds, are you?"

"No, I think the bonding company missed this one."

In a strange way, Dad and I were at opposite ends of the same boat. We had dropped out of sight with our respective medical problems at exactly the same time, and now found ourselves on the outside looking in at a critical moment for our company. Bob and Jerome had made the most of the opportunity created by Dad's decline and departure. He was still the president of the company, but in name only, too sick to assert the power he had once wielded absolutely. Dad had his opinions, and they could be strong ones, but that's all they were now. He had issued his last command, held his last end-of-day meeting from the heavy leather chair behind the big oak desk in the office on Casanova Street. He whiled away the days on a chaise longue on the patio in Sands Point. A nurse brought him his medicine.

I knew my father could offer me no real backing if I chose to take a stand at the office. So I resigned myself to going with the flow, trying to protect myself, him, and the company by doing what I could to help us surmount this enormous challenge my uncles had taken on. At the same time, there was something to be said for rolling up your sleeves and going along for the ride. We were, after all, building the World Trade Center, and that stuff rubs off.

My biggest problem was finding out what the hell we were doing. Bob and Jerome were a cabal, and you had to know something to get Rudy to reveal information. Donald just wanted to be left alone, and my brother-in-law Jack was happy so long as he was taken care of. There were no moral imperatives in this for him.

"Karl," my father asked, "do you know why the Port Authority asked our company to bid?"

"They must have heard of your reputation and thought you're still in there."

"Bull. Do you know the reason they called us in the first place?"

Of course I knew. I was the one who told him. But I let him explain the situation, waiting for the point that always came, that moment of astuteness and wisdom that assured me it was still him in there. ". . . So Bethlehem and American Bridge told Tobin, 'If we don't build them, you'll never see your Twin Towers.' So Tobin got steel from everywhere he could find it. The only thing left was to find a sucker to put it all together. A sucker that bid too low."

"What about the fame we'll get, even if we don't make a helluva lot of money?" I asked.

"The gang that built the Tower of Babel didn't get much fame, did they, Karl?"

We sat in silence for a few seconds, and then my father said he'd had enough sun and arose to go inside. He brushed off my help, too proud to be handled. I looked down and lowered my head as he shuffled past, so he wouldn't see that small pools had collected in my eyes.

THE NEXT DAY, at the office, we all sat around the engineering desk eating lunch. I didn't pass on my father's insistence that we use the guy derricks. I asked Bob instead if he thought the manufacturers of the hoist would be interested in joining us in the design of the cranes.

"We've talked about it," Bob said. "They're not interested."

"You asked them?"

"No, I didn't ask them," Bob said, laying his hands on the table with the sandwich bridging his two thumbs and forefingers. "I didn't ask them because I think it's a stupid question."

The pressure to figure out the crane question was weighing heavily on everyone's mind. Jerome never challenged Bob on technical questions, but even he thought his plan was foolish and doomed to fail. And then, a few weeks later, a kind of miracle happened. The phone rang, and on the other end was a voice with an English accent. The voice of our savior.

He asked for Mr. Koch, and I said he had one of them. "Mr. Koch, my name is Eric Favelle," he said. "I'm from Australia, but I've come to the United States to try to market a crane that we manufacture in Sydney. I'm in the office of Boyd Clyde Hoist and Derrick in Detroit, and they tell me there's a chap in New York who is building the World Trade buildings who might have need of such a crane."

"What type of crane is it?" I asked, interested but not jumping out of my seat.

"It's a tower crane," he said, "but not of the conventional type."

"What's the capacity of your crane?" I asked, that one question enough to decide whether the conversation was worth continuing.

"I understand you have to pick fifty tons out fifty feet. Our crane can do it."

"Hold on, sir." Now I was jumping out of my seat.

I pressed my hand over the receiver and motioned to Bob. "You better pick up on this with me. There's a guy here who claims he has a crane that can pick fifty tons out fifty feet."

Bob held out the palms of his hands, like a policeman directing traffic. Then he closed his fist except for his index finger which he pointed slowly toward the desk. "Put him on hold and hang up the phone," he said.

Bob picked up. "Hello, this is Robert Koch. Can I help you? Hello, hello. . . ." Bob searched my face "What line is he on?"

"He's on one. Same line you're on."

"Hello, hello. Dammit. Pick up on the other phone and see if he's there."

I picked up the phone and heard Bob's voice. "I guess we lost him, Bob."

"Don't give me this 'we' lost him. Damn! Did you press the hold button?"

"For Chrissakes, I know how to operate a telephone."

I leaned back in my chair. The circulation in my legs felt worse than usual. The phone rang again, and Bob snapped it out of its cradle. "Hello, don't hang up! Hello?"

"Mr. Koch?"

"Yes, this is Robert Koch. Can I help you, sir?"

"As I was saying . . . "

"Start over again, please," Bob said, apparently pretending there was only one Mr. Koch. "We had a bad connection before."

I desperately wanted to be in on this conversation. I slowly lifted the receiver and placed the phone against my ear, but held the mouthpiece high over my forehead so Bob wouldn't get all excited. He watched the mouthpiece go over my head, then dropped his eyes to his yellow note pad as Eric Favelle launched into an explanation of how his cranes differed from those being used around the world. The main distinction was in the counterweights, the tons-heavy metal slabs that were stacked on the bottom of a crane to maintain the balance of the boom—the crane's long arm—as it lifted its cargo. Most cranes had fixed counterweights, but Favelle said his design had a moving one that kept the center of gravity inside the tower itself, always keeping the crane in perfect balance no matter how much weight it was picking up. Very much different from conventional derricks that caused buildings to sway when they reached out and picked up heavy loads.

Bob confessed that he didn't understand how a crane could have a moving counterweight.

"The engineering of most of the European cranes, and, I dare say, most of the American cranes is simply to put a mass of weight behind the crane, opposite the boom. The amount of lift is thus fixed by the amount of weight, rather like a seesaw. But our boom is not fixed like the Europeans have." He explained that the boom on his crane went up and down, like the boom in a standard American crane, but its counterweight was also mobile: It was mounted on a set of rails on an inclined plane. If the boom was all the way out, the counterweight would be at the bottom of the inclined plane. "And the boom's load is all pleasantly balanced in the center, in the middle of the tower," Favelle said. "Now, as we boom up into the air, the cable pulls the counterweight up the inclined plane. When the boom is straight up, nearly perpendicular to level ground, the counterweight is very close to the center of gravity of the crane. In this way we always keep the center of gravity inside the tower of the crane."

This was the crucial point because the center of gravity traveling outside the tower was what made a boom and the building under it bend. But Favelle was saying that this didn't happen with his crane. "That's why our crane can be made so light," he said, "and that's why the buildings that our cranes go into need practically no temporary support steel to take these reactions that a normal crane would throw into the building. Am I clear?"

"Absolutely," Bob said. "It sounds fantastic. But how fast is this crane?

These buildings are more than thirteen-hundred feet. Add the boom and we'll have damn near a fifteen-hundred-foot lift." Conventional cranes lifted their loads at a hundred feet a minute. That would mean a fifteen-minute lifting period to the top of the tower. Way too slow. That alone could add a *year and a half* to the timetable.

"We can do much better than that," Favelle said.

"I need it to be five times better," Bob said. "I'm looking for something in the neighborhood of five hundred feet a minute. Three minutes from bottom to top."

"I can do it."

"Really? It can go that fast?"

"Absolutely."

"Where did you say you are now?"

"In Detroit."

"Do you have plans to come to New York?"

"If you find this interesting, I will arrive in New York tomorrow morning at eight o'clock."

I called Donald that night and asked him to meet me in the office the next morning so we could both meet Favelle. Bob was going to pick him up at LaGuardia on his way in. Donald and I were sitting at my desk at eight-thirty sipping our coffee when Bob came in with Favelle. Bob introduced him to Jerome and Rudy, and without breaking stride walked right by us, pulling Favelle by the arm into my father's office. "Come on back," he told Jerome and Rudy. "I'd like you both to hear what Mr. Favelle has to say."

Donald and I stood there dumbfounded, alone as we had been fifteen seconds before.

"Son of a bitch," I said.

"You take things too hard," Donald said.

"How the hell did *you* take that?"

"It doesn't mean anything, Karl."

"Bullshit, Donald. Don't you see what he's doing? You think you're being the peacemaker, the compromiser. You punch holes in my arguments, and everything they do to hurt us is perfectly fine. I'm going back into that office. They're not going to shut the door on our stake in this company!"

"Don't be an idiot. How the hell can you go in there?"

"Easy. I'm going to walk my ass to Dad's office, open the door, and sit down."

"You can't do that!"

"Watch me. And you should come in there with me. You owe it to me. You owe it to Dad. Shit, you owe it to yourself."

"I can't do it, Karl. They don't want us back there."

"That's the point! That's why we have to go back."

"Aw, hell, I have to get back to the field anyway. I'll see you later."

My frustration with Donald was nothing compared to the fury I had at this moment for my uncles. I walked through the door of my father's old office, as I had thousands of times before, and was taken aback by the sight of Uncle Bob sitting behind the big oak desk. His small frame was sunk deep into my father's great leather armchair. I couldn't resist the thought: *You need a booster seat, Bob.* He looked up as I came in, annoyed but not so annoyed that he would throw me out. Nor would he introduce me.

Rudy and Jerome were sitting at opposite ends of the conference table as Favelle gushed about the motors that drove the winches for his tower crane. ". . . So the oil absorbs the impact. It's a built-in safety device. And we don't have the giant levers and the long pedals. You can drive with hydraulics easier than pedaling a kiddy car." Wow, I thought. Hydraulic motors. "A baby could operate our machine."

"Now, come on," Bob said.

"I'm serious, dear chap, dead serious," Favelle said as he reached into his open valise and took out a photograph of the controls for the crane. This one slewed the crane—rotated it on the tower. That one was for luffing it, raising or lowering the boom. "See that?" Favelle said. "This little knob here, just push it two or three inches forward and your load comes up. The further you push it, the faster it comes. If the fellow should die at the controls, or hesitate to scratch his *arse*, it would snap back to zero. Dead man controls, you know."

"Impressive," muttered Jerome.

"How about the capacity?" I asked, my first opportunity to speak.

"We covered that." Bob cut me off.

Favelle, whose back had been to the door, turned to me, looking sociable but slightly bewildered. I walked across the room and extended my hand. "I'm Karl Koch the third, Mr. Favelle. I talked to you on your first phone call yesterday."

"Oh," he said, apparently realizing for the first time that he had spoken to more than one Mr. Koch. He looked at Bob. "I *thought* your voice had changed on the second call."

Favelle was about fifty, a slight, unassuming-looking engineer wearing one of those European-cut suits with wide lapels and all those extra buttons. He politely tried to catch me up. "As I was telling these chaps, we can pick fifty tons out fifty feet. That's what you need, is it not?"

"Yes," I said, as Bob looked on impatiently. "That's a terrific load. I've never heard of a crane with that kind of capacity. Where is your crane in use? In a shipyard?"

"Actually," Favelle said, "we haven't made one yet."

Apparently he hadn't gotten around to mentioning that yet. "I thought you had these cranes in operation," Bob said, crestfallen.

"Actually, not even in production."

"What's that picture?" Jerome asked.

"Well, your precise crane has not yet been built. These photos are for our Favco seven-fifty, which has a capacity of twenty-five tons."

"Half of what we need," Jerome said, suddenly sullen.

"I know that," Favelle said. "It's a simple matter to increase the size of the components."

"You gave us the impression that you had this crane in production," Bob said.

"I'm sorry if I misled you, gentlemen. However, I assure you that it's a simple matter to reach the capacity that you boys are talking about."

"So how long will it take to make this crane?" Bob asked.

"I would guess about three months. Of course, you know we import the steel for the boom from the United States, but we have enough on hand to make at least one boom. We wouldn't lose any time on that score."

So, how much? The Favco 750 model, Favelle said, doing some quick pounds-to-dollars calculation, is about $150,000. He estimated the fifty-ton crane would be about $400,000. "That's over three million dollars," Rudy said to Bob.

"Do you have any better ideas?" Bob replied.

"Listen, fellows," Favelle said, "if we're talking about eight cranes, I know we can do better."

Jerome, who usually excused himself at the first unfurling of a blueprint, wanted to bring the discussion back to the technical aspects. He still wasn't convinced. Favelle spread a collection of drawings and calculations on the green glass top of the conference table, and we spent two or three hours studying them, probably the longest business meeting I'd ever been in with my uncles. He explained how a two-hundred-ton crane could lift a quarter of its weight without toppling itself, along with the tower it was building. He showed a diagram of the hydraulic retractable feet that enabled the crane to jack itself up a story at a time. Favelle captivated us with his Aussie charm, managing to make a discussion of slew speeds and fall capacities sound like poetry. Of course, what was really poetic was that a phone call, really in the nick of time, might have saved us from extinction. This could be The Crane.

Bob asked Favelle if he could assemble a fifty-ton crane for us to come over and look at. "I'm sorry, we couldn't begin on that approach," Favelle said. "You gentlemen are the only chaps in the world who would use anything this big. Unless, of course, they are going to build another building this size in the near future."

"I doubt that," Bob said.

Favelle suggested we come to Australia now and look at the smaller versions. "We have a hundred of these cranes working in the streets of Sydney and throughout the provinces. You can see them at work. If you like them, we can put a crane together for you. However, we would certainly require a firm order."

Bob said he could come to Australia in a couple of weeks, making it clear to the rest of us he was going alone. "I guarantee you'll be amazed," Favelle said. "And you'll love my country."

"I'm not going as a tourist," Bob said.

"I can tell by your looks that you're a man who loves machines," Favelle said smoothly, "and you'll love my machine. It will do the job for you."

My father once told me that with the exception of Henry Ford a man could be a great engineer or a great salesman, but he couldn't be both. But Eric Favelle, this affable Aussie, handled the technology and promoted his crane with equal gusto. "What were you going to use before I came in here, guy derricks?" he asked.

"No, we were running our own calculations out. We were going to build our own tower crane."

"Good Lord. You fellows are more ambitious than I am. Well, you can file all of those calculations, boys. My crane is your answer."

He had everyone's adrenaline pumping about this steel-lifting marvel that seemed to be sent to us from heaven. Life was so much better than it had been twenty-four hours earlier that Bob's whole demeanor changed. He turned to me as we were breaking for lunch, held my arm, and asked me, almost sweetly, to meet with a group from Hobart Welding. "Listen, I'm sure they'll need a lot of data," he said. "Give them everything we have. I'll talk to you later." It was an *assignment*—a delegation of responsibility! Even if it was only to keep me away from lunch with Favelle, it was the first time I could ever recall Bob entrusting me with a job he would ordinarily do himself. "Sure, Bob, I'll take care of it," I said, awfully glad I'd decided to crash the meeting. "Have a good lunch, fellas. So long, Eric."

Waiting for the people from Hobart, I had a quick lunch with Jerome, who was looking at drawings that described some of the structural members of the towers. "Look at this!" he exclaimed. "Five-inch plate!"

"Five inches thick?" I asked.

"This is some hunk of iron. And we have to weld this five foot across. Here are the fifty-ton columns. You're an inventor, Karl. Maybe you can conjure up a machine that can do this without using men."

"Well, we certainly have to go to semi-automatic welding," I offered. "Even if we can't get a machine."

"Yeah, I know. It might be a good idea for you to sit in with the welding people tomorrow morning. We're going to need all the bright ideas we can get."

Thank God for Eric Favelle, I thought as I headed home across the Whitestone Bridge that night. The promise of the Australian tower crane was a huge turning point for us, even if at that moment we couldn't be absolutely sure Favelle wasn't just blowing smoke—was there such a thing as a heavy-construction equipment snake-oil salesman?—or that scaling up the twenty-five-ton crane wasn't as simple as he made it out to be. For the first time since I'd come back to work, I was truly excited. For the first time since Donald had first told me we were bidding on the Trade Center, I pictured the completed Twin Towers in my head, the Koch name waving from a banner right next to the American flag at the topping-out ceremony. What an accomplishment it would be, what a monument to all those decades of hard work and determination by my father and grandfather. And for the first time, my uncles were treating me like a member of the team. That was the kind of euphoric spell Eric Favelle brought with him from the Outback and sprinkled on the Koch boys of Casanova Street.

"SAY, JEROME," BOB said. "I want to go over the plaza drawings with you this afternoon. Let's get the southeastern section together and plan the way we can get temporary support material for that area. You know, we have to brace those columns."

Jerome nodded, and I volunteered to procure the timber we would need. "Okay, Karl, you handle that," Bob said.

"What about the studs? There are three salesmen in the outer office right now."

"You'll have to handle that, too," Bob said.

". . . and the welding equipment?"

"You talk to Hobart about that."

"And what about—"

"Karl, you have enough jobs for now."

"Yes, but we'll need barges," I persisted. We were more than a year away from sailing the first floor panels across the river—we didn't even have a plant yet—but there was so much to plan and organize that I felt driven to do everything at once.

"All right," Bob said. "Call around and find out what you can about barges."

As we got deeper into 1967, Bob was wrapped up with the engineers in the office and Jerome and Rudy were knee-deep in setting up the floor-panel plant. Jerome had found a spot down in Carteret, an old fabrication plant on the banks of the Arthur Kill, a narrow waterway separating New Jersey from the western shore of Staten Island. Eventually, we would be moving our whole operation there, leaving Casanova Street after nearly thirty years. It was sad news to me.

Thinking in the narrowest of terms—I know David Rockefeller and Austin Tobin must have had more than this in mind—one of the great benefits of the World Trade Center was that my uncles couldn't possibly exclude me from being a full participant in the operation of our company. There was just too much work to do. And I needed it. With my mobility severely curtailed, the more work I could do from the office, the better. I was in the hospital twice more for surgery that spring and summer and had at least one more bone graft ahead of me. I was coming to understand that I would probably never again be without pain and disability. But I was back to work, busy and happy, rescued by this great venture. The Trade Center pulled me out of the worst period of my life.

With my uncles and Rudy so focused on other things, I concentrated on procuring materials and supplies and gearing up for the administration of a payroll many times larger than any we had ever employed. I was trying to computerize the payroll, with the guidance of a friend of mine, Joe O'Brien, who was the only person I knew in this brand-new field. My best estimate was that we would carry about five hundred men at our peak, though Bob, perhaps thinking about our bid number, insisted it would be fewer. "Anything more than two-hundred-fifty men on one building, they'll be pushing each other over the side," he said. Okay, I said. We're doing two buildings.

I was also trying to design a purchase-order system to handle what was already a throng of suppliers and equipment manufacturers paying calls on our office in the Bronx. They all wanted a piece of the World Trade Center. They wanted to be able to say, "Those are our bolts holding up the World Trade Center," or claim theirs was "The Official Welding Wire of the Twin Towers." I might not know a thing about a product before I spoke to the salesman, but I could use what he told me with the next one through the door. By the time the third salesman arrived, I was an expert. Then I took the best of each of them and turned it into the official specifications for the job and announced to the best prospect that these were the Koch criteria for the contract. Suddenly, everyone I met was only too eager to meet my requirements. Bolts, studs, cable, chokers, shackles, safety netting, oils, welding machines, trucks—whatever we needed, America's largest manufacturers were at our doorstep, aiming to please. Eventually, the stud man gave me free use of his machines for the life of the job. The bolt man would be glad to package and deliver the bolts directly to the site, throwing in distinctive markings for specific areas, at no extra charge, of course. The discounts were phenomenal, unheard-of. I put all my misgivings about our bid out of my mind. I was having too good a time.

Bob flew to New South Wales, Australia, in July of 1967 and found his way out to the world headquarters of Favco Industries. Eric Favelle gave him a tour of the shop, introduced him to his engineers and technicians, and showed him more drawings. He took him to Sydney to see one of the tower cranes, the 750, in operation. It had only half the capacity we needed, but it did everything Favelle said it did—lifting, slewing, luffing, jumping. Bob ended the visit by buying a 750 right off the floor. We would bring it over, test it on a smaller building we were working on, and if all went well, place the order for eight giant-sized cranes.

Bob had called Guy Tozzoli and Ray Monti the day we first met Favelle, but on his return home he could report that he had seen one of the Australian cranes in operation, and it worked. He gave the plans and specs for the 750—and for our yet-to-be-built model, the 2700—to Jack Kyle, the Port's chief engineer. The Port men were thrilled, and a few weeks later, seventy tons of components arrived in New York Harbor aboard a ship called the *African Moon*. We joined a contingent from the Port Authority in welcoming Eric Favelle and the first Australian crane to the Port of New York. A PA photographer caught the moment when the fire-engine-red control house was lifted off its timber cradle, and the name KOCH appeared in three-foot-high white block letters. Eric Favelle knew how to seal a deal.

The entire group followed the crane as it was trucked to our test site: a forty-four-story office tower Jack and Donald were putting up on Forty-fourth Street, off Sixth Avenue. The Port Authority engineers spent hours chatting with the Aussie technicians and climbing the ladder, peering into the cab, writing down every detail of the jumping procedure. The crane was a downright curiosity to us hardened New York construction men. The crane worked flawlessly, and the battalion of engineers agreed that there was no law of physics that would prevent the crane from being scaled up to pick fifty tons out fifty feet.

True to his word, Favelle was able to do better on the original price and knocked $50,000 off each crane. We placed our order: Eight Favco Model 2700 cranes at $350,000 each. A total of $2.8 million—a lot more than we had expected to sink into equipment but without question a fabulous investment. The Port Authority happily gave us an advance. Favelle had the fanciful idea of painting an eighteen-inch kangaroo on each crane to signify its roots—this remarkable Aussie machine that would jump 110 floors.

That winter we said good-bye to Little Pittsburgh and the pickle man, and moved our operations over to Carteret. Meanwhile, in downtown Manhattan, the most fought-over sixteen acres of New York real estate since the Revolution was slowly being reduced to a cavernous hole in the ground. The demolition team had done meritorious service for urban renewal. The excavation force had rolled in for the big dig. The foundation builders were ready to construct a barrier that would make the Berlin Wall look like a picket fence.

And we were counting down to the steel of the century, waiting for our kangaroos to jump off the ships sailing into the Port of New York from the coral seas of the South Pacific.

14

TOWN
OF
BEDROCK

WE WERE A little late to the party. By the time the Koch company was signed on and gearing up for the erection of the towers, the project was already underway. It had begun even before the Port Authority had first called us in the midst of the Big Steel debacle—one reason, of course, why the Port was in such a bind. By the time I hobbled out of the hospital and back to Casanova Street that day in the fall of 1966, the demolition derby was in full swing downtown. A building a day was coming down, and old Radio Row was being hauled away unceremoniously by the truckload. The surviving fittest, like the revered Trinity Church and the venerable New York Telephone Company building, seemed to look on with mutual shrugs: There goes the neighborhood.

Leveling the site took a year, but it was a cup of coffee compared with the next stage—digging it up. A maze of delicate utility and phone lines had to be exhumed and reconfigured, a painstaking job unless Guy Tozzoli was prepared to explain why Wall Street had no dial tone. But with New York Telephone's headquarters right next door, local phone service was only the half of it. Under the site happened to run the main trunk lines that connected New York and other major cities in the United States with the rest of the world. Even the hotline to Moscow was down there, somewhere under Greenwich Street. Moving the wire, which ran under the PATH tubes to New Jersey, turned into the biggest relocation job in the history of New York Telephone. To do it, technicians had to work in two huge vaults the Port Authority built to provide access to the tunnels, where the connections would be made. Sections of cable were brought into the vaults, where the technicians, working in round-the-clock shifts, sat on benches splicing each

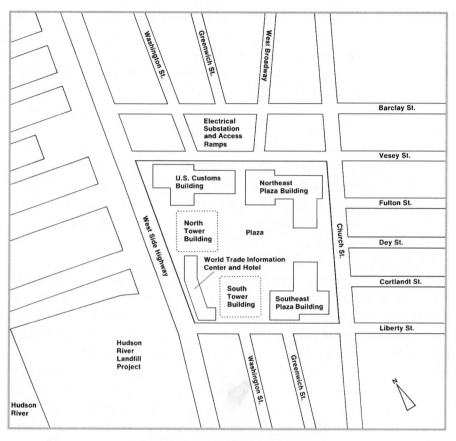

SITE PLAN FOR THE WORLD TRADE CENTER

one—managing to make the connections without interrupting conversations. Then the newly connected cable was dropped into the tunnel to continue its journey.

As laborious a task as rerouting the phone lines was, it was just scratching the surface. That winter and the following spring of 1967, while we were frantically trying to come up with a crane to erect the towers, Jack Kyle and Martin Kapp were going in the opposite direction. Kyle was the chief engineer for the Port Authority and Kapp worked under him (appropriately enough) as the head of the Division of Soils and Foundations. Kapp and his department would oversee the excavation of the site and the construction of the foundation. These were usually mundane and unheralded chores, but in this case they were every bit as extraordinary as the erection of the Twin Towers themselves.

Every skyscraper is rooted by a massive, sunken structure that's out of sight and out of mind but is, in relative terms, a kind of skyscraper in reverse—an earthscraper. Considering that the city's basement is already a labyrinth of intersecting subways, phone cables, electric lines, sewer, water, and steam pipes, it's hard to imagine there's any room left for the earth-clutching foundations securing all those soaring towers. Being "the tallest of the tall ones," as it was put so decisively by *The Ironworker*, the international union's monthly magazine, the World Trade Center required the biggest, deepest, strongest foundation. But it wasn't just size that counted, but location, location, location. To anchor the towers, the excavation had to burrow more than seventy feet, all the way to bedrock. It was the downside of putting the tallest buildings in the world on ground more befitting sandcastles. The concrete jungle of lower Manhattan was just a facade for some of the mushiest land this side of the Amazon.

Until the seventeenth century, the site of the World Trade Center was in the Hudson River. It was a natural harbor where fur traders from Europe moored their boats and went ashore to do business with the Indians of New Amsterdam. But as the city grew in the century and a half after the birth of the nation, the dirt and rock dug out for cellars and eventually subways was dumped at the shores of both the Hudson and the East River to create new land. On the west side, the shoreline was extended nearly seven hundred feet out. So the deal banged out between the city and the Port Authority that allowed the Trade Center to proceed—moving the site's one million cubic yards of earth over to the river's edge to create twenty-four acres of land—was in the fine tradition of adding fresh real estate to the south end of the teeming island of Manhattan. Essentially it meant the landfill would merely be moved. There was no telling what the excavators might find in the process: timber from old wharves, artifacts, maybe even a sunken ship.

Among the first of the forty-three "principal contractors" hired by the Port Authority to build the Trade Center was West Street Associates, which was actually not one company but five, a joint venture of heavy-construction firms created to share the load, and the $27-million fee, of excavating the site and underpinning the towers. One of the five was Spencer, White & Prentis, a partnership of foundation experts that was practically an automatic call for architects and engineers who suspected underground complications awaited them. In New York, the firm was never wanting for work. Beneath the concrete crust was a world unto itself, thousands of years in the making.

One hot summer day in 1966, Robert White, one of the partners, was showing around an old friend of his, Edith Iglauer, a writer for *The New*

Yorker. Iglauer became a regular at the site during the two years of pre-erection construction, and later published an 8,000-word piece that must still stand as the most exhaustive magazine article ever written about a building foundation. "Some foundations, like those of the Empire State Building, are so routine they aren't interesting," White told Iglauer as they walked toward West Street to watch a test of the equipment that would be used for the construction of the main foundation walls. "But on this kind of filled land there is nothing but trouble." He looked anything but troubled—actually, he seemed pleased.

It wasn't the fill per se that was the problem. It was the layers beneath it, and it was the water pressing in from the Hudson. Of particular concern was the area around Greenwich Street—the original shoreline—where the Twin Towers, the Customs Service building, and most of the plaza would be built. Test borings in that area indicated that the foundation builders could expect to find eighty feet or more of mush that couldn't possibly handle the foundation for buildings whose combined weight would be 1.25 million tons—more than the collective girth of every one of Austin Tobin's Port Authority bridges, plus all those built by Robert Moses. White figured this was what they would find: "Ten or fifteen feet of fill near the surface—rubble, old bricks, old anything. Then you have five to twenty-five feet of Hudson River silt—black, oozy mud, often covering old docks and ships. Below the silt, there's maybe a dozen feet of red sand called bull's liver, which is really quicksand—the bugbear of all excavating. The more you dig in it the more everything oozes into the hole. We expect to find it here, but we know how to deal with it. Under that is hardpan—clay that was squeezed dry by the glacier and its accompanying boulders. Finally, beneath the hardpan, there's Manhattan schist."

Manhattan schist was the end of the line—bedrock. It's what lays beneath the surface of the city, a gradually inclining rock ledge whose depth varies wildly, actually breaking through the surface in Central Park while descending below sea level at around Fourteenth Street and staying down there all the way to Pennsylvania. There is no better way to fasten a building to the earth than to sink its foundation into bedrock. That's why Midtown Manhattan was such an ideal place for the early skyscrapers: The schist is close at hand in that area, in some places so close that the blasters union had to be called in to allow the buildings to have basements. At Rockefeller Center, the bedrock is only eight feet below the street.

It was seventy feet down at the Trade Center. But the problems went beyond the depth of the rock, or the sogginess of the fill, or even the weight

Vesey St.

Existing PATH tube

Tracks f
new PATH termin

West St.

THE EXCAVATION JOB

The world's biggest basement:
the "bathtub" inside the 3,100-foot concrete
retaining wall that provided the World Trade Center its
foundation. A million cubic yards had to be dug up to reach
bedrock seventy feet below sea level. The exposed tubes enclosed the
PATH railroad. At the far right, just outside the bathtub, is the IRT South Ferry subway.

of the buildings. Going down seventy feet meant digging a big hole. Digging a big hole meant Hudson River water seeping into it. And that could mean problems with the neighbors. Even aside from the hopeless task of trying to pump it out, the falling water table could cause streets to sink and buildings to move. And if all this wasn't enough, there was one more thing: two rail tunnels—the tubes for the PATH train to New Jersey—ran right through the foundation site, and no, they could not be shut down or relocated, at least not until much later in the project. Trains carrying nearly eighty thousand passengers rumbled through the five-hundred-foot iron tubes that traversed the site. The excavation would unearth and expose them, and a way had to be found to jack them up as the foundation was constructed around them.

After much testing, studying, discussing, mulling, and hand-wringing, the Division of Soils and Foundations decided the best solution to all this was a gigantic concrete enclosure, essentially a four-sided dam, that would wall off the western half of the site. At 980 feet by 510 feet, it would be the

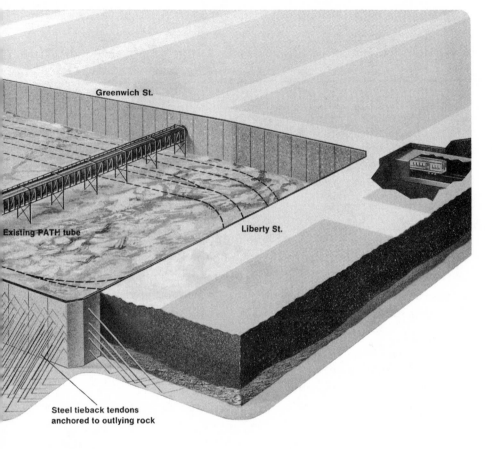

Greenwich St.

Liberty St.

Existing PATH tube

Steel tieback tendons
anchored to outlying rock

world's biggest basement—or, as the engineers preferred, the Big Bathtub
(though one to keep water out, not in). It would have concrete walls and a
bedrock floor. Besides solving the problem of creating a foundation that
could withstand the external pressures of water and earth, the bathtub would
provide half a million square feet of usable space: six underground levels
accommodating a new and bigger PATH station, a shopping concourse,
mechanical rooms housing the towers' air-conditioning equipment and
other utilities, truck docks, storage space for tenants, and a parking garage
with two thousand spaces.

Great concept—not so easily done. As strange and impossible as it may
seem, the wall had to be put in *before* excavation could begin. That, after all,
was the whole point. But how do you drive three thousand feet of three-
foot-thick concrete wall straight down, *seventy* feet into the ground? All the
possible methods were cumbersome and time-consuming—meaning expensive—and most certainly not designed with this kind of scale or these kinds

of conditions in mind. The most common approach would be to drive steel sheathing down to the rock and then pour in the concrete. But that would involve laborious bracing and shoring, and with the size of this foundation could be harder and take longer than erecting the towers themselves. And that was the *best* option. There were eight more, each unfeasible for more or less the same reasons: just too hard, slow, and costly. Time to get creative.

John M. Kyle Jr. was a short, affable man whose favored on-site headgear was a white hard hat marked "Lincoln Tunnel, Third Tube, Last Bolt, June 28, 1956." At sixty-two, he was the current holder of the exalted office of Chief Engineer of the Port of New York Authority. His predecessors included two giants of civil engineering, the great bridge designers George Goethals and Othmar Ammann. "The chief engineer," Austin Tobin once proclaimed, "is responsible for the integrity of all Port Authority construction." Jack Kyle had been intimately involved with everything the Port had built in the past twenty-five years. When he sat at the meeting in which my uncles discussed the crane situation, Kyle was noticeably unopposed to the idea of our coming up with something novel that would free us from the hook of the guy derricks. Kyle was known as a creative engineer, always interested in new ways to do old things. He also knew as well as anyone that this project, a new thing, was destined to be pioneering at every turn, that it would rise or fall on the imagination of the people building it.

Struggling with how in hell to get that bathtub built, Kyle went to Europe to check into the work of a company based in Milan called Impresa Costruzioni Opere Specializzate—"company for special jobs"—that built subways and other underground structures in areas near water in Paris, London, and other cities. The company, and a Canadian affiliate named Icanda Corporation, used an ingenious new technique called the "slurry trench method." It was a European inspiration virtually unknown in the United States, but based, ironically, on the use of a fluffy gray clay found in Wyoming. The substance was called bentonite, after the town of Fort Benton, where it was discovered in the mid-nineteenth century. When it was mixed with water, bentonite took on a unique quality that suggested it was created by divine intervention for just one purpose. The "slurry" mixture, 94 percent water, expanded to the consistency of pea soup, and when it was poured into a trench, it had the uncanny ability to absorb huge quantities of groundwater—while simultaneously maintaining enough strength to hold back the earth, keeping the trench from caving in. With the slurry trench method, first used by gas- and oil-well drillers around 1900, concrete could be poured into a trench and displace the bentonite. Nobody seemed to understand exactly how it worked. But it did, like magic. Kyle and Kapp, his soil man, realized that *this* was how in hell they were going to build their bathtub. It was the latest Great Idea, another perfect solution for a project that was, from the moment it was conceived, not so much a pair of towers to be built as a mountain to be climbed.

Using the slurry method, Kyle's staff devised a system for creating the bathtub wall in 152 sections, each about the size of half an Olympic swimming pool. Gangly drilling machines imported from Italy churned the earth, burrowing a trench twenty-two feet long and three feet wide, digging seventy feet deep until it hit bedrock. With each scoop of earth removed from the trench, it was replaced by an equal volume of slurry mixture, so that the trench was always full and the sides intact. When all the earth was out and the trench was filled with Wyoming bentonite slurry, a muddy crawler crane lifted a huge, twenty-five-ton steel cage, shaped and sized to fit the space exactly, a hundred feet in the air and then slowly lowered it into the slurry-filled trench. Ever so slowly, the cage (which Edith Iglauer thought looked like a giant bedspring when she joined the usual group of "sidewalk superintendents" outside the gate one day) disappeared into the fluffy beige soup. Then the much heavier concrete was piped into the bottom of the trench, forcing the slurry to the top, where it was sucked up by an outflow pipe and pumped to the next section.

Thus was a virgin wall buried underground, not to see the light of day until earth movers working from inside perimeter began to dig it out. With a dozen drilling machines working simultaneously, the excavation line got lower and the wall came into view. The men drilled slanted holes that extended through the concrete, through the earth outside the bathtub, and diagonally down straight into the bedrock. Then, steel tieback tendons were inserted through the holes, with one end socketed in the rock and the other anchored to the wall. The tiebacks braced the wall without taking up space inside the bathtub.

With each twenty-two-foot slice of land they dug out, the men moved on to the next section, getting into a rhythm that started to outpace the demolition still going on above. (There were two last holdouts, according to Edith Iglauer: a man unwilling to give up his apartment—fifth floor, river views, $85 a month—and a monkey that had escaped from a condemned pet shop, survived on bananas swiped from nearby markets, and made the demolition team chase him for months.)

Day by day through 1967 and into the first half of 1968, the project took on the industrious aspect of an ant farm, many things going on at once as

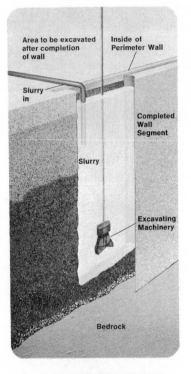

Area to be excavated after completion of wall

Inside of Perimeter Wall

Slurry in

Completed Wall Segment

Slurry

Excavating Machinery

Bedrock

THE SLURRY TRENCH

1. The perimeter wall was built in 22-foot segments like this one—152 in all. Excavation of the trench went to the bedrock. As material was scooped out, bentonite slurry was piped in to fill the deepening trench.

2. When the trench segment was finally dug out, a 7–story 25-ton cage was lowered into the slurry. This formed the skeleton for the concrete wall to come.

3. Now the concrete was poured through a big hopper down the pipe to the bottom of trench. The slurry had served its interim stabilizing purpose and was forced out as the permanent wall rose to ground level.

Guides for Tiebacks to Outlying Rock

Concrete in

Slurry out

Concrete

men from assorted companies wearing variously colored hard hats simultaneously went about their respective, seemingly unrelated, tasks. They were
the first wave of what would eventually be, at the project's peak, a force of
seven thousand workers, men of every conceivable construction specialty.
For now, the only ones in this town of bedrock, a place right out of history,
were the advance team. Even as the hole in the ground got bigger and bigger, old buildings were still being razed and cleared at ground level elsewhere
on the site. Meanwhile, a continuous parade of giant yellow Euclid dump
trucks struggled out of the hole, carrying great russet heaps over a temporary
ramp to the riverfront. There, the trucks deposited their loads behind an
enormous three-sided steel retaining structure called a cofferdam, stirring the
brackish water before returning empty to the bathtub for refills. Yard by
yard, load by load, the land moved west to the Hudson's edge. A six-block-
long rectangle that was jarringly precise—nothing is this perfect in New
York—began to take shape, the beginnings of Battery Park City.

Back in the hole, it wasn't long before the operation became almost as
much an archaeological dig as it was an act of urban renewal. It fell to Henry
Druding, the senior Port Authority engineer in charge of the site, to schedule visits by all the professional and amateur historians and scavenger arche-
ologists requesting access to the site. When a reporter for the *Times* visited
one day, he found Leo Hershkowitz, a history professor from Queens
College, down in the pit. "I could stay down here for a week," Hershkowitz
called up gleefully, barely audible above the thunderous drone of the excavation equipment. He held up a pottery jar caked in mud. "Salt-glaze! They
used this stuff around Seventeen-hundred to Seventeen-fifty."

But it wasn't colonial condiments that was most intriguing. In 1613,
Captain Adriaen Block sailed to New Amsterdam under the sponsorship
of Dutch fur merchants and went up and down the Hudson trading with
the Indians before anchoring his ship, the *Tijger*, at the south end of the
island, where the vessel promptly caught fire and sank. Three hundred
years later, in 1916, a few ship timbers were found during the excavation
for the Seventh Avenue subway, but the city couldn't be enticed into digging further on the chance of finding the buried *Tijger*. By the time of the
Trade Center excavation, city historians, thrilled at the prospect of digging into the past, concluded that the *Tijger* might be buried under the
corner of Greenwich and Dey streets—smack in the middle of the Trade
Center site, though, tantalizingly, at the very edge of the excavation for
the towers.

In Henry Druding's temporary office on Dey Street, meanwhile, was a growing collection of artifacts: pottery, clay pipes, hand-blown bottles and glasses, a bedroom slipper, a Portuguese fishing gaff. Many of the items had markings tracing them to eighteenth-century England. There was a pre-Revolutionary British halfpenny, three cannonballs, and a shoe that could go on either foot. An expert told Druding that's how they made them before 1865. Many of the household items, and some animal bones, were found beneath Greenwich Street—the original shoreline. In the hallway, meanwhile, Druding kept a corroded anchor with a huge, ten-foot shank, a prize find to go with a collection of ship fittings he was saving for a maritime museum on the drawing board for the South Street Seaport. Another anchor was so heavy, about half a ton, that it took nineteen men to move it. But, alas, the *Tijger* was never found.

The press delighted in the unearthed treasures—and you knew what some people had to be waiting for. But there were no bodies buried here, only the broken relics of earlier times. The most pristine discovery was a canister from the cornerstone of the gigantic Washington Market, built in 1884. The building filled an entire square block between Fulton and Vesey, on the east side of Washington Street. It was a city-run assemblage of 175 meat, poultry, cheese, produce, and other food merchants to which Costco might trace its roots. The time capsule included business cards, an opera program, a lithograph of the newly elected President Grover Cleveland, and a letter signed by three dozen occupants of the market who "wish to be remembered that we were doing business in it and hope that it may long remain as it is, built for and not be changed into any other thing but a market." In 1956, the market was torn down for a parking lot.

Eventually, the digging uncovered something of current importance, and the only items actually intended to be found: the two PATH tubes, one that had been under Fulton Street, the other under Cortlandt. With the trains continuing to run, the tunnels were nestled on cradles whose underpinnings were deeply rooted in the bedrock. The tubes were unearthed nearly three-quarters of a century after they had been built, and after all that time in the cool cocoon of the earth, the summer heat was a shock to their cast-iron skin. The sudden heat caused the iron to expand, so it was decided to cut a two-inch slot in each of the tubes to relieve the pressure. As soon as the cut was made, however, a PATH passenger who saw sunlight pouring through the hole got off at the nearest stop in near hysterics and reported that the tunnel—which she had no idea had just traversed a vast, open trench—was breaking apart. The Port engineers decided to wrap sheet metal around the opening.

✶　✶

EARLY IN 1968, getting ready to join the great undertaking later in the year, we rented an office on the sixth floor of a building on Liberty Street for our construction headquarters. We had moved out of the Bronx and set up our new fabrication plant in Carteret, but needed an office close to the job. You couldn't get any closer than Liberty Street without actually being down in the bathtub. If one of the big steel companies had gotten this contract, they would have established a field office on the construction site, relaying reports to the home office in western Pennsylvania, where decisions of any consequence would be made. It would have stood out in the company's history, but not by all that much. A World Trade Center constructed by U.S. Steel would have lent a decidedly detached, distinctly corporate atmosphere to the proceedings. But to us this job was personal. It had uprooted us from our home of three decades. It would be our lifeblood. We would survive or perish here.

Not that anyone would have noticed or cared the way people do when a corporate giant is in turmoil, but the company that was going to build the World Trade Center was coming into the project primed for battle—with itself. I was right in the middle of it. I saw where things were heading almost from the moment my father began to withdraw, and my uncles' made not the slightest effort to keep my brother and me in the dark about how they viewed the lay of the land. In the fall of 1967, after a year in which they had worn Donald and me out with their divide-and-conquer approach to day-to-day business, my uncles made a move: They proposed to my father that Jerome get a seat, the fourth, on our little family company's board of directors, joining Grandpa, Dad, and Uncle Bob. With my grandfather ensconced in retirement and my father ill and increasingly detached, allowing my uncles to fill the power void—instead of staking a claim of my own—was tantamount to throwing in the towel on my career.

I decided that I had to make a move of my own. Soon we would be immersed in the biggest challenge of our lives, and that didn't strike me as the best time to flex my father's muscles. Taking a page from his own book, that October I asked my father to give me some of his half-ownership in the company. I explained to him that it was the only way I could maintain any rights and responsibilities—to say nothing of respect—within the family business that he and I both cherished. But taking a page from *his* father's book, he said no. Turning the page, I quit. I stayed home and rode my bike. A few weeks later, Dad came to my house and told me he had come to a decision.

During those few weeks, my father had spent some serious time with his friend and attorney, Bob Auld, relating the entire history of the company and discussing what he might do about the future. My father knew he would never again lead the company, and concluded that I was right about how the balance of power was shifting by the month. I didn't need to tell him that it would shift even more if Bob and Jerome had half the votes on any major decision—with the other half held by the two fading elders.

"There are two factions present in your business," Auld wrote to my father in an analysis of the situation, stating the obvious. "Your father's family and your family. And apparently because of seniority in years, jealousy of you, or whatever reason, harmony such as you and your father enjoyed is impossible. The exact solution must be made through some compromise. I personally doubt that your brothers will ever accept your sons as equals and therein lies the entire problem."

If he waited until he was gone to pass his interest on to his sons, Dad concluded, it might be too late. His brothers would likely have already driven us into the ground, or out the door. He sat in my living room and told me he had thought long and hard. Perhaps he had thought of his own power play thirty years earlier. He was giving me a third of his stock, he said. He would hold the rest for my younger brothers. And he was not giving Jerome a vote.

That Christmas, when I arrived with Vivian and the children at Sands Point, an icy silence greeted our appearance at the entrance to the living room. But we continued on as a family of sorts. We had no choice: We were about to start building the World Trade Center.

LIBERTY STREET WAS the southern border of the site, and the building we were in was slated to join the ranks of the demolished, eventually to be replaced by one of the new structures developers were dashing to put up on the outskirts of the Trade Center. Tenants were moving out in droves, so we had our pick of offices and got the place for a song. It was directly in front of the spot where the south tower would be built, a perfect if somewhat frustrating sightline for a man not yet forty with legs less mobile than his eighty-six-year-old grandfather's. I would have to limit my time over there on the steel and do my work from here. So close, and yet . . . I got myself a good pair of binoculars.

From my window seat, I could take in the entire expanse of the giant hole in the earth. All day long, men and machines descended the long timber ramp on the eastern edge of the excavation. They were putting in the last few sections of the perimeter wall—trenches cut, slurry in, earth out, concrete in, slurry out—the system as routine by now as if it were right out of the foundations textbook at the Manhattan College School of Engineering. Over in another area, the men from Icanda continued their relentless digging. Down, down, down they went, descending below the waterline of the Hudson, each mechanized shovel burrowing through the geological layers like a spoon through parfait. Spoons would have been preferred by the hard-hatted historians and urban anthropologists who were by now as much a part of the bustling subterranean village as the men driving the machines. But the operation was at full bore now, and whatever diversion the cannon balls and bedroom slippers had once provided, the novelty of the buried treasure had worn off.

Like my uncle Bob, I was a man who appreciated a good machine, and I was captivated by the specialized, literally cutting-edge Italian equipment I saw the Canadian excavation team using to chew through everything from buried timber to bedrock. Huge iron clamshells scooped up the black muck of river silt, then the red quicksand called bull's liver. The Icanda men used a three-ton bucket with shark-like teeth to chop through the hardpan clay formed by the glaciers. When they reached bottom, they moved in with machine hammers to chisel out a flat surface on the schist, in some places keying the rock like dentists in order to tie the slurry wall to the rock with cable. The Canadians rented a rotary oil drill from Texas and a rock slicer from Milan, but New York was a tough town in all ways. Neither could handle the hard rock of literal Lower Manhattan. Unable to beat the schist out of the bathtub floor, the men were left to pounding rock like a very well-equipped chain gang. Gradually, the rock crept across the floor like tile. When I saw that, I knew our work was not far off.

So fascinated was I by the activity outside my window that many days I found myself pulling up a chair, glued to my binoculars. I had to tear myself away to do my own work, which was absorbing and vital in its way, if not quite so riveting. Serving as our purchasing agent for the Trade Center project, I spent what seemed like half my day on the phone with Bernie Robinson. Bernie had a small equipment company we'd done business with for years, mostly to buy welding equipment. Suddenly he found he was a major supplier for the construction of the World Trade Center. I called him for everything, most of which he'd never heard of. "Bernie, I need bolt baskets." Bernie said, "Describe it to me." "Oh, a metal basket with a handle on it, maybe a foot long and eight inches wide and six inches deep . . ." I started sounding like a J. Peterman catalogue for the construction crowd. ". . . Made out of perforated metal. Solid but light." Bernie called me back a few hours later to say one of his customers could make the buckets for me, eighteen bucks apiece. Good, I said, give me a hundred, and put a rush on it.

Jack Daly called to talk about hard hats. We needed at least five hundred. "Good ones, not crap," my brother-in-law said. I found that the best ones, also the most expensive, were the ones miners wore. I called Bernie and said I needed five hundred—and make 'em red. "I'm not a distributor," Bernie said. "Become one," I told him. "Use my order as your stocking inventory, and sell me the hats at cost." Bernie said, "Well, not at cost. I'll add ten percent." I had decals made with KOCH printed in red on a white field. We bought five hundred hats to start, and would add another thousand during the course of the job—two for every ironworker. "We're the only contractor in New York that buys two hats for every man," Uncle Bob complained. "Maybe three." The hats were so popular that they began to disappear. I had the shop make a KOCH branding iron.

Every day, I added more to the list when I called Bernie: I bought Chicago Pneumatic impact wrenches by the dozen, at $1,500 each. Burning torches, gauges, burning hose, welding shields, safety goggles, spud wrenches, drift pins, bull pins, safety belts, safety nets, wood floats—all of these by the hundreds, sometimes the thousands. And every time I ordered something new, Bernie became a distributor for it. (Today he has a shop in Queens that's set up like a supermarket, with aisle after aisle of tools for ironworkers.)

As I accumulated equipment and watched the progress down below, I imagined what it would all look like one day. From the solarium in the hospital up at Columbia two years earlier, I had gazed downtown and imagined the towers redesigning the skyline, making the buildings below look like shrubs. But it was an abstraction then, and now it was real. I was right there, ordering spud wrenches and safety nets and five hundred hard hats. I had studied the architectural renderings often enough that it wasn't hard to envision this place when we were finished. I looked out the window and saw all the bankers and brokers and international traders taking their noontime constitutionals across the plaza. Thousands more were inside the towers—assistant vice presidents and executive secretaries and exporters visiting from Shanghai all streaming down in one of those supersonic cattle cars. The new PATH station was awash with commuters, and the concourses with their shops and restaurants were filled with people going every which way. And out there on the river, maybe someday—I'm Robert Moses for a moment—there would be modern apartment buildings with parks and sports complexes on their roofs. The West Side Highway would be a memory, in its place a space-age transit system and a marina and maybe just one more park.

Ruined legs and all, it was hard not to feel that life was very good.

15

THE
CURSE OF
LIBERTY STREET

It would seem to be a law of nature that twins cannot be born simultaneously. One has to come first. So it was that the north tower of the World Trade Center was to rise first from the floor of the big bathtub, six months ahead of its twin.

It was on Tuesday morning, August 6, 1968, that we descended seventy feet into the pit with eight men and a crane, ready to set the inaugural piece of steel before a line of blissful-looking men in uniform, all narrow ties and short-sleeved white shirts with matching Port Authority hard hats. It was a humble beginning. Our eight men were the first of seven thousand who would eventually have a hand in the biggest construction undertaking ever attempted—at least the biggest job since the Pyramids.

The crane was a bright red Manitowoc 4000W crawler, top of the line and the finest one in our fleet. The week before, Tony Frandina, our master mechanic and all-around indispensable employee, had made sure it was in perfect operating condition. It was a task he did not take lightly. Tony had a special affinity for the Manitowocs, as we all did, and it pleased him to get this one ready for its big day in the city. The crane and the company that made it were named for their hometown, Manitowoc (pronounced Mat-e-ta-wok), Wisconsin. With its 150-foot boom and four spreader cables suspended from a giant vulcan hook, the 4000W could lift 150 tons at a clip. It had a continuous loop of battlefield-style crawler tracks, and it moved with a rumbling groan that suggested a Sherman tank storming Normandy. There was a day one of these ungainly but endearing beasts slid off a barge in heavy seas on Long Island Sound, somehow landing perfectly on its crawlers on the sandy bottom eighty feet down. The insurance company called it a total loss, but we didn't have the heart to leave the poor bastard drowned at the sea floor. We used the settlement to fish it out and let Tony nurse it back to health. He spent six months painstakingly rebuilding the soggy machine and back it went to lifting and luffing.

To Tony, the World Trade Center was magic, and he was as full of pride as anyone named Koch that we were building it. And as far as he was concerned, when you got the job of your life, you gave your crane the once-over of its life. Especially since the Trade Center was to be something of a swan song for the esteemed crawler. This one and two others would raise the bottom floors and then turn the stage over to the young turks from Australia. The Manitowocs would carry on dutifully, but the kangaroos would get all the glory. The Aussies would be on top of the world, a place far beyond the reach of their esteemed colleagues from Wisconsin. Tony gave the crane's Cummings diesel engines a complete tune-up, put new rope on the drums and greased and oiled them, and carefully checked every one of the controls. Then he called Gerosa Trucking to arrange for the disassembled crane to be picked up from our new base of operations in New Jersey and taken to the Trade Center site.

Uncle Jerome called his brother-in-law, my uncle Tom Bracken, and told him the Manitowoc was his if he wanted it. One of the few things my uncles and I agreed on was that Tom was hands-down the best crane operator in New York. We wanted to put our best man on our best crane, and Tom took the job as the honor it was. He was already in the seat of the Manitowoc when the sun rose over this yawning hole in the ground in the heart of the financial capital of the world that hot Tuesday morning. His son Tommy, a member of Local 15, whose men serviced cranes, came aboard as his oiler.

Jerome showed up early with John LoVerde, my old friend and pioneering steel detailer. The biggest steel job in history simply could not occur without the fabricators working from the drawings and specifications rendered by John LoVerde, the Henry Ford of the detailing profession. The Port Authority had given him the contract for the north tower. With 100,000 pieces to detail, it was more than ample work for him. (Detailing a virtually identical twin might seem simple enough, if not downright redundant. But every piece of steel had a number, and, like twin people, there were differences between the towers that weren't easily detected. The south building, for instance, was six feet shorter than the north.)

Ray Monti, the construction manager, was also there early. "Hi, Karl," he said when he saw me on the ramp. "Where's your Uncle Bob?"

"He'll be here later," I said.

"I'm sure he will," Monti said. "Did you know your uncle and I were both in the Seabees? We both have '*We build, we fight*' in our blood. I know he wouldn't want to miss the beginning of the greatest steel project ever built on Planet Earth."

"Yeah," I said. "Especially when he's doing it."

Eventually, down the ramp came a parade of two dozen men in jackets and ties—Austin Tobin and Guy Tozzoli and assorted others from the Port Authority, the city, and various professional firms and contractors. Jerome, standing with Jack Daly, got a chuckle out of everyone when he asked if the bolts for the base plates would be adjusted in beer cans. Not on this job, he was told—here we check them with theodelites, the most modern surveying instrument. The men in the pit chatted happily on this day so long in coming, even as excavation droned on around the site of the south tower.

It was eight o'clock when the five-man raising gang came ambling down the ramp like an Apollo crew marching to the launch pad. They wore their apple-red KOCH hard hats and went over to a truck that was straining under the load of the first piece of steel to be set—a thirty-four-ton monster chosen not for any structural or logistical reason, but because the Port wanted a good photo opportunity, and it went without saying on this project that the bigger the better.

The piece meant business. It was a grillage—a massive assembly of beams and plates that measured eight by ten feet in perimeter and was at least shoulder-high to everyone in attendance. All grillages are formidable—they are used to hold columns that are too big to be secured by simple base plates—but this one and the twenty-seven others to be set were bigger and heavier than most because of the burden of height and weight they would bear. The prefabricated units would be the framework upon which the core of the entire building, a million tons, would ultimately rest. Together they were engineered to perfectly distribute the weight of the heavy structural columns over a wide area. They were like giant shoes, each one serving as the footing for one of the columns that would eventually contain all those Otis elevators speeding up and down like a vertical subway.

The grillages, as well as the base plates for the columns of the exterior walls, came from Dreier Structural Steel of Long Island City, the only fabrication shop in New York City with a contract to provide steel to the World Trade Center. At 2,800 tons and $700,000 it was a minuscule order by the colossal standards of the Trade Center. But it was somehow fitting, almost ceremonial, that the only hometown fabricator brought over the first steel, the underpinning for the tens of thousands of tons that would arrive over the next three years from all corners of the country, a significant percentage of it fabricated from raw steel forged overseas.

With the crowd of bigwigs looking on, the ironworkers took their positions, two hopping on the truck to hook on, two waiting at the anchor bolts, and a signalman between them. Uncle Tom climbed aboard the Manitowoc and maneuvered the hand and foot controls with the aplomb of a master, swinging the crane over so the men could hook on the piece. Tom picked the massive hunk tenderly, seeing how she floated, and then swung it over and gently lowered it to the floor. The connectors below guided the grillage into position so that it swallowed the extra-large anchor bolts protruding from the poured concrete base, which was bonded to the bedrock with heavy rebar rods. Later, after all the grillages were set, they would be leveled and aligned, and then the men would spin nuts by hand down the anchor bolts. They would finish the task by torquing them tight with an oversized wrench, getting extra leverage by putting a pipe over the handle and grunting the nut tight against the steel. With the assembly firmly in place, the grillage and its concrete base would later be encased in concrete, joining the footing—and, by extension, the base column and eventually every piece of steel up to the roof—to the bedrock of Manhattan schist. The World Trade Center was now officially under construction by the Karl Koch Erecting Company.

Two more Manitowocs were to arrive on the job that week, along with crews to run them. There were two dozen more grillages to set in the core, followed by three times that many base plates around the perimeter. That the exterior-wall columns would be set in garden-variety base plates—grillages lite—might seem paradoxical. It was the structural innovation of these buildings, after all, that the outer walls would be load-bearing and carry the heaviest steel, primarily to brace the towers against the whipping winds of Lower Manhattan. But because the exterior load would be distributed among many more columns than those in the core—eighty columns spaced ten feet apart around the entire perimeter—each individual one wasn't as heavy. So setting them in grillages would have been overkill, even for a project so ambitious that the biggest builders in the biggest city had once pleaded, *Be Reasonable*.

It took nine days to set all the grillages and base plates, and another four to level them. Coming close on their heels were the first of six hundred truckloads of structural steel—12,000 tons of columns, trusses, and welded beams—enough to get the tower out of the ground and up a few floors. The steel was coming from two of the twelve out-of-town fabricators, Mosher Steel Company of Houston and Atlas Machine & Iron Works of Arlington, Virginia, by way of a rail yard the Port Authority had leased across the

THE WALL AND THE CORE

A tower cross-section—almost an acre of unobstructed space on each floor from lattice outer wall to concentration of interior core columns.

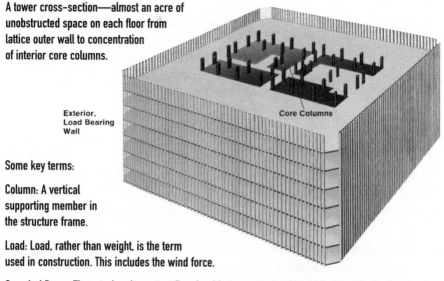

Exterior,
Load Bearing
Wall

Core Columns

Some key terms:

Column: A vertical supporting member in the structure frame.

Load: Load, rather than weight, is the term used in construction. This includes the wind force.

Spandrel Beam: The exterior element, at floor level between stories, by which the vertical columns are tied together. The walls of the tower buildings were spandrel-column welded assemblies.

Truss: A horizontal assemblage of members which make a rigid framework; designed to provide maximim strength with minimum weight. The floor sections in the tower buildings were trusses.

Hudson in Jersey City. It would be the first test of the complex delivery system Ray Monti had spent the better part of two years devising.

Even when the Port thought all the steel for the Trade Center would be coming from a single company, to be erected by employees of that same company, Monti had been puzzling over how to overcome the logistical paradox of building these towers. For a project so big it could only be built in a city like New York, you needed a lot of space to put things—mostly, all that steel. But in any jam-packed downtown, let alone one as choked on man and machine as Lower Manhattan, you couldn't put your stuff where you were building, or even near it. There just weren't a whole lot of empty lots and private roads left in Manhattan. Monti had to find another place, and it had to be a strategic place, and it had to be a strategic place on the water. Then he had to devise a *Mission: Impossible*-style system for having each ration of steel delivered precisely when it was needed—not too soon, and certainly not too late.

All this would have been largely the headache of Bethlehem or U.S. Steel. But when the job was broken down into little pieces, it became the

Port Authority's—specifically, Ray Monti's. It meant not only supervising and inspecting the work of a dozen far-flung companies, but coordinating their delivery schedules with one another and, of course, with the erecting company. For Monti and Tishman, that meant dealing with a dozen different plant superintendents—men with Texas twangs and California cadences and midwestern inflections as flat as the plains, all of them feeding an old family erecting company from da Bronx that had just moved out to Joisy. Welcome to Noo Yawk, fellas.

Monti's plan was based on a system called critical path method, a technique for scheduling the delivery of material in tight, efficient sequence. CPM, as it was called in the trade, had come into vogue a few years earlier, and Monti had used it successfully on the construction of the Port Authority's futuristic heliport at the World's Fair. His plan for the Trade Center, which made the heliport look like Guy Tozzoli's old erector set, called for the fabricated steel from the various plants around the country (except our floor panels down in Carteret) to be delivered by rail to the Penn Central's Greenville Yards in Jersey City, where it would be unloaded and sorted. The essence of CPM was precise timing. The fabricators couldn't simply deliver their material whenever they finished it, even if they were ahead of schedule. They had to send the steel when it was sent for. The Greenville Yard wasn't big enough to be a warehouse. It was a staging area, from which the steel would be delivered to the site, most of it aboard trucks rumbling through the Holland Tunnel, with pieces that were too large to be trucked sent across the river on barges and held at Pier 13, adjacent to the construction site. Some of the largest pieces required two railroad cranes working in tandem at the Jersey yards, with the 800-ton-capacity derrick boat *Century* unloading on the New York side.

There would be pressure on everyone up and down the line, to be sure, but with or without CPM there was no avoiding the weight that fell on our shoulders. According to the schedule, once we completed the most structurally and architecturally tricky part of the tower, at the ninth floor (fifteenth including the underground levels), we were expected to virtually fly to the top—erecting three stories every ten days. It was like getting through local traffic, then breezing on the highway.

Unfortunately, the highway was more like the Long Island Expressway than the autobahn. But if we didn't meet the schedule, neither would the project. The entire job depended on the steel being set when it was supposed to be set—on our "speed-ability," to use my father's quaint phrase. We needed to raise and bolt up the steel members, skillfully and at a good clip, in order to avoid delaying the nearly simultaneous next stage of the erection—which was also our responsibility: installing the floor panels, which we had to assemble, deliver, and set in an equally efficient manner. If we were slow, it would delay the men from Dic Concrete who were scheduled to trail us by ten stories pouring the floors. And if *they* were set back, so would all the subcontractors Tishman was managing: the plumbers, electricians, wall and ceiling and floor contractors, and dozens more that would follow in our wake, first up the north tower and then up the south one. It's why the Port Authority—which always seemed to be announcing another cost overrun that inched the project past the half-billion-dollar mark—wanted those performance clauses in our contract.

Of course, while it was a simple matter of the engine leading the train, the engine couldn't do much without coal being shoveled reliably. To a large extent, we were at the mercy of the suppliers' ability to deliver error-free fabrications on a timely basis, and dependent on the Port's finely tuned transportation system working as well in practice as it did on paper. Which was why we *didn't* want the performance clauses in there. We could only hope that the nearly two years the fabricators had to make their products was as much time as it sounded like. Just like the rest of us, they were depending on other people. In some cases, a fabricator had half a dozen different suppliers of parts for the single component it was producing for the Trade Center.

With the first major shipments of steel on their way, we would soon see just how well Monti's method worked. Meanwhile, our own new waterfront plant in Carteret gave us the luxury of sending the floor panels and our equipment and supplies directly to the site on barges. The thought of taking the Kill Van Kull instead of the New Jersey Turnpike, the prospect of erecting the entire job without ever seeing the Holland Tunnel or Canal Street, was enough to make us giddy.

"THE BARGE IS DOCKING," I told Jack Daly as he came through the doorway of the office on Liberty Street.

"Good," he said, "I'll buzz John and tell him to hustle some men to meet it. I see you got your cranes."

"Yeah, they're putting them together now. Did you get all your foremen?"

"Half a dozen."

"Who are they?"

"Guys we know. Hambone, John D, Backett. Artie Van."

"We're gonna be busy guys, Jack."

When the two crawler cranes were assembled, they clanked and groaned their way into an assigned niche and joined the one that had come a week earlier. The steel from Mosher and Atlas started to arrive—so far, so good, for Monti's system—and the cranes' diesel engines snorted as they swung the first, giant pieces lightly into the dead air of the pit and then lowered them into position over the anchor bolts with a deep thud. With the burden of carrying the dead load of the whole building, the base core columns were fifty tons apiece, almost solid steel.

Once the base columns were set, bolted, and secured into the grillages and base plates, all 108 footings were buried beneath a layer of gravel and then a slab of concrete was poured six inches thick. Now the tower had its foothold, and its basement floor. It was hard to imagine that this was just a drop in the bucket: By the time the second tower topped out, enough concrete would be poured to lay down a five-foot-wide sidewalk from the Twin Towers to the Washington Monument. (The calculation came from the Port Authority's prolific publicity department, which also later produced the astounding if unverified claim that if you pulled all the buildings' electrical wire out into a single strand, you would find yourself in Mexico.)

Now the only place to go was up. The trio of growling Manitowocs crawled around the mud in the bathtub as the first crews of ironworkers began making their pieces from the bottom up. That was the usual direction, of course, but in this case it was literally *rock* bottom: They had to erect six stories just to reach the street. It was like running a marathon from a mile behind the starting line. Between the two towers, filling the hole would be the equivalent of erecting half a dozen six-story buildings—without even touching the space outside the towers that would sit beneath the plaza. Into the Trade Center's sub-basement levels would eventually go a community of virtually secret official operations: an armory for the Secret Service, an emergency bunker for the city's police commissioner, a precinct with jail cells for the Port Authority police, and space for both a massive telephone switching station and a communications center for the Federal Aviation Administration linking the Port Authority's three New York–area airports.

The ranks of columns—some of them forty tons apiece, some a mere twenty—swelled daily. They stood, silent sentries, until the cranes began to drop horizontal beams on them, tying the columns together and forming the first hint of the skeletal grid that said this was going to be a building some day.

For now, these were days spent chasing steel and trucks and men as the steel went up out of the ground and then one, two, three floors. Jack traveled from foreman to foreman, crane to crane, gang to gang. *Let's get into A area, Hambone! Gus, watch Hambone's progress. When he has the steel tied, move your bolter-uppers in. If you can't get in there by the time he's finished, call me on the radio. . . .*

It wasn't long before we hit the first roadblock in Ray Monti's critical path. One of the trucks broke down on the timber ramp going down into the pit and backed up the ones behind it for three-quarters of an hour. Jack called up to the office and told Jerome to tell Jersey City to hold the last three trucks. "I've got steel backed up my ass!" he said. Jerome told him one of the trucks had already left the yard but he thought he could stop the last two. "Tell them to send a car out to stop the first one!" Jack said. "I have them backed up into the street! It's like goddamn rush hour at the Lincoln Tunnel. I don't want any more steel!"

Bob got on the phone just in time to hear the last part. "Oh, Christ," he said. "We've been screaming at Greenville all day to move those trucks out."

"Bob, I can't help it," Jack said. "Look out your window."

Bob had been on the phone the last hour. "Who's the foreman?" he asked. "Why didn't he pass the truck?"

"The driver's green. He was afraid he'd go over the side."

"Chrrrr-ist!" Bob yelled and ran for the elevator.

"I'll try and get that truck back," Jerome called after him.

Bob ran across the street and started waving wildly at the young driver stopped behind the broken-down truck. Judging by the look on the kid's face, he must have thought Bob was some pedestrian gone mad. Bob just kept waving and yelling, and the driver figured this guy must be in charge and followed his directions around the stalled truck and down to the foot of the ramp. Then Bob pointed toward the crane he wanted him to pull up next to. Jack appeared out of nowhere after Bob finished unclogging the backup, saw the rig moving toward a crane, and ran up to the cab of the truck. "Where the hell are you going?" he yelled up to the driver.

"Over to that crane."

"Hold on." Jack took off his hard hat and wiped the sweat from his brow. He pulled a set of prints from his back pocket. "Okay," he said, and the truck rumbled off.

BY LABOR DAY, we had fifty men working in the hole, raising and bolting up the basement and sub-basement levels. Meanwhile, another dozen men were involved in an operation at the piers, one whose progress we followed with terrific anticipation. The first four Favco 2700 tower cranes had arrived on schedule, sailing into New York Harbor even as we were putting down the first grillages. They came in on a tramp steamer, eight hundred tons between them, the largest self-climbing derrick cranes in the world. The kangaroos painted on the housing assured the nickname for these jumping Aussie cranes would catch on instantly.

The kangaroos came with batteries included but assembly required. Each was broken down into more than a dozen parts: boom, mast, winch unit, machinery deck and cabin, rear platform and power pack, slewing ring and mount, base section, tower section, bogeys, single- and double-fall hooks. And the heaviest piece of all, the star of the show: the mobile, forty-ton counterweight. When the ship steamed into the harbor and docked at the first pier at the mouth of the Hudson, the Raymond International derrick boat *Century*, renowned and well-traveled in its own right, came alongside and swung the pieces over to its own deck. A tug towed the laden derrick ship eight wharves upriver to Pier 13, the Trade Center's personal port, just across the West Side Highway, where one of our Manitowocs lifted the pieces to the dock.

Our crews would spend the next three months assembling the cranes under the guidance of Eric Favelle's technicians from New South Wales. They would put as many parts together as possible at the dock, taking care not to exceed the lifting capacity of the Manitowocs. It would be the crawler cranes' job to set the quartet of kangaroos, planting each one in a corner of the tower's elevator core. The big, red cranes from Wisconsin would be erecting the erectors, introducing the Aussie phenom that would become the world's preeminent skyscraper builder.

We wouldn't actually need the kangaroos until we reached the fourth floor of the exterior wall, which gave us time to get the cranes installed and ready to go, and for our operators and mechanics to get to know them. The cranes were completely different from anything we or any other American steel erector had ever used, and not only because of the mechanical gymnastics that allowed it to go where no crane had ever gone before. It was powered by a system of diesel-fired hydraulics that made them stronger, faster, and safer than any other crane in the world. But there was a potential downside. As with every machine, the more complicated the technology the more ways it could break down. In this case, the crucial parts were the crane's three sizes of hydraulic pumps, each powering a different motion of the crane. The largest one, the main pump, was for lifting (commonly called hoisting). The two smaller ones were for luffing (moving the boom up or down) and slewing (rotating or swinging the crane). All three pumps were made by Joseph Lucas Ltd., a major British company regarded as the manufacturer of the world's best hydraulic pumps.

Earlier in the summer, when the crane's components were first being assembled at the dock, I had gotten a call from Bernie Buongiovanni, the rep from the Delaval company, the American distributor for Lucas. Bernie said Les Goddard, the head of international sales for Lucas, wanted to fly in from London for a visit. Just a few days before, Bob had had a sudden attack of appendicitis and wound up in the hospital, out of work for a couple of weeks. Jerome was running the plant in Carteret, and Rudy was busy with various engineering problems. So I was holding down the Liberty Street office when the pump boys came to town—Goddard and one of his technical people from Britain, along with Bernie from Delaval and Terry Murray, one of Eric Favelle's crane technicians from Australia. I gave them a tour of the biggest pothole in New York, showing them where the Lucas pumps would power the Favco cranes that would fill this crater with steel. We went back in the office an energized group, everyone talking about how great it all was, what a beauty the 2700 was, how she would purr with those top-of-the-line Lucas pumps.

So what about spare pumps? I asked, sucking the euphoria from the room. Since these cranes had been custom-built for us—we were essentially helping Eric Favelle design and market a new product—we'd had some options, and Bob and Eric had wisely decided to have them built with two complete and redundant operating systems. Instead of one pump for each motion of the crane, there would be two. It was like jet engines on a plane. Two gave you optimum power, but if you lost one, you could still fly with the other. If one pump had a problem, it wouldn't shut down a quarter of our production. Still, if I had learned anything from my father, it was that preparation could make an ordinary man look really smart. We needed to have spare pumps on hand. This job was just too big and too tight to leave anything to chance. I told Goddard and Buongiovanni that I wanted every pair of pumps on every crane to have a backup—eight of each size pump, twenty-four spares in all.

We started with ordering the smaller pumps, the IG1000s and IG3000s, which was as routine as ordering spools of welding wire. Bernie had plenty in the warehouse in central New Jersey. But when we hit the big one, the 4000, Bernie said he had none on hand and turned to Goddard, who said we didn't need them. I hope we don't need them, I said, but I want them. One for each of the eight cranes. "You don't need them," Goddard insisted.

"Any maintenance is simply taken care of with the proper spare parts and an able technician." I said that wasn't good enough. "Do you know how long it would take?" he said. All right, I said, make it six instead of eight. "Do you know how much they cost?" I said I didn't care about that either. "Fifteen hundred pounds—that's thirty-six hundred American dollars for every pump." All right, make it four. I felt like I was in some bizarre role reversal. Which one of us was the salesman here? We actually seemed to be arguing about this.

Bernie suggested lunch. I didn't have the time, but figured maybe it would help get the pumps out of Goddard. I took the group downstairs to the Bull and the Bear, and we lined up at the bar and ordered drinks while we waited for a table to be cleared. Goddard remarked on the cold American beer. "We drink ours warm," he said. "Kills the taste, don't you think?"

"I'd like to give you a purchase order for the spare four-thousands," I replied, starting up again. "I'd like to order four spare pumps right now."

"God, man," Goddard said, "That's nearly fifteen thousand dollars American. Don't be a fool. Lucas pumps are tried and proven. I can assure you they are the finest pumps in the world. You would never use these spares."

"Then I never use them. That's my problem. But I want them. We can't afford to shut down even one crane, even for an hour. We've got too tight a schedule."

"Have you ever flown on a Boeing 727? Every pump on that plane is a Joseph Lucas Ltd. pump. As a matter of record, ninety percent of all the planes in the air depend on our pumps. And we have never had a single failure. With proper maintenance and usage, our pumps are virtually indestructible." He was starting to get loud, and the businessmen at the bar turned to listen. "There is no company, there is no pump in this world comparable to the Joseph Lucas Ltd. pump!"

I couldn't believe I was actually in a fight about this. Did he have so much pride in his product that I was insulting him? Goddard leaned closer to me. Saliva was bubbling from his mouth. "Good God, are you some kind of *Jonas*? You're wishing all this bad luck down on yourself."

I couldn't think of another thing to say, and accepted the spare parts.

AFTER THE KANGAROOS were as put-together as they were going to get at Pier 13, the rest was up to the bolters-up in the tower. The men loaded up the pieces on a big flatbed and hauled them across the West Side Highway and down the ramps, into the pit. The Manitowocs were busy dropping columns and beams into the waiting hands of the raising gangs that were toiling away in the bottomless cellar. We broke two of the crawlers free to install the kangaroos, finishing the assembly and preparing them for their grand entrance.

Over the course of construction of the Trade Center, thousands of pictures of the towers would be taken, from every possible angle and perspective—even, for a while, from taller buildings looking down like the Jolly Green Giant's average-sized parents. And no matter how high they went, whatever elevation the top of the tower might be at the moment the photographer pressed his shutter, the four Australian cranes were always on top, like points on a crown. But they had come from Down Under, and at the Trade Center they started out down under, too. Their feet were anchored to the very bottom of the bathtub.

Operators at the controls of the Manitowocs began by setting the bases of the cranes' towers. They dropped the bases to the connectors on the floor, who guided them into position inside the four corners of the elevator core. Bolters-on anchored the bases to the concrete. Then came the towers themselves. They were constructed of four thirty-foot sections bolted together to reach the full height of 120 feet. Half the job was done at dockside, so that the men had only to connect two sixty-foot sections inside the elevator core and bolt the assembly to the base. They perched the machinery deck and cabin on the tower, then attached the counterweight and boom. They laced the hoisting and working cables, thick as an ironworker's forearm, through the lifting blocks. Later, jumping beams and ladders would be placed inside the elevator shaft, and outrigger beams would be attached to the base of the tower, so that eventually it could be released from the rock anchors and make three twelve-foot jumps up the climbing ladders to a new perch thirty-six feet higher up the building—a jump every three stories. They didn't call them kangaroos for nothing.

The sight of all four cranes sitting high atop the bare steel, towering over the fledgling structures they would raise up to the heavens, was nothing short of stunning. Recorded history would not do them justice. Most of the pictures taken as the towers grew made the cranes look as though they were cut off at the knees. Where were the towers in these tower cranes? They seemed to be all boom. It was because two-thirds of the towers' 120-foot length was nestled in the core, hidden behind the rising structure that surrounded them like a steel curtain. Like some rare astronomical opportunity, there was only a brief time—in those early months before the elevator core had risen too far—that you could really see the cranes in all their glory. "They look like four giant ospreys sitting on nests on top of your building," said my wife, Vivian, charmed the first time she saw them. Personally, I thought the kangaroos looked more like giraffes.

Before it could go into operation, each crane (and its operator) had to pass a test by inspectors from the Port Authority. The crane operator was instructed to pick thirty-five tons and put it out seventy-five feet, and hold it there, three feet off the ground for about twenty minutes. The inspectors used a surveying instrument to make sure the tower of the crane stayed plumb—meaning it didn't budge under the strain of the reach and the weight. Its might thus demonstrated, the crane was free to go about building the elevator core around itself.

The first two cranes were working by October, and the third and fourth joined them six weeks or so later. But picking the pieces for the elevator core was just limbering up. They wouldn't make their biggest splash until we reached the fourth floor of the tower's exterior wall. It was there that Yamasaki's design took a radical turn. The Mosher and Atlas steel, hefty but straightforward columns, would all be up. Now would come the dramatic, three-pronged exterior pieces that would extend from the fourth all the way up to the ninth floor in a single bound. The columns were variously described as treetops or tuning forks, but at fifty-six feet tall and weighing in at fifty-two tons, whatever you called them they were huge. The sections were of such massive proportions that each one needed its own rail car to make the trip from the Pittsburgh–Des Moines plant to the yard in Jersey City, where we had to use special lifting bridles to ease the trees onto king-sized beds of timber, where they would rest until shipped over to the site.

The trees, which numbered seventy-six in each tower, nineteen per side, would be the Favco tower crane's first real test. The baby kangaroo we'd used to test the concept—low-bidding on an office-tower job in the theater district just to try it out—had done the equivalent of opening off-Broadway. The 750 had performed flawlessly and gotten rave reviews, but it was half the size of the 2700. We were confident in the machines—so far, everything Favelle promised proved out—but the fact was we were putting a prototype into service on a job that would kill us if we failed. The attention of the world was on us. We had safety netting for the men, but none for ourselves.

Few had seen the kangaroo in action uptown, but there was a buzz in the industry by the time we commenced erecting the Trade Center. The first week of the job, months before the kangaroos would take over, Bill Brennan had stood on Liberty Street watching the activity in the hole. He was an old friend of my uncle Tom Bracken's, and greeted Tom warmly when he emerged from the pit at lunchtime. "Come on over here, Karl," Tom said. I was standing with my college roommate Nick Matich, who had also come to the site just to have a look. "I want you to meet one of your new kangaroo operators."

Brennan had seen the test crane in action on Forty-fourth Street. "Slick as a whistle," he gushed. "The boom went out, the counterweights slid down those rails in the back. She kept her balance sitting up there on top of that tower." The operators he'd spoken to loved the test model; the controls were so easy to use it was like moving up from an Army jeep to a Cadillac Sedan Deville. "Looks like a good job running one of them. That's what I'm going to do. How 'bout you, Tom?"

"Not me," Tom said. "I plan to stay right here on the ground with my Manitowoc. If I go up there, I might bump my head on the sky." He rubbed the top of his head convincingly, and we all laughed.

IN THE FALL, the Manitowocs crawled away and the first two kangaroos—one operated by Bill Brennan, the other by George Koshefsky—went to work. The battle-tested crawlers still had fourteen acres of plaza steel ahead of them, but for now, they had a pass. Brennan and Koshefsky raised the first core columns, and a few weeks later, after Thanksgiving, they were joined by Tom Roemer and Billy Barker, forming the first foursome of kangaroo riders. Roemer was legendary among the ironworkers of Local 40 simply by virtue of his ubiquitousness. He had worked for every steel erector in town at one time or another and had run every kind of equipment, so it was natural that he would be one of the first kangaroo operators. He liked the ease of the controls, but his instincts told him not to trust them. The operators' manual said everything was automatic—if the crane unexpectedly lost power, it would brake itself. Tom once told me that he kept thinking, *How do I know it will? What if it doesn't?* One day, Terry Murray from Favco snuck behind him and shut the motor. The crane hit the brakes, just as Terry had been trying to convince Tom it would. Tom was startled and pissed, but he trusted the kangaroo a little more (and Terry a little less). Still, he needed time to get used to this concept of man surrendering control to his machine.

Recovered from his appendectomy and back in charge, Bob gazed out the window of the office and marveled at the kangaroos poised to leap floor by floor a quarter of a mile into space, rewriting the engineering textbooks along the way. How fortunate it was that the Port had agreed to advance us two and a half million bucks for the eight cranes, though to refuse would have been unimaginably and uncharacteristically stupid on their part. To even the books, they reduced our monthly payments by $40,000, pocket change to them but equity to us. When the job was over, we would own the cranes. Jerome had done the math: These cranes were capable of erecting thirty-five tons a day, a rate of speed that he translated into a $38,000 weekly profit for us—and that didn't include the fifty-ton trees, Yama's little gift to us: they could be set in less than an hour apiece. As my father always said, the crane doesn't know how much it weighs; the heavier the piece the better—we get paid by the pound. From the window of our office, gazing out at the swarm of men and machines slowly raising Tower A, Bob looked like Caesar sitting on the heights, directing his generals.

With my legs putting a severe crimp in my ability to run around the site, never mind walking the steel, I did most of my supervising through the lenses of my big, black binoculars, which John Kelly, the Local 40 steward, noticed peering out one day. He informed his men to be on their toes. "Koch is watching," he told them. Most of everything else fell to Jack. And a lot was falling. He'd get help in January, when Donald finished a major repair job on the Kosciusko Bridge—as if the Trade Center wasn't enough to keep us busy—but for now it was just Jack and his walkie-talkie out there. He went through batteries the way a raising gang went through a keg of bolts. He gave himself a handle—Red One—and kept in close touch with the foremen. When he wanted one of us in the office he called Central Control. His voice came crashing through the squawk box, instantly filling the office with the stress that only a man dead-square inside the tower could feel. *Where's the steel for Crane Two? I need welding machines for the third floor—the men are still using the ones on the first floor. I'll need another eight men for the plumbing-up gang and another ten welders.*

We were flying by the seats of our pants, scrambling to fill what seemed like an endless need for specialized labor. The biggest problem was hiring enough ironworkers who were certified welders. The Port Authority had demanded the most cost-efficient construction, and when it comes to the economics of securing metal to metal, welding beats bolting. Welding is individually more laborious, but you make up for it in the steel you don't have to buy—the bracing, plates and fasteners—for a bolted job. On a project of the magnitude of the Trade Center, it saved the Port millions in steel costs. Of course, it also shifted a major burden to us, because we had to go out and find the welders—not a simple thing in a city where the overwhelming majority of buildings were bolted, not welded. This was sort of

Minoru Yamasaki had never designed a high-rise building before, but the Port Authority chose him over every major architect in the world for the World Trade Center. "Yama" came up with more than 100 models—including one for a 150-story tower—before presenting the Twin Towers. (*Detroit News*)

Guy Tozzoli became head of the Port Authority's World Trade Office in 1962 and spent ten years turning an idea into reality. He is shown here with the model presented to the public in 1964. (*Bob Gomel/Timepix*)

Floor panels in our yard in Carteret, about to be shipped by barge to the World Trade Center site. (*Courtesy of the author*)

(*Right*) We tried using a Sikorsky skycrane helicopter to transport floor panels during a tugboat strike in 1969. The helicopter couldn't handle this seven-ton section, and the pilot had to drop it to the bottom of Kill Van Kull near the mouth of New York Harbor, where it remains today. (*Courtesy of the author*)

(*Below*) With the "slurry trench" method, seven-story steel cages like this one were slipped into the earth to construct the 70-foot-deep concrete foundation walls around the huge excavation called the "bathtub." (*Ironworker Magazine*)

(*Opposite*) This is the South Tower under construction. You can see what we called the treetops, or tuning forks— these are the dramatic three-pronged exterior pieces from the fourth to the ninth floors that weighed 52 tons apiece. (*Courtesy of the author*)

(Above) The beginning of the North Tower. The kangaroo cranes, which had never been used on any other American steel erection, are ready for action. (*The Port Authority of New York and New Jersey*)

Steve DeSmidt, the son of our foreman, John DeSmidt, took these photographs of iron workers up on the towers. (*Steve DeSmidt*)

Erecting the 22-ton exterior wall panels on the 104th floor. (*The Port Authority of New York and New Jersey*)

The South Tower's general foreman, John DeSmidt, inspired his men to try to gain on the North Tower. In the background is the East River with two of its famous crossings: the Manhattan Bridge, on top, which my grandfather helped build (and which he fell off) in 1908, and the Brooklyn Bridge. (*The Port Authority of New York and New Jersey*)

Topping Out Day Number 1: December 23, 1970. That's me with my brother-in-law Jack Daly in the center and our longtime company engineer Rudy Loffredo on the right. (*Courtesy of the author*)

My family with me on Topping Out Day Number 2, May 1971. From left, Vivian, me, Vivi, Jill, Cynthia, John, and Karl. (*Courtesy of the author*)

In August 2001, I was working on an expansion of the AT&T Building when my partner Andy Zosuls insisted I pose in front of the World Trade Center. It was the first time I was photographed with the Twin Towers in thirty years. Two weeks later, the first hijacked plane flew over this building and hit the north tower. (*Andy Zosuls*)

The completed World Trade Center. *(Dmitri Kessel/Timepix)*

September 11, 2001
(*AP/WideWorld Photos/ Patrick Sison*)

I insisted on going to Ground Zero, but when I got there I realized it was a mistake. "I buried the Trade Center once," I told Andy Zosuls. "I can't bury it again." (*AP/WideWorld Photos/Paul Chiasson*)

like the Hospital for Joint Diseases finding its operating rooms backed up with patients who needed heart bypasses. They had all the orthopedic surgeons they wanted but what they needed were heart specialists. There just were not that many welders in New York, at least not as many as we needed.

Each perimeter column from the grillage to the fourth floor had three spliced joints—three columns standing on top of each other—so that meant 240 places that had to be fused. With each joint requiring a dozen passes of the welding torch, there were there were three and a half miles of welding just to that point. Jack was constantly on the radio commenting on the slow pace of the work, and asking for more welders, ten more, twenty, thirty . . .

"There aren't that many men in this business!" Bob told him when he got to forty.

"That's not all," Jack told Bob, continuing his litany. "We'll need forty more bolter-uppers."

"You'd better come up to the office," Bob said.

"I can't now. Crane One is having problems. Have to see what the trouble is."

Nobody expected the kangaroos to be maintenance-free. A machine is a machine. We had the backup pumps, most of them anyway, and plenty of spare parts and expect technicians. Besides, there was sure to be a shaking-out period for the cranes, and a learning curve on the project in general. There wasn't a job in the world that wasn't all about solving one problem after another. We could expect bigger problems from this project, and more of them, but then again we had a lot more men to fix them. Jack said the Aussie mechanic was working on the crane and didn't think it was a big deal.

Jack came up to the office after the workday, and we started going down the list, Bob giving orders to us as my father had to him: Get two men for the plumbing-up gang—take them from the southeast area. Work the welders an extra half-hour. We can't put on forty bolter-uppers, but we can get fifteen. Now, what about the crane? Jack said it looked like something blew out one of the pumps.

Which one? I asked. The main hoist, Jack said. When I heard this, I resolved not to get all excited. The Aussie's working overtime, Jack said, and thinks he should have her back up in the morning. I stood at the window and looked out at the cranes at rest, thinking harsh thoughts about Les Goddard. *Yes sir, Lucas Industries—finest fucking pump in the world.*

✱ ✱

THE FAVCO TECHNICIAN had barely taken the pump apart when Jack was back on the radio the next day squawking, "Bob, Red One to CC. Bob!"

"Yes, Jack," Bob said, picking up the mike.

"Crane Three is having trouble. It looks the same as Crane One."

Now, this was ominous. Two of the four kangaroos were already having problems. The *same* problems, with the *same* pumps. The pumps that we didn't have backups for because we didn't need them—because there wasn't a pump in the world that could compare with a Lucas pump. This had the makings of a goddamn situation.

The pumps drove the motors that rotated the drums that held the wire rope that was threaded through the block that was attached to the lifting hook that picked up the fifty-ton columns that we had gotten these cranes for in the first place. But we couldn't pick them because the drums weren't rotating. The motors were blown. The pumps were shutting down.

"Are you filtering the oil?" Bernie Buongiovanni asked when I called to ask again about replacement pumps.

"Christ, Bernie, of course," I said, as though I had a problem with my TV set and he was asking if it was plugged in.

"How often do you change the filters?"

"Every day at noon."

He thought the filters we were using were fine, and the oil was just the grade Lucas recommended "Are you running them hot?" he wondered.

"Hell, no! We have an automatic thermal cut out that we check every night."

"Why did you fellas put such tremendous pumps in these cranes, any-way? They're capable of putting out four thousand imperial gallons an hour."

"I know, and we get four hundred feet a minute travel."

"Why do you need such high speeds?"

"It's a tall building, Bernie. When we get near the top, that's thirteen-hundred feet. We can't spend twenty minutes lifting every piece."

"Do you operate at high speeds all the time?"

"Only on the descent, which isn't that far yet. When we lift a heavy load we travel at half-speed so we don't put a strain on it."

"When do the pumps fail?"

"When the pump is under load."

"And you're only at half-speed."

"Right."

"Beats me," said Bernie. "Better talk to Goddard."

Bob, meanwhile, called Eric Favelle, who for once was speechless. He was a crane engineer, not a pump mechanic. He knew what the pumps needed to do, but as far as fixing them when they broke down, he was useless. He said he'd call England, but for now all he could offer was the best efforts of his mechanics in New York.

The mechanics opened up the housing and took the main-hoist pumps out for a look. The pumps were no bigger than a Hoover upright but weighed five hundred pounds. The Australians' diagnosis was that they were running dirty. Foreign bodies and contaminants were getting through the filtration system and choking the pumps. So they suggested cleaning the system at night—which meant paying three men double-time—and getting finer micron filters from England. In the meantime, we could switch over to the good pump—the beauty of having a second system. But the finer filters weren't fine. The pumps kept breaking down. We gave up trying to fix them in place. Instead, we took the whole motor out and sent it to Delaval. Since we had no spares, we replaced it with a secondary motor from one of the other cranes. Of course, now *that* crane had no backup system to switch to when *its* first system broke down. And it seemed inevitable that it would.

As if this weren't enough, it seemed our lovely kangaroos were not big fans of cold weather. By early December, the nighttime temperatures were already dipping to near freezing, and when the men arrived in the morning, they found the oil congealed, thick as grease. The pumps had small radiators to keep the oil warm, but they were already blown. They couldn't handle the New York winter—in fact, they couldn't handle the late fall. "You got the feeling the Australians didn't know how cold it got here," Roemer recalled years later. "I remember one guy flew in, the middle of winter, in dungarees, a cotton shirt, no coat. I told him, 'You better get yourself some warm clothes, son.' I looked down and he had these pointy dress shoes on. 'And get yourself some work boots.' His nose was running. He said, 'Bloody cold, mate.'"

Apparently they hadn't done any better at preparing the kangaroos for the weather. The northwest crane was completely out of service by the first frost. Night after night, Favelle's men were purging entire hydraulic systems, draining and cleaning them to get them to work in the morning.

Les Goddard, naturally, defended his pumps. He and his technical people at Lucas agreed wholeheartedly with the Australians that the problem was our fault: We were guilty of poor housekeeping and running dirty oil—even though the Australians were *there,* working with us from day one, a point taken by Ray Monti. He doubted the dirt theory.

Dirty or not, the oil was all over the place. The pumps were spewing it like a mortal wound, and men were slipping and falling across the planks. I called our old neighbors on Casanova Street, the horse-feed people, and asked if they could get their hands on a truckload of cat litter. They delivered, and we had the stuff all around the tower. When the wind blew, we kitty-littered the whole neighborhood.

WHILE WE WERE frantically trying to keep the cranes going—paying bags full of overtime to mechanics pulling all-nighters, with only Band-Aids and denials coming from Australia and England—we found ourselves in another snag. Another case of a great idea gone wrong. All you had to do to see it was look up toward the fifth floor, on any side of the building. The tower was encircled by empty floats.

If you look at a picture that shows the lowest section of either of the Twin Towers, you will notice a horizontal line that extends around the entire 832-foot girth of the building, midway between the front doors and the arches formed by the bottom of the treetops. This spandrel of steel was called the belly band, and it was another way in which Yamasaki gave an important structural element an aesthetic flourish. If the tower was like a stack of boxes inside a tall carton, the belly beam was a strong band wrapped around the bottom to help contain it. At the same time, it divided the massive structural pedestal from the elegant vertical lines flowing to the upper reaches of the tower. The belly band was composed of eighty sections bowtied shape, twenty per tower side, that were five feet high and ten feet wide. The panels had to be welded—each piece to the one next to it and to the column between them. All told, it came to two thousand feet of one-inch weld, an overwhelming job.

IN THE EARLY days of planning, Bob had begun talks with Hobart Brothers, a company in Troy, Ohio, that was so big into welding that it published a quarterly magazine on the subject called *Hobart Weldworld*. The company's founder, Clarence Charles (C.C.) Hobart, was a trained lawyer who loved technology more than torts. He became an electrical pioneer of the early twentieth century who, with his son, Edward, made arc welding—which replaced riveting in shipbuilding in the 1940s—the most widely used method of fusing metals in manufacturing and construction. Hobart's company held more than thirty patents, and was like an advocate for a better-welded world. The company lived to join metals, and took great pride in its innovations. During our two-year roll-out for the Trade Center, Bob had told the Hobart people how much welding there would be on the Trade Center, and you could just imagine C.C. Hobart's eyes lighting up from the great beyond. Bob had intended to make a deal for conventional—if top-of-the-line—welding equipment. But the ever-ambitious Hobart wanted him to consider something much better—something revolutionary. With the Trade Center, "revolutionary" was by now almost part of the job specs.

In their shop, Hobart used a fully automated welding machine called an electroslag welder. What made it unique was that the slag bath—melted metal—was electrically charged. It could fuse joints in one continuous operation, at a speed that was light-years ahead of manual welders. Hobart—aware, of course, of the Trade Center's tremendous showcase potential—sold Bob on the idea of letting them develop an electroslag for us to use in the field. If they were able to make it work, it would be the most groundbreaking of their innovations, and a huge benefit to us. It could save us hundreds of thousands of dollars in man-hours.

Bob informed the Port Authority that we were planning on a new much more efficient way of welding the belly bands, and Rudy told the column fabricators and the detailers to change the profile of the welded connections at the pieces' matching ends.

Hobart worked furiously to develop the machine, and finally flew Bob and Leslie Robertson to Ohio on their Lear jet for a demonstration. The welder performed flawlessly in the shop filling the joint like hot lead in a mold. It was like magic. It eliminated the need to weave the weld into the joint with a dozen painstaking passes. A few months later, men from the Port Authority, Hobart, Skilling, and Koch gathered near the belly band itself to watch an ironworker weld in seven minutes what it would have taken him *two days* to do manually. But halfway through the fusion process, an arc flashed deep inside the copper shoe and the weld was broken. Another demonstration was attempted, but with the same sad results.

We sent the equipment over to our plant in Carteret, where the Hobart technicians labored for days to get the machine to give a continuous weld. They clamped the shoes on a test joint, inserted the rod through the wire guide, and proceeded with the weld. When it was finished, we sent specimens cut from the weld to the Port Authority engineers, who examined it with an electron microscope to quantify its strength. Meanwhile, Jack was on the phone to Carteret two, three times a day. He had floats suspended around the entire circumference of the building, sitting empty. He had welders waiting to weld. "When can I get the machines back?" he asked. "When can I start the weld? The men are ready to move up."

The test process was repeated several times until we finally satisfied the Port engineers that the molecules were all in the right order. They accepted the weld, and we sent the equipment back up to the job, where Bob and Jack were waiting restlessly with three dozen idle welders. But again, halfway through the first weld, the system stopped working. Back it came to Carteret. We went through the testing process once more. After a few days, it seemed to be working. Back on the truck to Manhattan. Again it failed in the field. The problem seemed to be the size of the joint: It had been enlarged to accommodate the electroslag, but now it seemed *too* large. The machine couldn't maintain the continuous weld. Every time we were in the shop, the technicians *just* managed to get the system to work, after many hours or even days of trying. But out in the field we didn't have that kind of time.

Jack kept calling and I kept saying, "Not yet, not yet. We're getting close."

Then three days passed without any calls. Finally I called him. I had nothing encouraging to report, but I couldn't take the silence.

"Throw all that crap away," Jack said disgustedly. "I've already started the men welding the joints with ball bats"—oversized rods used in manual welding.

"You're welding by hand?" I asked.

"You're damn right! I have sixty men welding and they're eating it up."

"That costs like hell."

"Is your machine working?"

"No."

"So what do you want me to do? Put bubblegum in the joint? It has to be welded."

It wasn't a disaster that we had to weld the old-fashioned way. That's how we had bid the job anyway. The trouble was that Bob had told the fabricators to change the profile of the connections, doubling the space of the joints to accommodate the electroslag on the assumption that the machines would work in the field as they had in the shop. So now we had twice the work that we would have had if we'd planned to weld them by hand in the first place. Bob reluctantly agreed with Jack and gave up the electroslag.

I hung up the phone and found the Hobart technician tinkering with the welding machine.

"Pack this gear up," I told him. "We're not going to use them."

"These aren't our machines," the man said. "You bought them."

"Take them back," I snarled. "Sue us if you want to, but just get them out of here."

So much for revolutionary innovations. Hobart later abandoned electroslag welding completely. It was a total flop, not one of their prouder innovations. And, for us, between the cost of fixing the crane pumps and doing twice as much welding as we had to, whatever contingency money Bob and Jerome had put in our bid was starting to look like the emergency twenty in the mason jar. Everything we did was turning to disaster.

And *still* that wasn't the worst of it–the worst was yet to come. As my grandmother used to say, some houses just have an aura of disaster about them. You had to wonder if our house on Liberty Street had some kind of curse radiating from its old, plaster walls. When we took this job, word around town among contractors and the unions had been that Koch was crazy. By Christmas, we had to be crazy to think they weren't right.

16

ON
THE
BRINK

MORE THAN MEN of other trades, ironworkers are a brotherhood of free spirits who, above everything, don't want to be controlled. At least they don't want to *feel* controlled. It's why they hated being watched. Their fierce independence was such an ingrained part of the culture that one of the rules they negotiated into their contract was that an ironworker would not punch a clock. Instead, when he came onto the job in the morning, he went to the superintendent's trailer and picked up his "brass," a silver dollar–sized tag with his number stamped into it that spent the night hanging from a hook on a large board in the office. The assistant superintendent gave each man his brass when he came in for the day, leaving his spot on the board empty so it was instantly clear who was on the job. At the end of the shift, the men returned their brass to the board, a day's pay wealthier.

By the time we reached the fourth floor of the north tower early in December of 1968, we were handing out enough brass to equip a small marching band. All told, we had more than three hundred men on the pay-roll, ten times the number we had on a typical job—and still, almost unfath-omably, only half the number we would reach after we began the second tower in the spring. Our weekly payroll, including all the things the union men called fringes or bennies and we called burdens, already exceeded $250,000. (A dollar today was worth $4.65 in 1968, so adjusted for inflation, that would be the equivalent of more than $1.1 million.) It was a staggering amount—a description that would turn out to be literal.

The site was crawling with steel erectors of every sort, all of them topped out in red KOCH hard hats: journeymen ironworkers and their apprentices—everything from hookers-on and bolter-uppers to the welders who were the artisans of the trade—crane operators, oilers, and mechanics; and several tiers' worth of collectively bargained union supervision, foremen, assistant foremen commonly known as pushers, the walking bosses who were like the foremen's foremen, and finally the shop steward, the highest-ranking union member on the job and a man with as much real power as anyone in our company.

As we were putting our workforce together, the Port Authority informed us that the entire job was under a directive to try to fill at least 10 percent of the jobs with men who were members of racial minority groups. As one of the largest single contractors, it meant we were supposed to eventually employ sixty or seventy black ironworkers. (Native North Americans didn't count as minorities at the time.) Ironworking was traditionally a trade passed down from father to son and was dominated by a few ethnic groups of European descent—Irish, Scandinavians, Newfoundlanders, Germans. Finding black ironworkers for the Trade Center job looked to be a real problem: There just weren't many to be found in New York. We were required to file a monthly report on our hiring, though the worst that would happen if we didn't meet the goals was a stern letter from the Port Authority. (Years later, I was organizing a bridge job in the city in which the minority stipulation was extended to women. I asked the union to send me a female ironworker. They sent me a woman who came to the job higher than the twelve feet from which she promptly fell without a hard hat. Not that gender had anything to do with her shameful death: The week before on the same job, a male ironworker, also full of drugs, decided he wanted to fly and leaped off the bridge into a stretch of netting. All he got was wet.)

The swelling ranks of our Trade Center workers were not without a bit of feather-bedding, as was painfully evident when we considered the money we were paying to fix the crane pumps overnight. According to the operating engineers' contract, every job employing more than five union members had to have a "master mechanic," a position I put in quotes because it was a political appointment that unfortunately had nothing to do with fixing things, even though he was paid as if it did. The rule was that the master mechanic, essentially a shop steward whose ostensible duty was ensuring safety, got paid for every hour there was a union member on the site—whether or not he was there himself. So when we had a union mechanic fixing the pumps in the wee hours, the mechanic got paid double time—and so did the "master mechanic," who was sometimes blissfully asleep at home. On the Trade Center, the lucky guy was Al Howell, who ended up making the *New York Times* because he earned $80,000 that year—more than three times the salary of the average major league baseball player. As Casey Stengel said, you could look it up.

Besides the three hundred men at the Trade Center, we had another thirty, plus office staff, at the plant in Carteret. And of course we had ourselves, those of us named Koch who had our own hierarchy. More labor meant more management, and the door was open. Through it had come Uncle Dan, who was back from Puerto Rico and working in the Carteret plant; and Vinnie Landers, his nephew, who had gone to Puerto Rico with him. My cousin Vinnie, whose mother was my father's sister Cornelia, proved himself an able steel erector, running jobs for us in Albany before joining my brother Donald and uncle Danny as an assistant superintendent at the Trade Center. My younger brother Roger, meanwhile, had just gotten an MBA and joined the company as the head of the accounting department, supervising a clerical staff of six and reporting to Jerome. And my boyhood friend Joe Sherry came in as timekeeper in Carteret.

Not all the relatives were on the management side of the divide. Three were employed at the Trade Center as union workers: Uncle Dan's son Dan Junior, a surveyor; Uncle Tom's son Tom Junior, a crane oiler. And Tom Senior himself, who could have come into the company years before, but had a much better deal as a member of the operating engineers' union and loved picking steel too much to give it up for some walking-around post, or worse, a desk job. Besides, it was Tom who took umbrage when my father paid off his sisters' mortgages, so he didn't figure to have a burning desire to go to work for him.

Because the economics of the Trade Center called for most of its steel connections to be welded rather than bolted, two-thirds of our workforce in the early stages needed to be welders and their helpers. But welded-steel jobs were so uncommon in New York that few members of the ironworkers' local bothered going through the training necessary to be certified in the specialty. Knowing we would need about two hundred welders on the north tower alone, one of the first things we did when we were organizing our labor force was to invite every ironworker with a New York City welding certificate to come work for us. Most of those who showed up were West Indian immigrants who had learned their craft working at the refineries back home. The oil was carried on ships from South America and Europe, then discharged two miles offshore through welded underwater pipelines to the tank fields on land. The companies had their own little welding academies, which turned out highly trained men. When we realized we had most of the available ironworker welders in the city and were still about 170 men short, we asked the men to get the word out back home that there was plenty of work up in New York. The call spread like wildfire at the refineries, and men started arriving in droves from Jamaica, as well as from St. Croix and St. Lucia—the answer not only to our very real problem of finding talented, experienced welders, but also to our obligation to try to employ minorities.

To get his certificate, each man had to perform a weld that didn't crack when it was bent 180 degrees. If he passed, he reported to the union to get his permit, and a foreman explained that the job involved standing on a sixteen-square-foot suspended wooden platform, welding beams and columns on the inside and outside of a building. And, oh yeah, this building would be eight hundred, a thousand, eventually thirteen-hundred feet off the ground. The looks on many of their faces suggested nobody had told them this.

Where they came from, ironworking was a horizontal job. John Kelly remembers giving a new man a safety harness and telling him to go upstairs to work.

"What do you mean go to work?" the man asked.

"There's where the work is," Kelly said, pointing up.

"Oh no, I want a job down here."

"We're not building down here, we're building up there."

The man looked up again, gave Kelly back the harness, and left.

But *most* stuck it out and unquestionably raised the level of our welding.

The ever-growing workforce might have been more manageable had we not had to face so many troubles with our equipment. "The way the freakin' problems are hitting us," Jack said one day, "I have to let the union foremen handle a lot of it. And this monster is so big I can go for days without seeing my foremen." Jack was not impressed with the work sense of some of these unfamiliar foremen. He would walk into an area to check its progress and become enraged at the slow pace of the work. *Christ, Pete, you should have been out of here a day and a half ago. You're only a quarter complete—what the hell's going on?* What was going on was that with so many men on the job, and so many things going wrong, we had to surrender the close supervision that had always been one of our great strengths as a small, hands-on company. The Local 40 steward, John Kelly, would enter the discussion, which would invariably degenerate into a heated argument and force Jack to take a position. "Those men go tonight, I don't give a shit who they're related to—if they're ironworkers, I'm a horse's ass!" Jack screamed at Kelly one day, and then called Roger to tell him to lay off the men in question. Hearing this, Kelly would shout, "I want to see the boss," to which Jack said, "I *am* the fucking boss." To which Kelly would say, "Bullshit, I want to see Koch." To which Jack would say, "I'm the super, you see me." To which Kelly said, "Either I see Koch or I pull the job." The two of them stormed across the street to Bob's office.

"Kelly wants to see you," Jack told Bob.

"How ya doin', John?" Bob began cordially. "What's the problem?"

"Jack just fired three of my boys and I told him I wanted to see you."

"What happened?" Bob asked, turning to Jack.

"You know how you've been on my back about the men on the first floor never moving to the third floor?" Jack said. "I finally got down there to see for myself, and I found three of the men bullshitting in the shanty. The foreman told me they'd spent most of the day there. The whole job needs shaping up, and these three men think they have a political connection at the hall that gives them immunity from being fired. They think they're on a tit job, and we can't afford to put up with that shit!"

"Bob," Kelly interjected, "these three guys are good ironworkers. The three of them had fuckin' bellyaches from the shit coffee you guys hand out. I'm running this job for the union and I'm not letting Daly shove me or my men around. He ain't gonna fire these guys."

"John, let's get one thing straight," Bob said. "You're not in charge. Jack is running this job. Anything Jack can't handle, I'll handle. Let's smooth this business over. I'll tell payroll to forget about paying these men off. But John, we're not going to take any more bullshit from these guys. You go tell the foreman if they're caught in that shanty again, they're getting themselves fired."

"Bob, they're not ironworkers," Jack protested, annoyed as hell that Bob wasn't backing him up. "They're better off in that shanty than up on the steel. We'll have to send six men behind them to take care of the mistakes they'll be making."

"Hey, come on, Jack," Kelly said, reaching over and touching his forearm, "two of those guys have been in the business for eight years."

"They never worked for us."

"You ain't the only contractor in this business."

"I would never have them. They aren't ironworkers, they're card players."

Bob suggested a compromise. "Can you put them down sorting bolts?"

Jack thought a moment, then said, "Sure, we can do that."

"Yeah, that would be a good job for 'em," added Kelly, notching another victory for Local 40 to tell his boss about.

Our growing army of workers was a force to be reckoned with. And it wasn't long before the day of reckoning arrived.

✺   ✺

ON FRIDAY NIGHT, the thirteenth of December, four months into the job, Donald phoned me at home and said he had gotten a call from Jerome. "Bob's calling a meeting in Carteret tomorrow," my brother said. "They want us there."

"Gee, a party," I joked.

"He sounded pretty serious," Donald said.

"Who else is coming?"

"Rudy, Jack, you, me, and Roger."

"I wonder what's going on."

I picked up Donald and Roger in the morning and we drove to Carteret, filling the time talking about the pumps, the electroslag, and the sundry other problems we were struggling with at the Trade Center. We arrived at the office a little after nine, and saw all the familiar cars parked outside—Bob's Cadillac, Jerome's Lincoln, Jack's station wagon—plus one I didn't recognize. We went inside and found a tableau that immediately suggested something was wrong. Everyone was in Jerome's office, gathered around his desk, talking softly. Bob and Jerome stood silently by the window. The unfamiliar car turned out to belong to Jack Mintz. He was the company accountant.

Bob sat down and cleared his throat. He was subdued, but not so much that he couldn't have been calling a routine business meeting to order.

"I'm sorry about this," he began in a low, quiet voice. "We lost the company."

The words hung in the air, an impenetrable message delivered so abruptly that I couldn't for the life of me fathom what he was trying to say.

"What do you mean we lost the company?" I asked.

"We can't finish this job," Bob said. "We can't make the payroll."

"Hold on—I don't understand what you're saying."

"We're bankrupt, Karl," Bob said. "Jerome took out a $150,000 loan to make last week's payroll. We can't keep up. And we can't keep borrowing the money we need. We're calling in the bonding company."

"We're sorry it had to come to this," Jerome said softly, his eyes glistening. "It's a disgrace to Pop. But there's nothing else we can do."

"He worked so hard to build the company," Bob added, also on the verge of tears. The hair on the back of my neck stood up. Even now they were writing off their brother, my father, as if he were a nonentity, a bit player. As if it wasn't he who would be disgraced by the fall of Karl Koch Erecting Company, more even than Grandpa.

"How did this happen?" Donald asked, incredulous.

Jerome fell back in his chair. "We underbid the goddamn job."

I was paralyzed. There were explosive, poisonous thoughts filling my head, but they were all stuck inside. *You fucking bastards. So this is the road to your million dollars, Bob? When Dad got sick you were answerable to no one. Now you don't even have the decency to say it's* his *company you've destroyed, not just Grandpa's. Destroyed it for some goddamn ego trip. He's laying in his sickbed and you incompetent fools are blowing up his company. You're goddamn right, Jerome. You underbid the job, the goddamn job of the century. And now you're throwing in the towel without even a fight? That's the disgrace.*

"I'm shocked," I heard Jack Mintz say outside my head. "But I thought something was wrong when I drove past the site last Sunday. I said to my wife, 'Gee, they seem to be going pretty slow.' "

A Sunday drive?! You're the goddamn accountant! What about the cash flow? What about the budget? What about the bid? It's not about going slow, you fool. You try lifting fifty-ton pieces of steel with cranes gushing oil so bad you have to have Kitty Litter ready. But that's a mess we can deal with. And besides, if being behind sched-ule—which we're not—were the worst of our troubles, we wouldn't be sitting here today.

I kept my silence as Bob and Jerome talked about the payroll, the payments from the Port Authority, the banks. I was in shock. Nothing I could possibly say would do justice to the atrocity they were describing.

But more than that, it was what came from working in this business of erecting steel, from growing up in it: an ingrained disinclination to rail about incompetence and wrongdoing and failure, when what you really needed to concentrate on at the moment was figuring out how the hell to climb out of the hole all that stupidity had put you in. A steel job to me was nothing but a succession of problems that had to be solved or surmounted; when you were finished and you stepped back to look at your work, what you had in front of you was not so much a building or a bridge as a monument to resourcefulness and perseverance. When someone screwed up, I found, bogging down in recriminations only set you back further. And the worse a situation, the more pointless it was, like flailing against quicksand.

After a few minutes of expressions of regret by my uncles, I finally erupted. No one was saying a word, and I was furious. How dare they think that they could dissolve the company that easily? My father's pride was that we had always finished every job we had started—no matter what. It was one of his most fundamental lessons to me, and it was part of my very being. *You must always fulfill your contractual obligations. Your word is your bond. You could have a hundred cranes and your greatest asset would still be your reputation.* Now my uncles were destroying that, talking about wiping out in a blink of the eye something it had taken nearly half a century to build. And to them, it was only Grandpa who would be disgraced.

Finally, I erupted. "My father *never, ever* walked off a job," I said. "And we're never going to walk off this one." No one said a word or even raised their heads, just their eyes. "What are you going to do about it, Bob?"

"We're going to turn the company over to the bonding company Monday morning," Bob said. "So everybody take out all your personal stuff. Karl, grab all your father's personal stuff."

"We are *not* going to take our files, Bob!" I shouted. "We're going to finish this job!"

"We can't, Karl," he said. "It's dead."

"You're going to finish it," I insisted. "You got us into this fucking mess, Bob, now you're going to get us out of it. You are not going to stick it on Dad and Grandpa."

Bob smirked—and I knew it was a reflex to the mention of Dad's name.

"So this is the road you've led us down—the road to bankruptcy?" I said, dropping my self-imposed stricture against recrimination. I turned to Rudy. "You see what all your secret bids with Bob got us in to?" He didn't answer. He just bowed his head.

"It can't be finished, Karl," Bob said. "We don't have the money."

I turned back to my uncle, regrouping my thoughts. I realized that if I had any hope of keeping us afloat, I couldn't turn this into a condemnation proceeding and pull the trigger in the war that had been waiting to break out for years.

"We don't *need* the money," I said. "The Port Authority has the money." Everyone was gazing at me. Bob was glaring.

"Let me tell you how we're going to do it, Bob." A plan started spilling out of my mouth, the words coming fast. "I have the power of attorney for my father. I am not going to allow you to put this disgrace on him. I am now tendering his resignation as president and treasurer of the company. You, Bob, are now president of Karl Koch Erecting, and you, Jerome, are treasurer. I will take your job, Bob, as executive vice president."

I saw that I had everyone's attention.

"We are not going to go crawling to the bonding company. We're going to go to the Port Authority and tell them, 'We have this job and we fucked it up. We made a mistake, we underbid it, but it's too fucking bad because you're gonna support us. Otherwise, we may lose our company but you'll lose the Trade Center. . . ' "

To this day, I don't know where all this came from, other than some kind of panic-driven adrenaline rush. As naive as it might seem considering my misgivings about the Trade Center contract, I am still amazed at how quickly we got ourselves in such a horrendous fix. When that contract was signed, our company was free of debt and sitting on $3 million in the bank. And now it was all gone?

". . . Do you realize that they have a $650-million job, and if they lose us, they lose everyone?" I continued, as everyone in the room stared at me in silence. "We own the kangaroos. It took us two years to build them. You're going to go in and see Monti and Tozzoli, and I'm coming with you. And we're going to tell them that if they have any ideas of throwing us off the job or calling in the bonding company, they can forget them because we have the title to the cranes. If they throw us off, the cranes go with us. It'll cost them millions in lost time to replace them. If they try to take the cranes, we can tie them up in litigation. They've got to support us! They have no choice!"

Amazingly, not a single word was said by anyone in the room as I spewed out my impromptu plan, which actually had a number of flaws. First of all, my father's power of attorney gave me the right to resign him as president but not the power to appoint Bob to succeed him. But that was just a technicality. More important was that the Port Authority—an outfit not known for being easy to push around—could knock us out with one slap. They did in fact have an option other than succumbing to our threat and advancing us the money we needed to pay the men each week. They could simply call in the bonding company, which would then take over the job and seize our assets— starting with our most valuable ones, the kangaroo cranes that we had bought with our *first* advance from the Port, which we were paying off in monthly installments. Even if the bonding company decided we had just made a bad bid but were still competent to finish the job, they would become our bosses. And when the job was done, our company would be finished as well.

But it wasn't intimidation I was counting on. It was simple pragmatism on the part of the Port Authority—something they *were* known for. We accounted for only a tiny percentage of the expense of building the Trade Center—$20 million out of a job that was now up to $650 million (and would eventually clear the $1-billion mark). Yet our dollar value was far outweighed by our essential role in the construction. It really would make no sense for the Port Authority to throw us off the job at this stage and try to find another contractor. Our competence as steel erectors wasn't an issue— our aptitude as businessmen, maybe, but not our ability to get the towers up. Given the struggles that had attended this project since it was a glimmer in

David Rockefeller's eye, it was impossible to believe the Port Authority would do nothing to prevent what would be the biggest and by far the most embarrassing obstacle yet—when all they had to do was come up with a relative pittance, money they would have had to pay anyway had we calculated the job properly.

When I was through, I realized everything I had just said had come out impulsively, the whole plan born of a protective instinct to insulate my father from a public humiliation wrought by his brother's unbridled ambition. I wanted to save the company, but if I couldn't, I wanted to make damn sure that Dad wasn't the president and treasurer of record when the company he had so carefully built went belly up virtually the moment he looked away. It just so happened that the best quick fix I could come up with on the spot was also an appeal to his brother's ego. Bob had always thought he could do a better job than my father, and let everyone know it. When he finished a conversation with someone he didn't know, that person was apt to walk away thinking he had just talked to the most experienced and able steel erector in America. I was so intent on not surrendering my father's company in so dishonorable a fashion that I submitted his resignation without thinking it through, something I would one day never stop regretting.

"Anybody have any objections?" Bob asked.

No one did.

"Okay," said the new president of the Karl Koch Erecting Company. "That's what we'll do."

As INFURIATING AS I found their initial unwillingness to fight, I understood why Bob and Jerome felt so defeated, so impotent. They had seen this terrible bombshell coming (though, true to form, they had saved it as a Christmas surprise for my brothers and me), and they knew just as surely where it was going. Our situation in December represented only the first trickle of trouble that would drip off what was turning out to be an impossibly oppressive contract.

The problem was simple math: The money coming in from the Port Authority was less, a lot less, than the money we were paying out to all those men in the best hard hats money could buy. We had come into the job with a couple of million dollars in the bank, but we'd spent it all on the plant in New Jersey, the barges, and all that equipment and all those supplies. We were also paying off the advance we'd gotten from the Port for the kangaroo cranes.

Bob and Jerome saw the figures staring at them: We were on course to lose a million dollars in the first six months (quadruple that figure to equate it to today's dollars), and it would only get worse. If we had to borrow $150,000 a week to make the payroll *now*—when we were working on only one tower and ironworker wages were only going in one direction—they couldn't even imagine how big the hole they had dug would become a year down the line, never mind two. And never mind trying to fix all the problems surrounding us on the job. In a matter of a couple of months, we had gone from being on top of the world, primed for glory, to sliding into an abyss, the road to hell paved with leaking oil and broken slag, and hemorrhaging red ink. Only years later did my cousin Vinnie tell me that in the days before that Saturday morning, he had helped Bob and Jerome remove a truckload of personal files from the office.

A steel erector is paid by the pound. At the end of each month, we submitted a requisition to the Port Authority, an invoice, stating how much steel we had set, which the Port's accounting department confirmed by counting the pieces and calculating the weight, then paying us according to the $111-per-ton price of our bid. The structural design of the towers placed by far the most weight at the bottom: 60 percent of the tonnage of the entire tower was concentrated in just the first fifteen floors, from the grillages six stories belowground up to the treetops at the ninth floor. The entire rest of the tower—100 floors—had only 40 percent of the load-bearing weight. The bottom fifteen averaged 4,000 tons of steel a floor—compared to a tenth of that, just 400 tons a floor, the rest of the way up.

Those numbers would be jarring in one sense years later, but in quite another at the time. It meant that the work we finished by December should have produced our greatest return—our biggest profit margin. We should have been comfortably in the black, if not downright flush. But we were broke. And with those one hundred floors of relatively light steel the rest of the way up, our books would only get more out of balance. Once we were above the treetops, our monthly payment from the Port would be a fraction of what it had been below them, while the cost of labor would remain the same—until it got higher with the next raise in union wages.

The only thing that could possibly reverse our fortunes would be a huge speedup in productivity, setting more pieces in the same amount of time. But that was beyond the realm of possibility. Even if those hapless Lucas pumps weren't spewing oil and shutting down, even if we weren't laboring over the ill-fated Hobart electroslag, even if we could somehow set and weld the steel more quickly, it would be a treadmill we couldn't keep up with. Not with the new union contract, which far exceeded the customary increase Bob and Rudy had budgeted.

I thought back a year and a half, to the night I stayed late at the office on Casanova Street to read the contract my uncles were ready to sign with the Port Authority. I had challenged them over the alarming absence of a standard escalation clause to protect us from a jump in labor costs. We couldn't know then how big a raise the ironworkers would get in their next contract; all we knew was that whatever they got would kick in just as we were starting the job.

My father never, ever signed a contract without an escalation clause, and considering the hundreds of men we would eventually have to hire to get these colossal buildings up, not having one now seemed the height of insanity. *Of course* my uncles underbid the job. It was almost inevitable. Dad was the master bidder, a model of prudence. Bob was the ambitious risk-taker. Jerome went along. They were intent on building the Trade Center—and unaware of the enormous leverage we had because no other erector in America would touch it with a forty-foot beam. So Bob and Jerome had acquiesced to the Port's insistence that in lieu of an escalation clause we simply estimate the union raise and build it into our bid. Bob, Jerome, and Rudy projected a three-year 10 percent raise, which they thought was a safe harbor judging by the previous few contracts. But in June of 1968—less than two months before we laid the first grillage—the association of contractors that bargained with Local 40 on the behalf of all of us apparently was in a magnanimous mood and decided that we contractors had been a bit chintzy with the union in the last few contracts. The union's negotiating committee, meanwhile, saw all the work coming up in New York—with the Trade Center, of course, way at the top of the list—and, being no fools, held a strike threat over the bargaining table. In the end, the union raise was almost four times the 5 percent increase my uncles and Rudy had considered more than safe.

As scary as the contract was when I heard it back in June, I thought we could take the hit, thanks to our stroke of luck with the kangaroo cranes. If we were using the usual guy derricks to erect the Twin Towers, as was the plan when my uncles and Rudy first computed the bid, the union raise would have broken us right out of the box. But the kangaroos had such expansive reach that we would be able to erect the Trade Center with eight cranes rather than twelve. With two fewer cranes on each tower, the kangaroos would save us the cost of about forty men for three years—more than $5 million in our pouch. But if the cranes helped offset the first year of the union raise, they wouldn't be able to keep up with the increases due in the second and third.

So if the union raise wasn't killing us—yet—where had all the money gone? How could we lose $1 million in less than six months? The answer to that question was ironic. One of our company's most notable projects, and one of which my father was most proud, was the General Electric Building erected in Pittsfield, Massachusetts, in 1940. It was the first all-welded building in the country. It demonstrated that welding a building's steel joints was more economical than bolting them, and performed properly, every bit as effective. Welding the connections joined the columns and beams so seamlessly that it was as if the entire building were one solid, continuous piece of steel. But it had never caught on because there was one string attached, and it made architects, engineers, and builders uncomfortable: It shifted much of the burden of quality control from the shop to the field, where it was more difficult to maintain.

This was more a psychological barrier than a real one, and welding techniques had improved vastly in the last twenty years, which was why the fearless leaders of the Port Authority decided to call for welding when they first started talking to the steel companies back in 1964. The advantage of welding was that it reduced the cost of the steel you needed to buy. The saving was partly offset by higher onsite labor costs, but on balance, it was less expensive than bolting. That was in a normal building. On a project with as much steel as the World Trade Center, the savings could be huge. And now that the job had been divided up, with the Port buying the steel from fabricators and then paying us to erect it, all the savings were theirs and the added expense ours. Unless, of course, we accurately calculated the cost of welding over bolting and built it into our price.

Welding was a far more precise and sophisticated process than the more primitive method of bolting on. Bolting wasn't brain surgery. But in the context of construction, welding was. We had to buy new equipment for hundreds of welders. We had to maintain the steel at a constant weldable temperature, summer or winter, by having a man stand with a propane torch, constantly heating the metal so that it would accept a flawless weld. Eventually, we had to have a special shield to protect the welder and his weld from the high winds of the upper floors, and to protect workers below him from his molten sparks.

Though our ironworkers were already certified as welders, they had to be trained specifically for this job. They had to make sure to scrub their welds with a wire brush after each pass. They had to break off any slag with a chipping hammer to get a nice, clean surface, then brush the surface again before the next pass. When we first started, way down at the first columns from the grillages, the Port Authority inspectors said our welds were no good. There were inclusions—tiny foreign bodies that looked like dots on an X ray—that indicated the men were not being as meticulous as they had to be. So we had to hire our own ultrasonic welding engineer to teach them the right technique to produce flawless welds without slag, without inclusions, without voids and other impurities in the finished weld. And then that engineer had to check every weld in advance of the Port inspectors.

The challenge was welding the joints not only to the highest standards of quality, but also fast enough to catch up to the raising gangs, which of course couldn't jump the cranes until everything beneath them was secured. And speed just wasn't welding's virtue. The lower exterior columns alone were ten feet each in circumference, and there were eighty of them—each with three joints to weld just to get to the fourth floor. And each of these 240 joints needed at least 15 welding passes. So just to get us to the base of the trees, and just for the exterior columns, not the core columns, required *seven miles* of weld. While all this was going on, we were in the beginning stages of installing hundreds of thousands of shear-connector studs, bolts welded to the tops of beams designed to anchor the concrete that would later be poured on each floor. More than 200 tons of these studs had to be fused, another task that was new to our ironworkers, who had to use special stud-welding equipment. We eventually mastered all these systems, but not without having to place a great deal of the management in the hands of ironworker foremen, most of whom were new to us and we to them. The learning curve for all of us was wicked. So that's where the money was going: It was disappearing in the welding.

Because I was in the hospital when Bob and Rudy were estimating the Trade Center in the summer and early fall of 1966, I never saw their calculations. But judging from the simple arithmetic that ultimately unfolded, it became apparent that they didn't fully appreciate the intricacies and the sheer scale of work involved in setting and welding 400 million pounds of high-strength steel. To be sure, the GE Building in Massachusetts was not the World Trade Center. And when it came to welding, it was a different world in 1940. But as the company that erected the first all-welded steel building in the country, we should have had some clue what we were in for. Apparently, we didn't. There was to be one final irony: Among the many ways in which the Twin Towers were a landmark in construction was that they were to become a defining moment in the way steel was joined in American skyscrapers. After the Trade Center, welding high-stress connections rather than bolting them became the standard.

So it was official: We had underbid the job—grossly underbid it. There was no way to know how much money we had left on the table, since we didn't know how much—or even if—another erector had bid on the job. But as it would turn out, our price was an entire World Trade Center short. Ultimately, the Port Authority would pay us $30 million, half again as much as our bid. But when all was said and done, when direct union labor, overhead, equipment, temporary material, and profit were computed, a correct bid would have been about $40 million—twice what we had agreed to be paid.

How could we have been so far off? The reasons were assorted and intertwined, but it all came down to being in over our heads, at least financially, almost from the very moment John Tishman called Bob and popped the magical question: *How would you like to build the World Trade Center?*

THAT SATURDAY MORNING in Carteret was unlike any hour I'd ever spent with my uncles. For those few minutes, I held power. It was the power of a flashlight in a dark tunnel, shining on the way out. And once that way out was taken, my power was gone, never to return. Bob took control as president of the company after a formal vote, and made plans to talk to the Port Authority about this awful predicament we had found ourselves in. From then on, he kept me as far out of the loop as possible, even more removed than I had been. That I was ostensibly now the second in command and controlled half the voting stock meant nothing—as Jack once said, as long as Bob was in control I was "vice president of shit." Bob returned to his secrets with Jerome and Rudy, and closed me out of all dealings with the Port Authority.

I didn't quite understand it. The underlying message I'd intended to convey to Bob—once you got past my shock and anger and real panic—was that I still believed that he had the ability to overcome his near-fatal mistake. Despite the shambles to which he had quickly reduced the company after forty years of steady stewardship by Dad and Grandpa, I still believed it was Uncle Bob's time to have a turn at the presidency. And with a little help from our friends at the Port Authority, he would have a chance to redeem himself and the company. His business sense and emotional intelligence left something to be desired, but he was still a superb, incredibly hard-working steel erector. I wanted him to take control of the situation, and to know that I would be right behind him. But apparently all he saw in me was my father's face. I didn't know about the meeting with the Port Authority until after it took place, when Bob told everyone that the PA had agreed to bail us out.

It was that simple. "They're taking it off the top," Bob said, meaning that since the Port had thus far paid us less than a third of our eventual $20 million, they would make up our shortfalls each week from the remaining balance. And if we needed money for supplies and equipment, they would pay for that, too. What would happen when we reached the $20 million—a point that would obviously come long before the second tower was up—wasn't discussed. But the assumption was that the Port would continue to support us. All we had to do was find three empty desks at our office in Carteret for the Port Authority accountants who would spend four days a week for the next year checking every penny that came in and every one that went out.

It was disconcertingly almost anticlimactic. On Saturday we had "lost the company." On Monday, we had a sugar daddy. Aside from the presence in our office of the Port's bean counters, it was as if the debacle had never happened. And now we could climb into the sky with a safety net beneath us. Exactly what had transpired was a mystery, at least to us, the Sands Point Koches. But by now I knew it was futile to press Bob for details. So I let it go at that, just thankful and relieved—euphoric, actually—that the plan I'd spewed out two days earlier had worked. It wasn't until more than thirty years later, when I started asking questions so I could write this book, that I learned that it really hadn't been in doubt—and that it actually hadn't been necessary to resign my father and turn the company over to my uncle. You talk about leaving money on the table. Money was the least of what I wound up surrendering.

My first hint came in 1999, when Angus Kress Gillespie, an associate professor of American Studies at Rutgers University, published a book called *Twin Towers: The Life of New York City's World Trade Center.* Gillespie concentrated more on the political history and architectural and cultural significance of the Trade Center than on its actual construction. But he did interview Ray Monti, who told him that we had run into "financial difficulties" at one point and that "Koch"—Gillespie wrote that it was "Karl" but obviously it was Bob—had come to the construction-site trailer one morning, thrown his keys and his wallet onto Monti's desk, and said, "You've got everything else, now you can have my Cadillac, my twelve kids, my wife, and my house because I have nothing else left. And, besides, I'm going to kill myself, so it really doesn't matter." Monte told Gillespie that he had blithely replied, "Why don't you let me take you to lunch? Then you can kill yourself this afternoon." (Bob denied the episode in a conversation with my collaborator, but, of course, he was the only Koch with twelve kids and a Cadillac, and such melodramatics would not have been out of character for him. Monti has died since Gillespie interviewed him.)

Bob had chosen the path of least resistance, his fellow Seabee who knew what it was like to build and fight. Monti, of course, didn't have the authority to bail us out on the spot, but he did get things rolling, bringing the situation to Guy Tozzoli, who brought it to Austin Tobin and the entire Port Authority Board of Commissioners. My cousin Vinnie, who was chummy with our uncles and also friendly with my brothers and me, tells me that while he didn't know anything about Bob's pre-suicide lunch with Monti, Bob told him that he had gone to the Port Authority offices to meet with the top people, and brought Grandpa, of all people, with him. Apparently, if the Port people were going to rescue and stay with Karl Koch Erecting Company, they wanted to meet Karl Koch. Bob presented his eighty-six-year-old, long-retired father as the head of the company, something Grandpa hadn't been since 1936.

When we talked to him, Tozzoli revealed that there had never been a question in his mind that the Port would bankroll us for the duration of the project. Though one member of his senior management team, Mal Levy, wanted to bring in the bonding company to take over the job, Tozzoli said that wasn't going to happen. After the Port jettisoned the Pittsburgh steelers in the summer of 1966, he brought in the Replacements, and we were the quarterback of this team of scrappy men of steel. And from the very beginning, Tozzoli said, he was ready to do whatever it took to help us get those towers up. "I was ready to finance anybody that would do it," he said. "All I needed was a guy who knew how to erect steel. You guys, to me, weren't a contractor, you were a partner. You took a big chance because you were a little bunch of guys. I knew in my heart that I had to keep you alive."

What this said to me was that Tozzoli probably knew from the beginning that our bid was too low, and that he was pretty much waiting for the day we came to him, hat in hand. I told him that, later on, when I was talking to Monti at a party, a reporter came up to him and asked what the secret was for building the world's tallest buildings. Monti had pointed to me and said, "The secret is getting a very small contractor with a very big bond." But the truth was that a bond was all but irrelevant. "My board said, 'Tozzoli, you'd better get a bond,' " Tozzoli said, "so I got a bond. But the idea was you were always my partner."

It was only one of the things I wish we had known at the time. Years later, John Alonzo, the president of Graphics Steel Design, told me that the entire industry—especially Bethlehem and American Bridge, which were not disinterested parties, of course—was shocked when we took the Trade Center job. "Everyone thought you were going to get killed," John said. He remembered a man from Bethlehem telling him at the time: "Wait until Koch tries to pick steel once they're over sixty floors. The wind will be blowing, the clouds will be sailing by, and the pieces will be flying like kites. Koch has no idea what that's going to be like, and that's when they're going to find out how to price that kind of a job."

The guy was more or less right, though we found out long before we reached the sixtieth floor. But as it turned out, while we were falling the hardest, we weren't the only one of the Replacements having a rough time of it. Many of the small fabricators who were supplying the steel seem to have fallen into the same trap we did: They were so anxious to get such a big and prestigious job that they didn't anticipate just how big, and just how complicated, it really was. That was the carrot the Port Authority held out: Everyone wanted to get in on the world's tallest buildings. We saw it ourselves, in the suppliers that gave us unbelievable deals just to be part of it. One company *gave* us three free compressors, at $5,000 a pop. The scuttlebutt around the job later on was that almost everyone had lost money, and that we were the only ones who got out with our skin because we were so central to the construction, and we were falling so dramatically off the cliff, that the Port Authority *had* to save us. It was a strange turn of events, given that the Port was known for its killer legal department and death-defying contracts.

A few years later, the *Wall Street Journal* wrote about the unique arrangement that evolved after the Port Authority parted company with the major companies. Some people in the industry thought that the Port's decision to break up the job into small pieces might mark the end of an era, that no longer would U.S. Steel and Bethlehem be the only ones getting the biggest jobs. But the paper also found that at least some of the fabricators were willing to admit they had submitted bids that left them working for next to nothing. "It's a more complex job than we anticipated," said C.M. Pigott, president of Pacific Car & Foundry. His company had the largest piece, a $21.8 million contract for the 55,000 tons of exterior wall panels that would clothe one hundred floors of each tower. "We don't expect to make any money," Pigott said at a point when the answer had to have been pretty clear. When I read that, I had to wonder if the big steel companies had really been so overpriced after all. Had they done the job for their original estimate, *they* might have been the ones looking for a bailout. Of course, there wouldn't have been anything so unusual about that.

Simple as all that, we were back at it Monday morning, without missing an hour on the job. I never told my father what had happened. I couldn't. He would go to his grave never knowing how close we had come to losing his company.

17

TASMANIAN DEVILS

HALF PAST SIX on a frigid morning, Jack Daly and I drove down the West Side Highway, heading for a diner to get our first coffees to go for the day. Jack was in a poor mood—nothing new there. "They pulled two motors last night," he said. "Same thing happened to both of them. The cranes were hooked onto a load, and as soon as the operator dropped the gears into high—zonk."

"I'll call Delaval and get a reading on the motors," I said. "I'll put some pressure on them to hustle them back to us."

It was just after the new year, January of 1969. We were back in business as far as money was concerned, but there wasn't a thing the Port Authority could do to fix the Lucas 4000 pumps that were still breaking down on just about a daily basis. Austin Tobin himself could write a check for a million dollars and all it would pay for was the double time the crane operators and mechanics were piling up and a lifetime supply of Kitty Litter to sop up the oil. Not to discount the Port's spirit of cooperation, and its deep pockets, which made the cost of fixing the pumps the least of our worries. But spending the nights taking the pumps out, sending them out for repair, changing parts, waiting for them to break down again, was no way to build the World Trade Center.

"Except for that, the kangaroos are running sweet, right?" I asked Jack. I meant the hydraulic controls, the lifting capacities, and the other things that made us sink $2.5 million into these cranes. But, of course, it came off like an "Other than that, Mrs. Lincoln . . ." kind of question.

"They'd be sweeter if Favelle had finished making the freakin' things," he said.

"How's that?"

"That gang of Aussie mechanics are always fiddling with them, attaching some piece they flew in. There isn't a crane on the job that has the two systems intact. We're always stealing from one system to another. We paid Favelle for the cranes when he loaded them on the steamers in Sydney. Now he has a crew on the job finishing them."

"Come on, you're exaggerating."

"Exaggerating? Go climb up the crane tower. You'll see for yourself."

"Jack, you know my legs won't take me up there. I'd never get back to my desk."

"Then when I tell you our problems, believe me."

"Okay, okay, I believe you."

Jack leaned forward in his seat and muttered: "Shit, shit. *Shit!*"

The routine was by now all too familiar. Whenever a pump blew, the mechanics would shut down the crane and take the pump off the gear box and completely drain and clean it. If it was shot, they'd send it to Delaval for repair. When it came back, it would last a week, maybe two, maybe just a day. Eric Favelle was ultimately responsible, but all he could do was defer to Leslie Goddard, the international sales manager for Joseph Lucas Ltd. in London. Goddard would dispatch some engineers and technicians who would study the situation, go home, and come up with new filters. For nearly six months, Goddard and his technical people had been insisting the problem was that our dirty oil was blowing the motors. Favelle's people agreed, even though they were there day after night and had to know it wasn't. Nothing to it, Terry Murray, one of the resident Favelle technicians, always seemed to be saying. Just needs a finer strainer. "Lucas is sending new strainers in with a couple of fellows from London," Terry said. "They'll have the things here in the morning. I'll go pick them up at JFK." No, I said, you stay here and work on the cranes. I'll go.

In the morning, I went to Kennedy and waited in a coffee shop for the men from Lucas to make the drop, as if they were Napoleon Solo and Ilya Kuryakin, the men from U.N.C.L.E. After clearing Customs, they joined me at a table and took out bags of strainers and other little bits and pieces. I examined the goods, praying that I held in my hands the answer to all our woes, then stuffed the pieces in my pocket. Cheerio, said the men from Lucas, and turned around to wait for the next flight back to London while I returned to my car and made my way through the rush-hour traffic back to Lower Manhattan. The mechanics put in the new strainers and installed the rebuilt pumps in the bellies of the beasts.

Bits and pieces and prayers weren't the answer. No matter how fine the filter, when the operator got to a certain speed, the pump would blow out and the parts inside would break loose and tear the whole pump apart, gushing oil everywhere. Another night of double time. If both pumps blew in the same crane, we scrambled to take a backup pump from one of the others. It got so bad that when the second group of four kangaroos arrived dockside from Australia in February, in preparation for starting the second tower, we started cannibalizing *them* to keep the work moving on the first building. What did it mean that every day, a black vulture flew above us, and shit on us?

One day I went down to Delaval in central New Jersey, and Bernie Buongiovanni led me into a laboratory where the internal workings of the shattered pumps were spread out on white gauze. Moving from pile to pile, I stared at the pieces of shrapnel. "That's some goddamn mess," I said to Bernie, who could only nod empathetically. He said he had no idea what was wrong.

"Bernie," I said finally, "you are looking at a desperate man. We need new pumps. We can't go on like this." Bernie said he would call Les Goddard in London and tell him how bad the situation was.

Whatever Bernie said to him, it was enough to get Goddard on a plane to New York. The next morning, Bernie picked him up and brought him directly to the construction site, where Goddard climbed up to the cranes and began inspecting each one, searching for evidence of sloppiness on our part that would support his insistence that *we* were causing the breakdowns, not his best pumps in the world. His contention that impurities were getting into the systems had only one flaw: Goddard found our operation spotless. We had already made it as sterile as an operating room months earlier when he had first said our own poor housecleaning was making the cranes break down.

Goddard suggested we all retire to our office on Liberty Street. Virtually right outside our window, the grillages for the south tower were due to go into the ground in just a matter of weeks. It gave Goddard a perfect view of what we were facing: the prospect of trying to erect both buildings simultaneously with the pumps on *eight* cranes breaking down.

We all went into Bob's office. "Les," Bob said, "this is critical for us. You've got to straighten this out. We've done everything you've told us to do."

"How many pumps have you lost so far?" Goddard asked.

"Fourteen in four months," Jack said.

"We have seven smaller Lucas pumps on these cranes, and we haven't had any problems with them," I pointed out.

"Are those picking heavy loads?"

"They do when the crane booms up."

"That's a short haul?"

"Shorter than the main-load."

Goddard said that the problem was still that the mesh in the strainers was too coarse and was letting impurities through. His technical people were working on an even finer micromesh strainer that would keep the oil clean. And they believed that a secondary problem was that a tiny neoprene seal was failing. "Have you noticed that, Bernie?" he asked.

"Yes," Bernie said, "as a matter of fact the seals are gone in almost every case."

Goddard said his lab people had come up with a new, improved seal, an O-ring.

"When can you have them here?" Bob asked.

"Three days," Goddard said.

"That's not soon enough."

"How about the day after tomorrow?"

Jack and I were both fidgeting. "I'm sorry, Les, but I think the problem is your fucking pumps," Jack said. "They're no good. And saying it's our fault is a crock of shit."

Goddard stiffened. "If you want to reduce this conversation to expletives," he said, "I assure you I am as good as you, if not better." He turned to Bernie. "How many pumps do you have at your lab?" Goddard was a master at avoiding questions and deflecting criticism with a perfectly timed expression of indignation—as he had shown the last time he'd been in town, when he shut me up by accusing me of being "some kind of Jonas" when I pressed him about getting backup pumps.

"We have seven on the table," Bernie said.

"We will have more than an adequate supply of parts for that."

"Three or four of them are basket cases," I pointed out. I was polite about it, but picked up the argument we'd had downstairs at the Bull and the Bear. "How about spare pumps?" I asked once more.

"We won't need spare pumps," Goddard said, brushing me aside as if he'd never heard this suggestion before. "This will solve the problem."

Maybe yes, maybe no, but it was progress: The O-ring was something new. It seemed that for the first time, Goddard was acknowledging, or at least opening the door to the possibility, that the pump had at least some role in our grief. But he was still far from saying what Jack and I had begun to suspect: that these pumps just could not handle the load and lifting speed that the crane was demanding. That it had nothing to do with dirty oil. That whatever the merits of the rest of the product line of this eminent company, this time it had come up with a clunker—a genuine, honest-to-goodness Piece of Shit. On that score, Goddard was on another continent.

Two days later, I was back in the coffee shop at Kennedy, sitting with the men from Lucas and examining a tiny neopren ring, no bigger than a dime. So this is supposed to save the World Trade Center, I thought. Hard to imagine. There were a dozen rings in a little bag, enough for all eight 4000 pumps, plus some ominous spares. I stuffed the rings in my pocket and headed back to the city. They'd better work, I thought as I emerged from the Brooklyn-Battery Tunnel and headed up West Street. The tower was starting to look like a tower, its twin was about to be born, and by late spring we would be going at full throttle, or trying, pushing the kangaroos to their limits. Meanwhile, greeting me as I drove up was a fifty-foot trailer that had taken up residence alongside the north tower. It was filled with industrial-strength absorbent. With all the oil all over the place, we weren't using Kitty Litter anymore. We needed the hard stuff.

A FEW DAYS LATER, I was in Carteret when Jack called, screaming almost incoherently. Slow down, I told him, I can't understand you.

"Seven pumps! Seven pumps! Seven pumps! Seven pumps! Can you hear that? We lost seven pumps in the last three hours! The job is damn near stopped!"

Bernie Buongiovanni, of all people, happened to be in my office. I told Jack I would call him back, and slammed the phone down. "Seven pumps, Bernie, seven pumps!" I said. "This is it, Bernie! And don't tell me about another seal!" Bernie looked truly pained, if not especially surprised. It was at this moment that it occurred to me that the bailout by the Port Authority might not be enough to save us after all. If we didn't fix this, we might still be remembered not as the company that built the World Trade Center, but the one that *couldn't*—the one that blew it. "Let's get out of here, Bernie," I said. "Let's go someplace and talk." We started walking north on West Street, heading for Ponti's, a favorite downtown haunt of the construction industry, famous for its three-hour steak-and-scotch lunches.

"Seven pumps!" I was still repeating when we sat down, still unable to grasp the relentlessness of the trouble, the strife, we were having on this job. I ordered the first round of scotches. "I'm getting on a plane to England," I said to Bernie, "and I want you to come with me. I don't care what Goddard says, I'm getting those spares."

"No, Karl," Bernie said. "You don't want to do that. Believe me, it won't do you any good."

"How could it not do me any good? It has to. We're listening to this horseshit and the pumps are blowing us out of this job. I'm going, and you're coming with me."

"It won't be worth my time."

"I'll pay your way," I said. "It'll all be on me. Just introduce me to the people, and then you can go off and see the Tower of London."

"It's not going to help," Bernie repeated.

"How can it not help?"

It went on like this through a second scotch, through the steaks, through a third scotch and a fourth, until the drinks finally loosened Bernie's lips. "Bernie," I said, "you gotta tell me what's going on."

Bernie looked at me intently for a long moment. "Karl, I've got to tell you something," he said finally. He pulled his chair around, close to mine. "But you've got to promise me you won't tell them I told you."

"I won't, I promise," I said.

"Karl, you've got the only Lucas 4000 pumps in captivity."

I looked at him blankly.

"The reason Goddard is always putting you off about getting spare pumps is because there *are* none. There are sixteen of these 4000 pumps in the world, and you've got them all. Oh, excuse me. There's one in Tasmania."

"Can I get that one?" I asked cluelessly, not even sure where the hell Tasmania was.

Bernie chuckled. "It's nothing but trouble, too. Karl, the pumps are no good."

"What do you mean the pumps are no good?" I asked. "I mean, I know the pumps aren't any good, but what do *you* mean they're no good?"

Bernie said he'd better start at the beginning. "And you swear you won't say I'm the source of this, right? You'll have my job."

"Bernie, you've got my word."

"All right. When Goddard was in town that first time, before you started the job, remember how getting spares for the 1000s and the 3000s was no problem, but when it came to the 4000, you could forget it? He was fight-

ing you on it. I found out that it was because these pumps weren't in production. They were prototypes. They still are. Karl, it's an experimental
pump. You're testing it out."

I was trying to take all this in. Bernie explained how it all went back to
that first time my uncles and I had met Eric Favelle in our office on
Casanova Street, the day after he called us from Detroit saying he'd heard
we were in the market for a crane that was something special. We had told
him we wanted it all: strength, range, and speed—the power to pick fifty tons
of steel out fifty feet, and to lift it at the relatively supersonic rate of 400 feet
a minute. That would get a fifty-ton piece of steel from the street to the
110th floor of the Trade Center in a little over three minutes—a full ten minutes faster than anything out there. After that meeting and in the months
that followed, Bob had pressed the need for speed with Favelle, who was
nothing but agreeable. He had cranes to sell. Now all he had to do was come
up with a hydraulic pump that could drive a crane harder than any crane
had ever been driven before.

"He went to Lucas and told them what he needed," Bernie said. "And
they told him, 'Well, we've got this prototype.' " It was a pump that Lucas
was developing for an oil company that needed a high-capacity machine for
an offshore oil drilling platform in Tasmania, a little island in the South
Pacific, off the southern coast of Australia. The model numbers of these
pumps—IG 1000, IG 3000, IG 4000—denoted how many imperial gallons of
oil (thus the designation IG) the machine could pump in an hour. The more
oil it could pump, the more the capacity, the faster the crane's line speed.
"But all they did was take the 3000 and make it bigger," Bernie said. "Now,
that's a good pump, been around for years, and it's a workhorse. But when
you get into these higher capacities, it calls for a different design. You can't
just scale it up without changing the engineering."

Lucas slapped the model number IG 4000 on the larger pump and tried
it out in the oil rig off Tasmania. Meanwhile, when Favelle sent us the
smaller kangaroos that we used as a tryout on the office tower in Midtown,
he used the IG 3000 pump for the main hoist. It performed flawlessly, with
a line speed that would leave a guy derrick in the dust. Though its high
capacity was more than enough for the bigger kangaroos to boom up and
down, and even enough to lift, it wasn't quite enough to give us the line
speed that Bob had insisted on.

The 4000 pump in Tasmania apparently worked reasonably well at the
start, but by the time we were using them, it was delivering the same dismal
results in the South Pacific that we were now seeing in Lower Manhattan.

Lucas at that point might have conceded that the larger pump hadn't been adequately tested and that it might have a design flaw. The company might have given us the option of swapping them for the more dependable if slightly less breathtaking 3000 pump on the main hoist. But instead, Goddard and his people acted as if the pump had been around for years, and that we were somehow abusing them—apparently keeping their fingers crossed that by a small miracle and an even smaller piece of plastic, they might start working. "They didn't care about anything but the four hundred feet a minute that your uncle and Favelle wanted," Bernie told me. "So Lucas gave it to them, but never gave the pumps a good tryout. They tested them on their workbench." It wasn't until these pumps—these prototypes that were passed off as production models—were put to a real test that they proved worthless. The internal mechanisms couldn't stand the pressure at high speeds and blew out.

What Bernie Buongiovanni said was so devastating that it took a few minutes for it to sink in. It was unbelievable: Lucas had actually tried to sneak an unproven pump onto the biggest steel job in the history of the planet. Even worse, for six months they had refused to admit what was going on, even in the face of obvious failure and at the risk of bringing down this immense project, not to mention our less-than-immense company. They stubbornly, calculatingly continued to use us for their research and development.

"Ho. . . lee . . . shit." That's all I could manage when he finished. "You're telling me they watched us go through all this and kept feeding us all this horseshit, while we're trying to build the goddamn *World Trade Center?*"

"Yeah," Bernie said contritely.

"So what's all the shit about strainers and O-rings?" I asked Bernie.

"They honestly think that's what the trouble is," Bernie said. "I thought so, too, at the beginning. But when we were at that meeting, I was wondering what Goddard was going to say when you asked him about the spares, because I *knew* there were no spares."

"Why didn't you tell me?"

"Karl, I'm sorry. But how could I?"

"I'm calling the son of a bitch." I looked at my watch. Three in the afternoon, eight at night in London. "First thing in the morning."

"Don't forget your promise," he said.

The next morning, I was up at four and an hour later I was in the office and on the phone with Les Goddard. If anything, I was even madder than I'd been twelve hours earlier, and armed for battle. "Les, this is Karl Koch,"

I said. "Yesterday we lost seven pumps. Seven pumps, Les. Now where are those fucking spares?"

"Now, listen, I'm not going to listen to your tirades," Goddard said. "Calm down and let's discuss the situation. There must be something wrong with your operations in those towers." Now, that was the wrong thing to say to me at the moment.

"I've had enough of your bullshit games. I happen to know we have all the 4000 pumps there are. I know the only other one in the world is in Tasmania, and that's why you've been lying to me for six months."

London was silent.

"Now that I have your attention, I have one thing to say to you, and after I'm finished saying it, I'm going to call the managing director of the whole Joseph Lucas Ltd. enterprise and tell him the same thing. The failure of your pumps could very likely cause the Koch Erecting Company to go under on this job, and if that happens I promise you I will take Joseph Lucas Ltd. down with us. If I have to spend the rest of my life doing it, that is my solemn promise to you. Now, here's what we're going to do. I don't want those pumps anymore."

"What do you mean you don't want them?" Goddard asked.

"I want to replace them with the 3000. I'll install them at my cost and trade you even. I've already checked with Buongiovanni, and he has enough on hand."

"Yes, but the speeds," Goddard said. "You're not going to get your line speeds from the 3000."

"The hell with the speed. I need pumps that work. Now I'm going to hang up and give you an hour to talk to your boss and get your act together. And then I am going to call him and we are going to settle this."

As soon as I got off the phone, I called Bernie at home, waking him up to tell him what I'd done. I told him Goddard was so dumbfounded that he didn't even ask how I knew about the pumps. "but if they ask," I said, "we'll say I found out from one of the Aussies on the job."

"I had my own cover story," Bernie said, "but I like yours better."

I sat at my desk and watched the clock. At six, the sun was about up, and I called Lucas back and asked for the managing director. When he got on the line, he said he'd been waiting for my call and wanted to include Goddard in the conversation. I gave him a little background: how we might be erecting the world's tallest buildings, but we were hardly the world's biggest steel erector. And now, because of his company's pumps—and, I might have added, because of its deceit—we were in very serious peril. "I don't have to tell you about the international publicity we have on this," I told him, a preamble to repeating my threat. "Our name is on those cranes in letters four feet high. If these pumps take us down, I'm going to take you down with us."

"Mr. Koch," the man said in a heavy Scottish accent. "I want you to know we are behind you."

"How are you behind us?"

"We are very distressed, I assure you. This is a disaster, and we can't have it. We will put all the resources of our firm behind you. After our conversation, I plan to call Bernie Buongiovanni and tell him to put his complete facilities at your disposal. We will beat this one together."

"It's too late for that. I want to replace all the 4000 pumps with 3000s."

"Don't you realize how expensive that would be for you?"

I had to be sure I heard right. "No, they're not going to be expensive for *me,*" I said. "I'm not buying them. I'm exchanging them. I want you to call Bernie and authorize it. My trucks are already on the way to Delaval."

Before the week was out, we had switched the main-hoist pumps in all eight of our cranes, and just like that, the oil stopped spewing and the kangaroos got well. They lifted and luffed and slewed as if they'd all had heart transplants—as if they'd been reborn. They weren't quite as fast as they might have been if the 4000 pumps had worked. But, really, it was a case of losing something we never had. Moreover, whichever size pumps were in there, the cranes still gave us a line speed far beyond what we would have had with guy derricks. Even at a slower speed, the kangaroos could do in four or five minutes what might take a guy derrick fifteen minutes, because the new cranes could lift a piece of steel with one monstrous length of cable. Guy derricks would need to use four separate sections. The difference between the 3000 and the 4000 pumps was so relatively slight that it was truly beyond comprehension how much time, money, energy, and suffering we had wasted trying to attain such an ungodly speed as my uncle had demanded.

Now we had to believe the worst was beneath us. With the cranes hoisting steel like a charm and the Port Authority accountants closing our wounds, all we could see when we looked up was infinite blue sky. Even that damn black vulture had quit circling and disappeared, as good an indication as any that we were back from the dead.

THE LONG-RUNNING FIASCO with the pumps cost us at least half a million dollars in overtime and downtime, to say nothing of the misery, which was immeasurable. Still, there was no question that the Favco kangaroo cranes saved us much more than they cost. In fact, they saved us, period. How much it would have cost to build the two towers with standard guy derricks, and how long it would have taken, is incalculable. Even whether we could have done it at all, and survived, is a question I still can't answer with satisfaction.

Eric Favelle's engineering genius was evident every time you looked up and saw the kangaroos at work. When the crane boomed out, its four eleven-ton counterweights moved down the incline beams, exquisitely counterbalancing the shifting weights of the steel, always keeping the center of gravity within the twelve-square-foot tower. And though Favelle had to bear a ton of responsibility for sticking us with those sputtering Lucas 4000 pumps, it was counterbalanced by the shifting weight of well-meaning: He was simply trying to give us what we said we needed, and no doubt believed the Lucas people when they said we were just one more strainer, one more O-ring away from making those pumps work. He was almost as much a victim of Lucas's ineptitude and duplicity as we were.

Still, even when the pumps were failing, it was clear by the fifteenth floor of the first tower that the kangaroo was a magnificent machine. Their cabs perched on the towers inside the four corners of the elevator core, the operators maneuvered their 110-foot orange-and-white booms like puppeteers. Crowds gathered to see the show, the way they once did to gaze up at the aerial ballet of the rivet gangs that erected the tower half a dozen subway stops north, the tower whose days as World's Tallest Building were now numbered. Hour after hour, section after section, the four cranes lifted the pieces up the sides of the tower, each responsible for a quadrant. Then, when the point came when the cranes had nearly disappeared behind the steel curtain they had erected around themselves, they performed their most famous and spectacular maneuver. The Kangaroo Jump.

Every three floors, the iron creatures hoisted themselves up, the height of self-sufficiency. The operation was a display of both strength and grace by the machines, and efficiency and coordination by the men, who swarmed over the rigging with surefooted agility, like a pit crew in space. First, each crane's eight crew members placed guide plates between the sides of the crane tower and the supporting structure of the building. This was to ensure a straight climb, since the twelve-foot-square crane towers were designed not to be so rigid that they might snap under strong winds during construction, especially as they achieved higher and higher altitudes. Then men scrambled a hundred feet down to the base of the towers to proceed with the jacking process, protected from falling too far by planks and netting placed over the elevator shaft.

In our shop in Carteret, we had designed and fabricated steel jumping beams with retractable outriggers for each of the crane towers. These outriggers were attached to the base and the midsection of the tower. The jumping beams and the jumping ladders were set up in the building's shaft by a tugger crew in advance of the jump. Now the towers and the cranes were ready.

The actual moment of lift was sublime. When I think of it now, or if I happen to be walking by a construction site and see one of the younger generation of kangaroos at work, the jump reminds me of one of my grandchildren holding the stem of one of those frozen push-pops and forcing the treat up through its cardboard cylinder. After seeing that all was ready, the pusher gave the order for the lifting to the signalman, who was always in radio contact with the operator who worked the controls for the pumps running the hydraulic jacks. The hundred-ton jacks pushed against the central climbing beam, hoisting the entire 200 tons of tower and crane twelve feet straight up in a smooth, silent movement that seemed so simple and effortless.

The cranes climbed the steel in twelve-foot leaps, and then the whole process was repeated twice more. The men removed and reset the outriggers and pulled and pushed the jumping beams into and out of position. The three giant heaves put the cranes thirty-six feet higher than they'd been when the men came to work that day. With all four cranes at rest in their new positions, standing tall above the setting floor once again, they were ready to bring up three more floors' worth of core columns, exterior wall panels, and floor-panel decking. Two weeks later, the foursome of cranes and the thirty-two men who attended them would be ready for another Kangaroo Jump.

"Isn't it always kinda nice when y'build somethin'?" John DeSmidt said, his Iowa-Louisiana drawl intact. "Look at that thing I made for mah wife." It had been years since I had last seen John. He was almost eighty now, hard to believe when you looked at him. He was still fit and full enough of life to occupy himself with a little hobby ranch on the west coast of Florida. The thing he made for his wife was a bench whose seat was creatively pegged to the side frame. "I'm not a carpenter. I just enjoy buildin'. Guess I always did."

John built a lot of things, and one of them was the south tower of the World Trade Center. Next to old Charlie Ruddy, John was probably the best foreman we ever had. He was primarily a bridge builder; he worked the

Kosciuszko, the McComb's Dam, the Manhattan, "damn near every bridge in New York," he said when he got tired of listing them.

John finished up the Kosciuszko, in Brooklyn, late in 1968 and went directly to the Trade Center, where he began working as one of the foremen on Tower A. In those first months, we were all learning on the job, struggling to keep our sanity and our solvency while getting the first tower off the ground. So no one foreman was designated the general foreman, the boss. All of them covered their areas and reported to Jack. Under the circumstances, we had no choice but to make it a group effort, like a barn-raising. By the time we were getting ready to start Tower B in the early spring of 1969, the biggest problems had been solved and things were calming down. We could start the second tower with the luxury of a normal chain of command. The choice for a general foreman for the second building was easy.

When Bob called John DeSmidt up to the office, John thought he was in trouble, maybe even getting fired. That was just normal in the industry. No matter how good a man was, when he got summoned by the boss, his first instinct was that he was in trouble. Shortly before the beginning of the Trade Center, John Kelly got nervous when he was called in by his boss, the legendary Local 40 and state AFL-CIO president Ray Corbett. But all Corbett wanted to tell him was that he had chosen him to be the shop steward for the biggest steel job the union had ever had.

Bob told John DeSmidt that he wanted him to run Tower B—the whole thing from the setting of the first grillage to the moment the flag was raised at the topping out two years or so later. Because John was regarded around the city as a bridge man, the union grumbled about him being a general foreman on the Trade Center, the highest ranking ironworker on the job other than Kelly, the steward. "I wasn't a high-rise man, that's what the union thought, so they put out a story that I couldn't do the Trade Center," John recalled. Of course, you could say that about our whole company. In the preceding decade, we had been almost strictly a bridge reconstruction outfit. "But I think a bridge man can do any goddamn thing a high-rise man can do, don't you?" John said. "I don't think you can say the opposite. You get hell of a picks on a bridge."

The union could dictate a lot of things, but keeping John DeSmidt from running the south tower was not going to be one of them. Being the building's general foreman, the walking boss, was an enormous responsibility, but it barely fazed John. Aided by a crew of assistant foremen and reporting directly to Jack Daly, he ran the tower the way he ran every job— if torqued up a rotation or two—"like a nasty bastard," he says now with a gleeful smile.

Ironworkers, especially bosses, each had their own approach to the perils of working on high steel. As long as I'd known him John's way was to turn on the mean machine for those eight hours, and it went double on the Trade Center, where he suddenly held the responsibility for the safety and performance of more than three hundred men. This wasn't like replacing cable and fishing for striped bass under the moonlight, like we'd done on the Buzzard's Bay Bridge. "He was like a man I didn't know," his son Steve told me one day in New York. Steve walked onto the Trade Center job as a seventeen-year-old apprentice, a punk as they were called then, a week after graduating high school. "I couldn't believe how much he cussed," Steve said, chuckling at the memory. "My first day, I was looking at him and couldn't believe these words were coming out of my father's mouth. He was good to the men, but he was serious, he was very serious."

One morning, John was in the superintendent's office handing out the brass to the men, an administrative chore normally handled by Vinnie or one of the other assistant superintendents. Bob came by and asked John why he was doing that—didn't he have more important things to take care of? "By God," John said, "I want to know a man's name if I see him up there holdin' up a column"—meaning standing around, loafing. And he handed out the brass just about every day forward until he knew the names of every one of the 367 men who eventually came under his command. It wasn't just bluster. If there was any doubt that John was qualified to run a tower, it evaporated almost from his first day on the job. His eyes were sharper than that black vulture's, and any man who hadn't had the privilege of working for him before learned quickly what veterans knew well: You didn't try to get away with anything with John DeSmidt. One day, he saw that the men were jumping a crane without bolting the beams on all four corners of the core. They bolted just two opposites—literally cutting corners. "I want that son of a bitch safe!" he bellowed. You can bet those men never did *that* again. And you can bet it made them think twice before doing anything that smacked of taking the easy way or coming to work without the full power of their senses focused on doing their jobs correctly, safely, and swiftly.

John loved hustling the men, never more than on days when the kangaroos were jumping. He would watch to see which crane was ready to go first, then quickly join the gang and pitch in, puffing up the men, saying how good they were, which invariably got them to go even faster—and pushed the other three gangs to try and catch up. There was nothing the men liked less than to see another crane standing high above theirs. It was like a connector nudging his partner, "I got my end!" When the first crane completed its thirty-six-foot jump, John would pull off his gloves, flash his trademark grin, and say, "You guys can be in my gang anytime."

John moved over to the south tower when the north one was at the twenty-third floor, a point at which the erection was as close to being on cruise control as it was going to get. Three kangaroo jumps earlier, the raising gangs had finished setting and welding the 56-foot trees, marking the completion of what for all practical purposes was the tower's 120-million-pound foundation and base. From the tenth floor to the roof, it was a matter of sustaining the pipeline of steel and floor panels, truck after truck rumbling through the Holland Tunnel and barge after barge floating up the Kill Van Kull to keep the kangaroos fed and the vertical assembly line moving. It would be one hundred stories of setting columns and beams, placing floor panels, jumping the cranes. And then setting columns and beams, placing floor panels, jumping the cranes. Followed by setting columns and beams, placing floor panels, and jumping the cranes. You couldn't quite call it monotonous, but every steel job had a high degree of repetition, or at least you hoped it did: A tedious job was a job without trouble, if such a thing existed. The minute it got interesting, you knew you had problems. And so far, the Trade Center had been nothing if not interesting.

As the Tower A crews bolted up and up, John and the second team of ironworkers were downstairs starting again from the bottom. Three Manitowocs were back, crawling around the bottom of the bathtub setting the grillages and the base plates, followed by the base columns in the elevator core and around the perimeter. Tower B was now officially launched. And if we thought we were running a big job before, all we had to do was stand at the window of the office across Liberty Street to realize that we were essentially running the *two* biggest jobs of our lives, separately and simultaneously. We were still adding men by the gangful, struggling to meet our ever-expanding need for experienced ironworkers, especially certified welders. We had exhausted the supply of men from the Manhattan and Brooklyn locals, and the pipeline from the Caribbean refineries was also running dry.

Already employing every available ironworker in the city, we started taking men from other parts of the country, who were allowed to work by "permit" from the New York locals. The Trade Center would turn out to have the largest number of out-of-town ironworkers of any job in the history of the city. But while the welders from the islands were very qualified and capable, some of the other permit men who came from outside the city were not quite so reliable. The truth was that you didn't need talented people in every job, but it was essential in the lead men: the welders, of course, but also the raising gangs and the bolter-ups who—even on a welded job—fastened beams to beams and beams to columns.

One day Jack was bemoaning the paucity of talented ironworkers in some of these key jobs and said we ought to go up to the Caughnawaga reservation in Canada and recruit some good men. We had some Caughnawagas already on the job, but their ranks in New York had thinned over the years as increasing numbers of the older men came down off the steel and the younger ones tended to look toward college or to seek less itinerant and treacherous fields of work. Jack thought we needed to go up and make a little splash to drum up business.

The Mohawk ironworkers were long known for their inclination to go from job to job, leaving one for another on a whim, lured by who-knew-what. The other thing they were known for, of course, was their fearless affinity for high steel. So you would think the ones who remained in the industry would have already gotten in their cars and come to the city, lured by the prospect of working higher than anyone had ever worked before. Maybe they were just waiting for us to reach a height worth writing home about before offering their services. But we needed them now—needed them to help us get up there. Jack had an idea for a Mickey Rooney–ish goodwill gesture: For years we'd heard about the golf course the Caughnawagas had on their reservation. How about we go up and put on a golf tournament, Jack suggested. I was game.

We told the thirty or so Caughnawaga men already on the job to spread the word home, and I went to a trophy store and bought the biggest one they had, a four-foot-tall prize that barely fit in the trunk of the car we rented to get us to the reservation after we flew up to Montreal. We drove up along the St. Lawrence, and arrived on the reservation to a welcome so affectionate that it was as if the men had been waiting for some Koch men to drop by for a visit since the Thirties and wondered what had taken us so long.

We pulled our golf bags out of the car and got our first look at the homeland of the Indian men who were so much a part of the lore of high steel, and of our company. I was disappointed to see that it bore no resemblance to an "Indian reservation" as I envisioned one. It was just a sleepy, rural, blue-collar community of three hundred or so people who lived in small houses on quiet streets. There were two points of interest: the nine-hole golf course, with its modest clubhouse, and out in a clearing, all by itself in the middle of nothing, a single, thirty-foot steel column sunk into a concrete base.

"What are you building out there?" I asked the chief, half in jest.

"That's to train the young braves to climb columns," he said.

I asked him how they trained them to walk on beams. "They learn that," he said enigmatically.

We hosted breakfast, lunch, and dinner, and drew about twenty men to the tournament. Bad legs and all—no golf carts at this course—I managed to lead the field after the front nine. As we were about to tee off again at the first hole to begin the back nine, the chief smiled and told me that I might be going home with that trophy but without my scalp. Not to worry—my legs couldn't carry me to victory. Les Albany, a foreman already working at the Trade Center, overtook me on the fourteenth hole. But the goodwill paid off. We added about thirty more Caughnawaga men to the job.

One of them was Bobby Montour, who became John DeSmidt's bolting-up foreman. There were two varieties of bolts on the Trade Center—the A490 and A325—each with a different strength, according to what it was fastening and where. Bobby would go home to Brooklyn each night with a roll of plans and make up lists of what bolts went to what points. In the morning, he would hand the lists to his three apprentices. Then the kids would go to the scale box—a pickup-truck body filled with kegs of assorted sized bolts that was hoisted to the working floor by one of the cranes—and start counting out the bolts and putting them in burlap bags, one for each point to be bolted. They would write down how many of each size and strength were in each sack, like the little plastic bags of hardware that come with something you might buy at Sears and have to assemble yourself. "And everything had better be there when the men got there to do that point," recalled Steve DeSmidt, who was one of those punks, recalling the moment with real dread. After all, his boss's boss was his father.

As the second tower rose up out of the bathtub toward street level, the crawler cranes assembled the second group of kangaroos inside the four corners of the core. And perhaps for the first time since the beginning of the job nine months earlier, it was possible to go to work and find real peace. It was a beautiful sight, the kangaroos working their tails off, all eight of them now, lifting and slewing so efficiently, like a perfectly synchronized team. Soon it was summer, the summer of 1969, and man was on the moon and the Mets—the *Mets*—were in a pennant race, and the north tower was reaching skyward, seemingly unstoppable, its twin following behind.

18

GAUDEAMUS
IGITOR

ONE NIGHT BACK in 1962, my father looked up from his desk and said, "Well, that's it, take me home." He had just finished reviewing our bid for the Robert Moses Bridge, adding his customary $50,000 to the number Bob and Rudy had come up with. I put my jacket on and started out his office door. I was half a dozen paces down the hall when he called me back. He was standing next to his old desk, this piece of furniture that was like his second home.

"I bid the atomic bomb plant behind this desk," he said, running his fingers across the top.

"I know, Dad," I said. "A lot of other jobs, too."

"I want you to have it."

I was taken aback. "Thank you, Dad," I said after a beat.

"Don't let the other fellas sit behind it," he said.

I just looked at him and nodded, but he reached out and held my arm. "Do you understand?" he asked.

"Yes, Dad," I said, "I do. I'll start using it the day you stop."

"Good," he said, and then we went home.

Nobody knew it yet—except, perhaps, Dad himself—but the Fire Island bridge was to be his last bid, and one of the last jobs we would build while the company was under his active management. Only later did his innocuous words, "That's it, take me home," become poignant and unforgettable to me—and only then did I realize that saying he wanted me to have his desk was his first acknowledgment that he was on the way out. It also said to me that he expected that one day I would lead the company. He knew Bob would have his turn first, but he invested great symbolism in making sure I had the desk Jerome never sat behind it after my father retired, but Bob often did. And whenever I saw him there, I was more amused than resentful. He was very much a pretender to the throne, in my mind. When we moved out of Casanova Street to our new home in Carteret, I had the desk put into my office. I got no argument from my uncles.

Whatever my office furniture, it had long been clear to everyone involved in the company that I wanted to run the business some day, and that that day would eventually come. Yes, Bob deliberately left me out of the main operations he was involved in, but I felt that in time, I would replace him before anyone else did. Bob was the boss and I had no intentions of making any play for his power, but it was also true that his screw-up of the Trade Center bid had done nothing to strengthen his position.

Though I split my time between Liberty Street and Carteret, my office at the plant became my main base of operation during most of the construction of the Trade Center. I put three phones on top of the desk for better efficiency—two outside lines and one to the shop, where we were busy running day and night shifts to keep up a pace that required us to construct and ship out nearly 5,800 floor panels—six million square feet—over the course of the three years of construction. I often had a receiver in each hand, working the wires as fiercely as a stock trader in a bull market. Between vendors, suppliers, engineers, inspectors, fabricators, field technicians, Jack, Rudy, and Bob, I was never wanting for conversation.

One day I got a call from my old friend Dr. Mountain, the man who had burst into the hospital in Westchester just in time to save my legs from being amputated. Dr. Mountain was calling to ask a favor. His chief operating room nurse's twenty-three-year-old son-in-law was looking for a job. There was nothing I wouldn't do for Dr. Mountain, and when he told me that the guy was a very bright, conscientious former Green Beret with a degree from Baruch College, I told him I just might have something for him. With the south tower beginning to take floor panels, we had gone to two shifts a day, and needed a good foreman for the night crew. We had tried two or three men, but for some reason none was able to whip them into shape. Their output was way behind the day crew's. Dr. Mountain's call had the feel of perfect timing. I was intrigued by the prospect of putting the underachieving night shift under the command of a former Army Special Forces captain not far removed from the jungles of Vietnam. I called the kid and told him to meet me in front of the RKO Theater in Flushing at six the next morning.

The floor panels were a critical element of John Skilling and Leslie Robertson's goal of meeting the Port Authority's demand that economics be front and center in every consideration of the Trade Center's construction. Nothing unreasonable or unusual about that, of course, especially for a project whose announced cost had blown past half a billion dollars before the first piece of steel went up. What was unusual was the design the engineers came up with. It gave new meaning to the saying, "One man's ceiling is another man's floor."

The floors were giant prefabricated sections of decking in which telephone jacks, power outlets, ductwork for phone and electrical power lines, and heating, ventilation, and air-conditioning ducts all came in one neat package. Each twenty-foot-wide panel consisted of six supports called trusses or bar joists designed to both bear the load of the floor decks and hold their duct and utility work. The trusses were nearly three feet deep and were welded to the corrugated steel decks. (They looked like the supports you would see nowadays if you looked up at the ceiling of a warehouse store like Costco.) The floor sections were either sixty or thirty-three feet long, depending on where they were located in the towers, and their widths var-

THE FLOOR PANELS

This is the floor panel and truss in detail, showing the network of utility and air-conditioning ducts. After we assembled the truss and the deck, and then set the piece on the tower floors, the corrugated top was covered by a concrete floor slab and tile surface.

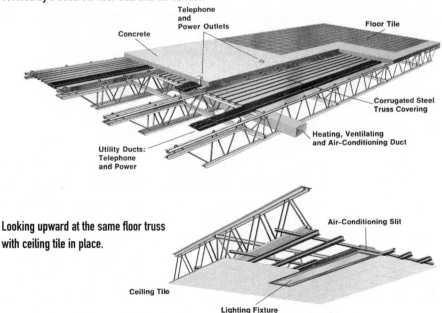

Telephone and Power Outlets

Concrete

Floor Tile

Corrugated Steel Truss Covering

Heating, Ventilating and Air-Conditioning Duct

Utility Ducts: Telephone and Power

Looking upward at the same floor truss with ceiling tile in place.

Air-Conditioning Slit

Ceiling Tile

Lighting Fixture

ied between ten and twenty feet. They were sized and structured to extend from the building's core all the way to its outer wall, while providing that exterior wall with its lateral support. After the decks were bolted to the wall panels and the core columns, a four-inch layer of concrete was poured over them, to be followed, eventually, by floor tile and carpet on top and ceiling tile and flush lighting fixtures beneath.

The floor panels and the engineering from which they flowed were designed to provide strength while saving money before, during, and after construction. The long, self-supporting floor spans eliminated the cost of buying, fabricating, and erecting many thousands of tons of steel for interior support columns, lateral beams, and steel framework that would have gone into a more conventional design. And, of course, the Yamasaki-Skilling plan allowed the Port Authority to meet its goal of making the Trade Center as rentable as possible by offering the widest open office spaces east of the Hudson. Meanwhile, the design accelerated the time of construction immeasurably. A more traditional one would never have allowed us to reach a cruising speed of erecting three floors every two weeks.

We didn't fabricate the floor sections so much as assemble them. We received the trusses from Laclede Steel in St. Louis and the corrugated decking and the power and telephone ducts from Granite Steel in Granite City, Illinois. Our men welded the components together in the shop, and then an overhead crane took the finished panels out and a truck transferred them to a stack of previously finished pieces in our twelve-acre yard at the water's edge. Now they were ready to be sailed on 300-foot-long barges upstream to New York Harbor and delivered to the Trade Center dock.

"HOP IN, HANS," I said, pulling up under the marquee of the RKO Theater on Northern Boulevard the morning after Dr. Mountain's call. "We've got about an hour's drive to Carteret. Tell me about yourself." Hans Liebel was a very respectful young man who had spent his tour in Vietnam with the Green Berets giving weapons training to a force of mountain guerillas. He had gotten a combat promotion, becoming a captain at twenty-two after most of the other officers in his company were killed. Before going to Vietnam he had gotten a degree in business administration. When we got to the office, I walked Hans through the shop and the yard, showed him the material coming in by rail and truck, and explained how the floor panels were assembled. We walked down to the water, looked over a 300-foot barge loaded with three dozen floor panels, and watched the tugboat hook on and depart for the

Trade Center dock. Inside the office, I had Hans sit across from me, pushed two phone extensions in front of him, and told him to listen to every one of my conversations. At the end of the day, I offered him $10,000 a year to run the night shift. He said that as much as he'd love to earn that kind of money, he didn't have any experience making floor panels.

"You'll learn," I said. "From what I've shown you, do you think you understand the system well enough to put all the right pieces in the right places?"

"Yes, sir," Hans said, "I think I could."

"Then you're hired. But there are three conditions. The first is that you have to work with me for at least one year and you *cannot* quit under any circumstances. The second is that I can fire you anytime I want. What do you say?"

"What's the third condition, sir?" Hans asked.

"Stop calling me sir!"

Hans accepted the job, but at the start of his shift two days later he was in my office, telling me he was sorry, but he had to quit. "I'm an embarrassment," he said. "My shift only made one panel last night." The day shift was making six panels a shift.

"Remember our deal, Hans?" I asked. "I can fire you, but you can't quit."

Hans agreed to stay. But the next night he was back, quitting again. He had doubled his production, but still felt unworthy. I knew a lot of ironworkers who took great pride in their work, but this ex–Green Beret was too much.

"Hans," I said, "I'm holding you to your contract. Now get back to work."

Over the next few weeks, Hans somehow got the night crew so whipped into shape and fired up that apparently they believed him when he said that it was a matter of honor to make more floor panels than the day shift. It was like one of those movies where a slovenly group of Army misfits turns itself into an elite force. Soon, Captain Hans had the night crew turning out six panels a night. As much as anyone, he was one of the reasons the floor-panel contract turned into something that was otherwise foreign to us: profitable and trouble-free. But of course, it couldn't be that easy, not on this job.

BY MARCH OF 1970, the Trade Center had gathered a lumbering momentum that somehow managed to push it past whatever obstacles lay in its path. And Lord knows, there were many of them. Some were dauntingly complicated—those were the ones that always seemed to find their way to us. Others were more like niggling inconveniences, any one of which had the potential to turn into a major breakdown: shortages of parts, slight mistakes in fabrication that kept Piece A from fitting Piece B, transportation glitches, bad weather.

We were nearing the end of our second winter now, and both years had been brutal. The winds blew, and there was no place to hide. When they reached thirty miles an hour, we had to shut down the cranes. The operators and raising gangs went ten floors below the setting floor by elevator to wait until the wind gauge told them it was safe to go back up to work. One time we had a winter storm that left the erected steel encased in ice that fell to earth in chunks so potentially deadly that the West Side Highway had to be closed. On the coldest days, the men dressed with two sets of thermal underwear, and some carried butane hand warmers that they normally used for hunting. When they came to work after an overnight or weekend snowfall, the first thing they had to do was shovel the snow off the beams.

With the first tower still only two-thirds complete and the second one about a third of the way up, the Trade Center was already nearly sold out. More than seven hundred tenants had signed leases in the two buildings, a far cry from the early days when Guy Tozzoli was out hustling space in buildings that were nothing but a big model and a lot of publicity. So now the pressure was on Ray Monti to deliver the buildings. Never was the "critical path method" more critical. Now that some floors were being started even as others were being finished, many more varieties of material than steel and concrete had to be delivered on a meticulous schedule. Besides our 200,000 individual pieces of steel, there were hundreds of thousands of smaller parts—42,000 doorknobs, for instance, and 21,800 windows and 250,000 square feet of marble and travertine. It was almost obligatory for journalists to come up with a list of fantastic calculations to convey the enormity of the project: Somebody figured out that it would have 3,000 miles of wiring and 10,000 lighting fixtures, enough to illuminate a highway from New York to San Francisco. The towers' air-conditioning could cool 15,000 homes. Somebody who had really run out of ideas reported that if you laid all the connecting pipe in the foundation in a straight line, it would stretch from Knoxville, Tennessee, to Daniel Boone's grave in Baghdad, Kentucky.

More important than the sheer numbers of parts, though, were the sequence and timing of their assembly—which materials had to be delivered before which other materials, precisely when and where and in what amounts. The information was fed into the cutting-edge electronic technol-

An artist's rendering of the north tower. Structural steel is shown placed up to the 65th floor, with aluminum facing up to the 50th floor level. The pier in the right background was the receiving area for waterborne building materials. In the left background is the 23.5 acre land fill area that became Battery Park City.

ogy of the day, enormous computers that pumped out tightly integrated diagrams that allowed Monti and the one hundred Port Authority engineers who worked for him to see how a shortage of any material or an interruption in any phase of the work would affect the project as a whole. Monti, the Seabee veteran, saw the operation in military terms. He once compared the construction of the Trade Center to the D-Day invasion. He called his office "headquarters company" and it included a "war room" and was staffed by four "line commanders."

Monti's key deputy was Bill Borland, who ran a staff of fifteen engineers who traveled to all the fabricating plants around the country (including our plant in Carteret) to inspect their materials and work and make sure they were producing what they were supposed to be, and on schedule. But Borland had another responsibility: to make sure the shipment of all material to the site ran like the trains in Italy under Mussolini. It might have been the most difficult job on the entire project: up to fifty truckloads of steel, each carrying an average of eighteen tons, had to be delivered at precisely the right time, hour after hour, day after day. Borland's goal was to keep steel deliveries to the site to within half an hour of their scheduled times—no earlier, no later. But whether it was steel or anything else, an unplanned stoppage of work anywhere on the project, even a small one, could have a devastating rippling effect. And when it came to labor peace, it wasn't the size of a trade union that counted but where, and how critically, its members fit into the gigantic machinery of the construction.

The union representing tugboat captains and crewmen was a relatively small group with a few hundred members, but it had as much power as the ironworkers who had parlayed the implied threat of a strike into a huge raise. The tugboat captains were our truck drivers. If they didn't work, we didn't get our floor panels from our plant to the job. The reason they had the job in the first place was that barging the floor panels to the site seemed to be the only realistic way of doing it. So it wasn't very surprising when they went on strike in March of 1970. Unions love when a contract expires right before or during a major job; they'll never be in a better bargaining position. It happened to us during the construction of the atom bomb plant in Oak Ridge, and it happened when the ironworkers' contract came up in New York as we were about to start erecting the Trade Center. In Tennessee, my father gave the union what it wanted rather than lose time we couldn't afford. But whether it was tugboat captains or ironworkers, we weren't in control in New York.

As the strike loomed, Ray Monti had started looking for a trucker to transport the huge floor panels to the Trade Center. When Monti told the biggest truckers that the biggest panels were twenty-by-sixty feet, they all said the same thing: Forget it. Don't even bother making another phone call. But with the strike on and our store of floor panels at the site dwindling by the day, if ever there was a time for Monti to call on his Seabee ingenuity, this was it. What he came up with wasn't a great idea, but it was an imaginative one. Why not get the biggest, strongest helicopter and *fly* the things across the water, one by one? Monti called Sikorsky Aircraft in Stratford, Connecticut, and asked how much weight their biggest bird, the S-64 sky-crane, could lift. Ten tons, he was told—and the Port Authority could have it for just $18,000 a day. Sikorsky just needed a day to bring the Skyhorse, as it was nicknamed, from St. Louis.

Monti later told Rutgers professor Angus Kress Gillespie that Malcolm Levy, his boss, was livid when he told him what he was doing. Monti and Levy were not the best of buddies to begin with. "You're crazy!" Levy yelled at Monti over the phone, according to Gillespie. "We don't have the authority to do that!" Monti said it was either the skycrane or they let the job shut down.

On Saturday morning, I was standing near Tony Frandina and the Sikorsky ground crew when the blue monster with the white band painted on its nose rumbled into view and hovered over the yard. The ground crew members, garbed in orange flight suits, stood beneath the skycrane as a hook came out of its belly and was slowly lowered toward the ground, where a floor panel awaited the first ride. Figuring we might as well know from the get-go whether the Skyhorse could handle the job, we decided to start at the top and see if it would be able to lift the biggest panel, a sixty-by-twenty-foot, seven-ton section. The *rump-rump-rump* of the motors was deafening as the big bird floated aloft, about fifty feet above the floor panel. One of the ground crew-men grabbed the hook and prepared to catch the O-ring attached to the four slings holding the panel. I had brought my two young sons, Karl and John, and warned them to stay in the car when the helicopter showed up. But as the operation proceeded and the ground crew hooked onto the huge panel like some Special Ops raising gang, I looked down to see my sons standing next me. I revised my orders. "Don't leave my side," I told them.

The piece started rising, as if floating up. But it was no more than ten feet off the ground when it started to spin. The downdraft from the rotors was pushing against the 1,200 square feet of deck, and the pilot, Lee Ramage, knew he wouldn't be able to lift it and still control the chopper. He whirled the bird around and quickly released the panel, which fell to the ground, crashing into another panel and instantly turning both of them into scrap metal. After some consultation, we decided to try again, but with a different approach, picking the panel vertically this time. Ramage rose his bird in the air again and hovered over the water, then Tony and the Sikorsky ground crew hooked up to another panel. Ramage managed to get it in the air, high up over our building. But then the panel started swinging erratically, and Ramage maneuvered back and tried at least to let it drop more gently than the first one, with limited success.

For the rest of that day and the next, we tried to figure out a way for the helicopter to pick up a seven-ton panel of steel and fly away with it. We tried using one of the smaller pieces and removing the decking, to see if the skycrane could manage a lighter load. The panel was thirty-five by twenty feet, weighing in at under four tons, and if this didn't work, it was time to give up. This time, the skycrane managed to lift the section and fly it up to the Trade Center, taking the same route as the barges so that if things went bad, Ramage could drop the panel into the water, not onto somebody's house on Staten Island. The Port Authority arranged for the police to stop traffic on the two bridges Ramage had to fly over, the Goethals and the Bayonne. The next day, we tried a larger piece, this one with half its deck. The skycrane, holding the panel snake-like, got this one aloft, too, and made the fifteen-minute trip up to the Trade Center. It looked like we might have it figured out. We could detach the decking, which came in sections small enough to truck to the site, and transport the trusses by skycrane. Then we could set the components in the towers and weld them there. So much for prefabrication. But desperate times. . . desperate measures.

Now, the final test: the largest panel. Again, Ramage got her up and began flying upstream toward New York Harbor. He got past the Goethals all right, but as the drivers halted on either side of the Bayonne Bridge watched spell-bound, the panel started to wobble and swing, so wildly that Ramage was in danger of losing control of his craft. He had to push the red button that drove an explosive charge to cut the cable. The panel crashed into the water just beyond the bridge, between Broadway in Bayonne and the foot of Clove Road on Staten Island. It sank to the bottom, never to resurface. Ramage continued on to the Trade Center site, where Monti was waiting. When he saw the Skyhorse coming across the bay near the Statue of Liberty—with nothing underneath—Monti got on the radio and asked Ramage what happened. "We pickled it," the pilot said. The load had gotten so wild that he had to let it go. It wasn't the weight that was the problem. It was that these floor sections were just too unwieldy to fly. Back near the Bayonne Bridge, police launches and cars were swarming, wondering what the hell that was that had dropped into the Kull from the big, blue helicopter.

By now we and the Port Authority were used to rescuing each other. Jerome decided to make a phone call. "Hello, Tom. . . ."

It was Tom Petrizzo. He was a trucker—not a big one, but as far as we were concerned, the best. Somehow or other, he did things that needed doing. Tom was the most ingenious of men, and when Jerome told him about our problem—not that he hadn't heard about it; the floor panel that went *ker-plunk* was in all the papers—Tom simply said, "If you want the panels up there, they'll be up there."

I had met Tom a couple of years earlier, on the job that directly preceded the Trade Center. We were replacing the old deck on the Kosciusko Bridge when he pulled up in his car and asked the ironworkers, "Who's running this job?" They pointed to me. "Who's your trucker that's gonna haul these new panels that you're gonna put in?" Tom asked me.

"Who the hell are you?" I replied suspiciously.

"I'm a trucker," Tom said.

"Then *you're* the trucker that's gonna haul these panels."

"I'm not shittin' ya," he said. "Who's gonna truck these?"

"I'm not shittin' ya either," I said. "You're the trucker that's gonna do the job."

"You're kidding."

"If you can do it, you're hired."

"Yeah? Where do I sign?"

"Go down to Carteret and see my uncle Jerome. Hurry up before he signs somebody else. And you better have a good story."

In the two years since then, we had learned that Tom always had a good story. When we called him about the floor panels, he was so casual that it seemed he wondered what the fuss was all about. He could truck the panels up. All it took was a little cooperation from a few police departments and some coordination. "The first thing I had to do was get an escort," Tom recalled when I talked about it with him years later. "I went down to the state troopers in Trenton and described what I wanted to do. They gave me one state trooper for each county. But I had to get the county or city escorts myself. So I set it all up. It was a lot easier than I thought it would be."

One night at ten o'clock, Tom lined up ten forty-foot flatbed tractor trailers at our plant in Carteret. A crane stacked three floor panels on the bed of each truck—thirty panels in all. Tom got in his car and led the convoy, with what must have been half the Carteret police department in front and the other half behind guiding the procession onto the New Jersey Turnpike, where they were joined by the Jersey state police. It was bigger than a presidential motorcade—you never saw so many flashing lights and whistles and wailing sirens. Each time they hit a county line, one police department would hand the convoy off to the next one.

The trucks rumbled across the Goethals Bridge—the very first structure ever built by the Port Authority, opened in 1928—where the Port Authority had made a makeshift roadway so the trucks could go around the tollgates. Now onto Staten Island, where New York City police took over the escort duties. They led the trucks across New York City's suburban borough to the Verrazano Narrows Bridge—the most recent major Port Authority project—and onto the Brooklyn-Queens Expressway. On every road and every bridge, Tom and his trucks had something every New York driver dreamed of: a commute completely devoid of traffic. Not light traffic. *No* traffic. The police shut down three major bridges because the panels were so wide that the cargo came into oncoming lanes.

With the Manhattan Bridge all to themselves, Tom and his truckers ambled over the East River, across a wide open Canal Street, and down a deserted Westside Highway. They finally arrived at the Trade Center at three in the morning, five hours after they had started out. Tom and his drivers left the flatbeds at the site, and retrieved them the next day after our cranes had unloaded them. They performed this miraculous operation again the next night, and on the night after that. At that point, Tom arrived at the Trade Center and found a greeting committee: the tugboat captains, who wanted to know what the hell he was trying to do to them. "What do you mean what am I doing to *you*?" Tom replied, completely unintimidated and unimpressed. "I'm making a living here."

"We're on strike!" he was told.

"Well, God bless you, I'm not," Tom said. "But you know what? A handful of you guys usually bring this shit over here. Do you know two thousand guys are gonna be out of work if they don't have these panels? I'm gonna haul 'em till you dummies come back to work."

The tug captains weren't the only ones paying attention to what Tom was doing, and getting real pissed off. When he and his men went to retrieve the empty flatbeds the morning after the first triumphant delivery, they found their chains and binders were gone. The same thing happened the second day. Meanwhile, Jerome got a call in the office from the head of one of the major truckers that had told Ray Monti before the ill-fated helicopter gambit that trucking the panels was impossible, forget it. He told Jerome we could "get rid of that kid," because he now knew how to truck the floor panels. "The kid's staying," Jerome told the guy. "And if you keep stealing his chains and binders every night, every morning I'll buy brand new ones for him and I'll charge them to you."

Tom Petrizzo wound up hauling floor panels twenty-two nights in a row, delivering 660 pieces before the tugboat captains and crews settled their contract and went back to work. In only three weeks, Tom transported more than a tenth of the floor panels for the entire three-year project. Of course, it played havoc with Ray Monti's critical path method, but as any Seabee knows, when you're building and fighting, sometimes things get messy. Tom, another unsung hero of the Trade Center (if not to the tugboat union), did what none of his much bigger competitors had the gumption to do, and single-handedly kept several thousand men employed. "I loved every minute of it," Tom told me, like a man recalling the greatest glory of his youth.

THERE WERE TWO other strikes during our three years building the Trade Center. The Teamsters went out, shutting down concrete deliveries, but only for a couple of days. And there was a citywide strike by the International Union of Elevator Constructors, whose members operated the temporary elevators that took the ironworkers to the floors being assembled. Though it didn't shut us down, it was an extremely disruptive strike. After all, this was a building whose workers had to go straight up to get to work.

Getting the men to their stations each day was an ongoing concern from the beginning of the project. The original plan had been for the single construction elevator to bring both men and material upstairs. But when we and the trades who followed behind us started to reach the higher floors, the trip upstairs got longer and longer—and so did the wait downstairs, especially when the elevator took a shipment of material that took a while to unload. Soon there were long lines of men waiting for the elevator to come back down, and groups of workers upstairs waiting for material to come up. The PA approached us with a proposition: Use our cranes at night to hoist the materials needed by the other trades on the upper floors, and they would take care of all the operators' overtime plus pay us a fee. Anything that improved our cash flow was a good deal for us, and we started hoisting electrical and plumbing material, floor and ceiling tile, hardware, and whatever else was needed. The lines of men in the morning all but disappeared.

When the elevator men went on strike, the setting floor was the forty-fourth story. That meant that the ironworkers had to climb forty-four flights of stairs to get to work. The commute was even more arduous for the crane operators, whose arrival on the setting floor was the end of just the first leg of their journey. Even when the elevators were operating, they still had to climb a series of ladders inside the crane towers, and then a catwalk, to get to their seats at the controls. (The crane operators, like the ironworkers, got "climbing pay," and usually stayed put for their entire eight-hours shifts, eating their lunches in their cabs rather than add any more climbing to their workdays.) Each day during the strike, the men trudged up the stairs in the morning and down in the afternoon—all except Hambone. He wasn't climbing.

Hambone was a crane foreman whose real name was Walter Beaubais. He was a French-Canadian Indian who was gung-ho fast about erecting steel, the hell with safety, which made him a major thorn in the side of the union steward John Kelly. "He wanted to get steel up, steel up, steel up," Kelly recalled, and acted as if he were unaware of the most basic safety rules—using tag lines on loads, planking every two floors. "Him and I had quite a few words quite a few times down there," Kelly said. "I used to tell Bob, 'He's going to kill somebody or he's going to get himself killed one of these days.'" When the elevator men struck, Hambone had no intention of trudging up forty or fifty flights of stairs in the elevator core. He tied a choker around a fifty-five-gallon drum when a crane was taking up a load, jumped into the barrel and crouched down so nobody would see him, and got himself a ride to work. What he didn't know was that Kelly was upstairs and saw him emerge from the barrel. Kelly went berserk and told Bob he needed to do something about this guy. Bob assured him he would fire Hambone if he took a barrel to work again, but apparently the message didn't get through to Hambone, who kept on doing it. The next time Kelly saw Hambone in the barrel Bob kept his word and told Hambone he was gone.

"So Hambone went over to the George Washington Bridge and worked seven days a week, twelve hours a day, piling up the overtime," Kelly recalled one day years later, sitting in the dining room of his house on Staten Island. "I had a union election the following June and I see Hambone coming down to the hall and he's got a carload of Indians with him." Kelly figured Hambone had it in for him and was bringing his friends down to vote against him. But Hambone told him, "I'm still voting for you, Kelly—you made me a bundle of money."

Kelly, the son of a filleter at the Fulton Fish Market, was that relatively uncommon man, a first-generation ironworker. He had started in the business in 1955, while still in high school in Brooklyn, when he walked across the street and asked his neighbor if he could get him a job for the summer. Kelly's neighbor was Ray Corbett, the business manager and later the president of the ironworkers local. Corbett was a Newfie whose trade was passed down to him by his father. The Corbetts worked together on the Empire State Building—one of the most famous photographs of the construction shows the two of them climbing the antenna—but the younger Corbett's greater passion was for the union. Working on terra firma, Corbett added a host of conditions and fringe benefits to the ironworkers' contract, not only essentials like health benefits and paid vacations, but also such extras as a "topping out fund," a bonus paid to workers when they erected the last piece of steel on a building.

When young Kelly asked for a job for the summer, Corbett sent him to punk on the Nyack Bridge. Kelly took to the work immediately, as well as to the work his neighbor did down at the union hall. Corbett took Kelly under his wing, and eventually helped him become one of the youngest members of the local's executive board. When the Trade Center was starting, Kelly asked Corbett if he would appoint him shop steward. "And he acknowledged me," Kelly said. By tradition, it meant Kelly was the very first ironworker we hired for the job.

It was a strange position, shop steward. He was appointed by the union, but he was technically our employee—I say technically because the reality was that more often than not it was *he* who was telling *us* what to do. It didn't mean we always complied, but his percentages were pretty good. In practical terms, Kelly's job title might have been pain in the ass. Some days he promoted himself to son of a bitch. And he was damn good at his work. He didn't let us get away with a thing, especially when it came to safety. If he had one job to accomplish over these three years of ironwork, it was to see every union man grab his last paycheck and go home to his wife and kids. History told us it was a lot to expect that not a single ironworker would die on this mammoth project, but Kelly established right out of the box that he was going to do everything in his power to maximize the chances. We might have had the best relationship with the unions among the erectors, but to Kelly that meant little. We were still the Company. And on this job, he was going to watch us like a hawk. He toured the whole job just about every day, looking for problems.

One day he found a big one, not in the towers but outside them. That big, sunken bathtub was finally all dug out, and now it needed a cover—and the towers needed a plaza. The bathtub was unlike anything we had ever worked on, or in. It was vast—enough space to play sixteen football games simultaneously—and its interior was extremely complex. It was in this cavernous space that the new PATH station would be built, along with concourses, a huge, multi-level parking garage, and storage, utility, and mechanical spaces. So while some areas were framed for flooring, others remained open—so open that the men sometimes found themselves working at the edge of a sheer drop, all the way to the concrete floor that sat on bedrock, without anything to catch them if they fell.

It was just a few beams, and Jack thought we could get them up and connected without anything bad happening. But when Kelly saw this, he said hold everything. The maximum drop allowed by law was twenty-four feet—two stories—and there were places where the falloff was twice that. Kelly got into his latest screaming match with Jack, and finally threatened to shut down the whole job, which, of course, he could easily do and be well within his rights. Jack relented, and tried to figure out how to make this unique space safe. Kelly called Teddy Gleason, the head of the longshoremen's union, to see about getting cargo netting to string. But we decided that would be too heavy. We ended up with nylon netting. When he saw it, Jack said, "You'd think we were goddamn fishermen instead of ironworkers, for Christ sakes."

"Well, gee, Jack, that's too goddamn bad," Kelly said. "God forbid if someone fell."

Falling in the plaza would be bad enough, but it was nothing compared to the risks that came with a misstep in one of the towers. And it wasn't getting any safer as the weeks passed. Kelly was the chairman of a safety committee for all the unions. He and the other stewards met every two weeks to talk about safety problems and to prepare the most serious grievances for John Tishman, bypassing the contractors. Besides the five hundred or so ironworkers, there were the union stewards for the electricians, concrete men, carpenters, elevator men, and the workers from Alcoa—the tin knockers—who were starting the biggest aluminum siding job on earth.

The elevator shafts were the most hazardous places in the towers. It was sixty, eighty, a hundred floors of sheer drop, with minimal protection. There were guardrails, but they were always being knocked over, broken, without being replaced. Over the course of the job, six elevator men fell down those shafts to their deaths. Five sheet metal men fell off the building and also died, and several concrete workers. Two pedestrians were killed when a load of planks rolled off a truck as it was coming out of the hole. By the end of construction, seventeen people would lose their lives in the construction of the Trade Center. And not a single one was an ironworker. Considering the history of the trade and the numbers of men involved, that is almost beyond belief.

But the job was not without its share of injuries. Near the end, an ironworker named Willy Kingsberry was working on the television antenna tower when a hand winch got loose and smacked him across the bridge of the nose so hard that his entire face collapsed. For a year, it looked like it was held together by wire. There were also some memorable scares. Once a heavy column was being hoisted up to around the eightieth floor and was just about there when suddenly the crane lost hydraulic pressure and the operator was unable to bring the piece any higher. And then he realized the brakes weren't holding it. He tried to slow it down, but it began picking up speed. The more it fell, the hotter the brakes got, and the faster the column began to fall. The operator grabbed a phone—the piece wasn't in free-fall, so he had time. "I'm losing the piece!" he screamed to the tag line man. "It's going down, everybody out of the way!" It happened too fast for anyone on the ground to react. They just stood there and watched as the column came crashing onto a mat, hitting so hard that the ground shook. Everyone just stood in shock. But it wasn't over. There was some slack in the cable, and looking up the men saw that the whole rig was hanging over the side of the building. "Everyone thought for sure it was coming down," recalled Steve DeSmidt. "And then it just swung back over. Just like that. And nothing was damaged. All they had to do was repair the engine. That was it."

Mishaps like that, though, were uncommon, especially for a project that ran so long that there were some ironworkers who started out on the job as apprentices and left as journeymen. It was normally a three-year process that was impossible to complete on a single job. And even with the occasional mishap, without a single death of an ironworker, the largest steel project ever turned out to be the safest.

TOWER B WOULD NEVER overtake Tower A, but with John DeSmidt riding herd, the men of the south would make a race of it. John loved using a man's competitive drive to get the most out of him, and he took real pride in closing the gap between the two towers. He knew George Backett's men on the north tower had an insurmountable lead, but if he could get his men within fifteen floors when Backett's men topped out, John would be a happy man. Competing with the other tower meant more to John than surpassing the Empire State Building, which wasn't that big a deal to him. "Now, I was in this a long time, and twice I built the biggest building in the world and three times I built the longest bridges," he told me. "Every damn one of them, the record was broken." (John was counting the Trade Center twice: He was among the men who erected the TV tower a few years after the north tower was finished, giving the Trade Center the edge over the Sears Tower in Chicago, though not everyone counts the TV tower.) But looking over at the north tower of the World Trade Center was something different. John had nothing against George Backett, but there was little doubt in his mind that if the construction didn't have to stop at the 110th floor, eventually his men would make up the deficit and pull past.

The rest of the world wasn't paying much attention to John's building, at least not on October 19, 1970. That afternoon—at 2:51, to be precise—one of the three-story-high wall panels was placed, extending the north tower to an official height of 1,254 feet, outdoing the Empire State Building by four feet. It was the 103rd floor, with seven to go. Of course, the triumph was tempered somewhat by the fact that it was a record that would stand about thirty-eight years shorter than the Empire State's did after it surpassed the Chrysler Building in 1932. In Chicago, construction of the Sears Tower was already underway. It would beat the Trade Center by 100 feet.

Still, it was a moment worth celebrating. Improvising on the tradition of unfurling an American flag at the topping out, the ironworkers raised an American flag and brought it with them on their ever-upward journey. Fridays became flag day as the towers grew endlessly on and on, floor by floor—"as though being constructed by battalions of exuberantly unstoppable madmen," Russell Baker observed in the *New York Times,* "determined to keep building until the architect decides what kind of top he wants."

Tom Roemer, one of the first kangaroo riders, loved going to work knowing that before the day was out he and his fellow crane operators would break the record yet again. The operators sat in their cabs, forty feet above the top working level, always the four kings of the rising tower. From the angle of their positions inside the elevator core, the crane operators couldn't see straight down to the street. The only way they could judge their growing height was by comparing it to the surrounding buildings, and to the view in the distance. "On a clear day, you could see up to West Point, out to the Robert Moses Bridge," Tom recalled. He had worked on the Verrazano Narrows Bridge a few years earlier, and it had provided him with his highest point up to the Trade Center—a mere 690 feet, half the height of the Twin Towers.

At these elevations, Tom and the other operators got a clue what Lee Ramage went through trying to bring the floor panels to the site with his sky-crane. The panels were hoisted flat off the ground, and sometimes when they reached the roof, the wind would catch them and they'd stand on end 1000 feet above the street. It was harrowing just watching—never mind being up there trying to get them under control. The operator had to handle the controls just right to bring the panel into the wind like a ship at sea, gaining enough control so that men below could handle the panel without being knocked off the building.

The operators on the west side of the building had it worse. For them, just getting the panels up to the setting floor could be harrowing. They were hooked so that they would come up on a 15-degree angle in order to get past the lugs on the spandrel plates on the columns. The wind would come rushing down the Hudson, blowing from northwest to southeast and driving the panels up against the building as they were being lifted. The operators had to boom way out to keep the panel away from the building. Even when it looked as though the panel was coming in safely, it was too soon to relax. One operator once was swinging a panel into its final approach to the floor when the wind suddenly caught it and jammed the section into the spaces of the triplet columns of the exterior wall. It was a testy job unjamming it. As the operators were going through these stressful maneuvers up in the sky, our crane engineer, Jim Markel, often came up and stood on the catwalk, talking to the operators: "How does it feel? How's it going?" He'd done all he could do at his drafting table; some moral support was all he could offer now. Tom, for one, appreciated it.

As the crane operators and raising gangs were finding out, the World Trade Center was being built in an area of Manhattan that called into question why it was Chicago that was called the Windy City. In fact, the Skilling engineers had devoted much effort to designing the building with the wind in mind. Long before construction began, they had studied the effects the wind might have on tenants of the towers—how much sway they would tolerate. It was an issue apart from the strength of the buildings. They knew that the towers could be perfectly sound structurally and still move with the wind. It was already known that 100-mile-an-hour winds made the Empire State Building sway three inches.

During the design phase, the engineers in Oregon lured people into a trailer behind an old car dealership with promises of a free eye exam. To test motion tolerance, the trailer was rigged with springs that made it sway. In New York, meanwhile, an office dangling from a cable was put into an airshaft of the Lincoln Tunnel to see how people would react. It seemed they had a high tolerance: They wouldn't notice up to eleven inches of slow sway.

The ironworkers had a much higher tolerance. Their workplace had no walls. So they either got used to the height and the wind, or found another line of work. Steve DeSmidt had never walked on high steel, though his father had been doing it for decades. Steve had just graduated high school and within months he was eighty stories up. "When I first went up I was very shaky," he recalled. "You don't trust your feet, you don't trust your knees, you don't trust your legs. I was trying to hold onto my lunch in one hand and with the other one I was etching my fingerprints in the columns. But then after you get used to it, it's like you're almost jumping from beam to beam. And then what happens—and a lot of guys have told me the same thing— there's almost a feeling that you want to jump. I used to sit there at lunch-time. I'd sit on the edge and unwrap my sandwich and I'd drop the paper out in the breeze and watch it float over the city as I'd eat my sandwich. And you get this feeling that you want to know what it feels like to just . . . jump."

I have been up there and I have been around ironworkers my whole life, but when I heard this, I had to clarify what Steve was saying. "When you say jump, you mean jump from beam to beam?" I asked.

"No," he said. "Jump off the building." He laughed, realizing how absurd it sounded. "Just like float, you know, like fly. Just this urge. You're com-fortable with it, you're not afraid of it anymore, and you feel like you can. And you almost have to watch yourself."

THE TWENTY-THIRD of December 1970 came up cold, damp, and gray. It was nearly two years and five months after the hot morning in August when the first grillage of the first tower was set upon the bedrock at the bottom of the bathtub. Now there were 117 levels of steel sitting on that grillage. Down on the street, the most honored piece of steel of the 100,000 in the building was about to be hoisted. Ironworkers crowded around it, passing around a Magic Marker and scribbling names all over it—their girlfriends', their wives', their own. The name Koch was all over the job, but not *Karl* Koch, so I made it official with the black marker. Then an American flag was wrapped around the column, and it was ready to go upstairs. It was the topping-out piece— the highest piece of steel to be erected.

Up in the sky, one of the kangaroos hoisted the column up from the street—the 1,300-foot-long trip took under five minutes—and when it reached the top the crane operator set it down on the deck. I had just beaten it there with my elevator ride. Everyone was up on top now, my uncles and brothers and cousins, Rudy and Jack, and we took turns holding the flag and posing for pictures, as crane operators and mechanics came out on their cat-walks to watch. Then the flag was fastened onto a twelve-foot pipe that was tied to the column. Dozens of men cheered as the crane raised the piece— with the flag on top, the column looked like a massive flagpole—and then the piece was set and bolted-on. There would be more work to do in the months ahead—setting lower pieces, along with the steel for the base of the TV tower that would come after the Trade Center was opened—but the north tower of the World Trade Center was now officially topped out.

We're halfway home, I remember thinking.

It had been a hell of a bumpy trip so far. The struggles hadn't ended with the debacle over the crane pumps in those first months two years earlier, and we had never really shaken our financial worries, even after the Port Authority pulled us in from the precipice of bankruptcy. The Port accountants spent a year in our offices babysitting our books, but it was no secret that eventually we would top out on the advances they were giving us each week against our $20 million bid. And right on schedule we reached that point, at around the time we reached the hundredth floor of the first tower. Now we were really out of money. But there was no doubt that the Port would keep the spigot open. With one tower up and the other halfway there, they assured us they would continue writing checks for the payroll and paying our bills. Meanwhile, they looked for ways to help us make up the gap between our foolish bid and reality. After some negotiation, we agreed to sell the Port our kangaroo cranes, with the purchase price going toward our expenses. (They later put them up for sale in an ad in *VIA,* the Port's official publication.) Wherever they could, they threw us extra work. The Fuji Bank, which would be occupying floors 79 through 82, wanted to install a 10,000-pound safe. It was too heavy to put in without extra load-bearing support, so we welded plates onto both sides of columns in the core, all the way down to the basement. We also were given extra work installing dampers that Leslie Robertson designed to reduce movement of the building in the wind.

It was staggering to consider all we had overcome to erect the tallest building on earth and live to tell about it. When my lifelong friend Joe Sherry gazed up at the topped-out tower, he said, *"Gaudeamus igitor."* It was a Latin phrase we had learned at St. Anastasia School. It meant, "Let us therefore rejoice."

When I heard those words, I had an idea. A few years earlier, during one of my hospital stays, I had met a man named Robert De Lazzero, the owner of a firm in the Bronx called Port Morris Tile and Marble Company. He was like me, an orthopedic mess. During a trip to Italy in 1963 to buy marble from the same quarry that had provided Michelangelo the material he had used for his *David,* De Lazzero and his wife had narrowly escaped death while staying in a village at the foot of Mount Toc. A massive landslide into a reservoir behind the Vaiont Dam sent a 200-foot-high wall of water roaring down a narrow valley, drowning more than 2,000 people. De Lazzero had survived, but had to have years of surgery. We met during one of his visits to Columbia Presbyterian, and he told me he had recently gone back to Italy to shop for a huge job. He had a contract with the Port Authority to provide 425,000 cubic yards of gray marble for the lobbies of the towers of the World Trade Center and 40,000 inch-thick cream-colored pavers for what was to become the Austin J. Tobin Plaza outside. "Wow," I'd said. "I'm doing the steelwork on the Trade Center." After we topped out the north tower, I called De Lazzero and asked him to make me eight six-inch square blocks of marble and attach to each one a specimen from a welder's exam, a piece of steel bent into a U-shape. On the plates of the marble pedestal, I had *Gaudeamus igitor* inscribed. I gave one each to everyone who had been in the office in Carteret that Saturday morning in December of 1968 when we were on the verge of bankruptcy—Bob, Jerome, Donald, Roger, Jack, and Rudy—along with my cousin Vinnie. I wanted to share my joy with my family and my partners. "See?" I said. "We bent but we didn't break."

It wasn't until the day of the topping-out that my father saw the World Trade Center for the first time. Late in the day, after I had gone back to Carteret, my sister Marie and her husband George, along with my brother Donald and Dad's nurse drove him into the city so he could finally have a look. Dad was in a wheelchair. Donald helped him out of the car and wheeled him to a good spot. "Well, Dad," he said, "what do you think of the World Trade Center?"

My father gazed up in silence, obviously in awe. Then they went inside, rode up a freight elevator, and got off at one of the higher floors so he could see the innovative structural design.

That weekend, I visited my father at Sands Point. He said he had seen the Trade Center, and that from the outside, it looked as though we had done a good job. "But Karl," he said, "there's no steel in that building."

"There's a lot of steel in that job, Pop," I said. "Two hundred thousand tons."

"I didn't see any steel," he said.

"The whole wall is steel," I said. "It's like a birdcage."

Dad stared into my eyes. It wasn't the wall he was talking about; it was the floors. "It's wide open," he said. "Is every floor like that? What's going to hold that building up?"

"The floor paneling system," I explained. "That gives the outer wall its lateral support. It's the modern way of building skyscrapers."

Dad shook his head. "The design is bad," he said. "It isn't strong. There should be steel columns across the whole floor to keep those ceilings up. Where are the beams and columns?"

"They're spanning the open floor area with trusses, Pop. It's a new, modern design."

Dad was getting impatient with me, as if I just wasn't hearing what he was saying. I tried to reassure him that the floor panels were a good substitute for vertical steel columns, but he was not to be convinced. He listened to me with his lips pressed together. I thought my father was living in the past, too firmly anchored in the construction methods of his day. I had recently read an article in which an architect had said that the Trade Center was the first building of the twenty-first century. But I didn't want to keep arguing.

When I played this conversation back in my mind thirty-one years later, it seemed almost unbelievably prescient. I remembered that Marie, George, and Donald had taken him to see the tower on the day of the topping out, and when I went up to Connecticut to interview Marie and George for this book, one of the things I wanted to ask them about was what they remembered about that visit. Marie said that when Donald pushed the wheelchair off the freight elevator and into the middle of one of those wide open spaces that would soon be the home of some bank, Dad had looked up and down at the steel framing, then panned the wide expanse of space. "He just said, 'You're *craaa*-zy,'" Marie recalled. She said they were all taken aback. Dad was obviously upset, but nobody could understand why. And nobody wanted to ask. They were an old man's children, letting their sick father be. I had never heard this—Donald, who has since died, never mentioned it—so I turned to George for confirmation. "Yeah, he did say that," my brother-in-law said. "It's really the only thing I remember. 'You guys are *craaa*-zy. You're out of your minds.' But with your father, it was always hard to know what he was thinking."

When I thought about it all these years later, my father's reaction made perfect sense. He had spent his entire career erecting buildings only one way. In his day, whether it was the Library of Congress or the Hotel Pierre, or even something relatively recent like the Marine Midland Building not far from the Trade Center, the inside of a building was a catacomb of steel. So of course the first thing he would ask when he went inside the tower was, "Where's the steel?"

And it wasn't surprising that by the time I saw him a few days later, he was filled with real concern. "It isn't strong, Karl," he said before I decided to drop the subject.

Topping out the north tower of the World Trade Center, December 22, 1970.
(The Port Authority of New York and New Jersey)

19

TRIUMPH
OF
TREACHERY

They said: Come, let us make a city and a tower, the top whereof may reach to heaven; and let us make our name famous before we be scattered abroad into all lands . . . But God confounded their tongue, so that they did not understand one another's speech, and thus scattered them from that place into all lands, and they ceased to build the city.

—FROM THE BIBLICAL STORY OF THE TOWER OF BABEL

B̲Y THE SPRING OF 1971, if you stood on Austin Tobin Plaza and looked straight up—you might have to squint—you could see the end of our vertical odyssey. The tin knockers had the north tower all dressed up in their aluminum best and were a good ways up on the south. Tenants were moving into their new offices on the lower floors even as we were still erecting the upper ones. As if to emphasize the whole point of this ten-year struggle, the Port Authority made sure the first tenants of the World Trade Center were undeniably engaged in world trade. A week before we even topped out the north tower, a company with the no-frills name Export-Import Services Inc. moved into an office on the tenth floor, the first of an eventual seven hundred occupants of the Twin Towers.

John DeSmidt had the south tower crew edging ever upward, so efficient and unstoppable that his memory has compressed the time like a beater on a rivet. "We damn near topped out Tower B the same time they did Tower A," he recalled. "A couple weeks behind is all, boy. If we had another month. . . . Yes, sir, two weeks or three at the most." It was actually six months between the official topping outs, though John and his crew did place their highest piece only weeks after George Backett's crew set their last piece of support steel for the antenna that would go up years later. John is also fond of pointing out that his tower took one month and $1.5 million less to erect than the other one. Some of that was the advantage of the learning curve, but some of it was John's talent for inspiring men at work.

With the job finally winding down that spring, nearly five years after Bob and Jerome had first submitted our undersized bid, I began looking to the future, eager for our company to build on what was, in the end, a huge triumph of perseverance, ingenuity, and fortunate timing. The Trade Center had brought us fame and turned us into a much bigger player in the industry, and it made us smarter. We knew things we didn't know before. Col. William A. Starrett compared building a skyscraper to a military operation, and it's hard to imagine another erector feeling more like it had actually gone through a war than we did. At the topping out, a quarter-mile up on a blustery day, I handed off my camera so I could have a picture taken of Jack and Rudy and me holding the flag. When I look at that photo now, I see the faces of men about to come home from battle.

So now what? Nobody would deny our right to the Yellow Pages chestnut "No job too big," but we weren't rushing out to put up the next World's Tallest Building. Whoever was was building the Sears Tower—God bless 'em. Certainly there would be big jobs ahead, but what the Trade Center told me was that we should expand our horizons. The floor-panel work was practically a revelation to me. Fabricating and assembling was a profitable business—just don't try using helicopters to deliver your goods—and we should be in it. We had that big space in Carteret, and we ought to be smart about what to do with it.

I started researching that end of the industry, and what I learned was that America was stuck in the past. We were making steel with obsolete machinery, equipment in use since World War I. The state of the art was in Europe, particularly and ironically in Germany and Italy, whose factories had been destroyed during World War II and had been replaced afterward with help from the United States and its Marshall Plan. By now, these countries were using cutting-edge punch-card computer systems that controlled modern machinery, conveyors, and transfer tables. The new systems used a fifth of the manpower that American plants used to get the same job done.

The south tower was to top off in May, and I made plans for Vivian and me to fly to Europe and visit some of these plants. Importing the technology, I thought, could not only give our company a profitable new line of work, but maybe even spark a veritable revolution in our country's steel industry. Maybe that was a little cocky and self-important, but ambitious thinking came naturally to me in those days, and considering what we had just accomplished, why not?

Before leaving on our trip, I went up to Scarsdale to see my 89-year old grandfather and tell him I would be visiting Germany, the homeland of his side of the family. I climbed the stairs to the second floor of the big old house, and found Grandpa laying on a bed in one of the smaller rooms. He looked so frail. I reached for his hand, this hand that had pounded so many rivets, and it was limp. I asked him how he was doing, and he assured me he was just fine. "Grandpa," I shouted, trying to overcome his deafness, "I'm going to Europe. I'll be stopping by Baden-Baden, the town where your parents came from. You remember you told me that once? Do you want me to bring anything back for you?"

"No," he said. "I'm fine."

I told him about my plans for the trip, and filled him in on news of the family. We'd recently had a Koch family day at the Trade Center, all my siblings and cousins bringing their families up to see the family project. It looked like one of the Scarsdale Christmas gatherings, with hard hats. My older son, nine-year-old Karl IV, looked so proud in his red KOCH hard hat. I could already see him walking steel one day, running jobs, waiting his turn to lead the Karl Koch Erecting Company. Grandpa seemed pleased to hear it.

All my life Grandpa was the gregarious one, the one telling stories and asking questions and kidding around, the one always on top of what was going on. He'd lean close to you and ask with a twinkle, "Got any secrets you want me to help you keep?" He must have asked me that a hundred times. Now here he was, the life in him all but drained. But we were a stolid lot, we Koch men, so I couldn't turn to hugs and kisses or tears. Grandpa never did that. Dad never did that. Instead, I reverted to what I was accustomed to, what I saw my father and uncles do. When in the company of close male relatives, talk business. I told Grandpa about the new conveyor systems I was going to see. Then I said good-bye to him and the next day flew off to Europe with Vivian.

We started our tour with three factories in Germany. Vivian was at my side at meetings and dinner engagements, and she gamely looked over the equipment with me until she got bored and went sightseeing on her own. Continuing my penchant for almost getting killed, we narrowly avoided a head-on collision with a bus on a highway in the Black Forest. This didn't make me any calmer when I left Vivian behind in Cologne and got in

Ferdinand Pedinghause's Mercedes to go see a factory that was using his fabricating system. Ferdinand had planned to fly me up in his private plane, but it was raining too hard. Instead we hit the autobahn at about 120 miles an hour. I looked around for a seat belt, and there weren't any. Pedinghause explained that he and his brother, who had both tested cars for Porsche, had once been in a bad accident. His brother wore a seat belt and was crippled for life, Ferdinand said, while he wore none and was thrown clear, sustaining only minor injuries. So no seat belts for Ferdinand Pedinghause. "Don't worry," he said. "If we crash at this speed, seat belts won't help anyway."

Ferdinand showed me around the factory and then we got back on the autobahn. We made it back to the city that evening in one piece, picking up Vivian and then going out for dinner. The next day, Vivian and I drove to Basel, Switzerland, a stop on the way to another plant in Milan. Ferdinand, meanwhile, had an appointment to show the plant to a Russian fabricator. It was still raining, but he couldn't bear the thought of another three-hour drive, so got behind the controls of his plane and took off. Not long after takeoff, though, his engine became flooded and he had to make an emergency landing in a pasture. Ferdinand got the plane down safely but the wheels hit a drainage ditch, and the plane flipped over, killing them both. When they found Ferdinand and the Russian, they were both strapped in their seats, each with a snapped neck and not a scratch between them. That made two brushes with death: If the Russian had my appointment and I had his, I'd have been the one sitting dead in the passenger seat out in the wet field.

By the time Vivian and I arrived in London, we were shaky. We checked into our hotel, Grosvenor House, and found a message waiting for us: Call home immediately. Our first thought was the children, who were staying with Vivian's parents. I reached Donald, who told me the children were fine. It was Grandpa. He had died three days earlier, while we were traveling. We cut our trip short, and as we were making arrangements to come home I realized that on the day that Grandpa had died, we had been in Baden-Baden, the town from which his parents, my great-grandparents, had emigrated to America.

When we arrived home, Donald told me that Dad didn't know about Grandpa's death yet. None of his brothers had come or called, and my siblings decided that I should do it and waited for me to come home. My father had always said two things about Grandpa. One was that he wanted to make our company successful enough so that Grandpa didn't have to drive rivets anymore. He accomplished that. The other was that he didn't want to outlive his father because he loved him so much and didn't think he would be able to bear his death. No son ever took better care of his father than Dad took care of Grandpa.

I sat before my father in his room. He had been struggling with Parkinson's disease for eight years now. It was an insidious disease, and I realized that it might not be very long before I might lose him—or I might have to watch him deteriorate slowly for many years more. It was only a week earlier that I had been to Scarsdale and tried to shake Grandpa's hand. Now I took my father's hand and told him Grandpa was gone.

He didn't say a word. He just squeezed my hand. I wondered how long it would be before Dad, like Grandpa, no longer had the strength even for that simple connection.

WE DIDN'T DISCUSS IT—there was really nothing to say—but there was a profound business consequence to Grandpa's death: It meant that Dad's brothers were finally voting partners in the family company. Bob and Jerome inherited their father's stock and were now no longer just officers of the company but part owners, something they had felt was their due virtually their entire adult lives. Bob was fifty-three, Jerome fifty-one. Each had been working twenty-six years for the company that bore the name of their father, their brother, and—to their infuriation, I'm sure—their nephew. Now they owned half of Karl Koch Erecting, with my father and I controlling the other half—an equal but extremely volatile division of power. I resolved not to think about it and set my mind to trying to work together with my uncles to chart the course of our post–World Trade Center life.

Over the week or two after Grandpa's death, I gathered all the notes I had taken during my trip to Europe and all the research I had collected before going, and wrote a proposal to present to my uncles and brothers about how I saw the future of the company. I called the paper "Wake Up, Sleeping Giant" and couldn't wait to expound on how I thought we could lead the American steel industry into a new era. I was pleased when Bob and Jerome called a board meeting and asked me to present my proposal. With Donald and Jack also in the room, they listened patiently as I outlined the new automated systems being used in Europe and how easily we could adopt them in Carteret, New Jersey.

When I was finished, Bob said, "Let's take a vote. Jerome, do you want to go ahead with Karl's proposal to go into the fabricating game with all of his superhuman machines?"

"No," Jerome said.

"My vote is no also," Bob said. "Now *we* have a proposal: Jerome and I want to buy out you and your father."

I was stunned, but only for a split-second. I understood immediately what was happening. It was a paradox of our relationship that my uncles' secrecy, their private culture of invitation-only meetings behind closed doors had long since removed any element of real mystery from their maneuvers. I might not know what they were thinking, but whatever it was, it wouldn't surprise me. The only thing that caught me unawares now was the swiftness of their move. Grandpa was barely gone, and Bob and Jerome were already seizing power, trying to get rid of my father and me, and presumably my brothers Donald and Roger and perhaps even my brother-in-law Jack—any vestige of my father and his family.

I had long known Bob's feelings, of course. What I didn't know, not until a conversation with my mother one night during my journey back in time to write this book, was that the bitterness between my father and uncle didn't start when he and his other brothers joined Dad in the family business after the war. It had started nearly a decade earlier, going back at least as far as 1936, when my father was pressing my grandfather for an equal partnership in the company. According to my mother, Bob, then only eighteen, argued strenuously against the partnership between his father and much older brother. I never knew this, but it shed new light on their hopeless relationship. I had always thought it stemmed from my father's authoritarian ways. I'm sure that didn't help. But now I realized it might actually have been provoked in part by Bob's own attitude—his deep frustration at not having had the good fortune of being born first. No wonder he and Jerome couldn't even wait until all the sympathy cards were in to make their move. They had been waiting a long time for this power, and they began using it with a vengeance.

When Bob said he and Jerome wanted to buy my father and me out, I quickly regrouped my thoughts. "Is this a two-way street?" I asked.

Bob asked me what I meant.

"Would you accept counteroffers to buy *you* out?"

Bob looked at his brother and answered for both of them. "Sure. Right, Jerome?"

Jerome nodded his head in agreement.

This did surprise me. If they wanted to buy me out, why would they so quickly, and without any discussion, seem equally amenable to being bought out themselves? Did they really want to own and continue running the business, or were they more interested in cashing in at the height of its prestige? Or were they just calling my bluff?

I got Donald, Roger, and Jack onboard and hired an accountant to put together a financial presentation for a banker he knew at Chase Manhattan. The bank committed a line of credit of $1 million to start, with the understanding that if we needed to go higher we could probably get more. Rudy Loffredo, meanwhile, told me up front that he was with my uncles. I told him I understood and respected his decision. I couldn't expect his loyalty to my father to extend to me. Bob and Jerome had treated him well, and he made a practical decision to go with the men he figured would wind up in control—his contemporaries, one of whom happened to be the president of the company.

Over the next three months, we engaged in a bidding and counter-bidding match that went up in increments of several hundred thousand dollars. We offered them a million, they offered us a million-two. We went to a million-and-a-half. They went to a million-eight. When I got to two million, Bob and Jerome's reaction suggested that they had only gotten into this because they thought my brothers and I didn't have the ability or connections to buy them out. When we presented a letter from Chase attesting to the soundness of our offer, they showed their hand. My uncles rejected the offer—and declared the game over. They suddenly asserted that I could not represent my father because he was no longer competent: Their argument was that a person must be competent to give *and* to take away his power of attorney. They claimed that Dad was *non compos mentis;* therefore, my power of attorney was not valid and I no longer represented his interests. As the ironworkers might say, my uncles had us "two-blocked"—when the lower block on a crane hits the upper block and can go no farther. "We're not for sale," Jerome said.

"*We're* not for sale, either," I said.

"We'll see what your family says when they see a million dollars on the table," Bob said.

It was at that moment that any pretense of civility evaporated and the environment of our office in Carteret became more polluted than the air around the Goethals Bridge. Already there had been an unspoken but conspicuous absence in the company: a celebration. Here we had just finished the greatest erection of steel ever attempted, a project that had taken two years just to plan and another three to build, and there was no collective acknowledgment of the achievement or of all we'd had to overcome. The fact was that of all the obstacles we'd faced—the cranes, the pumps, the welding, the money woes, the labor problems, the tugboat strike, the weather—none was as formidable as our own disunity. The towers were erected by a house divided. The real accomplishment was prevailing against every impediment, and still not destroying ourselves.

But now it seemed that it was just a delayed mechanism. We were like the builders of the biblical Tower of Babel who found themselves speaking different languages and about to be scattered. Could it get any more symbolic than for our patriarch, the co–founder of our company and really, our family, to die virtually at the moment we reached the summit, and while I was in the place of our forebears, looking for our future?

To fight my uncles, I hired Bill Shea. He was arguably the most powerful corporate lawyer in New York, a Republican power broker most famous for helping replace the departed Dodgers and Giants with the Mets and having the new stadium in Flushing named for him. (In our family, he was also known as one of my father's golfing partners, who had supported Dad's membership in the Sands Point Golf Club.) With the support of my mother, brothers, and sisters, Shea immediately applied to have me appointed my father's conservator under a brand-new New York State law that allowed a disabled person to have his interests represented by another person without having to be declared *non compos mentis*. In fact, I am a tiny legal footnote: I was the first conservator appointed under that new law in New York State.

My uncles couldn't deny the validity of the conservatorship, and I gave no ground to them in the fight for the company. Their next move marked a turning point in the history of our company and for our entire extended family—the beginning of a descent into a kind of betrayal and treachery of which I didn't think they were capable. In another effort to pressure my brothers and me to sell, they went after our father, their brother. At his first meeting as an officer of the company in 1960, Bob had voted in favor of a policy of paying salaries and medical expenses for both Dad and Grandpa in the event they were disabled by illness. Bob and Jerome had enforced this policy for their father until the day he died. Now they cut off their very sick brother.

They fired him. They *fired* him. I still can't just say it once.

They refused to pay my father's medical costs, which were enormous, and they ceased payment of his dividends. To remain at home, Dad needed fifty hours a week of care from registered nurses. My mother cried on the phone to Bob, begging him to send money. "Please, Bob, we have no money to pay the nurses," she would plead. According to my sister Pamela, who was there, Bob said: "Get your son to sell the company and you'll have plenty of money."

The most powerful lawyer in New York told me there wasn't a damn thing I could do about it, other than doing what Bob wanted. But I couldn't do it, not yet. Faced with the immediate priority of paying for Dad's medical expenses, we had to obtain a bank loan. The unrelenting medical costs soon used up that money, and the best Shea told us he could do was to arrange for a loan from the company cosigned by my brothers to pay my father's bills. My mother, meanwhile, asked Shea for help but the best he could do was arrange a loan from the company. So my father, sick and slowly dying, had to *borrow* money from the company that only existed because of him.

Money was finally coming in, but by now my mother was on the verge of a nervous breakdown. Mom couldn't take the strain of the exhausting care she had to provide for her husband. It became unbearable for her. With my father's care fully in the control of the nurses, she left for Europe with my sisters Pamela and Marie. The girls came home after a few weeks, but Mom decided to stay in Spain indefinitely. Eventually she found a man who gave her solace and peace, an attentive and gentle restaurateur named Carlos. She wanted to get a divorce, but an attorney we engaged told her it would leave her in financial ruin. Stay separated, the lawyer wrote to Mom, and your sons will take care of you. My mother would constantly call from Spain, asking about my father. And the rare times he spoke when I visited, it was most often to ask, "Where's Mom?"

Through all these travails, I could not escape thinking what a terrible error I had committed in resigning my father as president and installing Bob in his place three years earlier. To this day I carry the pain of that decision, which I knew only in hindsight hadn't been necessary to save the company. Now it was one of the reasons we were losing it. I never told my father that his brothers had cut him off, actually fired him.

I had long known Bob's feelings toward my father and me, but I had never figured him to be this ruthless. As for Jerome, I couldn't believe he was following Bob this deep into the woods. Jerome was naturally affable, and unlike Bob, he never spoke ill of Dad, at least in front of me. He always showed him respect. And he didn't detest me for being my father's son. In fact, he seemed to appreciate me. I remember once dashing off to the Trade Center site to deliver some documents and returning forty minutes later. He looked over the top of his glasses when I returned and remarked, "You got out of here so fast, your pants were still in your chair." He liked to call me

Bullet. Jerome could be playful, capable of real affection. We played golf together, and he would stand at the edge of the green, rattling coins in his pocket and loudly unwrapping cellophane from his cigarette pack as I was preparing to putt. I remember once making a long putt despite Jerome's best efforts at mischievous distraction. "See, Karl," he said, putting his arm around me, "I'm helping you develop nerves of steel." It was hard to put that man together with the one who was playing such cruel games now.

I was finding evidence that Bob and Jerome, frustrated in their attempts to get me to sell my father's interest in the company, were shuffling corporate assets without my father's or my knowledge or authority. They began convening meetings of the board of directors without notifying me, the third director. Among other things, they changed the signatories on the corporate bank accounts and voted to authorize themselves to sign contracts of up to one hundred million dollars "without additional approval of the Board of Directors, or any party." Meaning me, and the single largest shareholder of the company, my father.

Somehow, in the middle of all this, we managed to build on our Trade Center triumph. We won bids for two stadium jobs that were two of the most prominent jobs in all construction in the Seventies: the new Giants Stadium in the New Jersey Meadowlands and the renovation of Yankee Stadium.

It was looking more and more as though it would be impossible to prevail against them, especially with Shea's dire warnings that unless Dad and I were prepared to go on for years like this, the *only* prudent thing to do was negotiate the sale price. Donald, Roger, Jack, and I talked every day about strategies, about options, about the various potential outcomes. We started making rough plans for starting our own construction company.

But they wouldn't include Roger. In the middle of the battle, he decided to move to Florida to go into the real estate business. My baby brother had put in two stints in the family company, sandwiched around a trip to Vietnam, and he really wasn't sure which was worse. Neither of my brothers really had the stomach to fight our uncles, but unlike Donald, Roger could really take or leave the business. "In our family," he reflected years later, "if you didn't have a hard hat and work boots, you were a nobody. If you didn't get out on a job and climb steel, you were an overhead item. I got up a couple of times on the Fire Island Bridge and the World Trade Center to see if I would like it. I couldn't wait to get down." Roger felt he was "kind of like the odd wheel," but the bigger problem for him seemed to be the discordant forces that were pulling every which way in our offices. Roger told me he was leaving because one guerrilla war in Vietnam was enough for him. "They hate you, Karl," he said, telling me the obvious. "They're getting even against Dad. You can't beat them."

So now we were down to three: Donald, Jack, and me.

ONE NIGHT AFTER working alone in the office, I was cleaning up when I went to shut off the copy machine and noticed someone had left a document in it. I picked it up off the glass, and before I could read a dozen words I felt as though I was being hit all over again by those falling steel beams. I needed to sit down. What I held in my hands was a contract giving my brother-in-law, Jack Daly, a piece of Koch Erecting in the event my uncles were to buy my father's and my shares. Jack's signature seared the bottom line.

I sat there, speechless, devastated. Jerome had been in earlier drunk as a lord and had no doubt made copies and left the original. I made my own copy and returned the contract to the copying machine.

The next morning I called Jack into my office. I sat behind my father's desk and asked him to close the door. "Jack," I said, "when and if we sell this company, whose side will you be on—theirs or ours?"

"Yours, Karl," he said. "You, me, and Donald. Why are you asking me that?"

"Let me be clear, Jack," I said. "If I sell my share and Dad's, you and Donald and I are going into the steel business together as three equal partners as we've planned, right?"

"Yes, Karl," Jack said, searching my face.

I opened the top drawer and pulled out the contract and placed it in front of him. Jack's body became rigid.

"Is that your signature?" I asked.

Jack raised his eyes to meet my stare.

"I would be an asshole if I didn't go with them," he said. And then he just turned and left.

Jack and Donald and I had been like the three musketeers. We worked and drank and socialized together. He was our dear sister Roberta's husband, our brother-in-law. We had spent countless hours with our wives in each other's homes, incensed and pained, commiserating about the audacity of the uncles, planning our defense, our legal strategies—our future. I included Jack whenever I reported back to my brothers after a meeting or phone conversation with the lawyers and accountants. Apparently, he'd also been informing Bob and Jerome of our every move. Judas betrayed one man for thirty pieces of silver. Jack betrayed his father-in-law and three brothers-in-law—and ultimately, though she didn't regard it that way, his wife—for ten percent of a steel-erecting company. Roberta sacrificed her relationship with her family for her husband's deceit. It became apparent later that she was aware of the plan all along, and for that my mother never forgave her. For almost thirty years, Mom has referred to Roberta as "Mrs. Daly."

Now it was just Donald and me. I loved my brother with everything I had, and I never suspected he didn't have the will to fight on, especially now that he was all I had left. A few months after Jack's betrayal, Donald asked me to meet him at a bar on Long Island, where he told me that he was out, too. He said he had an opportunity to go into the dish business with a friend of his.

"*Do what?*" I shouted. "Selling dishes? Are you fuckin' crazy? This is our company. We gotta fight for it."

"There's no fight left," he said. "They've beaten us."

I pleaded with him. "I need you. We're a team. We're together. We'll always be together."

"I can't," he said. "I've got too much pressure on me at home."

Donald and I had always made every move together. No two men could have been closer. We were like two connectors, our lives forever bonded. But Donald absolutely refused to reconsider, and I became furious. Finally, after three hours, I said, as calmly as I could, "Okay, Donald. I'll tell you what I'm gonna do. We have always been a team. I've never done anything without you. You've never done anything without me. From now on, it's just me. I'm making all the decisions. You just follow and do what I say. I'm gonna screw a red light bulb up my ass. And from now on when you see that red light glow, you follow it."

Now I was truly alone. I knew I had to sell to my uncles, but I tried first to part only with my father's stock, so that he could have enough money to live. But my uncles said no: They would not buy his shares without mine. They wanted me gone. By now I was drained, in every way. It had been three years since this all began, three years of legal struggle and turmoil. Three years of true despair at the ugliness that had overtaken our company. You would be hard-pressed to call us a family anymore.

My uncles applied one final act of coercion. One Friday in the spring of 1974, I asked Jerome, "Where's my paycheck?" He said: "You don't get one. You've been terminated." I turned around and walked away.

I called Bill Shea and told him I would sell my share. But I instructed him to insert a clause in the agreement: Should my father die before the sale closed, the deal was off. I was only doing this so he would be able to live out his days in the house that he loved and not in some terrible nursing home.

The sale closed that July, and now I had to bear the full force of the loss. Not just the fact that I would never run my father's company, but that I was denying my sons the place I always dreamed for them. At least I'd had many happy and fulfilling years with Karl Koch Erecting. They wouldn't have even one. The closest they would ever get was the red hard hats they wore on family day at the Trade Center. And maybe they would sit at my father's old desk. After I left the company, Vivian had the desk picked up and brought to our home without telling me. It took four moving men and two dollies an hour to move it from the truck into the house. Vivian covered my eyes and led me into the living room, with all five children in tow. Then she uncovered my eyes, and let me take it in. I had no words. I opened a drawer and found a copy of *Manhattan Engineer* inside. It was the issue with my article on high-strength bolts. This must have been the last one left after he handed out copies to everyone he knew. The desk seemed so out of place in our living room. And yet, it was in a perfect place.

I COULD GET AWAY with never telling my father how close we had come to losing the company. I could skirt the fact that his brothers had fired him and denied him the money he needed to live on. There was no reason for him to know how my mother pleaded with Bob. But there was no way I could avoid telling my father that we no longer owned our company, that I had sold it to Bob and Jerome.

Dad was so ill now that his facial muscles were frozen in the so-called Parkinson's mask. Speech was extremely difficult, his communication reduced to slow nods, though on occasion he smiled and laughed. His mind was trapped inside a body that appeared catatonic. I went to Sands Point to give him the news, and it was the hardest thing I ever had to do. I told Dad everything, how I'd had to sell the company to get money for his care, how I'd had no choice. I told him several times to make sure he was getting it, but each time he would just nod.

The guilt I felt was unbearable. To this day, I will occasionally awaken from a recurring nightmare in which my father is healthy and we're talking about the company. I realize from his questions that Dad doesn't know we sold it to his brothers. In the nightmare, I cannot bring myself to tell him again. So I keep talking as if nothing were wrong. The same dream, and it always wakes me with a start.

Soon before the sale was closed, Vivian and I flew to Spain to visit my mother and get her signature on the legal documents. Vivian wanted to visit

Portugal before we went home, so we flew from Madrid to Lisbon, where she arranged a trip to the shrine at Fátima, where the Blessed Mother Mary was believed to have appeared to three peasant children. We entered the enormous cathedral the Catholic Church had built to hold the thousands of pilgrims who came to Fatima each year seeking miracles from the Blessed Mother.

I had a great devotion to the Blessed Mother when I was a child. I thought I might become a Maryknoll priest when I was in sixth grade, and on Good Friday that year, I knelt in the second row of pews and prayed for three straight hours. I started at noon, symbolizing the same three hours Christ hung on the cross.

Vivian and I slid into the second pew of the otherwise completely empty church. The altar blazed with candles. Vivian prayed uninterrupted for an hour and a half while I sat there musing over my life. My mind was full of hatred for my uncles. They obviously had good lawyers and had aligned their forces. Jack and Rudy were strongly supporting them. My forces had scattered and run away. I had nothing left but a murderous hate for these two men. Herb Fine, who had represented me in an unsuccessful lawsuit stemming from my accident seven years earlier, told me, "Karl, they've changed you. Just in the time I've known you. That's how they've hurt you."

Herb was right. The bitterness was like a cancer, eating its way through my very soul. It had changed the man I was. I had grown to hate my uncles. In fact, I was actually entertaining thoughts of having my uncles killed. Was it just a fantasy, a release? I can't honestly say it was. Up until now, the venom had all been theirs. But their greatest act of treachery, their worst insult, was firing my father. That was the phrase I kept hearing in my head: They "fired my father." Every time I thought about it, my mind filled with thoughts of vengeance.

Vivian was on her knees praying next to me, and I knew what she was asking for. I managed to get my rebuilt knees to bend just enough to kneel and began my own prayers. *Dear Blessed Lady, dear Lord in Heaven, don't pay any attention to Vivian. I don't expect any miracles for my legs. I'll take care of them. Please just take care of her and our children.* I asked for blessings for everyone in our family. For Mom and Dad, for everyone. And, just for good measure, I said a prayer for everyone whose name I could recall and a prayer for every-one I couldn't recall. And lastly for anyone that I might meet in the future. I sat back feeling I had covered everyone and satisfied the obligation of being in Fatima. Then I realized I'd forgotten one person. What did *I* want? What should I pray for in my own behalf?

I accepted the pain of my legs. I was blessed with a loving wife and beautiful children. I didn't want money. Then it became suddenly apparent. *Dear Blessed Mother, there is one thing that I beseech you for. Take this murderous hatred from my heart that I have for my uncles. It has changed me for the worse. If you do that for me, I will renew the faith and love for you that I had when I was a boy."*

The flames on the candles seemed brighter. Suddenly, I realized I could take a full breath without feeling that crushing pressure in my chest. I thought about my uncles. I felt nothing. I thought about the horrible things they had done, and how they had treated my father. Still, nothing. I tried to envision the act of killing Uncle Bob, something I'd sadly had no trouble doing before. It didn't work. I didn't want to kill him. Was it the power of suggestion? Self-hypnotism? It can't be that easy, I thought. Maybe my mind was playing tricks on me. I got on my knees again. *Lord, if you have really wiped away this hate, and I am not imagining this, send me a sign. I need a sign to know that it won't come back.*

Instantly, a priest strode briskly onto the altar and went directly to four banks of candles, about forty candles in all flickering light throughout the chancel. As quickly as he could move, he took his long-handled snuffer and extinguished each candle in rapid succession. He did this until the only flame left burning was the sanctuary lamp and the altar was in semi-darkness. I immediately assigned symbolism to what must have been routine. The self-destructive hate was being extinguished, leaving only one bright light of salvation. At that point, I was ready to take anything as a sign, because all I knew was that everything had changed in an instant. *Dear Lady, thank you. I'll keep our deal.* I guess that's what they mean by "an epiphany." It was the most pivotal moment in my life.

OVER THE NEXT few years I must have resembled a man trying to find himself. I became a serious golfer and invented a putting training device, which was endorsed by professional golfer Lee Trevino. I owned and published a weekly business newspaper with a circulation of about 10,000. I invested in movies. The first one I put money into was *The Man Who Would be King*, starring Sean Connery and Michael Caine. I figured it had to be a hit because it was based on an excellent story by Rudyard Kipling. It bombed at the box office. I went to a different genre next time out: *The Rocky Horror Picture Show*. Financially speaking, it more than compensated for the failure of the Kipling film. But despite its success, which I will never understand, I have never been able to bring myself to see it.

I invested in one other thing: The D. Koch Construction Company. Six months after I sold my share of our company, I gave Donald $100,000 to start an erecting business with his wife's brother-in-law, Andy Zosuls. Donald had decided that the dish business wasn't for him after all. Meanwhile, not working at anything full-time eventually made me restless. But I couldn't bear the thought of doing anything having to do with steel. I got a job as a district manager for Equitable Life Assurance Company.

On a cold winter day in 1978, Simone Arama, Dad's housekeeper, called me from Sands Point. In her delicate French accent, she said, "Your father is not well, you should come at once."

I rushed to Dad's bedside. He had pneumonia and was failing. I summoned an ambulance, and then called Donald and asked him to get the word out to our sisters and brother. Donald met us at the hospital. The doctors were grave; the nurse told us to step outside while they worked on him. I refused, so Donald and I stayed rooted to the spot while they inserted tubes and hooked up intravenous lines and a heart monitor. I was lovingly talking into Dad's ear telling him he was a great father, a great son. Donald couldn't bear the scene, and so he fled to the hallway. I told my father that he had fought this horrible disease for a long time. It was all right if he wanted to stop fighting. Later, a doctor told me each time I had leaned down to talk to my father, his vital signs had shot up again.

"Every time I think of you, Dad, I'll say a prayer for you," I promised, beginning right then with the Act of Contrition. And then, this man who had worked so hard his whole life, this man who had taught me about honor, integrity, and sacrifice for family, this man who had been robbed of a restful retirement because of Parkinson's disease—this man passed away still holding my hand.

The funeral was an event. Bill Shea was chatting with his entourage of admirers. Bob was holding court with his siblings and other visitors. There were groups everywhere, congregating by what role they had played in Dad's life: a bunch of bankers over here, engineers over there. And way back there, the contractors. After the service and the gravesite ceremony, most of the crowd drifted off, heading for the house in Sands Point, where a mountain of food awaited. Vivian and I stayed back in the cemetery, hanging around while the gravediggers waited impatiently for us to leave. "Dad," I said again, "whenever I think of you, I will pray for you."

SOON AFTER my father died, Donald was diagnosed with non–Hodgkin's lymphoma, a debilitating illness that frequently put him in the hospital to undergo arduous chemotherapy treatments. He was still battling the cancer eight years later when I took him to a doctor in Boston who recommended a bone-marrow and radiation treatment that had succeeded in putting Governor Michael Dukakis' disease in remission. Though he knew the chemotherapy was failing, Donald said the bone-marrow treatment scared him more. Then I took him to a doctor recommended by George Crickelair, my plastic surgeon and friend. This doctor used a procedure involving immune therapy. When Donald refused, the doctor took him to a mirror and said, "Can't you see this therapy you're under is killing you?" I told Donald he was a stupid shit for refusing the newer treatments that might save his life, but all he said was, "Karl, you always worry too much."

Donald's illness pulled me back into the steel industry after a decade away. By 1985, he was too sick to keep up and I offered to help him. Apparently word got around. At one point, Donald said he had seen Jack Daly, and that Jack told him, "Tell Karl I said welcome back to the industry." Jack was now president of Karl Koch Erecting Company. Donald told me that Jack had been promising since he started D. Koch Construction that he would take him under the wing of Karl Koch Erecting and send plenty of jobs his way. Donald had waited in vain for years.

I went with Donald to a medical appointment one day, and on the drive home, he said he was ready to give up the steel business for good. He suggested we both sell our homes and move out to the East End of Long Island and go into business together. "You sell insurance, and I'll sell real estate," he said. "The rest of the time we'll go fishing."

"Donald," I said, "You've got a deal." And I meant it. The doctor had given him a good report that day. In fact, he said, "Don't worry, you're not going to die."

Two days later, Donald was dead. He had suddenly taken a bad turn, and died in the hospital the next morning. He was just forty-three.

Now, I drove into Manhattan to say good-bye.

When I got to Donald's floor in the hospital, I walked over to the bed and stood by him. His eyes were closed and his lips were tight, but they were still formed in his trademark little smile. It was as though Donald was saying, "Hey, Karl! Do you believe this shit?"

"Oh, Donald," I said. "You dear boy. You stupid shit."

At that moment, I was angry at him, angry at him for getting sick and dying. I choked back my tears. I knelt and prayed the Act of Contrition out loud, just as I had done for Dad. I pulled myself up and looked at his beautiful face. "So long, kid," I said and gently kissed him. He was cold as marble.

I was sitting in the funeral parlor a few days later when Jack Daly came across the room and sat down next to me. "It's a terrible, terrible thing," he said with his head bowed. He stuck his hand out and I let it hang. Then he moved off and headed in the direction of Donald's coffin. "Hey, Roger!" I called across the room. All eyes darted in my direction. Roger walked over and asked what I wanted.

"What's Daly doing next to Donald?" I asked.

"Mary Ann wants him to be a pallbearer," Roger said.

"You go tell him if he touches our brother's coffin I'm going to take this chair and bust it over his fucking head."

"Ah come on, Karl, take it easy," Roger said.

"Go tell him!"

Roger moved to Daly's side and spoke quietly. Daly looked at me through the corner of his eye, then turned and walked out of the room.

AFTER BUYING US OUT in 1974, my uncles, along with Jack and Rudy Loffredo, who also now had an interest in the company, continued down the path opened by the Trade Center. With Bob and Jerome taking turns as president, they won some big jobs, including the biggest one of the seventies: the Jacob Javits Convention Center on the west side of Manhattan. The Javits Center turned out to be another big job with big problems. There were fabrication flaws that Koch Erecting was responsible for as general contractor, and Bill Shea's law firm wound up defending the company in a major lawsuit.

In 1982, my uncles sold the company to Skanska, an enormous international construction conglomerate based in Sweden. Bob and Jerome were "ecstatic" with the sale, Rudy later told me, and they both took their money and retired. Rudy became president of the company for his new Swedish bosses, and with Skanska's unlimited financial resources they were able to grow even stronger. When he retired, Jack Daly took over.

After Donald's illness drew me back into the steel-erecting business, it didn't take long for me to rediscover my love of the work. I left the insurance company and started a steel consulting business, starting by finishing up some of Donald's jobs. The biggest one was the West Side Storage Yard in Manhattan, a subcontract for Schiavone Construction, the company that had started out as a little driveway paving contractor and which we'd once hired for work on the Williamsburgh Bridge. Now it was one of the giants in construction in the New York area. I asked Schiavone's president, Joe DeCarolis, to allow me to take over Donald's contract.

"Do you think being out of the steel business for ten years is going to hurt you, Karl?" Joe asked.

"It sure ain't gonna help, Joe," I replied honestly.

He smiled and told me I had a job.

Schiavone became my first major client. The deal was that I would bid and oversee bridge jobs. But before I signed on, I wanted to be honest with Joe DeCarolis. I told him that my main objective was beating Karl Koch Erecting out of jobs. Winning the bid for Schiavone was only the second most important goal.

Joe laughed—whatever my motivation, the result would be the same.

Actually, I had never bid a job in my life. But I got help from Donald's partner Andy Zosuls and their engineer Tim Brennan. We were low bidder, winning a $40.9 million contract to rehabilitate the Queensborough Bridge. The second-lowest bidder: Karl Koch Erecting Company, at $42.6 million. But a few days later after we won the bid, Joe showed me a copy of a letter Jack Daly had written to the New York State Department of Transportation. Jack asserted that while Schiavone was the lowest bidder, the company's legal difficulties meant it wasn't the lowest "responsible" bidder. Therefore, the job should be awarded to Karl Koch Erecting. Schiavone was later acquitted of bribing a union official and other charges, but by then the state had agreed with Daly and given the Queensborough Bridge job to Koch. I lost this round to Jack Daly, but I was to go on to win many other jobs for my clients over the years, work collectively worth more than half a billion dollars, many of them by underbidding the company that bore my name.

In 1989, the company was renamed Koch-Skanska, and it is now one of the most successful construction firms in New York, with annual sales of $102 million and a net worth of $52 million, according to Dun & Bradstreet. Despite its foreign ownership, it is still a family enterprise, employing a number of my cousins and nephews. Its current president is Bob Koch Jr. Jack Daly remains chairman of the board, and one of his sons and another of Bob's are vice presidents. Uncle Jerome died in 1989. Uncle Bob is eighty-four and living in Florida. I was hoping the years had mellowed him, and that he and Jack might talk to me for this book. But they both refused.

THE WORLD TRADE CENTER was finally dedicated on April 4, 1973, by which point its cost had reached $700 million, with the books still open. President Nixon, whose speechwriters may have been preoccupied with more pressing matters, sent a message blandly hailing the Trade Center as "a major factor for the expansion of the nation's international trade." It was supposed to be read by Labor Secretary Peter Brennan, but there was a strike going on by the railway carmen's union against PATH. Brennan—the one-time president of the Building Trades Council who had spoken in support of the Trade Center at the City Council hearing in 1966—didn't want to cross the picket line. Another no-show was Austin Tobin, who had retired a year earlier. "It was raining," he explained when a reporter called to ask why he wasn't there.

The Trade Center went on to an honorable life, earning its place in the modern culture of New York City. For years, critics, architects, urbanologists, and other interested observers debated its merits as a piece of urban architecture, the challenge being to comment on things other than the only reason anyone cared in the first place: the towers' bigness. People talked about how far you could see from the top of the towers, but just as remarkable was the distance from which *they* could be seen. These metal mountains were visible from Bear Mountain fifty miles up the Hudson.

It all took some getting used to. You didn't change the New York skyline so dramatically without hearing about it. "To anyone gawking from a car window during those last few grimy miles through New Jersey to the Holland Tunnel, it appears that there *is* no skyline anymore, just those looming twin towers," wrote Glenn Collins of *The New York Times Magazine.* "Even in aerial views of Lower Manhattan these days, the towers look like the two tallest kids in a choose-up basketball game."

Paradoxically, many critics considered the Trade Center a dinosaur. "There's nothing revolutionary about the World Trade Center," maintained a grumpy Lewis Mumford. "Tall buildings are outmoded concepts—this is Victorian thinking. Skyscrapers have always been put up for reasons of advertisement and publicity. They are not economically sound or efficient—in fact they are ridiculously unprofitable."

There was truth in what Mumford was saying. It turned out that the Committee for a Reasonable World Trade Center was right when it predicted that the Port Authority could fill one but not two towers with companies engaged in world trade. The Port wound up renting to anyone with a check and didn't turn a profit on the buildings until 1981, even though its address provided companies with a certain cachet. Eventually, control of the Trade Center, closely associated with the Port Authority for so long, changed hands: In 1999, a businessman named Larry Silverstein bought the 99-year lease for $3.2 billion.

But dubious economics didn't keep the Trade Center from triggering an era of can-you-top-this skyscraper building that went from Manhattan to Chicago to Asia. The competition became so fierce—amid arguments over whether "tallest" meant the height to the top of the roof, or the "structural or architectural top" or to the top of the antenna, or the number of stories—that somebody started a Council on Tall Buildings and Urban Habitat to set standards. (If you're talking about the *top* top, the tallest buildings in the world, at 1,483 feet, are the twin Petronas Towers in Kuala Lumpur, Malaysia, which surpassed the Sears Tower in 1996. The Sears Tower, though, had twenty-two more stories.)

People could debate the aesthetic and commercial merits of the World Trade Center all they wanted, but the fact was that the towers were the most photographed buildings in New York, if not the world (you'd need a Council on Pictures of Tall Buildings to establish this fact). It was a tribute to its size if not its character. After all, at the end of the day—five o'clock sharp—these were really just office buildings.

Despite the affection many New Yorkers had for the Twin Towers, for many years I could not even look at them. If I was coming into the city or was downtown and the Lower Manhattan skyline came into even a corner of my view, I actually averted my eyes. To me, the World Trade Center was the best and worst thing that ever happened to the Koch family. In construction circles, I was often introduced as "the man who built the World Trade Center." Besides being a gross and embarrassing exaggeration since thousands of men built it, this was not the job with which I wanted to be associated. Nothing against the job. Everything against what it was associated with—at least in my mind.

I have always felt terrible about selling the company for my father and later generations of our side of the family. In a moment of panic, I had removed my father from the presidency of the company and given it over to my uncle Bob, facilitating his eventual grab for all the power. Every jump of the kangaroo, every foot higher we went, had brought us closer to that point. My aversion to the Trade Center was, of course, all symbolic—it was our Tower of Babel. But then, so much about the World Trade Center was symbolic.

Eventually, even these feelings subsided. Nothing could change the role the Trade Center had played in hastening the disintegration of our company. But it also seemed pointless to deny the achievement of actually building those towers. I could finally look downtown and feel not pain but pride. One day in late summer, I was up on the roof of the AT&T Building, just a few blocks north of the Trade Center on Sixth Avenue. I was consulting for a company with a contract to expand the building, and with the job just about done, my friend Andy Zosuls, the engineer on the project, was taking pictures. He insisted that he take one of me with the Twin Towers in the background. I went to the corner of the roof, took my hard hat off, and held it in front of me as I leaned against the railing and turned slightly so the towers were off my right shoulder. I smiled, posing like a tourist.

This, too, was a symbol. It was the first time I'd been photographed with the towers in thirty years. The date was August 30, 2001.

EPILOGUE

September 11, 2001

WE SET THE LAST section of antenna on the AT&T Building the first week of September, and then I went home to take some time off. I was consulting for Francis Lee, whose company was doing the steelwork for the upward expansion of the telecommunications giant's twenty-eight-story national corporate headquarters building. It had been a year of intricate and challenging work, and I was ready for a break. On Thursday, September 6, I told my partner Andy Zosuls that I was taking off Friday and all of the following week. I was getting ready to retire again. I do that on a regular basis.

The following Tuesday morning around eight-thirty, I called the field office a block away from the AT&T Building and talked to Andy about some final details of the job. "I'm going down to the Trade Center," he said when we were wrapping up. He wanted to go to the Port Authority office on the 72nd floor of the north tower to check for any new work they were putting out for bid. It was about fifteen blocks down Broadway.

Just as I hung up the phone, Vivian called out to me. "Karl, come to the TV! Quick. A plane just hit the Trade Center!" Our daughter Jill had called on the other line while I was talking to Andy. Jill lives on the thirty-sixth floor of a building on East 39th Street, in an apartment with a clear view of the Trade Center out her window. When I got to the TV, I saw that horrendous scene, smoke billowing from the north tower. I rushed back to the phone in my office to call Andy back. "Don't go to the Trade Center!" I shouted. "A plane just hit the tower!"

"Wow!" Andy said. "I heard a plane go over us when we were talking. I thought, 'Boy, he's low. Where's he going?' I'm going over to our building."

I went back to the TV. What kind of fool would fly smack into the tower?

How do you lose your way on a beautiful, clear morning like this? What kind of plane was he flying? I looked at the hole blasted through the exterior wall and glanced at my watch—five to nine—and knew that dozens of people were probably dead. Watching the fire, I thought of the day back toward the end of the construction when I arranged for a tour by a group of doctors, a favor for George Crickelair, the plastic surgeon who had become my friend. One of them asked a Port Authority official what would happen in case of a fire. The PA man explained that the fire would be sealed off and everyone on the floors above it would be sent to higher floors—to the roof, if necessary—while those below would be evacuated. Then the firefighters would rush in to put it out. It's a big building, another doctor asked, what if it falls over? "If it falls over," the Port official said, "then we all end up in New Jersey." Everyone laughed.

I squinted at the TV screen, trying to see if people were heading to the roof. I pictured them huddling to the leeward side, and if all else failed they would be picked up by helicopters. The people below were well on their way out, I was sure. I looked at the TV screen and imagined hundreds of people rushing down and the firemen pushing their way up. "My God," I said to Vivian. "Look at all that smoke."

And then . . . a flash . . . another fire and more smoke—*in the other tower.* And I knew—I didn't need to hear it from someone on TV—it was a terrorist attack. Sick, evil bastards, I thought. Now I became much more concerned about the logistics of escape. I prayed they evacuated right after the first hit on the other tower. It was becoming harder to imagine what was really going on inside those two buildings. Would any more planes hit? I thought they had to be either military transport planes or giant jets. I was glad the towers took the impact; so far, they seemed to be doing okay. But for how long? "Those upper floors are going to collapse," I told Vivian. "They're not putting the fire out. The whole goddamn upper system may go in the street."

Jill was still on the phone, relaying to Vivian what she was seeing from her apartment window. Suddenly, I heard Jill screaming into the phone. "Oh my God, she says one of the towers collapsed!" Vivian said. I grabbed the phone and Jill repeated, "It collapsed! One of the towers collapsed!"

"No, no, honey, it didn't collapse," I told her. "It can't collapse."

"No, Daddy," Jill said, crying. "I saw it fall. Can't you see? There's no building there!"

"Look, the building is hidden by the camera angle and all the smoke," I assured her. "It's behind the other building."

I switched channels, hoping to find a camera angle that would show both buildings. But all I could see was the north tower and a tremendous amount of smoke. I switched channels again. Same thing. The people on TV were saying what Jill was saying, that the south tower had collapsed, but how could they know? They couldn't see. I looked for that tower, just a hint of it, anything to sustain my denial and choke back my growing sense of dread. It *had* to be the angle. The south tower *had* to be hiding behinds its twin. But why wasn't I seeing at least a glimpse of it?

And then I saw the impossible, saw it live: the north tower collapsing inward, straight down like a plunger. "The floor panels!" I cried out—I knew just what was happening. I could see it in my mind's eye: The fire burned until the steel was weakened and the floors above collapsed, starting a chain reaction of gravity, floor falling upon floor falling upon floor, *clunk-clunk-clunk,* the load gaining weight and momentum by the nanosecond, unstoppable. Once enough floors collapsed, the exterior walls and the core columns were no longer laterally supported and folded in. I couldn't stop saying it: *The floor panels. The goddamn floor panels.* The floor panels that we assembled from the pieces that arrived from the Midwest, and that we barged and trucked over to the site.

Down the tower went—my God, I thought, how many people were still in there? I saw the 360-foot antenna riding the building down to the street. Our company put that antenna up; I remember John DeSmidt telling me what a bitch it was. I remembered the day we topped out the building and raised the American flag on it, a celebration of three years of work and another two of preparation, and for the Port Authority, the culmination of an entire decade of toil and struggle. Now the entire building had fallen in only seconds. I saw it—but I still didn't believe it. This couldn't be happening. But it *was* happening, and I knew this because I was gasping for breath and my vision was blurred with tears. And then they were saying it on TV. Both towers had collapsed.

I left the room and poured myself a scotch. I sat on the living room couch and looked out over the blue waters of Long Island Sound and tried to process what I had just seen. I thought if a man lived from the day of creation to the end of the world, he would never see a sight like that. In the pit of my stomach I felt the reality of the horror. I knew you could populate a small city with the number of people who work in and visit the World Trade Center. They couldn't have all gotten out.

✳   ✳

By the time I got to what everyone was now calling Ground Zero, the whole world knew that thousands had not gotten out, that hundreds, in fact, had gone *in*, doomed rescuers who had heroically marched into something worse than an inferno. It was five days later, Sunday, the sixteenth. The day after the terrorists' attacks, Verizon had hired Francis Lee to repair its building on Washington Street, which was damaged by the collapsing towers. I needed to be at the Trade Center, and I was going in with Andy. We met the next morning and drove in together.

After getting off the phone with me that terrible morning, Andy had walked the two blocks over to the AT&T Building on Sixth Avenue and gone up to the roof. He was up there with Damir Plisic, the engineer on the job and another good friend of mine, and a small group of ironworkers. The tradition of topping out a building with an American flag applies to expansions as well as new construction, so when the men had set the highest piece a few weeks earlier, they raised an eight-by-twelve-foot flag that Damir had brought in from Long Island. His wife, Liz, had found the flag at a garage sale. Damir was born in Croatia and came to this country when he was six. He was now thirty-eight, exactly my age when we topped out the north tower.

After the men first put the flag up on the antenna, they noticed that it would sometimes become wrapped around the needle and need to be unfurled. The morning of the eleventh, a group of them were up there, working. They saw that the flag needed an adjustment, and one of them, Ray Fuerst, went up twenty-eight stories to do the job. He climbed the ladder inside the 150-foot antenna tower until he got to the thirty-foot needle. Then he had to climb the spikes jutting from the needle to get to the flag. As soon as he unfurled it, he saw the first of the two hijacked jets pass just four hundred feet overhead. He and the other men up on the roof barely had time to register their shock before they watched American Flight 11 crash into the north tower. They stayed up there, not believing what they were seeing. Andy said the men described how the pilot banked the plane and then accelerated. "Karl, he gunned the engine," he told me. I mulled the possibility that one of the last things the hijackers saw below them before they committed their mass murder was that American flag flapping in the breeze, the flag that belonged to an immigrant who came to this country and thrived. Twenty-one minutes later, by which time Andy had joined them, United Flight 175 approached from the opposite direction and slammed into the south tower.

Andy and I arrived downtown at 6:45 that morning five days later, got our security passes and went through the checkpoints, and then headed toward the Trade Center on foot. I couldn't call it Ground Zero. As we got closer to the place where the towers had stood, the scene was impossible to grasp with too wide a view, so I tried to take it in a little bit at a time. Even in the rubble, everywhere I looked I could see familiar things: the three-column exterior panels, still held together by their spandrels, the treetops that were so big each one needed its own rail flatbed. I looked for any signs of a floor panel, just one of the 5,800 I knew were in here, but I couldn't identify a single one.

At the Verizon Building, we were briefed by someone in authority who said there were some things we needed to be aware of. He told us that the CIA had some kind of arsenal in Building 7 of the Trade Center, so be on the lookout for that. And there's supposed to be millions of dollars in gold bars somewhere in here, from a Federal Reserve transfer station. And, yes, bodies, and parts of them. They handed us boxes with gas masks inside. They looked old. There was a date stamped on the box: 1952. Korean War surplus.

On TV the night before, I had seen my cousin Dan Koch Jr. being interviewed. He had been an apprentice in a surveying party during the Trade Center's construction, when he was seventeen. He had gone on to become an ironworker, and was part of the team that repaired columns after the first terrorists drove a bomb into the parking garage in 1993. Now he was back, doing his part for what was being called the recovery. Also down there was my elder son, Karl. He is the one of my five children most pained by the loss of the company that he once believed would be his life's work. Instead, he works for the Metropolitan Transportation Authority. The agency asked for volunteers to help out at the Trade Center, and Karl showed up in his old Koch helmet, the same red one he wore when I took him up to the open-air top floor of the south tower when he was nine years old. I look at the picture one of our men snapped that day and see the pride on his young face. And on mine. Karl and the MTA volunteers worked all day Saturday on rescue and recovery, but when one of the men fell apart after finding a body part, the professional emergency workers pulled the MTA men out. They instructed them to stand outside the debris and form a barricade so the victims' families couldn't see the burned and mutilated bodies being pulled out.

I couldn't stay, either. I only half-listened to the briefing, preoccupied by the devastating sight of ironworkers, these guys I've worked with for more than fifty years, not building up but breaking down, reaching over from baskets hung from cherry pickers with their wrecking torches, burning heavy weldments of steel into pieces small enough to fit into the truck headed for the Fresh Kills Landfill on Staten Island. I offered my two cents about the demolition methods, but it was a lost cause. Too many bosses. Andy and I brought six torches for the ironworkers, our small contribution, and then I was ready to leave. I was invited to stay and manage the night crew, but I couldn't do it. "I buried the Trade Center once," I told Andy. "I can't bury it again."

I WAS NUMB, off-balance, for weeks. A mix of memories and images bounced around my brain. I thought of how, only a month before, I had been to Windows on the World, the famous restaurant atop the south tower, with my niece Kim, along with my partner Andy and his daughter Nicole. Kim was my brother Donald's cherished daughter, and she had grown into a beautiful young woman. We had a lovely window table that gave us a breathtaking view of the Empire State building, and in the foreground we could see the AT&T Building that Andy and I were working on. In my mind, I kept picturing Donald sitting in my seat and imagined how proud he would have been of Kim. She had always wanted to go to Windows on the World, and, now, after the tragedy, I couldn't help but wonder why I had chosen that moment to take her.

Members of my family, meanwhile, went to great lengths to acknowledge my personal connection to the Trade Center. My nephew George Hendricks, a sculptor who works primarily in stone, sent me a design for a poignant memorial at the Trade Center site. He called it "The Circle of Life," featuring a kaleidoscope of the names of those who perished. My daughter Cynthia wrote me a beautiful and poignant letter. "You constructed the only building in the world whose destruction could unite not only a nation, but the world," she wrote. "The toil and effort and struggle you put into making sure that steel got built succeeded. No terrorists can ever take that away from you. Little did you know when you were erecting the steel for the World Trade Center nearly three decades ago that you were actually building the structure whose collapse would end up steeling America. For nearly thirty years, the World Trade Center was two powerful buildings standing side by side in defiance of the impossible. Now, it will forever be the symbol of this country's true strength—Americans standing side by side in defense of the possible."

Over the next few months, I was like anyone else in the country or the world who saw and read about the terrorist attacks and watched the collapse of the Twin Towers over and over on television, as if it were the Zapruder film. We all were tortured by that image, and by the thought of so many innocent people dying so horribly. And gradually we all turned our attention to what could be done to protect ourselves from falling victim to such heinous crimes. But in the midst of all these human emotions, these natural reactions as an American and a human being, I was also gripped by a need to understand the mechanics of the towers' collapse. I'd had a hand in building the towers; I wanted to know what caused them to fall.

The exterior walls performed beautifully as long as the floors were intact. About thirty-one columns were knocked out in the south tower when the plane hit and the load simply spanned around the lost section. Tens of thousands owe their lives to the towers' ability to resist being knocked over by the impact of 767s flying at more than 500 miles an hour. It was the ensuing fire that weakened the floor systems and then caused them to collapse as if they were imploding.

One plane hit the south face of the south tower at an angle, missing the core and piling debris in the northeast corner. The aviation fuel ignited the debris, engulfing at least five floors in the inferno. The other plane hit the north face of the north tower and slammed into the core. But while the planes came in differently, the effects were the same: In both cases, the intense heat weakened and deformed the trusses, causing them to collapse and eliminating the lateral support for the exterior wall and the core columns.

The trusses in two or three floors lost most of their strength and then deformed in the 600- to 800-degree heat. They deflected, or catenaried, like a clothesline—each truss pulling out the two bolts that fastened it to the exterior wall. As these floors gave way, the outer box columns started to bow outward, causing the bolts on the lower floors to pull out and sending floor after floor crashing down. The angle supports of the floors below were unable to withstand the impact of the floors crashing down from above, and they gave way. The floors collapsed, the exterior walls and core columns folded out, and the towers collapsed like a house of cards.

Thirty-five years ago, the Port Authority couldn't get enough mileage out of the word "revolutionary" when it promoted the Trade Center. In a publication called *The World Trade Center: A Building Project Like No Other,* it boasted that the towers were "radically different in that the structural design of the towers uses the exterior walls as the load-bearing walls. Most of the steel is on the outside instead of the inside.

The only interior columns are in the core, which contain the elevators. Thus, there is a maximum open, column-free floor space. The outer wall carries the building's vertical loads, and provides the entire resistance to wind. The wall consists of closely spaced vertical columns tied together by massive horizontal spandrel beams, which girdle the tower at every floor. On the inside of the structure, the floor sections consist of trusses spanning from the core to the outer wall. In effect, the towers are a huge four-sided lattice, bound together for enormous strength."

Would a less radical departure from traditional key structural elements have yielded a less devastating result? The first official government investigations of the collapses did not offer an answer to this question. A report released in May 2002 after a joint investigation by the American Society of Civil Engineers and the Federal Emergency Management Agency (FEMA), found that the initial impact of the planes wouldn't have been enough to bring the towers down. In fact, the buildings held up amazingly well against the tremendous force of the racing 767s crashing through the steel panels of the exterior walls. Although Leslie Robertson and his colleagues at the Skilling engineering firm designed the towers to handle the crash of the largest plane at the time, a Boeing 707, flying at low approach speeds—thinking in terms of a lost pilot, not a crazed suicide hijacker—they absorbed the shock of the slightly heavier Boeing 767's flying at much higher speeds. If the crashes had been the only stress on the buildings, the investigating engineers concluded, they could have remained standing indefinitely. It was the intense fires that brought them down. But these conclusions are fairly obvious. The real question is what the mechanism of structural failure was.

There are sure to be further investigations and reports. But everything already known, and conversations I have had with many in the field, only bolsters my initial instinctive reaction as I watched the towers come down on television. It is my considered opinion it was all about the floor panels, those light, highly engineered, open-web joist panels that resisted deflection and failure for only 54 minutes. Heavy structural beams, spaced at perhaps ten-foot intervals and fully fireproofed, would have in all likelihood resisted the fires for hours, not minutes, perhaps allowing firefighters to reach them and put them out. The vast majority of civilian victims were at and above the impact floors and fires. Had the building stood long enough, maybe many of them could have been saved.

Structural engineers like trusses because they are exceptionally efficient—light but strong. But firefighters have a saying: Don't trust the truss. They fail in fires because they heat up very quickly. And structural steel in general will start to lose its resistance at around 800 degrees. Estimates of these jet-fuel fires were that they burned at more than 1,000 degrees. The FEMA report found that the buildings were virtually defenseless against this monster fire. The impact of the planes disabled the sprinkler system; emergency elevators were damaged so firefighters couldn't use them to get to the fire quickly; and the fireproofing material sprayed on steel beams and trusses apparently was blasted off by the impact of the planes.

I discussed my thoughts with Charlie Thornton, a greatly admired engineer of my acquaintance. He is a partner in Thornton-Tomasetti Engineers, a world-renowned structural engineering firm that has designed many of the world's most prominent structures, including the current World's Tallest Buildings, the 1,483-foot Petronas Towers in Malaysia. Charlie was on a four-person team that investigated the destruction of the federal building in Oklahoma City blown up by domestic terrorists in 1995.

I told Charlie that I had thought immediately of the floor panels when the towers came crashing down. "Karl, we all know what caused the collapse," he said, as if what I was saying was so obvious it didn't need to be discussed.

I asked Charlie if he agreed with the position that there was no way to build a building that will withstand the impact of a 767 loaded with fuel. "You can't design every building for these extreme events," he said, "but there are things that could have been done in both of these buildings or in any buildings from this day on that buy you more redundancy. And we've done it now on maybe six buildings in the last five years."

For instance, he said, if the core of the Trade Center had been part of the lateral load system and had the floors been heavier and stronger, the south building might not have collapsed. "And if it did, maybe just the top would have collapsed," he said. "You can see that with only two little five-eighths-inch bolts, the minute the joists started to sag, they just yanked them right out." Had there been more and bigger bolts, they wouldn't have pulled out.

"Most of the tall buildings that we've designed recently, we share the load," Thornton said. "We share the wind and earthquake forces between the core and exterior. And in the case of the Trade Center, the tube was so stiff they didn't put any lateral load resistance in the core. And so, in a sense the core was a bunch of columns stacked on top of each other. But I still think that the weak link was the floor system with the spray-on fireproofing and that either the exterior or the interior was done for the minute you lost more than, I don't know, three, four, five, six floors."

Charlie added, "I think people will think twice before they use a long-span open-web joist-type design on a large, important building."

This doesn't mean that the World Trade Center was defectively designed. But now that we can all see the devastation of a suicide plane or even a war plane, let our buildings and skyscrapers be designed accordingly. We should build support floors with heavier structural steel members, using a multitude of high-strength bolts to fasten them to the structure. We should build "compartmental" skyscrapers that don't depend on a single structural design and have redundancies that will help the building stand up to forces bearing down on its lateral load in situations such as an earthquake. And we should introduce blast-resistance and redundant fire extinguishing systems.

As we're reminded everyday, this is a new era—nothing is the same since 9/11. It's bizarre to think, but now architects and design engineers need to work with police and fire departments, military agencies, and disaster experts. They must widen their art, because the concept of building safety changed profoundly on September 11, 2001.

Given the new reality of terrorism and realizing that no abhorrent act is beyond the terrorists' desire, I believe that a national panel of recognized authorities in architecture, engineering, construction, disaster, fire, military, and police must be formed. This panel should formulate procedures and implement national codes and regulations. It should review and approve any future designs of major and important structures. Having a license in the respective arts and building to codes that vary from city to city are simply not enough anymore in this new world of terrorism. The collapse of the World Trade Center and its satellite buildings has shown us that any structural steel–framed building standing today is susceptible to a similar disaster. An uncontrolled fire can destroy any building, so it is our obligation to determine how to protect the buildings now standing and the ones we build in the future, so that the people who are living and working within them are safe. The factors of economic feasibility and investment return cannot be the primary concerns any longer.

IN THE MONTHS after that infamous day, I reconnected with some of the men with whom I had shared the mighty struggle of building the World Trade Center. I called on crane operators, ironworkers, foremen, as well as the guys in charge, Guy Tozzoli and John Tishman. Austin Tobin and Minoru Yamasaki were gone, and so were Ray Monti and Eric Favelle. But there were others I hardly knew then, like Steve DeSmidt, who turned out to have a poetic appreciation of this business of steel. He still had his brass from the job, and brought it out to show me. It would have been a different experience, a pleasant one, if all I had wanted to do was reminisce, like Roger Kahn when he was writing his great baseball memoir, *The Boys of Summer*. But after September 11, we all shared a different kind of bond, regardless of our relationship back then.

When I went to see Rudy Loffredo, I wondered, Would he greet me with a handshake or a hug? I got a hug—and a kiss on the cheek. I found John Kelly, the union steward, in happy retirement on Staten Island, and he pulled out all his mementos. He still had the key chain we gave out at the first topping out. It was inscribed: "World Trade Center Tower A 110 floors 1,470 feet." I remembered John was a real son of a bitch back then—that was his job—but he couldn't have been friendlier now. He showed me a small cross he had made from a piece cut out of a downed column an ironworker had gotten for him at Ground Zero.

I went up to John Tishman's office on the thirty-eighth floor of a building on Fifth Avenue. He was now chairman and chief executive of the entire Tishman Empire, not just the head of the construction arm. We had a long talk about the Trade Center, then and now, and I told him I had cried for three days after the towers came down, and that there were moments when my entire body twitched involuntarily for just a microsecond. He looked at me wide-eyed and whispered, "I got that sometimes, too."

Everywhere I went, everyone I visited, I had the same conversation. Why did the towers come down the way they did? Was it a bad design, or just evil men and let's just leave it at that?

A shoemaker one day startled me by asking if it was my company's fault. We put those towers up, right? Of course it wasn't our fault; we erected the materials we were given exactly according to the plans. Every item of work was inspected and approved. Like everyone else—at least everyone but my father—I thought the design was a brilliantly creative way to put up an attention-getting building efficiently. But after September 11, I don't think anyone intimately involved with the design or construction of the Trade Center could avoid thinking about his role. The man most responsible for that design seemed to be the one most filled with regret and self-doubt. It has been a horrible year for Leslie Robertson, the Skilling engineer who designed the structural framework of the towers. Now seventy-three, he had his own firm, with offices that until September 11 had wonderful views of his most famous work. On that day, he was in Hong Kong, discussing a skyscraper to be built in Kowloon. He watched the horror on his hotel room TV while packing his bags in a fog.

To his credit, Robertson has not run away from the scrutiny of his design, the questions, including mine. He first emerged publicly on October fifth, three weeks after the attacks, at a previously scheduled meeting of the National Council of Structural Engineers Associations in New Hampshire. When someone in the audience asked Robertson if there was anything he wished he had done differently in the design of the buildings, he broke down and wept at the podium. But his entirely understandable emotional reaction didn't mean he felt he had done anything *wrong,* or that there was a flaw in the design. He held to the position that it was impossible to design a terrorist-proof building. Instead, he said, we should make sure we keep terrorists away from the cockpits of airplanes.

UNTIL IT STOPPED taking regular deliveries in March of 2001, the 3,000-acre Fresh Kills landfill on Staten Island was the largest garbage dump in the world. Six months later, it became almost a city of misery and destruction, the place to bring the wreckage and remains of all the life that was obliterated that Tuesday morning in September.

One day a few months after the attack, I drove out there and met up with a friend, a trucker who had been hired by the city to haul away all the scrap metal. I had called him with two purposes in mind. Seeing the landfill was only the second one. Mainly, I wanted him to tell me his recollections of how he had gotten the floor panels to the Trade Center during the tugboat strike of 1969. It was none other than Tom Petrizzo, the man who stopped traffic on half the bridges in the metropolitan area for twenty-two straight nights.

Tom picked me up at the gate and started driving around the landfill, pointing out the sobering sights. There were hundreds, maybe thousands, of crushed vehicles, including row after row of destroyed fire trucks. There had to be enough to outfit the entire fire department of a medium-sized city. We passed pieces of wreckage from one of the jets. "The fuselage of the plane, the motors, and the wheels are back there," Tom said. "See those guys inside here?" He pointed to a tent. "They're all FBI agents, NYPD, or ATF. They're finding wallets, watches, all kinds of jewelry and personal belongings. This is the coroner's area here. There was so much being found at the beginning they had refrigerator trailers."

Tom drove on to an area that he said had been a mountain of steel a couple of months earlier. "It was about thirty feet high," he said. Now most of it was gone, shipped out to Hugo Neu Schnitzer in Jersey City, the biggest scrap metal dealer in the country. By now a lot of it was on its way to China to be melted down and recycled. "There had to be three hundred thousand tons," Tom said. "How many tons in the two buildings?"

"Two hundred thousand," I said.

"In both buildings? Impossible."

"That's what it was," I assured him. "That's what I got paid for."

"Some of the columns that came in here were bent like U-turns," Tom said.

I asked him if he'd seen any floor sections. "No, that's what I don't understand," Tom said. "I didn't see one goddamn floor deck come here with a bar joist in it. They must have disintegrated. Because they did not get here. And I handled this from day fuckin' one."

"Did they send you any decking that was loose, no joists?" I asked.

"None," Tom said.

"None? Well, that's impossible. There were six thousand of them."

"There's stuff crumpled up, but go identify it as a floor deck if you can. Impossible. A lot of guys come and ask me, they know I was involved in bringing 'em over, but Karl, not one came where I could say, 'Oh, here's one.' I could not show anybody a floor deck and say, 'This is what I hauled over.'"

I couldn't believe it. Not one goddamn floor panel.

A COUPLE OF MONTHS after September 11, I was in an all-too-familiar place: the Harkness Pavilion of Columbia-Presbyterian Hospital. Thirty-eight years after my accident, I was back for more treatments. Once again, I was facing the loss of my leg. I'd already gotten one opinion that it had to go. I wanted a second one. A doctor at Columbia gave me one I liked better than the first. It resulted in surgery and a complicated mix of medications that included, of all things, Cipro, the anthrax antibiotic.

While in the hospital, I returned to a place I'd spent a lot of time all those years ago: the pavilion's eleventh-floor solarium. I looked downtown, all the way down to Wall Street. The skyline was as it had been when I spent so much time here in 1965 and 1966. As if Donald had never sat right here with me and told me we were bidding on the World Trade Center. As if those buildings had never been built.

Now I pondered what might be constructed in their place. It's a question many people asked me after September 11. To me, the site became sacred ground on that day. I believe we should build on it, but in a way that renews the original intent and purpose of the World Trade Center. Guy Tozzoli, the former Port Authority official who is the one person who can truly be considered "the man who built the World Trade Center," has always said that countries that trade together make peace together. He has been nominated for the Nobel Peace Prize several times for his efforts, and now is president of the World Trade Association. In recent years, economics forced the World Trade Center to step back from its original purpose and become office buildings occupied by anyone who could afford the rent. I hope new buildings are constructed on a scale that will allow them to be a true World Trade Center. I also would propose that space be given for a memorial—a promenade, a sanctuary, a garden path—devoted to reflection and memory. Let it be a place people can visit and from which they may draw comfort.

The events of the past year have reawakened a spirituality in many of us. Being back in the hospital in the late fall of 2001, I was reminded of a night in 1965. The door to my room opened a bit, and a man poked his head in. Seeing that I was awake, he came to my bed and asked how I was feeling. He was a rabbi; he might have thought from my name on the door that I was Jewish. I welcomed the visit. He saw the framed pictures at my bedside, and we began talking about family. I remarked how lucky I felt to be alive, and he began to tell me a fable.

There was in the South Pacific a tiny, lost island on whose shores shipwrecked sailors would turn up every couple of years. The natives would lift the parched and weak sailor gently in their arms as others pulled his craft into the brush. They would carry him to their village and place him in their finest bamboo hut and then gently administer to his wounds and sunburned and blistered body. When he was well enough, they placed a crown on his head and sat him on their throne. He was fed their finest fruits and best catches from the sea. They placed their softest cloths at his feet and presented baskets filled with pearls and rare seashells. Finally, after ten years, on the anniversary of his arrival, the crown was removed and he was escorted back to the beach. The craft he arrived on was pulled from the bushes and he was put back into it and pushed out to sea. This ritual happened repeatedly until one particular sailor washed ashore on his raft. Again the natives lifted him in their arms while others dragged his raft into the bushes. The whole cycle was repeated except that when he was finally well and they put the crown on his head, he spoke lovingly to them and sang to them. He shared the baskets of fruit and catches from the sea. He gave them back the pearls and the precious seashells. Again ten years to the day of his arrival they escorted him in procession back to the beach. They cried as they pulled his raft from the bushes. They dressed him in the rags he arrived in and lovingly lifted him in their arms and placed him back on the raft. The whole village stood by while he was pushed out to sea. They sang songs of lament as he drifted out farther and farther. Their eyes never left the little raft and their songs continued until that little dot on the sea finally drifted over the horizon. And every day thereafter, they went down to the beach and sang in his memory.

"Karl," said the rabbi, "that is the story of the Kaddish. It explains how we feel about our departed loved ones. They are like the sailor who returned the love the natives showed him. Even after they are gone, we celebrate our loved ones and pray for them." I have never forgotten that story, and it was why, as my father lay dying years later, I whispered in his ear, "Every time I think of you, Dad, I'll pray for you."

And I will always remember and grieve and pray for those poor souls who died at the World Trade Center. I will gently push them out to sea and sing songs and prayers to their memory.

The last support column from the south tower of the World Trade Center is raised by a crane at Ground Zero before being loaded onto a flatbed truck, May 28, 2002.
(Reuters/Mike Segar)

NOTES ON SOURCES

THIS BOOK HAS a history of its own. In 1974, finding myself separated from the business I loved, I sat down to write the story of the World Trade Center and how it set off the events that led to my selling the company my father built. I rented an office and spent many weeks with my old friend Joe Sherry writing and dictating ten chapters. Then I sent it to a friend who knew someone in publishing. But the partial manuscript wound up in a drawer for the next twenty-seven years.

After the terrorist attacks of September 11, 2001, it became apparent that amidst all the intense emotions swirling around the tragedy, there was also renewed interest in the World Trade Center itself. The Twin Towers' innovative design became central to what will surely be many years of discussion about why the towers fell the way they did and what might be done in the future to protect innocent civilians and rescuers should there be similar strikes by terrorists. In the wake of 9/11, my wife, Vivian, persuaded me that there might be interest in a book about how the Trade Center came to be built and about the history of our family company and its place in the twentieth-century culture of the American steel industry. Maybe the time had come to dust off my original manuscript. I knew, of course, that if I were to write a personal story, much of it would have to be about my father and his brothers and about how the family firm that built the Twin Towers saw its epic struggle trigger the destruction of the company as we knew it. My children and my wife, who have lived and often suffered with me through the events described in this book, thought that my story was worth sharing.

The book that resulted is based primarily on my own recollections, aided in no small measure by boxloads of material that I saved through the years. Foremost among them were the 46,000 words I wrote back in 1974, which included much of the dialogue I've included in this book. In addition, I found a tape I had made in 1969, in which I recounted many of the events that were taking place at the time, and a letter that I composed in 1967 and sent to my uncles, as well as the voluminous file of related legal documents. In addition, many documents and photographs related to the early history of Karl Koch Erecting Company were acquired from the National Archives and other sources. A personal memoir by my paternal grandmother, Cora Koch, helped piece together and fill in some of the blanks of the early history of our family and our company.

My collaborator, Richard Firstman, and I also interviewed dozens of people who played roles large and small in the events described here. Since the story reaches back many decades, in some cases I contacted the children of my father's contemporaries. Most of my relatives were glad to help me rediscover the past, but some were reticent. Unfortunately, two key people wouldn't consent to interviews: my uncle, Bob Koch, and my brother-in-law, Jack Daly. I would have preferred to include their recollections in this book about our family and its steel-erecting company.

We also relied on published sources, some of which were invaluable. In particular, *Twin Towers: The Life of New York City's World Trade Center,* by Angus Kress Gillespie (Rutgers University Press, 1999), provided a helpful road map by pointing us to many pertinent newspaper and magazine articles. Since the Port Authority's own collection of documents, clippings, and photographs related to the Trade Center were destroyed in the September 11 terrorist attacks, Professor Gillespie's files, which he donated to the Rutgers library, were the only available source for such archival material as the Port's weekly reports.

Following is a selected list of published material that provided primary source material for *Men of Steel:*

BOOKS

Bard, Erwin Wilkie. *The Port of New York Authority.* New York: Columbia University Press, 1941.

Caro, Robert A. *The Power Broker: Robert Moses and the Fall of New York.* New York: Alfred A. Knopf, 1974.

Darton, Eric. *Divided We Stand: A Biography of New York's World Trade Center.* New York: Basic Books, 1999.

Doig, J.W. *To Claim the Seas and the Skies: Austin Tobin and the Port of NY Authority.* Jameson W. Doig and Erwin C. Hargrove, eds., *Leadership and Innovation: A Biographical Perspective on Entrepeneurs in Government.* Baltimore: Johns Hopkins University Press, 1987.

Gillespie, Angus Kress. *Twin Towers: The Life of New York City's World Trade Center.* New Brunswick, N.J.: Rutgers University Press, 1999.

Mysak, Joe and Schiffer, Judith. *Perpetual Motion: The Illustrated History Authority of New York and New Jersey.* Santa Monica, California: General Publishing Group, 1997.

Nye, David E. *American Technological Sublime.* Cambridge, Massachusetts: MIT Press, 1994.

Pacelle, Mitchell. *Empire: A Tale of Obsession, Betrayal, and the Battle for an American Icon.* New York: John Wiley & Sons, 2001.

Yamasaki, Minoru. *A Life in Architecture.* New York: Weatherhill, 1979.

PORT AUTHORITY PUBLICATIONS

The World Trade Center: A Building Project Like No Other, 1990.
Weekly Report (of Port Authority Operations) 17 Dec. 1962.
Weekly Report (of Port Authority To The Commissioner from the Executive Director: 29 August 1966.
Weekly Report 16 Sept. 1968.
Weekly Report 20 Oct. 1969.
Weekly Report 17 Nov. 1969
Weekly Report 13 December 1969.
Weekly Report 30 April 1970.

MAGAZINE AND NEWSPAPER ARTICLES

Engineering News-Record, McGraw Hill Company, New York
"A Look at the New Record" (January 30, 1964).
"Big Steel Cage Goes Underground" (June 1, 1967).
"Contractor is Consultant on World Trade Center" (March 3, 1966).
"Contracts on Tallest Building" (November 24, 1966).
"Cost Plus Penalty" (March 2, 1967).
"Court Action Halts Major Project" (February 28, 1963).

"Designed for 110-Story Buildings" (April 2, 1964).

"Men and Steel Shape Trade Center Towers" (January 1, 1970).

"New Face for Lower New York" (October 23, 1958).

"Steel Ahoy" (November 9, 1967).

"Tieback System Gives Elbow Room" (May 9, 1968).

"Trade Center Builds Upward Fast" (March 13, 1969).

"Trade Center Opponents Say Bids Double Estimate" (October 6, 1966).

"Trade Center Plans Firm up—Cost up" (March 16, 1961).

"Trade Center Steel Contracts Let" (February 2, 1967).

The Ironworker

"Ironworkers Completing World's Tallest Building" (August 1971).

The New Yorker

Iglauer, Edith. "The Biggest Foundation" (November 4, 1972).

Seabrook, John. "The Tower Builder" (November 19, 2001).

VIA Port of New York–New Jersey Custom Publishing, New York.

"A New Lease on Progress" (June 1970).

"Australian Crane Makes Debut at Port of New York" (September 1967).

"Commerce Official Visits Port Authority" (September 1966).

"D-Day for World Trade Center" (April 1973).

"Design for Trade" (April 1966).

"First Steel Arrives and Plumbing Contract Is Let for W.T.C." (April 1968).

"Independent World Needs Trade" (January 1966).

"New World Milieu" (February 1971).

"Port Authority Executive Director Announced Retirement after 45 Years" (January 1972).

"Progress Brisk on World Trade Center Building" (October 1970).

"The Changing Face of Lower Manhattan" (December 1968).

"The Incomparable Port of New York by Austin Tobin" (April 1967).

"The Steel Goes Up" (October 1968).

"They Lift, Luff, and Slew" (September 1969).

"TV Eyes on the Trade Center" (May 1969).

"Work on World Trade Center Moves Ahead as Contracts Are Let" (January 1967).

"World Trade Center Column 'Trees' " (April 1969).

"World Trade Center Construction Proceeds" (March 1968).

"World Trade Center Efficient 'Kangaroos' Complete North Tower Assignment" (May 1971).

"World Trade Center Honored by ASCE" (September 1971).

"World Trade Week–1967" (July 1967).

The Wall Street Journal: Landauer, Jerry, "New York Port Agency's $30 million Saving on Steel Work Prompts AntiTrust Inquiry" (July 16, 1969).

New York World-Telegram and Sun: Klein, Woody. "Small Merchants Protest Trade Center" (March 30, 1962).

The Manhattan Engineer: Koch, Karl W. III. "High Tensile Steel Bolts," Manhattan College School of Engineering, Volume X N O 2 (January 1953).

The New York Times
  "A Section of The Hudson Tubes is Turned Into an Elevated Tunnel" (December 30, 1968).
  "Artifacts Are Dug Up at Trade Center Site" (June 10, 1968).
  "Biggest Buildings in World To Rise At Trade Center" (January 19, 1964).
  "City Ends Fight With Port Agency on Trade Center" (August 6, 1966).
  "City-Port Authority Talks on Trade Center Enter Crucial Stage" (June 7, 1966).
  "Hearing Is Held On Trade Center" (May 3, 1966).
  "He Broke A Stalemate" (August 4, 1966).
  "Lindsay Assails Charge By Tobin" (July 16, 1966).
  "Mayor Rebuffed on Trade Center" (July 13, 1966).
  "Questions On The Trade Center" (December 24, 1966).
  "Real Estate Men Fight Port Agency" (April 1, 1964).
  "The Wind, Fickle and Shifty, Tests Builders" (May 5, 1974).
  "Trade Center is Doing Everything Big" (June 6, 1969).
  "Transport is His Life" (September 8, 1961).
  "Work on Trade Center is Moving Into Higher Gear" (July 6, 1967).

Bergen Record
  "The Four-Letter Word That Started an Era" (January 25, 1962).

Newark Sunday News
  "New York Casting Cold Eye on World Center Plan."
  "61.1 Million in Trade Center Construction Contracts Let" (20 November 1966).
  "Young Engineers on Tough Job" (December 4, 1966).

New York Herald Tribune
  "Small Guys Finish Last" (May 2, 1962).

The World Trade Center: A Building Project Like No Other, The Port Authority of New York, February 1990, Port Authority of New York and New Jersey.

London Engineering News "Unsettling Effects In The Room At The Top" (May 18, 1967).

ACKNOWLEDGMENTS

Karl W. Koch III

I MUST ACKNOWLEDGE and remember, first, the terrible losses sustained by those killed during the construction of the World Trade Center and the thousands of victims of the terrorist attacks of February 26, 1993, and September 11, 2001. They and their families will always remain in my prayers. I think society owes them the debt of ensuring that great minds from all disciplines work together to avoid a tragedy like the one we all witnessed on that terrible day in September.

I am grateful to the brilliant Richard Firstman, my coauthor, collaborator, and friend. I am deeply indebted to Rick for his help in unwinding my tumultuous life and then putting the story into compelling and heartfelt prose. This book demanded a punishing schedule; so I must also thank Rick's wife, Jamie, and their children for tolerating the many nights and weekends Rick spent hunkered in his office writing the story of my life.

I must thank my literary agent, Faith Hamlin. From our first conversation, Faith believed in this project and cared a great deal about putting me and my story in the right hands. I am indebted to her for her continued support and kindness. Likewise, I could not have hoped for a more supportive and enthusiastic editor than Kristin Kiser. She and her colleagues at Crown Publishers made my first experience in publishing a very positive one.

I owe heartfelt thanks to my dear wife, Vivian, and my late father, Karl W. Koch, Jr., to whom this book is dedicated. I am also grateful to my late brother, Donald Koch, for his support during our difficult times.

I am deeply indebted to my children, for *Men of Steel* could not have been written without their tremendous help and support. A special thanks is owed to my daughter Cynthia for her unflagging help in editing and synthesizing the voluminous material that went into the book. My daughter Vivian and son John were indefatigable in their research help. Thanks, also, to my son Karl and my daughter Jill for their loving support, as well as to my grandchildren James Mathews, Emily Mathews and Brian Murray. I must also thank Andrew Mathews, Rustin Edwards, and Glenn Murray, for their computer support. A special thanks to Caroline O'Flannagan for her research support.

In 1974, I began the manuscript for this book. I thank my lifelong friend, Joseph Sherry, Jr., for helping me with that first literary effort. I must also acknowledge my good friend Phillip Kerrivan, who provided sage counsel and support during the tumultuous early 1970s. I am grateful to Dr. John David Mountain, who courageously saved my life and has been like a father to me all these years. Words cannot express how great this man is.

I am indebted to the following people who generously submitted to interviews: my mother, Marie Koch; my sisters, Marie Koch Hendricks and Pamela Koch DeMayo; my brother Roger Koch; my nephew Donald Koch, Jr., whose insights as an ironworker were an inspiration; my uncle Daniel Koch, my cousin Vincent Landers; Guy Tozzoli, President of the World Trade Center Association; William Faschan of Leslie Robertson and Associates; John Tishman of Tishman Realty & Construction Company; Anthony Frandina; Rudy Loffredo; Tom Petrizzo; and ironworkers John Kelly, John DeSmidt, and Stephen DeSmidt. My appreciation goes to the artist Richard Welling for his permission to publish some of his wonderful drawings of the World Trade Center's construction, as well as to the New-York Historical Society.

I would also like to express gratitude and deep affection to the following, who are listed in no particular order: Dr. Keith McElroy, who, against all odds, saved my legs and has been treating me for the past thirty-seven years; Dr. George Crikelair, whose art in plastic surgery hastened my recovery; Drs. David Andrews and Brian Scully, who have again rescued me from an amputation; my partner and mentor, Andy Zosuls, who is like a brother to me; Damir Plisic, a superb engineer and a great friend; Tom Roemer, an operating engineer whose name is legendery with New York ironworkers; Barbara Koch; and Nick Matich, my college roomate, who has been my close friend all these years.

I am also grateful to the following for their help with this book: Bill Tilly, Jr., who shared with me his recollections of our fathers and the work they did with Bristol Steel and Iron; Bobby Johnson, my brothers' great iron-worker foreman; John Alonzo of Graphic Steel Structures for his unfailing help whenever called on; Steven De Lazzero of Port Morris Tile & Marble Company; Huey Law at Favelle Industries in Australia for the documents and encouragement he gave me; and John Truitt.

Thanks also to John Denise, Mike Dombrowski, Dan Bledsoe, Leslie Robertson, and Ray Finnegan at The Port Authority of New York and New Jersey; Kevin Brennan, Safety Engineer at OSHA; Pat Grant at IMP Pump; Cheryl Catler-Peterson at Demag DeLaval; CDR James Blomquist, USN (Ret.); Angela Mattea at the Museum of the City of New York; Bill King at Yamasaki Associates; Jan Frank at Linda Hall Library; Donald Gill and Dr. George Billy at the U.S. Merchant Marine Academy Library; Renee Jawish at *Ironworker Magazine;* Bill Wethersby at *Architectual Record;* Dr. August Molnar at the American Hungarian Foundation; the National Society of the Daughters of the American Revolution; Carol Willis, director of the Skyscraper Museum in New York; Tiffany Kailor at the Pierre Hotel; Masako Yukawa at C. W. Post College, Long Island University; Mark Silverman, Karen Atkinson, Kay Houston, and Jan Lovell at the *Detroit News;* Len Tortora at L & L Camera; Paul Legant of Turner Construction Contracting; Janet Mahler at the James V. Brown Library, Williamsport, Pennsylvania; the Messiah Lutheran Church in South Williamsport; Mary Orwig at Lycoming County Historical Society, Williamsport; Barbara Wolarian, Office of the Architect, U.S. Capitol; the National Archives, Photo Division, College Park, Maryland; the Department of Energy; Robert Blomquist; Franz Jantzen, curator of the United States Supreme Court; Daniel Rawner at the Bureau of Labor Statistics; Linda Callahan at WGBH, Boston; Raynelda Calderone, Andrew Saks, and Maria Alos at the New York Public Library; the New-York Historical Society; Arnold Galz at Tosco-Phillips; Brian Kelly at the International Union of Elevator Constructors, New York, and Judy Lim-Sharpe at the Library of the U.S. Department of the Treasury.

A final word about the World Trade Center: Of the thousands of men who worked on the Twin Towers, seven hundred were ironworkers. These men of steel made the towers rise and removed the steel after the towers fell. The latter effort was heartbreaking for ironworkers, who are literally the builders of our cities. This book highlights only some of their contributions to modern civilization.

No thanks are adequate for the heroic firefighters, police, and medical personnel who worked at the World Trade Center from September 11, 2001, on. I must also acknowledge the unsung heroes at the United States

Merchant Marine Academy in Kings Point, New York. Under the leadership of Commander Eric Wallischeck, college students and staff conducted a three-week sealift across Long Island Sound to Ground Zero. They repeatedly ferried 1,500 medical personnel, firemen, and police officers to the disaster site, along with tons of water, food, and rescue supplies.

RICHARD FIRSTMAN

I CANNOT IMAGINE a more fulfilling and memorable collaboration than the one I have had on this book with Karl Koch. Reliving his life was a very difficult process for him, and I will always be grateful not only for the grace, integrity, and good humor with which he carried it off, but also for his extremely hard work and skill in writing about it truthfully and compellingly. Besides contributing a valuable resource in the manuscript he wrote many years ago, Karl also spent countless hours over many months writing and rewriting. I am grateful to him for his astuteness and his fine literary touch, and for trusting me with his story. We were true partners.

Likewise, little did I realize when we began the book that I would not only be collaborating with Karl, but also with his wonderful family as well. I am indebted particularly to Karl's daughters Vivian and Cynthia and his son John for their phenomenal work in helping to gather and organize much of the research material that went into this book. I could not have written it without the mountain of archival material that John hunted down and compiled, or without the memos and transcripts he whipped up. Vivian was tireless in her historical research and in her efforts to acquire and organize the photographs that appear in the book. And Cynthia came in twice from her home out of state to work with her father, then returned home to continue helping out via e-mail. Cynthia, a very talented editor, also teamed up with Vivian to pore over every page of the manuscript. I want to also give a very special thanks to Vivian Koch, Karl's wife, for the support and love she has shown me and my family (not to mention all the interviews she transcribed).

I thank Kristin Kiser, executive editor of Crown Publishers, who is what every writer wants: an enthusiastic, supportive, and skilled editor—with patience.

I'm sure I don't know half of what she did to get this book published so quickly and so well. This project had no business going smoothly, but somehow Kristin made sure it did (or so it seemed to me). I also want to thank Kristin's able and dedicated colleagues at Crown for their hard work in behalf of *Men of Steel:* Amelia Zalcman, Claudia Gabel, Amy Boorstein, Lauren Dong, Leta Evanthes, Andrea Peabbles, and Elizabeth Parson.

I want to express my thanks and affection to my agent, Faith Hamlin of Sanford J. Greenburger Associates, who brought me this project and gave it great care from beginning to end. I must admit that when she first mentioned this project to me, I was skeptical ("What do you mean, he *built* the World Trade Center?"). But Faith urged me to read what Karl had written and to talk to him. I did and realized she had indeed spotted a compelling book waiting to be written. I thank her for her support and good counsel these past few years.

Thanks, too, go to Damir Plisic, who showed me things I will never forget one morning in September 2001. And to John DeSmidt, Roger Koch, Marie Koch, John Kelly, Tom Petrizzo, and Rudy Loffredo, for their kindness and help.

Finally and most importantly, I want to express my thanks and love to my unbelievably patient and devoted wife, Jamie Talan, and our children, Allison, Amanda, and Jordan. With these words, I can finally say I'm home from work.

INDEX

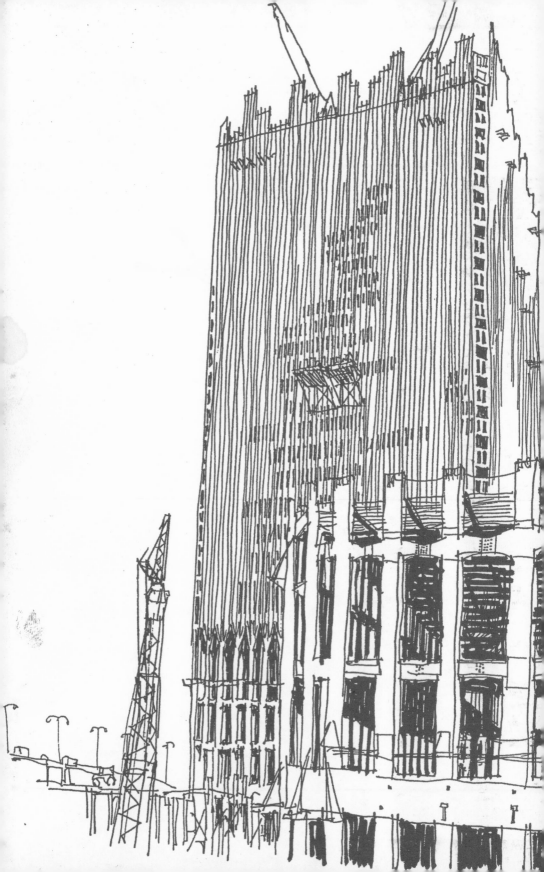